NIETZSCHE

HEIDEGGER

AND THE

TRANSITION TO POSTMODERNITY

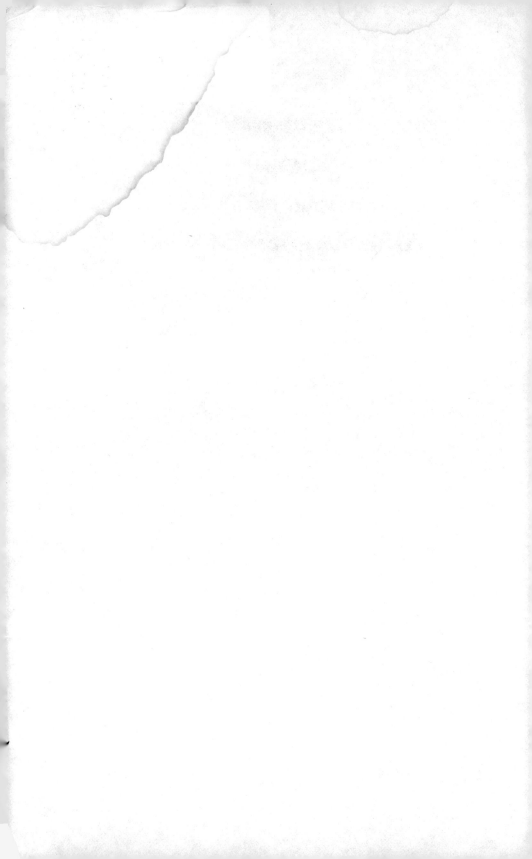

NIETZSCHE

HEIDEGGER

AND THE

TRANSITION TO POSTMODERNITY

GREGORY BRUCE SMITH

THE UNIVERSITY OF CHICAGO PRESS

CHICAGO AND LONDON

Gregory Bruce Smith is associate professor of political
science at Trinity College, Hartford.

The University of Chicago Press, Chicago 60637
The University of Chicago Press, Ltd., London
© 1996 by The University of Chicago
All rights reserved. Published 1996
Printed in the United States of America
05 04 03 02 01 00 99 98 97 96   5 4 3 2 1

ISBN (cloth): 0-226-76339-0
ISBN (paper): 0-226-76340-4

The Press gratefully acknowledges the support of the
Earhart Foundation in the publication of this book.

Library of Congress Cataloging-in-Publication Data

Smith, Gregory B., 1949–
    Nietzsche, Heidegger, and the transition to
postmodernity / Gregory Bruce Smith.
        p.   cm.
    Includes bibliographical references and index.
    ISBN 0-226-76339-0. — ISBN 0-226-76340-4 (pbk.)
    1. Postmodernism.   2. Nietzsche, Friedrich
Wilhelm, 1844–1900.   3. Heidegger, Martin, 1889–
1976.   4. Philosophy, Modern—20th century.
I. Title.
B831.2.S67   1996
190'.9'04—dc20   95-14678
                                                    CIP

For Betty

Contents

PART THREE
Heidegger's Critique of Modernity and the Postmodern Future

PART FOUR
Deflections toward a Postmodern Future

Abbreviations

AD	Friedrich Nietzsche. *On the Advantage and Disadvantage of History for Life.*
BAT	Martin Heidegger. *Being and Time.*
BG	Friedrich Nietzsche. *Beyond Good and Evil.*
BT	Friedrich Nietzsche. *The Birth of Tragedy* and *The Case of Wagner.*
DM	René Descartes. *Discourse on Method.*
DT	Martin Heidegger. *Discourse on Thinking.*
EH	Friedrich Nietzsche. *Ecce Homo.*
FD, SD	Jean-Jacques Rousseau. *The First and Second Discourses.*
GM	Friedrich Nietzsche. *On the Genealogy of Morals.*
GS	Friedrich Nietzsche. *The Gay Science.*
IM	Martin Heidegger. *An Introduction to Metaphysics.*
L	Thomas Hobbes. *Leviathan.*
LH	Martin Heidegger. *Letter on Humanism.*
N	Martin Heidegger. *Nietzsche*, 4 vols.
OTB	Martin Heidegger. *On Time and Being.*
P	Niccolò Machiavelli. *The Prince.*
PLT	Martin Heidegger. *Poetry, Language, Thought.*
PR	G. W. F. Hegel. *Philosophy of Right.*
PS	G. W. F. Hegel. *Phenomenology of Spirit.*
PW	Immanuel Kant. *Kant's Political Writings.*
QT	Martin Heidegger. *The Question Concerning Technology and Other Essays.*
SC	Jean-Jacques Rousseau. *On the Social Contract.*

SD	See *FD*.
ST	John Locke. *Second Treatise of Government*.
TW	Friedrich Nietzsche. *Twilight of the Idols*.
WCT	Martin Heidegger. *What Is Called Thinking*.
WP	Friedrich Nietzsche. *The Will to Power*.
Z	Friedrich Nietzsche. *Thus Spoke Zarathustra*.

PART ONE

The Essence of Modernity

Modernity, Postmodernism, and Beyond

With increasing regularity we have heard the last half of twentieth century referred to as a *post*-age: "postindustrial," "postmetaphysical," "poststructuralist," "postanthropological," "postmodern," and so on. To this litany could be added phrases asserting the "end," or at least the "decline," of modernity, of philosophy, of political philosophy, of ideology of the West, and of History. This melange of terms reflects a shared, at times inarticulate, brooding sense that something unique is happening around us. But it is unclear whether what is happening will culminate in a long hiatus or a relatively quick transition to something novel, or whether the early stages of a novel future are already settling in. In what follows I will argue that something is in fact coming to an end. I will do so primarily by focusing on the term "postmodern," speculating about what would be required if we were to use the prefix *post-* in a resolute fashion.

I am hardly alone in suggesting that the present is a watershed period. Recent events have made this observation commonplace. Regimes that openly flew the flag of the philosopher Marx have collapsed worldwide. It is unlikely that they will be restored. The same fate may await Marxist and neo-Marxist thought in its remaining forms. Who, for example, can still believe in History?[1] Without History, Marxism, in whatever form, is reduced to an egalitarian ethic that has to be willed. At best, that is a vague facsimile of Marxism as we have known it. Some have seen the collapse of Marxist communism as a sign of the impending global victory of liberal capitalism.[2] But the collapse of Marxist

---

1. I am in agreement with Lyotard, who states that "metanarratives," or grand philosophies of history, are no longer persuasive, and with Vattimo, who argues that modernity ends at that point where we can no longer believe that history is linear and unitary and progresses toward a fixed point; see Lyotard, *The Post-Modern Condition,* and Vattimo, *The End of Modernity,* esp. 7–13.

2. Fukuyama conjoins this notion with a reworking of the modern end of history

communism does not in itself make liberal *theory* more compelling, and
the liberal state is hardly without contradictions.[3] Liberalism—the primary *present* support for constitutionalism—has, like Marxism, increasingly reduced itself to an ethic dependent on willing. Without a
substantive foundation it is hard to know what makes one form of willing more compelling than another unless we resort to force, its softer

---

thesis in "End of History?" and *The End of History and the Last Man,* (New York: Basic
Books, 1992). While I find Fukuyama's account compelling and believe it deserves to be
addressed, I reject the notion that we have arrived at the *inevitable* end of history. The
end of history thesis can be compelling without being conclusive, and the movement of
modernity irreversible without having been inevitable. An extended hiatus of historical
novelty in which movement back is impossible and movement forward unlikely, is altogether plausible. I would attribute much of what Fukuyama takes to indicate the end of
history to the ramifications of the closure of modern thought. See in this regard my
essay, "The 'End of History' or a Portal to the Future: Does Anything Lie Beyond Late
Modernity?"

   3. There are several contemporary variants of liberal *theory*. The antecedents of the
two most powerful variants are Kant on the one hand, and Locke, Smith, and utilitarianism on the other. The Kantian variant has had its most powerful contemporary re-
statement in the work of John Rawls, who shares the core premise that links Rousseau,
Kant, and ultimately Marx. Following Rousseau, I designate that premise "metaphysical
freedom." There has been a significant recent reaction to this "deontological" approach
to political philosophy; see especially Shapiro, *Political Criticism.* I am in agreement with
Shapiro's critique of the limitations of the deontological approach, but will try to sketch
a different alternative. In this regard see also Galston, *Liberal Purposes,* and Salkever's
excellent *Finding the Mean.*

   If we are entering a postmetaphysical age, the metaphysical foundations of deontological liberalism will at best be theoretically difficult to resuscitate. But the other
most prominent variant of liberal theory is open to theoretical problems of its own. No
simple naturalism will readily prevail in our time—and the "state of nature" is too fan-
tastic an exaction to continue to persuade. "Possessive individualism" is too spiritually
hollow to sustain itself indefinitely; and reducing human life to self-interested competition and designating it "rational" is too impoverished a tactic to sway the minds and
hearts of any but the already convinced. To rely on articulating some present consensus
is hardly more compelling, in that any such consensus is necessarily the product of a
prior debate; what is at stake in the debates of our time is in fact precisely the nature of a
future consensus. For an extremely clear statement of this last approach consider Walzer, *Spheres of Justice,* xiv: "My argument is radically particularist; I don't claim to have
achieved any great distance from the social world in which I live. One way to begin the
philosophical enterprise—perhaps the original way—is to walk out of the cave, leave
the city, climb the mountain, fashion for oneself . . . an objective and universal standpoint. . . . But I mean to stand in the cave, in the city, on the ground. Another way of
doing philosophy is to interpret to one's fellow citizens the world of meaning we
share." As I will try to show, I do not think Walzer's two alternatives exhaust the available options.

cousin majority tyranny, or one form or another of reliance on the altogether traditional love of "one's own."[4]

For a variety of reasons, the ideas that have sustained men and women[5] in the modern age seem to have become less compelling in our post-age. Modern ideas seem to be on a more or less gentle, slippery slide to a loss of persuasiveness, but novel ideas seem reluctant to announce themselves.[6] In the interim, things are not quite right—who does not sense it? Wherever we turn there is a cacophony of voices. Everything seems adrift yet strangely unchanging.[7] We decry the absence

4. The last is precisely what a self-styled "liberal ironist" or "bourgeois postmodernist" like Richard Rorty ultimately relies upon. Rorty argues that theories fundamentally had little to do with the success of liberal politics; hence to lose the theories that accompanied its rise is of little interest. But having rejected the relevance of any theoretical foundations for our liberal bourgeois political and moral institutions, he resorts to a kind of postfoundationalist pluralism that anticipates the continued operation of those institutions. This simply accepts "our own" as the good, and assumes—wrongly, I believe—an inertia that will keep those institutions and beliefs in place even after the arguments implicated in their founding have been rejected. If theory is in fact insignificant, one wonders what difference Rorty's theory can possibly make. Be that as it may, the assertion that modern theory is irrelevant is empirically unfounded. I will argue that modernity is precisely the age of the conscious theoretization of *praxis*. See Rorty, "The Contingency of a Liberal Community" and "Private Irony and Liberal Hope," in *Contingency, Irony and Solidarity,* esp. 59–61. See also chap. 21, n. 15, in this volume.

5. Most Indo-European languages have separate words for male and humanity. Unfortunately English does not; but it is almost always clear which function the word "man" is carrying at any given time. To avoid tedious and infelicitous phrases, I will retain the traditional, generic usage of the word "man," and of male pronouns, when it is clear that the intent is to discuss humanity. When the intent might be ambiguous I will use other words or phrases.

6. Perhaps this is because it is only since World War II that we have finally cast off the last vestiges of the *ancien* and begun entering into the fully modern world. Only one or two more generations will have to pass and few will remain—especially in the "developed" world—with a living memory of any concrete elements of the premodern past. The premodern will become the preserve of history, a history that it is reasonable to expect will be repeatedly rewritten to meet what are perceived to be immediate needs. As the matter was articulated in a previous, provisional title for this work, we seem caught "Between Eternities."

7. Liberal pluralism, for all its obvious political and moral virtues, produces a world dominated by an endless motion, comparable to that of a flywheel, that seldom changes its location. If one believes that the present location is the best of all possible venues, then all is well; but then one should also willingly accept the end of history thesis. If we accept neither this thesis nor the contours of our present venue, we must consider in what direction we want to move. See in this regard Tocqueville, "How the Aspect of Society in the United States is at Once Agitated and Monotonous," in *Democracy in America,* 614–16.

I will argue that contemporary postmodernism seldom gets far beyond a left version

of leadership, but who can lead without a specifiable goal? We experience simultaneously the concrete intensification of modern principles and their theoretical disintegration. Intensification, fragmentation, cacophony of voices, and the monotony of constant, circling, changeless change. Who does not see it? But who has not grown weary of the endless, occasionally hyperbolic, restatements of the problem? And who has not had the enervating sense that we are playing a philosophical game where all possible moves and countermoves have been seen already—a game, therefore, no longer worth playing.

What follows will eventuate in no more than a modest suggestion. I wish to propose a way to get a purchase on our post-age, not a recipe for immediate practical adoption. In a way, the superabundance of recipes is at the heart of the problem. I begin by assuming several things. A central premise is that we human beings have no choice but to live out our lives on the evanescent margin between past and future. Regardless of the age in which we find ourselves, and whether or not we recognize the fact, the future is always lurking in the interstices of the present. More to the point, a limited number of possible futures exists *in potentia* at any point in time, while, given the inertial force of the past, a great number of other possibilities have become highly improbable. Philosophy is implicated in the process of giving birth to the future. As Nietzsche observed, genuine philosophy is always "untimely," critical and projected beyond its concrete present. To refashion a Derridean coinage, philosophy's public dissemination always leads to deferred ramifications. But only part of any profound corpus of thought will be plumbed and developed, and what part that will be is impossible to predict with precision. Ideas manifest themselves slowly, unpredictably, and in labyrinthine ways, but great tidal shifts in ideas have concrete ramifications.

I will argue that the thought of Nietzsche and Heidegger represents the *beginnings* of such a tidal shift, that their respective teachings are inextricably linked, and that another great constellation of ideas born at the dawn of modernity, reaching an early culmination in the thought of Rousseau and Kant and codified by Hegel, is today simultaneously reaching its most intense manifestation and disintegrating. It is precisely

---

of liberal pluralism. As Vattimo observes: "The left believes it can 're-found' itself by inheriting liberal theories and programmes, perhaps with their feet back on the ground. I shall not discuss the legitimacy of this procedure 'in general' here, for it is certainly also true that the political thinking and *praxis* of the 'left'—whatever that may mean now—assume the form of a 'secularizing' revival of the legacy of bourgeois thought" (*The Transparent Society*, 101).

in such an environment that novel possibilities might present themselves. As we think differently, we view the world and ourselves differently. In turn we act differently and changes in the configuration of our shared world develop. While no simple, one-to-one relationship exists between thought and the evolving configuration of the concrete world, it can be asserted that the present tidal shift in thought will have concrete consequences. In the work that follows I will briefly reflect on what is passing and then develop in greater detail a set of possibilities that I see lurking in the evolving Nietzschean/Heideggerian current of thought.

The texts of Nietzsche and Heidegger have quickly become part of our shared heritage. They have already been refashioned for practical use as well as for the unique purposes of academic specialists, sometimes with significant distortions, obfuscations, and transformations. Any act of interpretation unavoidably narrows our focus to something less than the whole; nonetheless, texts may be read in a more or less scrupulous fashion.[8] I will argue that a great number of now-prominent readings of the works of Nietzsche and Heidegger have been less than scrupulous. I am by no means alone in seeing this fact, nor in seeing the importance of Nietzsche and Heidegger for postmodern thought. Postmodernists such as Rorty, Derrida, and Vattimo, to name just a few, openly admit their debt to Nietzsche and Heidegger. But I wish to differentiate my understanding from those others. Contemporary postmodernism is a straightforward extension of modern thought; I am looking for possibilities in Nietzsche and

---

8. Arguing as I do that the history of thought is the history of deflections of seminal ideas implies that once a text leaves an author's hands it acquires meanings independent of, and not always the same as, the author's intention, which become a significant part of its concrete influence. Needless to say, a clever author tries to anticipate what meanings will be attributed to a text and how those meanings will advance his or her intention. The fact that we can see this indicates that we have some access—albeit imprecise—to the intention of the author, but the historical "meaning of the text" is never identical to the "intention of the author," and the two ideas must be kept separate.

My position falls somewhere between, for example, the hermeneutic theories of Hans-Georg Gadamer and those of Leo Strauss. I accept that the "hermeneutical situation" from which we *start* our attempts at understanding is not to be construed as an unsullied, self-grounding Cartesian detachment; but this does not imply that we are thrown blind into a situation we can in no way bracket. It is inappropriate to conceptualize the interpretive act as one of an autonomous subject completely extricated from the concrete present. But it is equally inappropriate to see it as hopelessly historical. There are many possibilities between those two poles; this is not an either/or choice. See Gadamer, *Truth and Method*, esp. 345–498. See also Gadamer, *Reason in the Age of Science*, and Strauss, *Persecution and the Art of Writing*, esp. 7–37, and *What is Political Philosophy?*, esp. 56–77.

Heidegger that open up something beyond modernity, and thus for something beyond contemporary postmodernism.[9]

It is difficult to fix precisely the origin of the term "postmodernism." Robert Pippin suggests one look to Arnold Toynbee's account of the fourth and last phase of Western history, which he designated post-modern. For Toynbee this is the phase of irrationalism, anxiety, and lost hope. Pippin suggests that the word was simultaneously deployed in literary criticism by Randall Jarrell as part of his characterization of Lowell's poetry as anti- or postmodern. Wherever it originated, the term quickly spread to architecture, art, cultural criticism, philosophy, and beyond.[10] Contemporary postmodernism is fundamentally a sign of disintegration, of transition, of waning faith in the modern ideas of Reason and Progress, and the Enlightenment project in general. It lacks faith in the modern autonomous subject as self-grounding and self-legislating. Nonetheless, it primarily represents the latest and most intense form of modern self-dissatisfaction, which is the shadow that has followed modern thought since its inception.

In architecture, modernism gave us buildings dominated by simple geometric patterns, unadorned and with no attempt to camouflage the functional, structural necessities of the edifice. Form followed function. To the long, unbroken lines of boxy modern buildings post-modern architecture adds gables, classical columns, and other forms borrowed from the past. There is a conscious, ironic playfulness in this effort. The result is a unique, if sometimes ugly, pastiche of old forms. But no truly novel forms are created.[11] In the social sciences post-modernism was initially linked with the concept of the "postindustrial society," in which service industries take precedence over industrial means of generating wealth, and information becomes the major form of capital. A "new class" sells this new capital in an increasingly global market dominated by computer and satellite information links. A "high tech" consumer society comes into existence where old urban areas are no longer necessary as hubs where capital, labor, raw materials, industry and commerce can come together. Decentralization and

9. For a discussion of the evolving uses of the term "postmodernism" in contemporary discourse, see my "Heidegger, Technology, and Post-modernity," esp. 370–72.

10. See Pippin's excellent *Modernism as a Philosophical Problem*, 156, where he suggests there is an underlying sentiment throughout: "Whereas in modernism, the typical modern experience that 'all that is solid melts into air,' or 'the center does not hold,' had prompted the creation of a 'subjective center,' an autonomous self-defining artist, for postmodernism there is no center at all."

11. For a valuable philosophical discussion of modern architecture see Kolb, *Postmodern Sophistications*. For a different view, see Steven Connor, "Postmodernism in Architecture and the Visual Arts."

globalization occur simultaneously. Since the initial discussions there have been myriad attempts in the social sciences to subvert subjectivism, rewrite progressivist history, preference the local, undermine representational thinking, decenter modern culture, and so on.[12]

In philosophy postmodernism is linked loosely with "poststructuralism." The poststructuralist focuses on the extent to which reality, including our own being, is constituted by our very acts of trying to use, describe, and understand what is. In attempting to explain reality we in fact constitute it—whether completely or partially remains open to question. Poststructuralism builds on the notion that reality, both human and nonhuman, is fundamentally malleable. We cannot, however, do our constituting of reality consciously or rationally. That would require a stable, unchanging actor facing a structurally stable world, and we are not beings with a simple, pregiven structure or nature. Hence the modern desire to consciously and rationally reconstitute the world is seen as a chimera. Any closure, or end of history, is simultaneously rejected.[13]

Without cataloging every discipline in which the term "postmodernism" has become current we can sketch a general postmodernist attitude, style, or tone that manifests itself artistically, culturally, and pop-culturally. Throughout postmodernism there is a fascination with the surface, conjoined with a perception that all of existence is a humanly constructed surface that has about it the aura of "contingency." It is asserted that all "difference" is a phenomenon of the surface, which continually reconstitutes itself in an endless and arbitrary process, beyond the control of any individual or group. There is no natural ground for

12. For an overview see Rosenau, *Post-Modernism and the Social Sciences;* the extensive bibliography is particularly useful.

13. For example, Derrida's version of "deconstructionism" argues that all of existence is a text. In "reading" (i.e., trying to understand) any text—whether a book, nature, a society, or ourselves—we *re*write it. All reading is "writing," a constant, endless process inherent to living that cannot be carried out consciously, at least not with the autonomous self-consciousness prior modernity had posited. Hence we can no more determine an author's intent than could the original author. There is no experience per se that is shared by all human beings; everything is a surface that constantly reconstitutes itself. Absence dominates all presence, and we are left to pursue the "traces" of an absent source. What is concealed, for example, on the "margin" or in the spaces between the lines becomes as important as what is present in the words of a text. Hence we try to avoid "logocentrism." Since all reading is writing, a flux of alternative explanations is inevitable. An urbane openness to diverse interpretations, which actually reduce to a cacophony of voices, is required; whenever anything in reality begins to ossify, the deconstructionist moves in to play the role of solvent. On deconstructionism and Derrida see my "Cacophony or Silence: Derrida's Deconstructionism and the Possibility of Political Philosophy."

difference; all difference is relational. This understanding leads to an ironic attitude toward life that inevitably transforms itself into a form of cynicism—a tendency to give in to a mocking superiority, the sense that nothing is worthy of passion or commitment because everything solid dissolves upon one's approach. An attitude of indifference, weariness, and exhaustion is often the result. All of this leads one to suspect a form of evasion, an attitude of avoidance, a blasé, unshakable refusal to face up to the terrors and general groundlessness of late-modern life (a groundlessness that is blithely admitted and celebrated). Only through such avoidance does nihilism cease to be a problem that needs to be confronted.

The fascination with the surface also predictably manifests itself in the characteristic postmodernist sortie through past forms, which are combined and juxtaposed in novel and at times purposely bizarre ways. In place of novelty and creation one gets "pastiche, collage, montage." "Postmodernists ransack history for shards because there is no here here; because historical continuity is shattered by the permanent revolution that is [modernity]."[14] This provides an explanation for the attitude of indifference and avoidance. We live in a world of abstractions; the concrete world withdraws; we are surrounded by the reign of triviality. Our world is an unworld. Such a situation is captured in Kundera's striking phrase, "the unbearable lightness of being."[15] The modern faith in man's ability to self-consciously re-create the world comes to be seen as a chimera, and no alternate faith is available. The postmodernist responds by adopting a defensive posture, a stance whereby he or she will not be unduly moved or hurt, an attitude, one suspects, of waiting without weighing, of biding time. This takes the form of a nihilistic unpacking and unbuilding that has nothing constructive in mind—deconstructionism with no eye to reconstruction. By its very name, postmodernism presents itself as a sequel, something that comes after something else; but it neither presents itself as *on the way* to anything nor designates anything unique as approaching. It is a phenomenon of a posthistorical age, passionless and jaded for fear that making do with the present—while maintaining a playfully sophisticated and detached distance—is the safest stance available.

I will argue that postmodernism, in its many contemporary manifestations, is anything but *post*modern, that it is in fact a perfectly logical extension of modernity. "Postindustrial society," for example,

14. See Gitlin's beautifully written and whimsical essay, "Postmodernism: Roots and Politics," 103.
15. Milan Kundera, *The Unbearable Lightness of Being* (New York: Harper & Row, 1984).

represents the very *telos* of modernity. It is Marx's posthistorical
world, the product of human labor, which creates a world no longer
dependent on the rhythms of nature, reduces numbing manual labor to
a minimum, and so on. Postmodernism, in its glorification of antifoundationalism, together with the an-archy toward which it points,
represents but the latest version of the "withering away of the state,"
and every other structure with it. Postmodernism is an extension of the
quintessential late-modern thought that all of life is an interpretation,
which in turn is nothing but an extension of the protomodern notion
that we can only know what we make. Postmodernism is primarily
Nietzscheanism shorn of the self-conscious "Will to Will."[16]

Further, postmodernism represents an extreme manifestation of
modernity's antinature animus.[17] When Machiavelli set out to conquer
Fortuna, he built on the notion that nature could be conceived as accident or chance and conquered by manipulative calculation. Hobbes
and Locke wished to quit the state of nature because, as they presented
the matter, it was a state inimical to the good for man. Likewise, Kant
opposed the realm of freedom to the realm of nature. The realm of freedom was where our true humanity was to be worked out. Hegel
showed that the realm of freedom, the human, *geistliche* realm, would
necessarily come to hold hegemony over the natural. Marx's communist society presupposed the complete victory of man over nature, both
technologically and spiritually. Postmodernism merely intensifies
modernity's antinature animus; there are no foundations and all difference is contingent.[18] Modernity set out to demonstrate the malleability

16. Of course, this is another way of saying that it is no longer truly Nietzschean.
See my "Cacophony or Silence," esp. 130–34, 153–62.
17. See my "Cacophony or Silence," 153–62, esp. 156.
18. Any alternative that is genuinely beyond modernity will have to construct a new
relation to "Nature" in full awareness of the "problem of Nature." See chapter 22, "The
Problem of Nature: Beyond the Sublimation of the Political." I will argue that Nietzsche and Heidegger open a path to a new relation to Nature.
I can give two general intimations of what I have in mind: (1) Wine making has, in
the last thirty years, come to be dominated by sophisticated new technologies and advanced knowledge in biochemistry. Yet every great vintner knows that the microcli-
mate and terrain of the vineyard, the quality of the grape, the natural process of
fermentation, the artful use or avoidance of finning and filtering, and fortuitous weather
are crucial to the final quality of the product. (2) Sailboat racing similarly now requires
onboard computers, technically efficient hull and keel designs, aerodynamic rigging,
and perfectly cut sails in conjunction with the mechanical ability to make infinitely
small adjustments. Yet one must still adjust to constantly changing winds, waves, tides,
and other natural forces. In both examples, technology is used to integrate human activity into nature with maximum efficiency, not to transform or negate nature. If a power-
boat steaming directly into the wind, indifferent to waves and tides, symbolizes the

of nature and in the end made it dissolve completely; Being withdrew and we were left to live in a world of traces—the rootless late-modern world that could be a historical terminus.

It is my contention that in the late-modern age those institutions that are without adequate roots will pass away most quickly, the post-modernists' and antifoundationalists' arguments to the contrary not-withstanding. Nothing can hang in midair indefinitely. We no longer live in a time when consensus—the short-term version of tradition—alone can support institutions; we must make arguments. Whatever we see as the best regime, the best life, the best social institutions, will in the future have to be rooted in a new philosophical understanding. It is the general contours of such an understanding that I want to address. I am not unmindful of the fact that limited constitutional government in its present form—until now supported by *modern* theory—has great benefits, for practical reasons that are too obvious to require elabora-tion. Nor am I unmindful of the existence of social injustice. But those are not my immediate concerns. I would argue that speculative thought is a legitimate undertaking in and of itself.[19] I would ask that the reader allow this exercise in speculative thought initially to proceed wherever it may. I will return to the relation between thought and *praxis* at the appropriate point. I realize that there is a danger in questioning the fea-tures of late-modern life that are the ground for significant dissatisfac-tion, alienation, and anomie. We run the risk of throwing the baby out with the bath water. The baby in this case consists of modern, limited constitutional institutions, individual freedoms, and technological emancipation from numbing labor and drudgery. Can we transcend increasingly autonomous technological and organizational domina-tion, growing cynicism, rootlessness, and worldlessness without los-ing what is valuable? I believe we can. But we will have to move beyond contemporary postmodernism to do so.

Furthermore, we can no longer ignore the dark side of modernity: the loss of community; moral, psychological, and social fragmenta-tion; the dissolution of the family; seemingly runaway technology; the loss of limits at a time of increasing technical sophistication (e.g., ge-netic engineering); destructive weapons; environmental imbalances; impending shortages; and so on. One need not be apocalyptic about these problems, but they are assuredly no accidents. A constant, frene-

---

modern relation to nature, a technically sophisticated sailboat can be taken as a meta-phor for a *post*modern relation.

19. According to my understanding, speculative thought is far more than the private daydream of someone engaged in Rortyan self-creation and imaginative, "utopian lib-eral" projections. See Rorty, *Contingency, Irony and Solidarity,* xiv.

tic, ongoing revolution in our social and moral existence now seems to be our inevitable condition in perpetuity. In such an environment no long-range, cross-generational perseverance will ever be possible, even though it is absolutely imperative in regard, for example, to various environmental issues, to say nothing of moral concerns. To remain within the modern horizon is to project an endless repetition of the agitated, monotonous present. What is that but the end of history understood as the end of historical novelty? That said, I am in no way opposed to the benefits of modernity; rather, I am arguing that we will have to reground them philosophically. I am arguing that modernity has more or less played out its philosophical possibilities and hence we must look elsewhere. For a variety of reasons, which I will articulate below, going back to the premodern is not a plausible option. Modern thought has so successfully transformed the world that no appeal to tradition or authority, to ancient or medieval philosophy, can be immediately compelling.

Modernity was born as a revolutionary, fighting doctrine. However, a revolutionary creed that substantially actualizes its ends loses its revolutionary thrust and is left simply to defend the present. The "progressives" become the "reactionaries"; the "conservatives" want change but know not in what direction, having lost sight of the essential things truly worth preserving. Such modern distinctions cannot continue to have persuasive force for much longer. We must move beyond these, and many other, late-modern categories. Further, unless we furtively hold on to some variant of the modern notion of inevitable progress, culminating in some version of the end of history—and in one way or another I believe that maneuver is deployed by both the right and left of late modernity—surely something novel will follow our distinctive present.[20]

20. I hope that what follows will be spared the thoughtless indictment of being "neoconservative," especially as the term has been used by authors like Habermas and Ferry and Renaut. The term makes sense only on the basis of a faith that there is nothing beyond modernity—i.e., on the basis of a hidden end of history thesis. Those who toss the term about argue that anything different from their own late-modern position must be a form of going back because in their universe there are no other alternatives. In the process, these authors show that modernity has been forced to make its last—and presumably everlasting—stand with some variant of metaphysical freedom, or willing the abstract universal. I will return to these issues below. See in this regard my "Ancients, Moderns and Postmoderns."

I would admit that the only persuasive evidence that history does not end with ongoing, agitated, changeless modernity would be the production of a novel speculative idea together with a showing that it could plausibly be actualized. Nevertheless, the burden of proof is on those who think the spectacle of ongoing novelty has ceased. What fol-

My argument is that whether or not we like it, we will increasingly be confronted by theories that emanate from the philosophies of Nietzsche and Heidegger. This can be seen in the paradoxical move of the Continental (i.e., French) left toward Nietzsche and Heidegger. The Anglo-American world has tried not to take notice, but Nietzschean and Heideggerian thought—under the rubrics of deconstructionism, poststructuralism, postmodernism, versions of feminism, and countless isms yet to come—have still made substantial inroads. The various waves of isms will no doubt be short-lived, but the thought of Nietzsche and Heidegger has put something into speech that will not go away. I would contend that until now the thought of Nietzsche and Heidegger has primarily been refurbished for use in pursuing thoroughly modern ends; on this level, contemporary postmodernists have tried to prop up fundamentally liberal notions of egalitarian pluralism, individualism, and autonomous metaphysical freedom. At an opposite pole we find those who fall into the trap of reading Nietzsche and Heidegger as aiming at something articulated in purely negative terms. That maneuver usually transforms itself into a merely empty, formless, *anti*modernism. We must be more original in our approach to Nietzsche and Heidegger. I predict that the now-extant attempts to deflect the primary thrust of Nietzschean and Heideggerian thought back onto the modern path will fail and, more to the point, that without other more consistent deflections, altogether undesirable outcomes could ensue. There are disquieting possibilities lurking in the thought of Nietzsche and Heidegger—neither is a friend of constitutional

---

lows is addressed to those interested in the future—to address oneself to any other audience is to assure one's own obsolescence. I will argue that without some as yet unseen refurbishing, the several extant variants of late modernity will inevitably become less and less compelling, even when propped up by the increasingly frequent returns to Locke, Kant, or Hegel that we have been witnessing. The return to a previous moment in modern thought is no more possible than a simple return to premodernity in any of its forms. Such maneuvers, what I would call "holding actions," are not to be despised, but without the eventual arrival of a relief column any holding action will ultimately fail.

One of the most sophisticated uses of this tactic can be found in Pangle, *The Ennobling of Democracy: The Challenge of the Postmodern Era*. For Pangle, postmodernism is *the* problem. He begins with a rather curious choice of "postmodern" authors, criticizes them, and then moves on to an interesting amalgamation of modern liberal and premodern ideas. While Pangle sees the limitations of both his classical and modern sources, he sees enough of value to forge a synthesis of elements taken from both. Yet, apparently, he finds no elements of value in any postmodern (meaning here, post-Hegelian) sources. In the last analysis I doubt that any synthesis that totally eschews post-Hegelian sources can hold for long. See my review of Pangle's book in *Perspectives on Political Science,* 1993, and my "Ancients, Moderns and Postmoderns."

government—which are important both to note and to avoid. At this point, it is too late to simply negate the influence of Nietzsche and Heidegger.

The intellectual present always confronts us with an inertial trajectory that cannot be simply reversed. It can, however, be deflected in a variety of ways. By studying the most powerful ideas in the present— and I believe these are to be found primarily in the thought of Nietzsche and Heidegger—we can assess our general, late-modern trajectory into the future, as well as possible deflections of that trajectory. This cannot be done with anything resembling precision. Nor can it be accomplished from some autonomous, Archimedean point. In my use of the term, speculative thought is the articulation of such possible deflections based on an assessment of present inertial forces both in thought and in the concrete world. No autonomy or determinism of ideas or consciousness is implied. Yet it is assumed that we are beings moved as much by ideas as by economic reality, instinctive human nature, or other blind, material forces. At the very least, the environment of ideas always overlays the substratum of concrete existence, and the two never diverge completely or correspond simply.[21] No one has the privilege of standing outside either their material reality (both human and nonhuman) or the evolving context of ideas. Instead, one must operate within those ideas gaining ascendancy, understand them, and determine how the available alternatives will affect human beings living in the particular world of the present.

I make no attempt to solve the unsolvable chicken-egg problem regarding the relation between ideas and their material context. Was, for example, Machiavelli—generally considered one of the intellectual fathers of modernity—the product of his world and its material and intellectual context or the father of a new context? The important fact for my purposes is that, whether Machiavelli set a new world in motion or presented one of the first and most prescient articulations of a world

21. A position frequently put forward in the "sociobiology" literature comes close to asserting the complete hegemony of nature in human affairs. See Edward O. Wilson, *Sociobiology: The New Synthesis* (Cambridge, Mass.: Harvard University Press, 1975), and *The Sociobiology Debate: Readings on Ethical and Scientific Issues,* ed. Arthur L. Caplan (New York: Harper & Row, 1978). Contemporary postmodernism comes close to asserting the complete historicality and contingency of drives and desires by transforming them into social constructs. In this regard, the work of Michel Foucault is indicative. I take a stance between the simple hegemony of material and efficient causality and the completely social construction of reality. Our existence has an underlying natural basis which must be completed by education, i.e., "ideas." Where the line between the two is to be found is never easy to say. For an interesting treatment of this issue see Masters, *The Nature of Politics.* I discuss the topic thematically in part 4.

already evolving, his thought represents *a leading indicator*. I make no claim for the thought of Nietzsche and Heidegger other than that it represents a similar political and moral leading indicator. Furthermore, I do not try to explain the existence of great thinkers, although I assume a difference between a genuinely comprehensive thinker and a derivative one.[22] I do not know why great thinkers have existed where and when they have, but one can proceed without such knowledge. Nor can I predict when another will turn up; we must make the best of the resources we have—even if they are less than ideal—and not sit idly by waiting for a great thinker to bail us out.

I offer as an empirical premise that there is no evidence that the force of an idea is in any simple way related to its capacity for apodictic demonstration. To believe otherwise is to engage in what I would call the "fallacy of logic," i.e., the fallacy that overestimates the status of logic and what it can accomplish. After all, the value of logic cannot be established by logic. And the plausibility and persuasiveness of such modern ideas as the state of nature, History, the categorical imperative, metaphysical freedom, and so on certainly did not rest on logic or apodictic proof. Yet those ideas have had, and continue to have, powerful consequences. Conviction is carried in a variety of ways. Factors other than logic, some of which we will consider, operate at least as powerfully as logic. Logic itself, like modern science in all its forms, rests on a prior act of faith: e.g., the belief that the world is in fact orderly and that reality corresponds with our statements about it. The reduction of philosophy to a form of apodictic proof not only unnecessarily constricts our view of philosophy, it represents the presentation of philosophy within one, historically determined idiom. What is at stake is precisely the future status of that idiom, and a reflection on the variety of possible alternate idioms.

Finally, great thinkers do not simply *will* or create their ideas *ex nihilo*. The power of their ideas comes from their having articulated a shared experience with more force and depth than anyone else.[23] Persuasive ideas do not simply float in the sky; they are related to experiences shared by more than a few. Still, it is never entirely clear what the

---

22. I reflect on this distinction in my "Who Is Nietzsche's Zarathustra?: Part II." The evidence convinces me that an element of the mysterious accounts for the coming-to-be of great thinkers. Needless to say great thinkers never operate in a vacuum. But rarely is the context that supports a great thinker so novel that it is not reproduced in a variety of places without producing the same result.

23. Here I agree with Vattimo that "any philosophy that wishes to remain faithful to experience cannot but argue on the basis of some sort of approximation of general experiential traits that must be assumed to be apparent to all" (Vattimo, *End of Modernity,* 6).

deferred ramifications of ideas will be; philosophy has its effects in unpredictable ways, and there are unavoidable differences between
thinker and layman. This is a significant ground of historical freedom.
If logic ruled, History would reign. In some sense, something like
Hegel's view of the inevitable sequencing of ideas would eventually be
victorious; we would eventually arrive at idea exhaustion, or closure,
and the history of philosophy would end. The notion of philosophical
persuasion that holds in the work that follows represents a return to
authors like Plato, Machiavelli, Rousseau, and others who understood
the unavoidable, subtle interpenetration of philosophy, poetry, logic,
and rhetoric. I will argue that this view is one that Nietzsche and
Heidegger understood as well, albeit in different ways. They *consciously* intended for their thought to have an *effect*. What that effect will
be is still an open question.

In the last analysis, what I have to offer is no more than the simple
dignity of thinking about our situation. Theorists must occasionally
disentangle their theoretical efforts from their political and moral commitments at least long enough to reconsider their compatibility. What
is required is the willingness to engage in a kind of thought that is not
precommitted, ideological justification. Otherwise, thought can never
do more than rationalize already existing relationships, leaving us to
drift toward the future without choices. Since I see no indication that
the premise that we have no choices has or can be proven, I will proceed
on the opposite assumption, that we can in some way shape our future.
If no such possibility exists—if we are all in the grips of an overpowering Fate—efforts like the present one will be ultimately superfluous,
more or less sophisticated, mandarin pastimes. I do not accept that
conclusion any more than I think we can or should dream up utopias
from out of thin air. What is needed is to think toward the philosophical possibilities that will exist in the future and consider how they
might support the pursuit of the just, the decent, the good, and the
noble. I admit that the modern world has supported the possibility of
justice and decency. But it is also true that justice and decency existed
before the twentieth century, which has invented more novel barbar-
isms, and on a quantitatively greater scale, than all past ages put together. Is it possible that there is only *one* way to defend the noble, the
good, the decent, and the just?

2

The Modern Longing: Protomodernity

In what follows I will argue that several central notions link protomodern thinkers. Those ideas did not spring immaculate from the
void.[1] Nonetheless, a few key, distinctively modern ideas were
plumbed, developed, and eventually deflected in a distinctive direction
over a five-hundred-year period. The pivotal deflection of protomodern thought was performed by Rousseau and led to the central

1. The issue of whether modernity represents a radical break or rupture with the
past, as the protomoderns themselves believed, has been hotly debated. For example,
in *Meaning in History,* Löwith argues that modernity is not fundamentally based on a
radical break with the past, that protomodernity's mythic self-understanding was deluded. Löwith argues that modernity is a self-deceived repetition, which takes over, sec-
ularizes, and transforms significant elements from faith and tradition, but is illegitimate
precisely because the borrowed categories will not work outside their original environment.

Funkenstein presents a softer version of this thesis in *Theology and Scientific Imagination.* In what could be called a "contingent convergence" thesis, he tries to show a cross-
ing of theological language into science and a simultaneous secularization of theology in
the seventeenth century. Funkenstein notes that that prior to Kant modern science still
addressed ontological questions about the nature and origin of reality, a concern conditioned by the crossover of theological categories. But that crossover was contingent and
cannot be recovered; in Kant's wake, he admits, theology and science are severed once
and for all. After Kant, knowledge of "the thing in itself" ceased to be an object for
science. According to Funkenstein, this diremption of science and theology solved numerous protomodern aporias. Still, contemporary science's indifference to ontology is
not altogether sanguine.

Riley offers an even more limited thesis in *The General Will before Rousseau: The
Transformation of the Divine into the Civic.* He argues that the concept General Will represents a secularized transformation of an idea whose original source is Christian—to be
found in a peripheral remark by Saint Paul. But Riley does not make larger claims about
the continuity of modern and premodern thought.

In *The Legitimacy of the Modern Age,* Blumenberg argues that modernity does represent a radical break precisely in line with modernity's self-understanding (which is an
indication that history is open to radical revision by thought). According to Blumenberg, modernity rests on the self-assertion of a self-legislating, self-grounding Reason.

late-modern notion, metaphysical freedom. That idea was in turn codified by Hegel, bringing about *an* end to modernity. We thus arrive at a
moment of irreversibility.[2]

In trying to articulate the shared central notions of pivotal protomodern authors, I begin from what I believe to be the fundamentally

---

This goes hand in hand with a project for demythologization (enlightenment) and a notion of limited, "possible progress." What might look like secularized Christian ideas
are in fact "reoccupied positions." Modern authors thought—incorrectly—that it was
incumbent upon them to answer various questions that grew out of premodern perspectives. This led to such errors as trying to prove historical inevitability when accepting the more limited notion of possible progress was all that was required. It also led
modern thought in a materialist direction, when self-assertion was defined primarily in
terms of a quest for survival and security due to an attempt to reoccupy teleological
positions. This move, by authors like Hobbes, was not required by modernity's original impulse. In short, modernity betrayed its initial impulses in unnecessarily trying to
reoccupy premodern questions.

2. Numerous contemporary "return theses" focus on returning to previous moments of modernity. Blumenberg's thesis represents an attempt to return to an earlier,
allegedly more modest understanding of protomodernity. In *Sources of the Self,* Taylor
also argues for a return to earlier modern sources, claiming there are moral resources in
protomodern thought that have been obliterated by the impoverished language of modernity's more ardent recent supporters. Pocock has argued for a return to various protomodern sources as a means of recovering modern republicanism; see his *The
Machiavellian Moment.* Pippin argues for a return to his modest rendition of Hegel,
stripped of teleology and the inevitability thesis. We have seen a variety of arguments
for returns to Locke, Kant, Hegel, and so on. Strauss is alleged to be calling for a return
to classical antiquity, but I do not accept that understanding; see my "The Post-Modern
Leo Strauss?" and my "On Leo Strauss and His Influence." MacIntyre would have
us recover a form of Augustinianism; see his *After Virtue* and *Whose Justice; Which
Rationality?* I reject all possibilities of going back. Either Pippin is correct that late modernity is an end—and we will remain in an ongoing environment of critique and
deconstruction—or we must find a way to go forward.

I side with Blumenberg in seeing self-grounding, self-assertive reason as the central
modern idea. I will argue that that understanding of reason opened itself to being quite
consistently interpreted as will. This puts me on the side of the "radical break" thesis,
against Löwith, Hegel, Nietzsche, Heidegger, MacIntyre, and many others. But, I
would maintain that Funkenstein, for example, is fundamentally correct in stating that
this break did not occur in a vacuum; the response to late medieval nominalism is surely
an issue. Funkenstein is also correct in pointing to a convergence of language and idioms
in protomodern thought. But I would argue that this convergence tells us more about
the requirements of philosophic rhetoric than it does about substantive agreement.

Contrary to Blumenberg, I will argue that the protomodern impulse is quite
logically—albeit not inevitably—deflected into what Blumenberg tries to dismiss as
unessential, "reoccupied positions" and that we have arrived at a point of irreversibility;
we cannot go back to the more modest claims of protomodernity. I stress that I am arguing for irreversibility, not inevitability. By comparison, I would argue that Strauss, who
also sees a radical break at the origin of modernity, comes very close to the inevitability
thesis. His famous "three waves" seem to inevitably flow from one to the next; see

correct conventional wisdom that sees Descartes as the father of modern philosophy and Machiavelli as the father of modern political philosophy.[3] The central notion shared by them, and by other proto-modern thinkers, is a self-understanding that a conscious, fundamental break with all past thinking—as well as with concrete reality—was required and that self-grounding Reason was the tool for making that break. For example, Machiavelli observes that "in order that our *free will* not be eliminated, I judge that it might be true that fortune is arbiter of half of our actions, but also that she leaves the other half, or close to it, *for us to govern*."[4] Machiavelli likens Nature (qua Chance) to a flooding river that sweeps away everything before it. But when times are quiet, dikes and dams can be constructed to channel the flood. In that way Nature can be brought under the control of man's Will. In human affairs, consciously constructed laws take the place of dikes and dams, and channel the flood of untutored passions and emotions. The master of human flood control channels human nature for the sake of enlarging the efficacy of the Will. Man becomes at least partial master in a consciously constructed kingdom of his own.[5]

Strauss, "What Is Political Philosophy?" in *What Is Political Philosophy?*, 9–55, and "The Three Waves of Modernity."

Again contrary to Blumenberg, I am in fundamental agreement with Pippin's argument, in *Modernism as a Philosophical Problem,* that Kant sums up the essential modern longing by addressing his critical philosophy to the question of the possibility of self-grounding reason, and that the aporias left by Kant lead quite consistently to Hegel's reflections. But Pippin goes on to argue that in rejecting Hegel's reconciliation of Kantian aporias Nietzsche simply proves that self-legislating reason (qua Will) is the only ground, and that a critique of its possibility remains the enduring problem of philosophy in perpetuity. Consequently, for Pippin modernity is unending and postmodernity is, in any serious sense, an impossibility. For Pippin, there is no way back—Kant's critique stands "permanently at the door of such return trips" (p. 166). But there is also no way forward; modernity is the last epoch. I agree that there is no way back beyond Kant. I will argue, however, that there is a way forward.

3. In pursuing the central ideas that link different authors, I will inevitably ignore the great diversity that exists in modern thought. But we cannot be truly resolute in our search for something beyond modernity without first trying to articulate the essence of the modern. To my mind we simply must ignore the potential difficulties of this approach in order to make a beginning. Otherwise, we must sacrifice all positive, speculative discourse about postmodernity. That would mean no longer reflecting on the alternate futures available to us, accepting instead chance outcomes and drifting into the future. As I have already stated, I reject the premise that the future *must* be an endless repetition of the present or a fated dispensation beyond our power to shape.

4. Machiavelli, *The Prince,* 98–101, esp. 98; emphasis mine. Henceforth designated in the text as *P,* followed by a page number.

5. For an elaboration of this argument, see my "Machiavelli's *The Prince* and the Abolition of the Political."

Machiavelli admits that the natural situation for man is to live in relatively small, homogeneous societies ruled by unwritten customs, that is, in the situation Aristotle praises. But such societies are unable to conquer Chance. In the grips of Chance, natural societies are prone to almost inevitable ongoing hostilities—too small to become materially self-sufficient, too dependent on divisive, natural factors such as ethnicity and language. Only the conscious application of the Will can construct a means to conquer Chance; the Will, that is, of a Machiavelli who plots a course to the emancipation of humanity from tradition, religion, and, in short, the dead weight of the past. In projecting man beyond the past, Machiavelli makes conscious choice the ground of law, and makes it inevitable that political communities will turn to their "advisors"—i.e., their philosophers—for new laws. Machiavelli, far from being a simple realist, aims at the most idealistic of ends, the actualization of the philosopher-king. The new philosopher-kings—acting just offstage, manipulating "new" princes—will, in effect, rule in a nonnatural society constructed by the Will.[6]

Machiavelli's modernity lies in the key notion that accounts for his efforts. Machiavelli opposes Nature (here primarily construed as blind Chance) and Will. The Will or Reason of man, not Nature, provides the ground for the human good. Man, acting out of himself, must construct the conditions for his well-being. The Reason/Nature dichotomy is the key to this distinctively modern understanding, which is conjoined with the transformation of Reason into a form of Will. Finally, Machiavelli manifests the modern relation to temporality. The past loses legitimacy; the present is sacrificed to the future. Modern man is expelled from both the past and the present and set *in transition*—forever "on the way"—to a novel future.

Premodern thought never made such distinctions. Human Reason was part of the natural whole, indeed the peak or culminating part. The *practical* task of Reason in premodern thought was to be found in supporting the customs and laws that make possible the habits that are the

---

6. These new princes are manipulated by the puppet master Machiavelli in ways old, "natural" princes never could be. Old princes are told to preserve the ancient laws and customs and to refrain from unnecessary expansion. New princes are advised to expand and innovate, to introduce "new orders and modes." Their task is to initiate the movement toward larger, more heterogeneous societies with *consciously* constructed laws. But these new princes are manipulated in such a way that they help launch a new world in which they eventually become obsolete. For example, without the guidance of ancient customs, new principalities are in much greater need of the wise "advisors" discussed by Machiavelli in chapters 22 and 23. Someone must consciously write new laws after the new prince has leveled the past. It is unlikely it will be done by the relatively rustic, proud, new warrior-prince.

prerequisite for reaching man's natural end. Its *theoretical* task was to grasp the articulation of the whole, part of which involved finding the necessary place of the thinker in that whole. Reason was an activity that was part of the natural perfection of the individual, as well as the faculty that made possible the ascent to unity with the first cause, the One, the divine *nous*. Reason was not a tool for standing outside the whole; it was, on the contrary, the faculty for grasping how properly to integrate oneself into the whole. It was not the task of theoretical Reason to invent new modes and orders.[7]

The premodern relation to temporality was correspondingly different. The present took precedence. Happiness was possible in the present, not as some future prospect—*nous,* for example, could get in contact with the eternal whole in the present; *arete* was possible in the present. One could probably go so far as to say that the future had no Being whatsoever. The past had no particular dignity simply because it was old. Reason, not tradition, discovered the good, although custom was necessary to actualizing the good.[8] Nowhere in premodern thought does one see the Reason/Nature split, the belief that Reason is the tool by which we emancipate ourselves from Nature, stand outside it, and construct the arena of the human good from out of our self-legislating Will. Nor does one see the transformation of Reason into a form of Will. Finally, one does not see the priority of the future over the present and past. One sees the first signs of all these modern ideas in Machiavelli.

For Machiavelli, the fundamental problems confronting humanity had solutions that were primarily political. We conquer Chance by emancipating ourselves from the dead weight of tradition, by channeling newly emancipated passions and emotions through consciously constructed dams and dikes. Machiavelli's new and better future world is projected as one dominated by larger, more self-sufficient states, states that are far more complex than their "natural" predecessors,

---

7. Seen retrospectively, from the viewpoint of protomodernity, this tended to make premodern philosophy look conservative, limited to tinkering and reform rather than revolutionary invention. Premodern thought also appeared to have an aristocratic bias. Taking Aristotle as an example, since there was no pure, practical reason that could provide an alternative to the laws and customs of a specific community, there was a need for a well-trained, virtuous individual—what Aristotle called the *phronimos*—who could make prudent, on-the-spot decisions; the theoretically wise could not replace the practically wise. The rule of the naturally best equipped and trained few, either directly or indirectly, was unavoidable.

8. The sharp reason/tradition dichotomy is a modern invention. See my "Aristotle on Reason and Its Limits," delivered at the Midwest Political Science Convention, April 1991.

needing new laws and the rule, not of strictly "political" individuals competing for strictly political goods, but (if perhaps only behind the scenes) of those who "know."[9] Machiavelli and his kind ("intellectuals") eventually replace those who can be described as occupants of the "life-world" as the ones with the primary legitimacy to rule. In Machiavelli we see the first signs of what we might call an elitism of manipulative theorists qua "legislators," a pattern that is repeated throughout modern thought. And we see as well the longing for the eventual abolition of the political.

For Descartes, the solution to the fundamental problems confronting humanity required a new science rather than a new political program. Descartes thought that the most important problems confronting humanity could be traced to the limits imposed by natural scarcity, disease, consciousness of mortality, fear of violence, and so on; human beings are political primarily because of the competition necessitated by these limits. Transcend the natural limits—remove the reasons for fear and competition—and what seem to be unavoidable divisions and hostilities would become less compelling. No other political motive—whether the natural love of honor, fostered by natural *thumos* or *megalopsychia,* or the simple love of one's own—would incline human beings to political competition. Likewise, no *political* participation, as a means to the development of moral virtues, would be necessary. Descartes looked instead to a new physics, and ultimately a new human physics—medicine. Like Machiavelli, he proposed a *transition* to a novel future.[10]

To launch the new science Descartes was willing to call into question everything from "common sense" and traditional wisdom to the evi-

9. I will elaborate what I mean by the "political" in part 4. At present my argument is that the purely political person is in the process of becoming obsolete in the future Machiavelli projects; again, see my "Machiavelli's *The Prince* and the Abolition of the Political." For example, an abstract theoretical end like "conquering chance" would be entirely foreign to Machiavelli's new princes. Motives like honor and glory move them to action. A full articulation of strictly "political" motives will have to wait, but there are motives to action that are not political. Determining the nature of the motive of the theorist like Machiavelli, who aims at the conquest of chance, is an interesting challenge. Does Machiavelli aim at honor and glory as well? Does one attempt to transform the natural articulation of things out of benevolence, to achieve immortal fame among humans, to rival the gods? What can be said is that in contrast to premodern thought, the modern end of theory is no longer the pleasure found in the activity itself. The modern theorist is engaged in a practical undertaking. In the process—in the service of abstract ends—politics becomes more theoretical. This could also be described under the rubric the "colonizing of the life-world." See chap. 22, n. 7.

10. Descartes, *Discourse on Method,* 18. Henceforth designated in the text as *DM,* followed by a page number.

dence of the senses. Having bracketed received opinion and the deceptive evidence of the senses, he was left with the empty self, subject, or
ego. For Descartes, a radically unencumbered, self-legislating consciousness was the bedrock upon which to build. This is the quintessential modern point of departure. Descartes will not allow us to rely
on the passive receptivity of our naive, natural consciousness. The world
presented by our senses does not have the same Being as the world of
our clear and distinct theories.[11] A gap opens between the two, and the
modern delegitimization of the realm of appearance begins. We lose
faith in the availability and reliability of the world of appearance. In
consciousness, or subjectivity, Reason finds a stance outside the shared
world of natural, sensual experience. Later modernity (and, I will argue, any dispensation genuinely beyond modernity) must struggle to
find a way back to the world and to give Being back to appearance. It is
not clear to me that modernity ever succeeds, despite, for example,
Hegel's heroic efforts. We are increasingly left with the hegemony of
the self-grounding, disencumbered subject, without history, tradition,
or world, trying to reconcile itself with concrete reality.

11. The problem was to sort through the ideas that pass through consciousness, giving the imprimatur of knowledge to some and discarding the others. The "clear and
distinct" ideas, the ones for which a fundamentally mathematical articulation could be
given, were granted Being; all others were cast off into an epistemic nether world.
Thereby we humans became the ground of Being. We decide what will count as nature
for us. Using Descartes's new scientific method, we start with clear and distinct ideas,
deduce ideas that are contained in them, divide the wholes of sense experience down to
simple conceptual parts, and even treat "as-if" ordered things which are not necessarily
ordered. When we reassemble the theoretically clear and distinct parts into a whole we
no longer have any assurance that the new, artificially constructed whole bears any
resemblance to the initial whole grasped by ordinary, sensory consciousness (*DM* 27,
55, 78).

Descartes explicitly argued that the clear and distinct ideas found their ground in
God, that in articulating the ensemble of the clear and distinct ideas one articulated the
mind of the creator. The status of Descartes's belief in God has been the basis of a lively
debate which I will not here presume to resolve. We can leave matters at saying that if we
remove the ontological underpinning of God, and the seeming convergence with theological idioms, Descartes's teaching can seem to generate a form of reason that then dictates *its* laws to nature. This reading is consistent with Descartes's dream that *we* become
"masters and possessors of nature" (*DM* 45). Furthermore, Descartes admits that his
clear and distinct ideas may not necessarily correspond to anything in the external
world. In fact, he is explicit that we must treat "as though ordered materials which [are]
not necessarily so" (*DM* 7, 15, 27). He further argues that it is not only reasonable but
useful to have more than one explanation of the same thing (*DM* 47). There is no simple
correspondence theory in Descartes's thought. Descartes's science does not aim at the
description or explanation of reality; it aims at manipulation and domination of nature
for the sake of removing the natural limits that seem to stand in the way of man's happiness.

In perfectly Machiavellian fashion, Descartes opposes chance and the conscious decisions of "rational men." Reversing a metaphor used by Aristotle, Descartes observes that cities built by *conscious* design are better than ones that are the product of chance.[12] Things produced by a single, self-conscious legislator are better than those produced by many hands through trial and error, that is, tradition. For Descartes, this means that a general, scientific project must be posited by one person. As it is now fashionable to say, an architectonic paradigm must be posited, a theoretical frame for others to follow. Armed with a shared method, a relatively prosaic cumulative effort could take the place of what for Descartes was the spectacle of past philosophy—one brilliant speculative flash of light after another that did nothing to overcome the ongoing darkness. Disciplining a great number of individuals, over many generations, in the use of a shared method could take the place of the formidable education of the premoderns, through which only comparatively rare individuals could attain happiness.[13] Descartes becomes the legislator to those who follow the method, just as Machiavelli is to his new princes; the elitism of the master theorist qua legislator returns. A philosophy that has utility as its end replaces and delegitimizes premodern, contemplative, speculative philosophy. Reason is employed for the benefit of mankind, in the hope it will make possible, in the future, what Descartes understands to be the human good: the enjoyment of the fruits of the earth in good health over a long life (*DM* 45).

While the new philosophy would eventually emancipate men from some of the more oppressive myths that had burdened them in the past, no general enlightenment is envisioned. The ideas generated by the new philosophy are for the "learned and wise." Descartes vaguely leaves it to wiser people to judge the extent to which the public should be informed of the discoveries of the new science (*DM* 65). The mastery and possession of the world was to be conducted by the few on behalf of the commonality of mankind, but not with their total understanding or participation.[14] One suspects that laymen, determined by

12. Descartes, *Discourse on Method*, 10. Compare this with Aristotle's discussion of Hippodamus in *The Politics*, 70–73, esp. 214.

13. This cumulative application of a method is far less dependent on chance—i.e., natural endowment, good birth, excellent education, fortuitous circumstance throughout a life. Modern science, dependent as it is on a shared method, has a decidedly egalitarian bent.

14. In Descartes's vision, the new philosophy should be conducted outside the glare of the public arena in regimes that will tolerate it. The new philosophers, clothed in the modest public veneer of their provisional morality, would not engage in public debate.

their senses and dependent, as in some sense they always will be, on "provisional morality," would never become complete initiates of the new science. Machiavelli and Descartes, despite competing visions of how to transform reality, share the idea of Nature as an arena hostile to human well-being and locate man's salvation in a Reason that stands outside the given and consciously constructs laws. Each asserts the necessity of a lawgiver who posits a project for others. Finally, both express what amounts to a longing for the eventual abolition of the strictly political and its replacement by a spontaneous comfortable, prosperous, long life.

The Machiavellian teaching, which was immediately stigmatized as the work of the devil, had to be deflected to gain any wide acceptance, and the new scientific method had no immediate political and moral relevance. Hobbes's subsequent synthesis of the new moral and political approach and the new scientific method was not inevitable, but it was thoroughly consistent with what I have argued is the central protomodern idea. In Hobbes, the modern understanding of the relation between man and Nature is presented through the metaphor of the State

---

Nonetheless, Descartes makes clear that their work can best be pursued in a commercial republic such as Holland—one needs open societies for the open transmission of ideas. In suggesting that, at a future time, under circumstances transformed by the successful new science, commercial Holland might well become the universal ideal of a regime in which to pursue the perfect physics and the perfect medicine, Descartes sounds one of the first notes of the protomodern faith in commerce.

A similar picture of the new philosophers, outside and indeed "above" the political community, is presented by Francis Bacon in his "New Atlantis." Bacon's scientists are strictly isolated from what passes for the political community. Inventions, but not ideas, are occasionally sent down from their mountain retreat; popular enlightenment is not a goal, nor are all inventions disseminated. An elite that understands the whole of the new science in a way even the expert inventors never do screens inventions, using the inventors much as Machiavelli uses the new princes. Still, while some inventions are dangerous, there is a general faith in the benefits of material and technological progress: the statues in the community are of inventors, not political heroes.

The nonscientific community at the base of Bacon's scientific mountain retreat has a traditional basis, including a foundation in religion. The community administered by the new science still requires a moral foundation, as was the case with Descartes's provisional morality. Traditional family relations are rewarded, as is population growth; a "feast of Tirsan" honors a father with thirty descendants. Bacon's ideal society is pacific, noncompetitive, moral, familial, and closed to outside—i.e., premodern— influences. It moves at a slow, unhurried pace, the success of the new science having made political competition and participation obsolete. Once again, this is all made possible by a scientific method that "vexes" and "tortures" nature with experiments, resolving things into their parts so that reproducible causal factors can be identified and understood, making possible prediction and manipulation.

of Nature. Hobbes's State of Nature is clearly inconsistent with human well-being. Like Descartes's ego, its inhabitants are disencumbered selves, without traditions, social ties, families, and so on. Once again it is Reason that allows these disencumbered selves to escape by grasping the "laws of Nature," understood as precepts or general rules. These laws do not operate in the same way as the natural passions and instincts; we must "discover" them before they can become operative. In reality, however, this discovery is possible only after Hobbes's teaching is posted because it requires the legislative act of "name giving" that he accomplished. Without Hobbes's distinctive name giving, Reason cannot operate.[15]

The antinature animus of modern thought continues to assert itself and becomes even clearer in Hobbes's teaching. The Nature/Reason dichotomy returns, with Nature now conceptualized as Necessity rather than Chance, and again clearly opposed to the human good. Everything rests in advance on the self-grounding, legislative exercise of Reason by a Hobbes who gives meanings to the names—though hardly the meanings embedded in everyday speech. There is no pretense that the names Hobbes posits correspond to anything in the natural world.[16] As in Descartes, Reason must construct its own point of departure. This Hobbesian flight from natural, historically embedded speech is intrinsic to later modernity, and is repeated in twentieth-century attempts to create ideal, artificial languages. To arrive at the good it was necessary to act "as if" all manner of natural difference did not exist (L 120), as if all men everywhere long for the same things: a peaceful, predictable, long life, with comfort and freedom from consciousness of death.[17] Hobbes's modernity culminates in a universal

---

15. "Reason" has multiple meanings in Hobbes's thought. Reason is the faculty asocial, natural men use to discover the laws that allow them to calculate their way out of the state of nature. Later, however, Hobbes explicitly defines reason (science) as the ability to deduce the consequences of altogether artificial "names." Finally, reason is also, presumably, the faculty Hobbes himself uses in consciously defining the fundamental names—definitions that clearly differ from traditional, conventional usages. It is not clear that all these uses of the term "reason" are identical. Put another way, it is not clear that Hobbes's explicit teaching can account for the doings of the *legislator* Hobbes.

16. Thomas Hobbes, *Leviathan,* 36. Henceforth designated in the text as *L,* followed by a page number.

17. Building on his mechanistic, reductionist psychological teaching—i.e., following Descartes in reducing the human soul to simple parts and then reassembling the parts in a novel way—Hobbes is able to be indifferent to the natural distinctions among men that took priority in premodern thought. Thus, Hobbes can posit a potential equality. "Prudence," for example, presupposes only quantitatively equal experiences.

teaching; only one way of life is legitimate everywhere and always. Like all universal teachings it is thoroughly hypothetical, based on the ubiquitous modern "as if."

Since man's various natural inclinations were strong, in Hobbes's teaching their sublimation required an unlimited sovereignty. This is where Locke moved in to further soften and deflect the protomodern teaching. At the very least, Locke was unwilling to rely on Hobbes's subterranean limitations on the authority of the sovereign.[18] This led to what is one of Locke's central innovations, his discussion of property.[19]

Theoretical reason or "science" can be shared equally, requiring only the assiduous application of the proper, shared method. It was especially necessary to emancipate men from vainglorious competition, and by extension, from partisan political participation. Where Machiavelli relied heavily on the manipulation of the ambition and the love of glory of political men—and on the fear of the majority—Hobbes tries to rid himself of strictly political inclinations from the very beginning. For Hobbes, the love of glory and honor are explicitly delegitimized by Reason. They, like laughter and many other natural phenomena, are rejected by Reason as at odds with the human good.

18. Hobbes offered prudential arguments, which recall those of Machiavelli, why the sovereign should limit itself. For example, only a poor and weak sovereign would keep its subjects poor and weak; the self-interest of sovereign and citizen converge in the prosperous society. In the same vein, Hobbes tried to convince the sovereign of the importance of having counselors who are capable of scientific method (L 256, 258). A wise sovereign will have as an "advisor" those, like Hobbes, who understand the "science of politics." This is especially true given that, for Hobbes, man the "maker" is more important to success than man the "matter" (L 237). Hobbes, the maker qua political scientist, is of the utmost importance. If the future is to be an improvement on the present, behind the throne, just off the stage, must stand the thinker qua legislator, a modern image par excellence. The picture of a sovereign surrounded by Hobbesian political scientists is particularly reminiscent of Machiavelli's new prince and his advisors.

19. There is an obvious reason why Lockean interpretation has remained a growth industry and why it is so spirited and diverse: Locke is the most easily discernible source of American liberalism. By advancing an interpretation of Locke one defends a particular vision of American liberalism. Is America a regime with a moral foundation or a godless contrivance? Is it the Marxist nightmare of "possessive individualism," where all life is reduced to the "callous nexus of cash payment," or does it aim higher and produce a more dignified form of life? In discussing Locke, one always runs the risk of being unwillingly dragged into this larger, much vexed political debate. I will beg off entering into the larger debate with the excuse that at present my purpose is limited to adding a few brush strokes to the modern canvas I am trying to paint. I am not interested here in taking sides in the lively debates over whether Locke was primarily, for example, a prudent Hobbesian, a true Christian, a latter-day proponent of Aristotelian "polity," or a "possessive individualist." I do want to argue that Locke consistently deflects the central protomodern ideas I am sketching. And it is in his discussion of property that one sees one of the most significant deflections of the central protomodern ideas. For an indication of the larger debate consider Tarcov, *Locke's Education for Liberty;* Strauss, *Natural Right and History;* Quentin Skinner, *The Foundations of Modern Political Thought,* vol. 2, *The Age of Reformation;* MacPherson, *The Political Theory of*

Hobbes had understood that "plenty dependeth, next to God's favour, merely on the labour and industry of men" (*L* 185). But in his labor theory of property Locke elevates labor to a place in the argument it never had for Hobbes, and opens a possibility, later deflected, enlarged, and deepened by Hegel.

For Hobbes, the State of Nature was so insecure that devoting effort to the accumulation of property made no sense. For Locke, it is inevitable that there be property. In their natural state, things are so useless and valueless that Nature does not yield enough for man's continued existence. Man must transform Nature by his labor to survive, thereby producing his continued existence. For Locke, in the State of Nature, at least initially, fear for our self-preservation is directed more toward ex-

---

Possessive Individualism; Pangle, *The Spirit of Modern Republicanism;* Dunn, *The Political Thought of John Locke;* Gough, *John Locke's Political Philosophy;* and Hartz, *The Liberal Tradition in America.*

One of the most significant arguments for the "non-Lockean"—i.e., nonmodern—character of Locke's thought is found in Tarcov's discussion of the importance of Locke's *Thoughts concerning Education,* a treatise that has become important in the recent debates on Locke. To what extent, it has been asked, does Locke's concern with the education of a gentleman mitigate the seemingly modern, bourgeois teaching of the *Second Treatise?* Clearly Locke's education is aimed at a *bourgeois gentilhomme* rather than a traditional, Aristotelian gentleman. Locke's gentlemen will know the new science and understand commerce and industry and would be more at home in Locke's liberal, commercial regime than would Aristotle's "great-souled" man.

Having said that, it can be granted that Locke's political teaching takes into account the existence of certain kinds of human beings whose character the state does not publicly form as part of its business. Locke's state is, in his own words, an "umpire," not a teacher. It can be argued that Locke's political teaching alone, without Lockean gentlemen, would collapse. The question is whether Locke's political universe does not ultimately make obsolete the kind of human beings it presupposes. Put another way, if a Lockean regime does not publicly support the formation of character, can it hope that such character will be produced privately for an indefinite period? If not, would it be possible, and what would be needed, to regain what Locke presupposed but did not foster. I consider the claim that such reclamation can be accomplished using modern premises to be highly implausible.

A similar issue arises from reflection on the American founding generation. Here was an assemblage of gentlemen—leaning perhaps more toward the traditional variety than the bourgeois. To what extent did they create a regime that worked best with individuals like themselves, but that tended to make individuals like themselves obsolete? How could one *recover the conditions* for the emergence of such individuals, especially in a regime that not only eschews the public formation of character but, in a variety of constitutional ways, makes its private cultivation increasingly difficult? There was a time when a relatively closed gentlemanly class ran political and economic affairs in America, but we have come to see that as altogether invidious. Locke's intention aside, how could a *more inclusive* group of such individuals be constituted using available sources? I will return to this issue in part 4.

ternal Nature than the threats of other individuals. This alone would account for the difference between the State of Nature and the State of War. We are forced by the penury of the State of Nature to subdue and cultivate the earth and take "dominion" over it. Nature exists for the support and comfort of mankind but is fundamentally valueless, with no independent dignity: "It is labor, then, which puts the greatest part of value upon land, without which it would scarcely be worth anything."[20] In perfectly modern fashion, man is the source of value.

Our bodies are the only things that we initially own. When we labor we "externalize" ourselves, put something of ourselves into external Nature. The external world thereby becomes our property and Nature acquires value. In the process we gain self-sufficiency and self-respect; indeed, we create our "self" by our externalizing deeds. But according to Locke, as we acquire property trouble begins. It now becomes plausible to plunder rather than labor as a means of self-preservation. As we all possess by nature the full executive and judicial right, we have the right to judge and punish as we see fit. The chaos brought about by the resulting multiple precedents causes anxiety and thereby a reason for preemptive behavior. A state of war inevitably ensues, from which we must extract ourselves by the use of our calculating Reason.[21] For Locke, the protomodern longing remains. The key to human happiness is the secure, peaceful enjoyment of life, now with liberty and property. Once again, the more intense, natural, sublime, higher-spirited longings must be suppressed.

The best society is one populated by industrious, productive individuals who transform the natural environment through their collective efforts.[22] With Locke, Nature is still the problem, human activity

---

20. Locke, *Second Treatise of Government*, 21, 26. Henceforth designated in the text as *ST*, followed by a page number.

21. For Locke, unlike Hobbes, in the movement from the state of nature Reason dictates that we retain *two* natural rights—the right to life and the right to property. Lockean societies can move beyond the Machiavellian manipulation of fear and the love of glory, and the Hobbesian reliance on fear and the love of comfort, to the more predictable reliance on acquisitive industriousness and the love of self-sufficiency. And that reliance can in some sense be sanctified by the belief that a society so constituted leads to a material progress that makes the poorest member better off than the wealthiest in the state of nature (*ST* 25). The goal of Locke's society is the perfectly modern desire to lay the foundation for the "comfortable, safe and peaceable living one amongst another, in a secure enjoyment of their properties and a greater security against any that are not of [the same society]" (*ST* 54).

22. An alternate understanding is to be found in Aristotle. Aristotle divided all human activity into *theoria, praxis,* and *technē,* i.e., theoretical activity, political and moral action, and productive activity, with productive activity seen as a necessary evil, not the

in opposition to Nature still the solution. But Locke's deflection of protomodernity prepares the way for a less elitist and theoretically self-conscious means to a solution. *Collective,* productive activity attains a prominence it does not have before Locke. The place of the conscious exercise of Reason by a legislator at the fringe of day-to-day affairs is more limited. There are no advisors, political scientists, or method givers immediately visible in Locke's teaching. Locke prepares the way both for Adam Smith, the market mechanism, and various permutations of the modern "invisible hand," and for the later "scientific" Marx of dialectical materialism.

For present purposes we need go no further. Obviously the few authors I have discussed do not come close to exhausting the developments I want to call protomodern. They are indicative, however, of a shared protomodern set of ideas. Nature is seen, not as an ordered, supportive whole into which we should properly integrate ourselves, but as a condition—conceptualized as either Chance or Necessity—at odds with human well-being. Reason is presented as Nature's Other, not its culminating part, as the tool that makes possible the great escape from Nature, not a faculty that brings satisfaction through its mere disinterested use. How one consolidates the escape from the natural condition differs from author to author: science, institutional tinkering, manipulation of the passions (and eventually, by logical extension, behavioral conditioning), and the market mechanism are among the variations proposed.

The metaphors for the great escape from Nature and the subsequent consolidation are many and familiar. Nature must be "beaten," "struck down," "mastered," "vexed," "dominated," "tortured." There is a willingness to transform what spontaneously occurs in Nature, whether that be human passions and instincts, natural differences among individuals, or fundamental forces of nonhuman Nature. The end is always

---

primary means to happiness. To be happy required that one have the natural capacity for contemplation or the virtues and habits that made moral action and political participation possible. Neither activity was productive. Needless to say both *theoria* and *praxis* required leisure, and because of natural inequalities, to say nothing of chance, that leisure would never be available to all. The political community had as its primary end the education that leads to the habits and virtues that make *praxis* possible, albeit seldom for the majority. A stable political community was in turn the prerequisite for the theoretical life. In the end, the political community may have been judged from the perspective of the well-being of philosophy, for there seems to be a significant bias in Greek thought in favor of *theoria* over *praxis.* One sees no bias in Locke in favor of either *theoria* and *praxis.* The modern faith in science, technology, industry. and commerce replaces both. Neither is the means to happiness in Locke's thought; he gives that function to material progress and stable, predictable, peaceable relations.

the same (again the metaphors abound): "the relief of man's estate," "the betterment of man," "the improvement of man's condition," "man's greater security." In this vision, the good life reduces primarily to peace and security, material prosperity, comfort, long life, and emancipation from consciousness of death.

Protomodernity is antinature, anti-*praxis,* ultimately antipolitical (in the architectonic sense to which I will return thematically in part 4), centered on domination and manipulation, and by and large, until Locke, theoretically elitist—relying on the great legislative acts of a few "advisors," "counselors," "name givers," scientists, and method givers, who rule from behind the scenes. Seldom was any thoroughgoing, general enlightenment envisioned. Life for most would remain something like life in the cave. Only very late in protomodernity was popular enlightenment proposed, and I would argue, in a way that was not altogether consistent with the protomodern project. Nature becomes a problem, Reason a tool or instrument. The transformation of the natural world is the means to happiness, and those best at fostering that transformation—that is, the theorists—have the right to lead. Thereby, we overcome the past and, eventually, quit the present to endlessly pursue the future.

3

Modernity Deflected: Metaphysical
Freedom and History

The protomodern ideas I have discussed were eventually deflected in ways that could not have been predicted but that were consistently modern. At roughly the halfway mark of modernity to date, the kind of world and the kind of human beings that protomodernity was producing came seriously into question. The bourgeoisification of man came to be seen as his uglification and diminishment. Simultaneously, the dangers posed by modern science began to appear as great as its benefits. These reactions, against the political and scientific components of protomodernity, came together in the thought of Jean-Jacques Rousseau. Rousseau deflects modern thought far more significantly than has previously been done; but he too retains its central commitments, and hence his deflection remains perfectly, consistently modern. Assessing these past deflections of modern thought will aid us in determining what is possible in the present.

The thought of Rousseau stands like a prism between protomodern and late-modern thought. While critical of the moral and political dimension of protomodern thought, Rousseau takes over its central ideas and deflects them toward what is the central late-modern idea— metaphysical freedom. Rousseau likewise opens the path toward metaphysical freedom's seemingly inevitable adjunct, History. Again, I am arguing not that this deflection of protomodern thought was necessary or inevitable, but that it represents a perfectly consistent, altogether modern deflection of protomodern thought that makes a return to protomodernity unlikely. Protomodernity retained a conviction that a standoff with Nature was the best that could be hoped for. Once Rousseau opens the door to the complete conquest of Chance, the more modest protomodern standoff becomes almost impossible to reconstruct.

Rousseau's protomodern predecessors had thought the advance of commerce, industry, science, and the mechanical arts would lead to human well-being. For Rousseau, the attempt to become "master of the universe" had led to man's ruination.[1] Intellectual and technological advance had been purchased at the price of moral and political decay and a psychological diremption or "tornness" between the self-interested self and the citizen self. Everywhere one looked one saw cowardice, greed, love of luxury, softness, and, ultimately, slavery. In opposition to the industrious self-interestedness of the protomodern vision, Rousseau seeks a recovery of political virtues like courage, patriotism, camaraderie, and the hegemony of civic-mindedness and civic participation. Ultimately the picture becomes more complicated as Rousseau pieces together a mosaic of Spartan and Roman patriotic virtue, together with Genevan self-sufficiency, softened by Emilean domesticity, surrounded by an epicureanized philosophy that culminates in private reveries.

Like his protomodern predecessors, Rousseau begins with the metaphor of the State of Nature, but admits far more openly than they that his arguments should "not be taken for historical truths" (*SD* 103). Rousseau posits that in the State of Nature man was a natural, psychologically unified, happy savage, different from the animals only in being less fully endowed with "instincts." Man was thrust out of the State of Nature by a series of accidents. In the process he changed. He came to own property and became selfish, proud, vain, and, in short, *self-conscious*. Eventually he became a citizen living under laws, lost his natural freedom, and was enslaved. The new man was simultaneously citizen and bourgeois, free and slave, divided and torn. The task was to allow him to recapture unity while remaining human by transforming him again, this time consciously, into a citizen under an artfully constructed General Will. But the price for this new unity was that man would have to be *completely* denatured.

Rousseau's discussion of History—which takes man from the State of Nature to a divided modern consciousness and, he hoped, to a unified, denaturalized citizenship in the future—is a "hypothetical and conditional" reasoning, precisely "like those our physicists make every day concerning the formation of the world" (*SD* 103). Rousseau proceeds "as if" in the original state man was fundamentally formless, as if he were shaped and reshaped, by imperceptible steps, over a long period of time. Rousseau posits that what passes for instinct was learned

1. Rousseau, *Second Discourse,* in *The First and Second Discourses,* 195. Henceforth designated in the text as *SD,* followed by a page number. *First Discourse* is henceforth designated as *FD.*

—by imitating other animals, by responding to threats, and eventually through the tutelage of human laws and conventions. Original man was isolated, asocial, and unselfconscious, locked in the enjoyment of the "sole sentiment of. . . *present* existence" (*SD* 117; emphasis mine). Neither past nor future held any significant reality. The past was immediately forgotten and the ultimate future of death was insignificant.[2] Only present, concrete reality caused pain or fear, and both vanished with their cause. This "hypothetical history" is posited as "instructive." It shows that politics can be put in the service of the conscious transformation of man—conscious, that is, on the part of a legislator like Rousseau (*SD* 97). Chance could now finally yield to conscious direction. The altogether modern, hypothetical approach remains central to Rousseau's teaching, as does reliance on self-conscious legislative manipulation. The future held out the hope of the conquest of Chance, to be accomplished by a few, great legislators for the benefit of unsuspecting humanity.

As had Locke, Rousseau saw property as implicated in man's being thrust from the State of Nature. With the institution of property came civil society and the most complete change in man: law was substituted for "instinct" and duty for "physical impulse." This gave morality to our actions, but we were torn away from the State of Nature, losing forever our natural freedom.[3] But sweet as the natural state was, it was a mere yielding to Necessity, and was thereby slavery. Only obedience to the law one prescribes for oneself brings truly human freedom (*SC* 48, 56). Rousseau explicitly agrees with what he deems the modern premise: a moral law is "a rule prescribed to a *moral being,* that is to say, *intelligent [and] free*" (*SD* 94; emphasis mine). This freedom—man's "perfectibility," his "distinctive and almost unlimited faculty"—raises him above Nature and makes him tyrant of himself and Nature (*SD* 195). In the process, he becomes "metaphysically free," human, and moral. Man's true humanity is to be found in the fact that he is a free agent, although his freedom and perfectibility are to be found primarily in the species, not the individual (*SD* 113–14). Will replaces Nature as the foundation of our fundamental humanity.

2. Early man did not fear death (*SD* 116) any more than he was moved by pride (*SD* 195). His weak, evanescent "passions" were so easily gratified they held no great sway in the consciousness. Nothing naturally inclined man to be self-conscious—the fundamental bases of self-consciousness for Rousseau being reflecting on death and a concern for the opinions of other men.

3. Rousseau, *On the Social Contract,* 55–56. Henceforth designated in the text as *SC,* followed by a page number.

Rousseau's invention of metaphysical freedom is a thoroughly logical extension of the protomodern Reason/Nature dichotomy and the
modern transformation of Reason into a form of Will.[4] Rousseau understood that his teaching led to the apotheosis of the Will. The hegemony of the Will—its opposition to and eventual emancipation from
Nature—opened the problem of finding its limits. If man can be consciously shaped and reshaped, are we not at the whim of each successive "legislator"? Rousseau responded that the individual Will had to be
tied to, indeed "given up" and "given over" to, the General Will (*SC*
53). Those who refused to obey the General Will would be "forced to
be free." To become metaphysically free, the individual had to be incorporated into a whole, a community, a modern surrogate for the
polis. The requirements of a political community would impose limits
on the Will. Over time each separate community would become, in
effect, a different species. The Germans and the French would be equal
in their metaphysical freedom but different in their acquired "instincts." Although it implies no simple "biologism" or racism, Rousseau's teaching consciously intends to divide the species. For Rousseau,
metaphysical freedom goes hand in hand with nationalism.[5] Rousseau
intended to force man to be political, a citizen participating actively in a
relatively small, homogeneous community.

Every General Will eventually traces its existence to a legislator who
shapes a people out of disparate individuals by denaturing them. Rousseau indicates where he expects to find potential legislators: "May
learned men of the first rank find honorable asylum in [the courts of
kings]. May they obtain there the only recompense worthy of them:
that of contributing by their influence to the happiness of the people to
whom they will have taught wisdom" (*FD* 63–64). As with Machiavelli's advisors, the potential legislators are lurking just offstage. Because they are unlikely to be actual princes, they must "win over
without violence and persuade without convincing" (*SC* 69). Hence
great legislators must attribute their teachings to immortal beings,
using civil religion and censorship as part of their "persuasion." Consciously willed myths are needed and must not be too severely scrutinized. Egalitarian, communitarian politics thus goes hand in hand with

---

4. Rousseau understood that he was the father of a new approach: "Others will easily
be able to go farther on the same road" (*SD* 92). That road led from the "general will" to
the "categorical imperative" to the "Welt-Geist" to "species being" to existentialism to
the "original position" to critical theory to the general fascination with "narrative" and
the constant rewriting of history, whether universal or local, and so on. All of those
attempts are thoroughly modern.

5. See Cohler, *Rousseau and Nationalism*.

elitist manipulation and mythologization. Rousseau openly praises public ignorance about science and philosophy as an important component of his return to ancient civic virtue, charging that modern philosophy and science destroy the virtue the nonphilosophic can achieve.[6] Rousseau does not criticize modern science and philosophy as false. What he desires is the withdrawal of the knowers from public view, a thoroughly modern maneuver. The Rousseauian legislator would not go among the many in the mode of a Socrates who thought offering public education was incumbent upon the philosopher (*FD* 62–63). Rousseau's philosophic legislators need no teachers, while the many are sullied by real education. Hence the true philosopher must remain offstage. Rousseau's vision of a people that is relatively rustic, happy, friendly, confident, unassuming, self-sufficient, patriotic, and god-fearing cannot stand the glare of theoretical, philosophical investigation or education.[7]

Rousseau here makes a frontal assault on the substantive moral and political teaching of protomodernity, using as his primary weapon the central modern dichotomy, Reason versus Nature. Prior to Rousseau, the modern concept of Reason remained conditioned and limited by Nature. For Rousseau, Reason qua Will approaches total hegemony. This opens the way for one legislative transformation of human existence after another, proceeding endlessly. Rousseau must confront a problem that did not exist for those who thought a standoff with Nature was the best Reason could hope for. With Rousseau, the late-modern problem of finding limits on the Will emerges with all its nihilistic implications. From the beginning metaphysical freedom and History were concepts that ran the risk of being nihilistic.

Again, the limit Rousseau imposes, via the General Will, is fundamentally nationalistic. His limit is to be found in closed, homogeneous, tough, courageous, political wholes conditioned by other, similarly constituted wholes. Conflict was inevitable. But that was merely what Rousseau willed. Others of equal stature had every bit as much right to will something different. A battle of the titans lurked in

6. I believe that those like Taylor and Blumenberg who see enlightenment and demythologization as intrinsic to the modern project are simply incorrect.

7. The paradox is that it is not clear that Rousseau thinks his legislators, with their godlike practical tasks, will be happy. Happiness is apparently reserved for the disinterested, contemplative solitary walkers. Whether this is a partial bow to premodern *theoria* is a complicated question that at present must be bypassed. However, it is fair to ask if Rousseau's entire project is not undertaken so that the private few can withdraw into an epicurean garden as solitary walkers. If so, this epicureanization of philosophy points forward to Nietzsche and his depiction of the "free spirits" of the future.

Rousseau's deflection of modernity. After Rousseau, metaphysical freedom was increasingly disassociated from his demanding moral and political teaching. Kant begins this process by deflecting the idea of metaphysical freedom onto the path of the universal. With that deflection, the modern attempt to sublimate political conflict reemerges. Kant tries to provide a standard equally applicable to all, regardless of their nation. In the process he takes us from the irreducible competition between various *Volks* to an attachment to humanity by trying to construct a hypothetical, universal history of man with a cosmopolitan purpose.[8] Like Rousseau, Kant leaves it "to nature to produce someone capable of writing [a definitive hypothetical history] along the lines suggested."[9]

For Kant, we must proceed "as if" Nature itself were teleological and inclined man in the direction of metaphysical freedom; as if, using war and human selfishness—modern means—Nature brings about the full development of man's faculties, culminating in the development of Reason; and as if what strikes us as confused and meaningless is, in the history of the species, a slow, steadily advancing development.[10] Kant proposes an experiment: Act as if individuals unconsciously promote an end that, if they were aware of it, would not arouse their interest. Again we see that reason is "fully developed . . . in the species, but not in the individual"; but now it develops unconsciously without the effort of a great legislator. Reason eventually reaches a point where it is available to all and enables all individuals to "extend far beyond . . . natural instinct" (*PW* 41, 42). Like Locke, Kant tries to turn modernity away from its reliance on a few great theoretical manipulators. Of course, humanity still needs the father of the "categorical imperative."

8. With Kant, the modern oscillation between nationalism and cosmopolitanism—as if they represented an either/or choice—begins in earnest. If modernity is not transcended, that oscillation could remain in perpetuity.

9. Kant, *Kant's Political Writings*, 42. Henceforth designated in the text as *PW*, followed by a page number.

10. Kant accepts that merely natural beings are warlike and selfish. But war eventually causes the universal dispersal of mankind over the entire planet as the losers and the weak flee rather than fight. Selfishness, natural scarcity, and the random, geographical distribution of needed resources, move universally dispersed men toward commerce. Commerce breaks down natural differences and fosters universal amicability. In this way, nature itself fosters perpetual peace and universal republicanism. Ongoing scientific enlightenment leads to a relative homogenization of opinions and eventually, it could be hoped, to a universal enlightenment that culminates in a rational religion "within the limits of reason alone." All of which is conducive to the possibility of generating and deploying consciously willed, universally applicable laws which expand their hegemony over time and make feasible a realm of universal peace. At least we must proceed "as if" this were the case: both Nature and will *might* lead in the same direction.

For man to be moral and free he must eventually stand outside the realm of natural necessity and produce everything beyond the mechanical ordering of animal existence; "he [is] meant to produce everything *out of himself*" (*PW* 43; emphasis mine). This is the modern longing writ large. The complication for Kant is that it is a natural teleology that is posited as leading to this possibility. But natural teleology in and of itself can never vouch for man's freedom since it is an occurrence of the natural or phenomenal realm. At best it can lead up to a point where the efficacy of the moral realm of freedom is enhanced. The articulation of the relation between the two worlds of moral freedom and natural determinism preoccupied Kant's thought. Explaining precisely how freedom gets actualized in the phenomenal realm remained the great difficulty Kant never surmounted. He was led to this difficulty in attempting to supply the philosophical presuppositions for the possibility of the free, moral realm, which Rousseau had opened up. In the process he produced an irreparable rift.[11]

For Kant, if our free existence is to be more than an exercise in idio-

---

11. Kant was concerned that the determinism evident in early modern science (as articulated, for example, by Newton), which he accepted as intrinsic to modern science, would destroy the possibility of freedom. Hume's skepticism—his doubt about the apodictic character of concepts such as causality and necessity—had given Kant his cue. Kant accepted Hume's premise that it had become necessary to rethink the status of the fundamental concepts of modern science, but rejected Hume's understanding that such concepts originated in sense experience. Kant wished to give an apodictic foundation to the concepts of science while simultaneously saving man's freedom, to give a philosophical foundation to both early, mechanistic modern science and Rousseau's central, moral intuition.

Kant tried to show that all experience presupposed certain concepts—like causality—that were not derived from experience. Kant posits the existence of an ensemble of such categories together with the forms of pure intuition (space and time). These categories and forms of pure intuition are prior to and shape all possible experience. Reason is active and constitutive of all experience. The categories and forms of pure intuition are laws we impose on phenomena and are not true of anything "in itself." Our theoretical reason legislates to the world. In perfectly Cartesian fashion, we lay down the law of nature ourselves. Reality ultimately remains outside our grasp; we can assume no correspondence between the "in itself" and the world as it appears *for us*. What Kant saves is the reliability of the world as it is for us. But in the process, the realm of appearance loses any possible, ontological foundation.

Still, the fact that the categories we apply to experience are necessary and transhistorical vouches for the possibility of science. And the inability of our theoretical categories to reach the ontological reality postulated outside of us and beyond the grasp of phenomenal experience vouches for the *possibility* of everything from freedom to God and the immortality of the soul. Since we cannot know the "in-itself," we cannot prove the impossibility of freedom or God or the immortal soul. Therefore, we can proceed "as if" a realm of freedom existed, as if metaphysical freedom were a possibility.

syncrasy, it must obey necessary, practical laws. These laws of freedom must be comparable to the theoretical laws which shape our experience of reality, and like the theoretical laws must be based on our Will. Just as the theoretical Will is limited by *a priori* categories, the practical Will must be limited by an *a priori* law—the categorical imperative. We must follow a law we have given ourselves, a law that transcends the particular and has a universal form. Universality provides a limit on the Will, but gives it no form. What form it receives comes from the second part of the categorical imperative: treat all individuals as ends, never as means. Man, the moral being, must be cut off from all natural ends. In fact, an act of free will proves itself by being *anti*natural. In the process, morality, like the realm of appearance, loses its ontological foundation. An unavoidable gap opens between the "is" and the "ought." The specter of isolated, autonomous, formless, ahistorical, traditionless selves again raises it head. Since Kant opts for the universal over Rousseau's multiplicity of General Wills, no political fleshing out of the moral self is available. Reason is left to generate the ought entirely out of itself.

Kant hoped that if universal practical reason was properly deployed, there would be progress toward a greater hegemony of moral and free acts over natural impulsion, and thereby an increasing sublimation of, or at least alienation from, the natural.[12] The problem is that our non-natural Will must prove its freedom in the phenomenal world. Somehow the gap between the realm of Freedom and that of Necessity must be bridged.[13] The problems this leads to provided the opening seized by German idealism and ultimately by Hegel. Eventually, stripped of its relation to the abstract universal, the ought became dependent on historical contingency—e.g., historicism—or pure groundless Will—e.g., existentialism. Like Rousseau, Kant opens the door to the nihilism he tried mightily to avoid.[14]

12. Unlike Rousseau, it is not clear that Kant thinks man's phenomenal existence is fundamentally malleable and changeable. Since we can approach our phenomenal, natural existence only through unchanging, necessary categories, it would be impossible to know if that was true; we can only grasp our natural existence in one way. Apparently, practical reason, once it has become conscious of its task, must continually hold out against an unchanging phenomenal realm.

13. For a useful discussion of the various contradictions this leads to, see Hassner, "Immanuel Kant."

14. There is a significant literature—with which I am in substantial agreement—on the problems left in the wake of Kant's thought. See especially in this regard, Rosen, *Hermeneutics as Politics;* Bernard Yack, *The Longing for Total Revolution;* Kelly, *Idealism, Politics and History;* Riley, *Will and Political Legitimacy;* and Smith, *Hegel's Critique of Liberalism.*

In Kant's thought, the idea of metaphysical freedom is deflected away from the Rousseauian political universe of multiple conflicting communities, back onto the paths of a universal commitment to humanity and of commercial republicanism supported by modern science.[15] This underscores the fact that until Marx—with the exception of Rousseau—the modern faith in the benevolence of science and commerce is almost complete. The antinature animus of modernity is brought to yet a higher manifestation, and the egalitarian impulse of modernity is again heightened. The Cartesian suspicion of the ontological adequacy of the realm of the senses is given a deeper exploration, and the alienation of modern thought and modern man from the realm of appearance—and from ontological foundations—is exacerbated. The priority of the practical over the disinterestedly contemplative continues. Autonomous human Reason, both theoretical and practical, is active and imposes the law on the external world and itself. In the process modern life takes a turn toward an increasingly abstract existence.

15. Kant concludes that universal republican government is simultaneously the most supportive of a universal morality of duty and the most conducive to the universal peace that Kant, following protomodernity, posits as the only goal of any rational political striving. In perfectly protomodern fashion, Kant's longing is to be consummated on a bed of universal, commercial, republicanism. Nevertheless, Kant pulls back from positing the universal state and opts instead for a confederation of republics. His argument echoes a famous Nietzschean theme: A universal state "is not completely free from *danger*, lest human energies should lapse into inactivity" (*PW* 49).

4

Modernity's Codification and Closure:
The End of History?

In the face of the aporias left by Kant—as well as the German idealism that flowed from Kant's teaching—Hegel attempted a variety of reconciliations. For example, he tried to reestablish an ontological foundation for modernity and to recover a relation to the realm of appearance. But in the process he primarily succeeded in codifying the modern longing. For Hegel the absolute ground itself becomes Will willing itself into concrete manifestation. Hegel builds on the modern transformation of Reason into Will and tries to show that fully self-conscious Reason will ultimately accept nothing in the world but itself. Reason inevitably strives to transform the natural fabric of the World until it becomes the mirror image of itself.

Hegel's deflection of modern thought, like those previously cited, is thoroughly consistent with the fundamental modern longing to transcend primary Nature and thereby accomplish protomodernity's longed-for conquest of Chance. Hegel tries to show the ultimate outcome of the longing to transform the external realm of appearance into a manifestation of Reason. For my purposes, the key to Hegel's account is its distinctively modern amalgamation of philosophy and practical action, especially in the *Phenomenology of Spirit*.[1] That amalgamation is succinctly stated by Marx: "It is not enough that thought

1. What follows takes a fundamentally anthropological orientation, not that this is the only or primary orientation of Hegel himself. Whether one reads the *Phenomenology of Spirit*, which will be the focus of the remarks that follow, or the Hegelian corpus as a whole, anthropologically or ontologically (cosmogonically), is for my purpose irrelevant. The result is the same. Once the absolute consciousness (reason qua will actualizing itself in the world) reaches its own end, certain things become true for finite consciousness. That is all I want to maintain at present. All citations are to Hegel, *Phenomenology of Spirit*, henceforth designated in the text as *PS*, followed by a page number.

should seek to realize itself; reality must also strive towards thought."[2] From the beginning, modern philosophy saw its task as a practical one, the transformation of reality and, in the process, of the sensible world. Unlike previous moderns, Hegel eschews the hypothetical. He tries to show that the transformation of the natural fabric of reality is inevitable and to specify precisely where it must come to rest. He does this by trying to demonstrate that the history of Reason was necessary, as a manifestation of the history of Being itself emancipating itself from natural determination.

Especially in the *Phenomenology of Spirit*, Hegel tries to show that it is not possible for a merely natural consciousness projected toward a simply natural world either to find satisfaction or to understand why it is dissatisfied.[3] Hence both world and consciousness must be transformed before true understanding and satisfaction will be possible. If human consciousness were equipped only with passive-receptive sensual experience—as Hegel depicts the natural consciousness—understanding and satisfaction would never have been possible. A passive-receptive consciousness could at best arrive at a form of skepticism, which would lead to various insoluble aporias. Since consciousness allegedly cannot be satisfied by this confusion, it is inevitably driven beyond its "natural" or "immediate" manifestation, to which it is thereafter impossible to return (*PS* 49). But in giving up the certainty of the natural consciousness, man embarks on a path characterized by doubt and despair. For Hegel, as for Rousseau, History—man's progressive alienation from Nature—is a tale of woe, although in Hegel's case, the shining grail of true science waits at the end of the path, albeit only for a few.[4]

The natural consciousness, which is primarily passive and other-

2. Marx, "Contribution to the Critique of Hegel's *Philosophy of Right*: Introduction," in *The Marx-Engels Reader*, 61.

3. Hegel discusses the limitations of a merely receptive, natural consciousness in the section of the *Phenomenology* entitled "Consciousness," which characteristically has three component parts—sense-certainty, perception, and understanding.

4. For Hegel, the older, Socratic dialectic, which begins with things as they are presented to the natural consciousness—or opinions about those things as they are articulated in ordinary speech—and then tries to rise to science, is doomed; it ends necessarily in contradiction and falsity, not truth. In that contradiction and falsity man's consciousness finds no satisfaction, and it is the longing for satisfaction, to overcome a sense of alienation from the absolute truth, that drives consciousness on, beyond its original manifestation, to an emancipation from natural determination, ultimately to the actualization of a realm of freedom where man reaches an accommodation with a transformed and domesticated realm of necessity (*PS* 51).

directed, is confronted with the difficulty that sensory reality presents itself as an ensemble of unities made up of manifolds—e.g., the unity "tree" is brown, green, cylindrical, hard, soft, redolent; it is a multiplicity composed of different, even contradictory parts. On the level of a merely receptive "consciousness," we can never find an adequate way of explaining the complicated relation between the "thatness" and the "whatness" of objects. Even when the natural consciousness has risen to the level of an articulate, theoretical consciousness, it cannot self-consciously grasp that the ground of unity is thought itself. In fact, consciousness is initially inclined to posit the self-standing, self-grounding status of the things themselves and to attribute any tensions that arise between the whatness of those substances and the thatness available to the senses to its own deception rather than to the "real" thing. Hence consciousness comes to view itself as the source of deception rather than truth. It is on this level that Socrates, for example, could postulate the doctrine of ideas or that Aristotle could posit his own distinctive metaphysical teaching about an underlying substance and it sensory attributes. But consciousness is equally prone to reverse itself and attribute falsity to things; having first blamed itself for deception, it then blames things for their unreliability. Mere receptive, contemplative consciousness can never get beyond the problem posed by the togetherness and apartness of a thing and its properties. It continually asks if it is the separate properties or the principle of unity that constitutes the truth of the objects it considers. For Hegel, this tension cannot be resolved on the level of a purely contemplative, theoretical consciousness. Thought must eventually rise to the level of seeing that the unity of the things that appear is not to be found in positing them to be self-standing and self-presenting.

Mere consciousness never realizes that it is primarily dealing with thoughts and concepts, not independent substances; hence it never arrives at the real truth. Consciousness fails to notice itself in its objects; i.e., it fails to notice, in precisely Cartesian fashion, that the ego supplies the medium in which the ensemble of qualities are brought together. Only "we," as latecomers or "phenomenological observers" (i.e., Hegelian philosophers), recognize this. Hence consciousness always treats things as alien objects that stand forth independent of itself. It cannot grasp that "Reason" is active in all experience and the ground of all truth. This gap between finite man and absolute reality causes an alienation which consciousness will not accept, and which it strives to overcome. The possibility of a philosophy that is merely a contemplative reflection on a self-standing reality other than the reflective self is chimerical. Hegel presumes to have demonstrated that, far from being capable of contemplation, consciousness is itself *productive*, closer to the classical understanding of *technē* than *theoria*.

The opening wedge for the solution to the "theoretical" problem presented by consciousness is action or *praxis*. The initial theoretical dialectic presented in the section "Consciousness" must dovetail with the practical dialectic presented in the section "Self-consciousness" if it is to move beyond despair and skepticism. It is for this reason that Hegel's discussion in the *Phenomenology* moves next to the famous dialectic of master and slave. On this level, we again begin from the natural consciousness, but this time in a practical aspect which will set in motion a dialectic that ultimately reaches its own peculiar impasse. The necessity of presenting what I am loosely calling a *practical* dialectic, at the point at which a *theoretical* dialectic reaches a dead end, helps explain the seemingly random order of the *Phenomenology*. For example, an argument which, in the section on consciousness, has already chronologically worked its way up to the time of Newton is, at the beginning of the section on self-consciousness, back in the primeval forests with the mere animal being of desire, and shortly thereafter with the master and the slave. The section on self-consciousness gets us chronologically back to Christianity, whereas the next section, "Reason," begins with Descartes and the Renaissance.

Each successive step solves a problem left by the previous one. For example, only because of the intercession of the practical dialectic presented in the section on self-consciousness can we see how the theoretical impasse of "Understanding" could ever get beyond itself and rise to the level of Cartesian idealism, in which the actual, external world is finally recognized as a projection of the self and no longer as a self-subsistent "object." In the section on reason we rejoin the theoretical dialectic, which helps man develop a new tool to overcome his alienation from the external world. The practical dialectic is rejoined in the following section, "Spirit," where, after the section on reason has chronologically taken us up to modern individualism, a theoretical idea of the bourgeois intellectual, we find ourselves back in pre-Socratic Greece. The chronological discontinuities can be attributed to Hegel's continually juxtaposing the dialectic of the theoretical and the dialectic of the practical, which he does for two reasons: (1) the dialectics must cross at certain points to overcome impasses that have been reached, and (2) they must eventually converge to bring about the final solution.[5]

---

5. The two dialectics will not simply and completely converge until the very end, absolute wisdom. At that point it will be philosophy, poetry, and religion, not practical action, that put us in closest contact with the absolute. Only then will the purely con-

Theory must externalize itself and become concrete, and actual practice must become abstract and theoretical.

Hegel codifies the modern longing by demonstrating that modern premises imply that human satisfaction is only possible in a world where the realm of appearance has been transformed by modern science and technology, on the one hand, and modern ethics and politics, on the other. For Hegel, the message of the *Phenomenology* is that either autonomous, theoretical contemplation or autonomous, natural practice, taken separately, leads to impasses that can be transcended only by their incremental convergence. That point of convergence represents the closure of modernity.[6]

For Hegel, the foundation of natural *praxis* is human desire (*PS* 105). Theoretical consciousness merely contemplates and becomes absorbed in external objects. What ultimately overcomes the externalization of theoretical consciousness and directs it in toward itself is the emptiness that forces upon consciousness the need to negate external objects rather than merely to contemplate them. As desirous, as an animal being, man cannot remain contemplative. As self-conscious, man is aware of his own desire and thereby certain of his own primacy as the most real thing, as the truth. Contrary to Rousseau, it is not fear of death and vanity that opens the self, but desire. Desirous man shows his disregard for the truth of external objects by simply negating them to satisfy his desire, e.g., in eating. But if man could not transcend this simple immersion in Nature as a being with animal desires, he would not be human; he would be indistinguishable from any other desirous animal, still a part of the realm of Necessity.

What desire does is to abolish Otherness, and in so doing to assert the primacy of the truth and reality of the desiring subject. But the negated Other simply reasserts itself—it grows back. Nature reproduces itself endlessly. On the level of simple animal desire no real certainty of self is possible; thus satiating that desire cannot ultimately be a source of truly human satisfaction. Desire can satisfy itself only if it has as its object another desire, i.e., another self-consciousness. Only by gaining "recognition" from another self-consciousness can desire achieve true certainty of itself as human. For humanity to dialectically emerge

---

templative individual achieve satisfaction. But this is only possible in a world in which practice comes to follow the abstract, impersonal laws of a thoroughly rational state that gives those not capable of absolute spirit a surrogate oneness with the absolute.

6. If one observes that that point of closure does not bring human satisfaction, it is at least as great a criticism of the original modern longing as it is of Hegel's philosophy which quite consistently codifies that longing.

from a mere immersion in Nature, the desire for recognition must win out over animal desire and the concern for biological preservation.[7]

For Hegel, if the desire for recognition was initially manifested universally, humanity would never emerge from the natural state. But for most individuals the desire for biological preservation is supreme; hence the many capitulate, proving their nonhumanity, and thereby give recognition to the few. There emerges a rift—the ground for what Marx would later call the self-alienation of men from their "species being"—between the self-consciousness of the "master," who is recognized, and that of the "slave," who recognizes without receiving recognition. Differentiation precedes the unity that will be possible only at the end of a long, historical effort. But the master can be truly satisfied only if he is recognized by something other than a purely natural object, by another human in whom he can recognize himself. This is precisely what the slave, having shown that his primary concern is for mere animal existence, is not. Hence the master is still confronted by a merely natural object and makes no real headway. But as a result of his "victory," the master is in a position to impose various projects upon the slave, who is forced to work in the service of the master and to transform the natural given in accordance with the master's desires. The products of the slave's work are initially merely negated by the master through consumption. The master thereby becomes increasingly a warrior–consumer and, as a consumer, remains a fundamentally immediate, animal being. The slave, however, in transforming the external given without immediately negating it through consumption, has rid himself of his simple attachment to natural existence.

The master never attains satisfaction, for consumption is not what is really desired; nonhuman Nature will always remain for him an external object, as will the slave. Only in another master could he recognize himself as Other, but their confrontation is always a fight to the death, negating any dialectical movement. The master is a dialectical dead end. As the epitome of the pagan master, he remains a tragic figure. He becomes all the more tragic for Hegel in that, having become a property owner as the result of the slave's work, he ceases to be the pagan

7. For Rousseau, natural man is an animal mechanism desiring self-preservation to which is appended sympathy, Rousseau's primary natural ground for a relation to others. In Hegel there is animality plus the desire for recognition, i.e., the love of honor. For Hegel, all the truly human characteristics of man grow out of the desire for honor. For Hobbes and Locke, to emerge from the natural state required the existence of a conscious relationship between free, equal, and rational individuals; for Hegel what is required is subjugation, inequality, and irrational self-assertion. From Hegel's perspective, Locke and Hobbes presuppose at the beginning what is only possible at the end.

master in the true sense and by the time of the Roman Republic becomes a fundamentally legal entity, ruled by a single imperial master,
ultimately succumbing to the ideologies of his slaves, e.g., stoicism,
skepticism, Christianity, and eventually modern individualism. This
represents Hegel's truncated vision of the status of *praxis,* at least of that
natural *praxis* which is autonomous and severed from theoretical projects.[8] Neither *theoria* nor *praxis,* in their natural forms, at least as Hegel
presents them, can be the ground of a truly human satisfaction.

It is in the consciousness of the slave alone that History becomes possible. By his work the slave transforms Nature and thereby begins to
overcome his simple immersion in a merely natural Otherness. It is the
slave's *technē* that becomes the engine of History. By seeing in the given
world a product of his work, the slave sees himself manifested in the
Other. For the slave, the ground for self-consciousness exists through
his transforming work.[9] The slave cannot initially be satisfied, for he is
still not recognized by the master and still fears him. And his transformation of Nature is based not on his own ideas but on the master's will,
which is determined by natural instinct. However, he has begun to be
ideally emancipated from Nature. The difference between the real and
the ideal in the self-consciousness of the slave is the ground for the
emergence of the various ideologies that help rationalize this disjunction, and that, for Hegel, ultimately encompasses all philosophy and

8. For a more comprehensive vision of natural *praxis* one must turn attention to Aristotle's discussion in books 3, 4, and 5 of *Nicomachean Ethics,* 1109b30–1138b14, 52–
145. Aristotle's considerably fuller discussion of the "great-souled man" is the corollary
to Hegel's truncated account of the honor-loving master. Aristotle's account of honor-
loving is at the heart of his understanding of why natural *praxis* can be satisfying, if perhaps only the "second best" means to satisfaction.

9. Steven Smith argues that "Hegel is not a pre-Marxist prophet of emancipation
through labor" (*Hegel's Critique of Liberalism,* xi). I agree that Hegel and Marx should be
kept separate. Likewise, there are a variety of ways in which consciousness externalizes
itself in Hegel's account, including religion, art, architecture, and so on. Labor alone
could never move history. But it is central, and without transforming labor self-
consciousness could never overcome its alienation from mere brute nature.

In Hegel, there are two potential grounds for the emergence of the truly human: a
fight to the death for recognition, and work—which in the technical sense is based on
fear—that overcomes the natural world and eventually replaces it with a succession of
human, spiritual, or cultural worlds. Work is humanizing in that the slave is forced by
fear to repress his natural instinct for gratification, thereby sublimating his desires. This
sublimation, not the immediate enjoyment or gratification of the objects transformed
by work, is the ground of human culture. The master—and the love of honor—is necessary to history primarily for providing the fear without which the slave would not
initially sublimate his desires. It should be noted that Hegel's is assuredly the modern
understanding of culture, which sees it as based on the *negation* rather than *cultivation* of
nature.

religion prior to his own work. All past philosophy and religion has been a more or less sophisticated form of rationalization on the part of a divided slave consciousness.

When the gap between the real and the ideal, between the slave's ideal, if inarticulate sense of his freedom and his real slavery, widens, the slave is driven more and more into himself to find the truth of his existence. In thought the slave senses himself as free. But since he is not in actuality free in the external world, he is driven to doubt the essentiality of anything but his own self-consciousness. The slave becomes a "stoic," for he must abstract as much as possible from all actual external content of consciousness—natural desires, feelings, concrete existence, masters, and so on—and become indifferent to all that exists outside of the consciousness. The slave withdraws into the pure, empty, abstract universality of thought. He has assumed an abstract indifference to natural being and become pure inwardness, pure empty self-consciousness.

The ground of self-consciousness has been opened, yet freedom remains abstract.[10] For Hegel, it is an easy step from stoicism, which refuses to be moved by the external world, to the "skepticism" that consciously rejects its essentiality and truth. As in the dialectic of understanding, the slave's consciousness ultimately refuses to grant truth to the world of appearance. But on this level, self-consciousness is locked in contradiction, for it must continue with the ordinary business of living and hence must accept all the customary beliefs that support a given way of life. The slave thereby contradicts the supreme detachment of his universal skepticism. When he becomes conscious of this contradiction he has emerged into the "unhappy consciousness," unhappy because it is *aware* that it is "torn" and "divided." The slave is now not only alienated from Nature, but also from himself. This internal tornness is increasingly what moves the slave, as the natural force of the master begins to become softened. Psychic tornness, not fear, increasingly becomes the engine of History.

The response of the unhappy consciousness is to transfer the location of the real truth to a transcendent realm, reproducing a maneuver performed on the level of consciousness. Self-consciousness now invents Christianity and longs to attain oneness with a transcendent reality.

10. As self-consciousness is the basis of philosophy, philosophy has as its psychic source man's alienation from his concrete world. This is far removed from the premodern understanding that philosophy originates in a disinterested, awestruck sense of amazement and wonder. To look ahead, it also differs from Heidegger's attempt to construct a form of thinking that is an amazed openness to "Being," understood as that which is *self*-presencing.

Thereby the slave replaces his worldly masters with an absolute master. Ultimately, in his longing for oneness with the transcendent, the slave brings the transcendent into the actual world in the person of Christ. But this is a fleeting moment, and self-consciousness gives up its search for the ideal in the actual world. Self-consciousness becomes all the more unhappy because of its alienation and remoteness from its posited ideal truth. It longs for the unchangeable and transcendent, but lives in the variable realm of slavery. Eventually the priest comes forth to mediate between the unhappy consciousness and the unchangeable transcendent, and through this mediation self-consciousness comes to attribute its unhappiness to its own fault, i.e., sin. The slave eventually sacrifices all decisions about the understanding of the Absolute to the intermediary consciousness of the priest and longs for the absolution that will bridge the gap. Through the mediation of the priest, the unhappy consciousness attains oneness with what it takes as the essential, absolute reality, abstracted as much as possible from the particular, actual world of which it is a part.

Self-consciousness is now related to the absolute essence, but alienated from its immediate world, a condition which will continue throughout the Christian era. Only as Reason will self-consciousness overcome its negative attitude toward the world and its own actuality in it. Only by consciously seeing itself as the source of the Being of the external world, from which the unhappy consciousness is alienated, will self-consciousness be projected back outward and transcend the impasse it has reached in the unhappy consciousness. For that we await Descartes and the stance of modern idealism, which will solve the impasses of both consciousness and self-consciousness, but only by introducing a new dualism—a radical separation of subject and object—which will itself eventually have to be overcome.

In Reason we do not solve the final problem, for the absolute truth is to be found not in the arena of Nature, with which Reason is preoccupied, but in either the spiritual realm of "ethical substance"—that is, in a community immersed in a spiritual, social, human world, not the natural one—or through Absolute Spirit: philosophy, poetry, and religion. But Reason is a necessary stage to allow us to take the actual world seriously again, rather than continually making it vanish, as occurs in both "Consciousness" and "Self-consciousness." And Reason is necessary to provide the ideas that can consciously inform the slave's *techně,* and his first and only true act of *praxis,* revolution in the service of ideas. A theoretical dialectic (Reason) must intervene to transcend the impasse of the practical dialectic reached at the end of the section on self-consciousness. Reason, in the form of modern, technological science and revolutionary *praxis,* must master and manipulate the external world, transforming it in such a way that human satisfaction becomes possible. As a result, humanity becomes increasingly conscious of its power through its ability to change the external given, and increasingly recognizes itself as manifested in the external given.

Through the work of the slave, the natural world is replaced more and more by a human, cultural, spiritual world, decreasing the need for work; hence the historical necessity of the now almost totally bourgeoisified masters dialectically passes. It is at this point that the slaves are ready to replace their old masters with a new abstract one; i.e., the State. And humanity is now in a position to overcome the natural given on the basis of consciously projected ideas rather than mechanically responding to mere natural desire or fear. It is the alienated bourgeois intellectuals who supply the slaves with these ideas. In the process, the State, and political life in general, comes to have a nonnatural basis. Politics now comes to be in the service of ideas rather than natural inclinations. Yet for Hegel those ideas remain fixed and determined; they cannot become the product of the mere, autonomous, human Will, as will be the case for Nietzsche. It is now that theory and practice can finally converge, because *praxis* no longer has a natural basis. And due to the success of self-conscious *technē,* increasingly there will be no autonomous, self-presenting, natural Other left. Only now is a contemplative consciousness possible, because we can know only what we make, and we have made everything of interest. In everything outside ourselves—from law to concrete reality—we see nothing but ourselves.

It is the modern, technological State, based on consciously projected ideas, that will allegedly bring universal recognition to all, because each citizen can recognize all others as equals and be duly recognized in return. With the State having replaced the natural masters, we reach the point where History will be continued entirely within the consciousness of the slave qua universal producer, consumer, property owner, and citizen. We have the complete hegemony of a unitary consciousness, and with it the beginning of the abolition of the political. As humanity increasingly negates Nature, it increasingly emancipates itself from it. This emancipation, plus man's new status as property owner, insulates him from Nature to the point that the fear of death becomes less and less a part of self-consciousness; the last vestige of the natural consciousness slips slowly away.[11] As human work completes

---

11. One could say of Hegel's *Phenomenology,* among other things, that it is a history of the necessary bourgeoisification of man. "Bourgeois" is the term Rousseau coined for

the overcoming of Nature, the need for *praxis* in the traditional sense—
that is, the partisan competition between different consciousnesses
pursuing different ends—is overcome. [12]

Because in the posthistorical world man has assumed a complete homogeneity of consciousness—i.e., has eliminated difference, thereby

---

the Hobbesian men who contract together to form the modern state. They do so for two
related reasons—to flee the preeminent *consciousness* of the possibility of violent death,
and in the hope of pursuing comfort. The more goods they have the more insulated
from nature they feel. Comfortable self-preservation is their end, with property providing an insulation from the consciousness of death. In short, "bourgeois" means far more
than merely capitalist; it means more generally "fearful and slavish." Hegel, like
Hobbes, tries to show why one necessarily arrives at the complete hegemony of this one
consciousness.

12. When there no longer remains any opposition between the I and the non-I, in
that the natural world has become totally a human world, totally the result of a projection of the ideas of the self, there is no more genuine "work" to be done, in the technical
sense. For in Hegel's technical usage work always negates that which is external as non-
I, and does so on the basis of fear. With the natural world replaced by a human one, the
opposition between subject and object is replaced by an identity of consciousness and
the given world. Since this identity exists, there is ostensibly nothing left to negate, so
that while men, like animals, will still labor (although as little as possible) and consume
(as much as possible) they will not engage in any truly human activity, i.e., "work."
Men will still be armed with technological skill, but increasingly it will be employed
aimlessly, severed from any articulate ends since its Other has dissolved as a guide to
transformation. Man's sophistication with regard to means will be emancipated from
any conscious, fixed ends other than increasing both the scope and intensity of animal
gratification.

Hence history is finished and the evolution of self-consciousness complete. In this
fashion the modern longing for autonomy can be shown, in a perfectly consistent fashion, to lead to its own overcoming. One is left with a primarily classless society peopled
entirely by worker-consumers, a world of individuals increasingly insulated from fear
of death by the humanized world in which they live and by the goods they own and
consume. Man has become emancipated from his fear not only of death at the hands of
his masters, but of the gods, and finally, perhaps, of external nature. All that is missing
is Descartes's dream of a perfect medicine that would lead to a final transcendence of fear
of death, especially since in a homogeneous society of equals there would be no need to
fight to the death to attain recognition. But since men are accepted as equals qua abstract
entities—not as particular, flesh and blood individuals—life is potentially reduced to an
abstract, passionless banality.

The most resolute reading of this outcome is by Alexandre Kojève (see his *Introduction to the Reading of Hegel*). With nothing to negate—neither another desire (self-
consciousness) nor the external world—man will neither "work" nor "fight to the
death" for recognition. But conflicts over recognition, and work based on fear and the
sublimation of desires, are the two characteristics which for Hegel define man as human. In the final state, therefore, man comes full circle and reverts back to his animality,
to an immediate absorption into the given world, and is given over to a new version of
the natural consciousness of pure immediacy. Man reaches identity with the given
world and with all others, along with a life consisting primarily of the immediate grati-

ostensibly overcoming all alienation from others—it is impossible to talk about elite rule, or about any conscious class that directs public affairs, in traditional political terms. With no simply instinctive or self-conscious ideational end to promote, the political as traditionally understood passes over, in the phrase of Engels, into the mere "administration of things." There will be no partisan competition over ends, merely technical debates over means and scrambling about to divvy up consumables. Universal comfortable self-preservation and recognition of the right to decency and civility become the only legitimate ends; hence the efficient functioning of an autonomous system of administration can replace self-conscious leadership, for the end is inherent in the system and theoretically incontestable. Future life will exist without limits, consisting of an unfettered consumption, based on the fundamentally unquenchable nature of mere animal desire.

Having arrived at this point I will advance a twofold assertion. First, Hegel's depiction of the modern transformation of theory and practice, and thereby of their eventual amalgamation, is a codification of the *telos* that was always implicit in the modern project: Theory becomes practical and practice becomes increasingly informed by theory; both lose their autonomy. Second, as a result we are left with an increasingly hegemonic *technē* in an environment of the diminution of the political. Late modernity arrives at a point where creeping global homogenization exists side by side with ever more sophisticated and limitless tech-

---

fication of mere animal desire. Hence, except for the philosopher, whose *eros* is replaced by the contemplation of the totally rationalized given—i.e., the philosopher contemplates himself—humanity is delivered from self-consciousness and given back over to the mere "sentiment of self." The dream of Rousseau is vindicated, and for more than a few. It is Marx who is left to idealize such a life—whose possibility, in his mind, was further in the future—as an expression of individual action qua art.

But as Kojève puts the matter, what henceforth passes for culture will not be based on self-consciousness—i.e., the attempt to actualize ideas—but on mere immediacy, blind impulse, or, more to the point, idiosyncrasy. Even art will have no other purpose than to express the immediate, idiosyncratic impressions of the particular artist. Architecture will exist on the same theoretical plane as the works of beavers and bees. "Art" will be comparable to the spider's web, and music to the sounds of cicadas and birds; i.e., there will be no truly human culture, but rather "art for art's sake" (Kojève, *Introduction to the Reading of Hegel,* 158–62). When everyone is finally in a position to participate in high culture, there will be none. There may remain veneration for the products of past cultures, but nothing comparable will be created. Culturally, man will be forced to live off his past—as manifested in the intellectual cannibalism of contemporary postmodernism. In this the universal desire for truly human satisfaction can be seen to be thwarted. I will not here enter into the controversy over whether this is the only way to interpret Hegel, although I find it very powerful. I will argue, however, that it is entirely consistent with the view of the world that Nietzsche and Heidegger try to oppose.

nology.[13] The present turn to ethnic nationalism represents one manifest form of backlash. Divorced from any simply natural basis by
which to distinguish one's group, however, and facing the disintegration of traditions born of premodern conditions, commitment to various shared ideological prescriptions will predictably become the
cement that binds as well as differentiates. But if Hegel is correct,
where will novel ideological prescriptions come from? Have we not,
in the aftermath of communism and fascism, exhausted all available
ideas?[14] What ideal other than consumption, comfort, and predictable
tranquility is it plausible to believe the majority of human beings might
pursue? While it would be premature to conclude that nationalism has
run its course—it is especially dangerous at a time when it has a seemingly limitless technology to support it—the present question is, If ethnic nationalism dissolves in the face of global commerce and global
technology, are we not faced with the end of history? If there remain no
natural bases for *praxis,* what other conclusion can be reached? Is there a
late modern basis for the generation of difference? In what follows, I
will argue that there is. But emancipation from various modern theoretical constraints is a prerequisite for its existence.

    13. This is an altogether consistently modern outcome.
    14. See my "The End of History."

5

Responses to Modern Closure:
Reconciliation or Transcendence?

Hegel was by no means unaware of the problematic nature of the modern transformation of human existence, nor was he altogether sanguine about it.[1] He admits that the rational world he depicts is one of old age and decay. The only solace, from his point of view, is that man's prior existence on the level of the natural consciousness was simply tragic. The natural consciousness as contemplative leads straight to skepticism, while on the practical level it cannot get beyond the master-slave confrontation. Those tragedies had allegedly been transcended, and the mature Hegel was unwilling to follow Rousseau and plot a return to ancient civic virtue. He had flirted with that idea in his youth, but the aftermath of the French Revolution had convinced him it was insane to try to transplant premodern institutions into modern soil. It is Nietzsche and Heidegger who try to recover the tragic. I will argue that they do so in an attempt to find a basis for an autonomous *praxis*—i.e., a *praxis* freed from modern theory. They likewise try to free philosophy from the need to dictate to *praxis*—i.e., from pursuing a modern legislative function.

The mature Hegel was determined to accept his modern fate and reconcile others to it. He knew that the most difficult task would be the reconciliation of the few—the erotically philosophic and those of aristocratic temperament—to modernity. He chose to make the best of modernity's virtues and to mitigate its vices, believing there was no acceptable alternative to the impending modern greyness. There remained no psychological incentive for change built into the increasingly universal, bourgeois consciousness. And no decent person would

1. Hegel's famous, melancholy statement bears repeating: "When philosophy paints its grey in grey, then has a shape of life grown old. By philosophy's grey in grey it cannot be rejuvenated but only understood. The owl of Minerva spreads its wings only with the falling of the dusk." Hegel, *Philosophy of Right*, Preface, 13. Hereafter designated as *PR*, followed by a page number.

undermine the equality and comfort of the vast majority. The "tornness" of the soul—both internally and in its alienation from the external world—that had been the moving principle of History had been
overcome, at least for the vast majority, as had, on the ontological
level, the self-alienation of the Universal Spirit. Whether one takes
Hegel's account ontologically or anthropologically the result is the
same; the tension in the soul of man that had created so much irritation,
and so many pearls, had dissipated. Even if this end is seen as greyness
and decay, philosophy itself can do nothing to transcend the problem.
Hegel argues that philosophy can assume no autonomous stance outside its world that would allow it to will a unique alternative; it can do
no more than reflect on and make palatable what has become a fait ac-
compli (PR 11).[2]

But how could Hegel, knowing what was at stake, advise future philosophy to pursue what can so easily be taken as a positivistic
glorification—indeed divinization—of the given?[3] In an age of unifor-

2. The philosophical person who understands the greyness of the present world and
the reasons for it, cannot simply will a different world, although Hegel intimates that
one might be lurking in America. What that might mean Hegel does not elaborate. He
certainly makes no effort to initiate a movement toward something novel. I will argue
that attempting to find that transition was left to Nietzsche and Heidegger. Hegel's was a
sober and prudent response to modern closure. In order that the few be reconciled to the
late-modern world, Hegel tried to make clear that there was absolutely no basis for transcendence, either in practical humanity or in philosophic man. Absolute wisdom goes
hand in hand with the impossibility of transcending the increasingly universal, rationalized given. Since philosophy has no capacity to grasp anything beyond the humanized world, the eros of the soul that longs for more will be disappointed, and a humanity
that looks to philosophy for "utopias" will receive none. Finally, a philosophy that
seemed to defend the same thing as the law could emancipate itself from contempt in the
eyes of the community of nonphilosophers (PR 8–9). And saving philosophy was one
of Hegel's highest goals. Hence he tried to reconcile philosophy to the reasonableness of
the modern world and to wean it from the desire to create and pursue utopias; a philosophy that continuously did that would gain public contempt. To return to my theme,
both theoria and praxis, in their original, natural manifestations, had to be radically limited and circumscribed if man was to find any peace and satisfaction in the world he
necessarily lives in and, in Hegel's calculation, cannot transcend. Hence the only salvation was to find a way to see "the rose [joy] in the cross of the present [the given world]"
(PR 12). The designation of the present as a cross to be borne, however, proves that
there remained in Hegel's eyes something tragic in that present for individuals like himself. One is reminded of Tocqueville's concluding observations in Democracy in America
(p. 704).
3. Consider the following observation from Nietzsche: "The decline of faith in the
Christian god, the triumph of scientific atheism, is a generally European event in which
all races had their share and for which all deserve credit and honor. Conversely, one
might charge precisely the Germans . . . that they delayed this triumph of atheism most
dangerously for the longest time. Hegel in particular was its delayer par excellence, with

mity, of what came to be called the "mass society," Hegel wished to preserve some basis upon which to differentiate the high from the low. He wanted to find a basis for a hierarchy in which "Objective Spirit," living in a community and state, was higher than "Subjective Spirit," mere idiosyncratic, self-interested, animal behavior, and both were subordinate to "Absolute Spirit," philosophy, religion, and poetry. In an attempt to avoid spiritual chaos, Hegel wished to find a basis for genuinely human life beyond the evanescent whims of egocentric individuals emancipated from traditional bases of authority. But above all he wished to find a basis for philosophy beyond feeling and sentiment, in the hopes of retrieving some of its dignity in the face of modern technological science, which would increasingly have no guidance in its transformation of the given except the gratification of animal desire. It was necessary to "rescue philosophy from the shameful decay in which it is immersed at the present time" (*PR* 2), from the spectacle of one fanciful, idiosyncratic attempt after another to dream up alternate worlds—a process proceeding endlessly and bringing with it public contempt and disdain. Philosophy had to become a "science." That meant it had to regain an ontological foundation—something it had lost in modern thought.[4] Philosophy would have to be severed from *eros* and *thaumazein* and turned toward contemplation and explication of the universal made actual. *At least that had to become its public persona.* This was the transformation of future philosophy toward which Hegel pointed.

What does it mean to say that Hegel attempted to save philosophy in an age of increasing uniformity, if that is one of the things he tried to accomplish? Since it is not obvious that any truly novel and unique philosophy—or religion, poetry, or art—can come into existence in the circumstances of late modernity, we can only conclude that he attempted to preserve and venerate that which had already been created as higher than anything that might yet be created. I will argue that the recovery of a ground for the emergence of novel forms of art, philos-

---

his grandiose attempt to persuade us of the divinity of existence, appealing as a last resort to our sixth sense, 'the historical sense'" (*The Gay Science,* #357, 306–7).

4. For Hegel, at the end of history, when individual consciousnesses are finally unified in the universal, bourgeois consciousness, Absolute Spirit regains identity, this time in concrete manifestation; the realm of appearance then *is* the outward manifestation of the absolute ground. Hence the world of appearance has an ontological foundation. Further, only by giving an ontological ground for law-abidingness and "community," a ground not based on consent, did Hegel think he could avoid chaos in the face of the collapse of traditional bases of authority. Hegel's ontological account is central to his entire enterprise; it cannot be dismissed as an unnecessary embellishment.

ophy, and religion is what both Nietzsche and Heidegger attempted. Hence for each, reality becomes dark and mysterious, far from rational or totally susceptible to mastery. In such a world, philosophy could turn away from the modern desire for control and regain a sense of wonder. Hegel on the one hand, and Nietzsche and Heidegger on the other, represent two different responses to the same set of circumstances. One points toward reconciliation, the others toward transcendence.

Hegel followed out the logic of modernity and concluded that all natural bases for difference, particularity, and individuality had been, or soon would be, overcome or at least thoroughly delegitimized. Only universally applicable principles derived from Reason could be valid. Nonetheless, in his political teaching Hegel tried to save as much difference and particularity as possible. He was as much aware of the totalitarian implications of completed modernity as of its nihilistic possibilities.[5] He tried to give an ontological foundation to the State, to depict it as an "ethical substance," and to show that morality required the habits and customs that only grow out of the shared ethos of a community. Yet "ethical substance" pointed toward dangers of its own, which Hegel tried to mitigate by positioning the family and corporation as mediating institutions between the individual and the modern bureaucratic State. For the same reason he took private property seriously. Following Locke, property was depicted as an external manifestation of the individual and thereby intimately linked not only to the longing for recognition but also to the development of "personality." Hegel understood perfectly the abstract nature of modern moral and political life. He realized that the only law that could be legitimate in modern terms would be an impersonal law, universally and impartially applied by bureaucratic functionaries to abstract persons. Equality and universality, however, threatened a potentially suffocating impersonality. Owning property and participating in intermediary partnerships could mitigate this abstract impersonality.

Likewise, while the bureaucracy was presented by Hegel as the most universal class—the one which acted according to universally applicable rules and in which particular interest and universal interest overlapped—the Rational State would still legitimately have other classes based on the principle of individuality and particularity—the commercial classes, both entrepreneurial and proletarian, and the "nat-

5. Hegel even supports the ongoing need for war, running in the face of the central modern tenet that universal peace is the primary end of any rational action. See Steven Smith's excellent "Hegel's Views on War, the State and International Relations," *American Political Science Review* 77 (1983):624–32.

ural" classes, the landed aristocracy and serfs.[6] In his Rational State Hegel attempted to save as much as he could of that particularity that was generated in previous ages, for there remained no ground for the reemergence of particularity, and hence no hedge against total and complete uniformity—that is, totalitarianism, in the precise sense. Far from being a totalitarian, Hegel tried to build dams and dikes against totalitarianism. I will argue, however, that without revitalizing the sources from which genuine difference grows, even a holding action of the magnitude of Hegel's will eventually fail.

Whatever pluralism might be implied in the class structure of Hegel's Rational State, law-abidingness and bureaucratic rationality were to be the foundations of authority. To legitimize the universality of law, it had to be grounded in the universality of the Absolute made actual; hence Hegel's deification of the State. For Hegel this was the only way to overcome the seeds of anarchy that flowed from the belief that all men are isolated, individual atoms, each of whom is free only in trying to invent his own set of rules. Hegel tried to sketch a middle way between totalitarianism and anarchy, using available late-modern resources.

In Hegel's understanding, the basis of right had to be laid elsewhere than in modern egocentric, subjective preference. Hegel thus presumed to provide a surrogate for the moral life of the ancient Greek *polis* by (1) legitimizing law-abidingness (freedom understood as rule-following behavior), (2) defending legalism (law understood as the embodiment of universal reason, hence more than mere conventionalism), and (3) advancing bureaucratic rationality as the support for modern "ethical life" and the means to becoming part of an "ethical substance." On that basis Hegel thought he could provide a foundation for community within the modern world. Unlike Rousseau, who actually wanted to find a way back to the *praxis* of the ancient world, the mature Hegel was content with a surrogate. This was the best he thought he could do. The end of history could not be circumvented.[7]

6. The reason for this attempt to preserve a particularity born of the past is similar to the Tocquevillean desire to save as many institutions from the past as possible—for example, in Tocqueville's case, religion, which he considered a vestige of aristocratic times. Like Hegel, Tocqueville also took seriously "voluntary associations" which could mediate between state and individual.

7. I have found it impossible to simply dismiss the end of history thesis even though I do not fully accept it. Hence I find myself in an ongoing confrontation with its presentation in the thought of Kojève. A recent work on Hegel admits the same fascination and need for an ongoing confrontation. Steven Smith presents one of the most thoughtful responses I have seen, citing five reasons—none of which I find ultimately decisive—for rejecting the thesis (S. Smith, *Hegel's Critique of Liberalism*, 229–31).

First, Smith writes that the end of history presupposes overcoming the economy of

Historical closure has become a possibility because of previous, altogether consistent, deflections of modern thought. As a result of the transformations of reality that have occurred, the slow decay of difference and the general abolition of Otherness, a historical irreversibility is possible. Lurking in modern thought from the beginning was a longing for a prosperous, comfortable, long-lived, pacific existence shared as equally and universally as possible. Modern science and modern po-

---

scarcity. Since raw materials can be recycled given adequate energy, this reduces to a scarcity of energy. We are told that a clean nuclear fusion reactor that uses more or less unlimited hydrogen as fuel and produces waste with a very short half-life may be only a generation away. Energy generated from solar power, wind, tides, and so on awaits only an efficient means of converting from direct to alternating current to be practical. I see no necessary reason why technology cannot in time solve the energy problem. Hence necessity may not bail us out of what is a fundamentally moral and political problem by imposing natural limits. We will have to find moral and political limits, and therein lies the real problem. What is the ground for the generation of new ends, "ideals," "values," limits, etc. History ends because of the potential exhaustion of novel ends and an inability to return to old ones.

Second, Smith notes that truly human satisfaction cannot be reduced to the gratification of bodily and material needs. This is assuredly true for some, i.e., the "few." But it seems perfectly satisfying to the vast majority, as thinkers from Tocqueville to David Riesman have observed. The momentum of late-modern, relatively classless, mass, consumer democracies cannot be underestimated. Where would we turn to legitimize the tastes and desires of the few?

Third, Smith observes that even for Hegel, America represented the possibility of something novel. I see no indication of this. As Joseph Cropsey has observed, America as a regime is the shore upon which each successive wave of European thought breaks. There is no indication that America has yet originated anything novel. See Cropsey, "The United States as Regime."

Fourth, Smith points to the various anti-Hegelian intellectual attempts at negation as an indication that the end of history has not arrived. By this he means everything from existentialism to deconstructionism. But I would use the same evidence as an indication of Hegel's victory. These efforts, though negative, are still totally determined by Hegel and his thought. Hegel never doubted the possibility of retrogression to previous moments of thought. The question is, will we see anything genuinely novel?

Finally, Smith argues that the shaping force of "culture" determines at least as much as the constellation of ideas that exists at any given time. But all the examples of distinct cultures that we would point to emerged in the past under circumstances that are daily being obliterated by our global, modern civilization. Anyone who witnesses the spectacle of folk festivals in which participants don native dress, sample traditional cuisine, and sing the songs of their forefathers knows the extent to which these become more and more hollow caricatures with each passing generation. Do the conditions exist for the emergence of any genuinely new, rooted cultural phenomena or are we left to try desperately to hold on to tradition? If the conditions under which genuine cultures emerge cannot be recovered, the end of history is a possibility. One cannot hold on to the past forever; in time traditions become stale precisely because they are at odds with the world in which one lives.

litical and ethical institutions were but means to that end. The dark side of that dream now seems to include homogenization, bureaucratization, the loss of the indigenous and distinctive, and the closure of novel possibilities in philosophy, religion, art, culture, and customs, together with the noxious residues of modern technology, the loss of limits on its use and the consequent global upping of the technological ante, and the potential for universal technological totalitarianism.

The thinker who remains committed to modernity must believe that these phenomena represent short term difficulties rather than an inevitable impasse or closure. But to cite the benefits that modernity has bestowed—political, moral, material, medical—in no way constitutes an adequate defense of modernity unless one can prove that what looks like closure is a chimera. To my mind, the still resolutely convinced modern bears a heavier burden of proof.[8] To avoid closure we

8. In finishing my sketch of modernity with Hegel, then jumping to a discussion of Nietzsche and Heidegger, it may seem that I have overlooked the crucial significance of Marx. Surely Marx and Nietzsche represent divergent post-Hegelian developments. I can say only a few words about this seeming omission.

With Marx, as with many contemporary authors, we have the problem of differentiating between the "early" and the "late" teachings. Added to this is the difficulty of separating Marx from later developments in Marxism. Marx's name has become an icon. As a modern icon, only the name of Locke has even remotely rivaled that of Marx. There was a time when many intellectuals felt the need to carry on their debates under the rubric of Marxism even if this meant doing considerable damage to the teachings of Marx. Needless to say, the literature is massive. As regards the late Marx—the Marx of dialectical materialism—we have a teaching that aspires to be a science. Marx rejected the notion that he was merely proposing an ideal, arguing that what he was elaborating was necessary. It is, therefore, a problem that predictions based on that science have been, almost universally, disproved by subsequent history. Even propped up by post-Marxian additions, like "imperialism" or "overdetermination," it is now hard to believe that any new, "structuralist" variant of Marxism can be persuasive. The counterproof is in the doing; we still await the author who can prove that this observation is incorrect.

This leaves us with the writings of the "early" Marx which have as their central themes such issues as "self-alienation" and "species being." But the early Marx's discussion of these ideas is an extension of what I have presented as the ultimate modern idea— "metaphysical freedom." The only unique idea is that the free and rational self inevitably arrives later than even Hegel thought. But nothing new is announced. The core idea is simply modern. I am in complete agreement with Bernard Yack, who has characterized Marx as a "left-Kantian"; see Yack, *The Longing for Total Revolution*. I will differ from Yack, and from Stanley Rosen, in *Hermeneutics as Politics,* both of whom extend this analysis to Nietzsche as well.

To my mind, it is Hegel who is the greatest of the moderns. He understood modernity's central impulses and tried to ground them as well as to deflect them away from their darker implications. By comparison, Marx's thought will be seen primarily as a *politically* interesting digression which has passed. Hence one can dismiss Marx and move directly from Hegel to Nietzsche on the assumption that Marx enunciates nothing that

must reflect upon what is required to move beyond the modern, using the resources presently available to us. In what follows I will explore the thought of two authors that I believe try to transcend the closure of modernity, to construct a *transition* to something novel. Again, I have chosen Nietzsche and Heidegger because it seems to me that the ideas that they articulate have gained such momentum that no thinker can now avoid confronting them. Many ardently modern thinkers have tried to prop up modernity using ideas borrowed from Nietzsche and Heidegger. I believe not only that those pastiches will fail, but that, in light of what Nietzsche and Heidegger have brought to speech, no simple revitalization of modernity will be possible. The options are limited: prop up modernity yet again—and it is unlikely it can be done with greater depth or dignity than was brought to bear by Hegel—or begin to think beyond it. I will try to show that Nietzsche, and to a lesser extent Heidegger, co-opt more modern ideas than they would be willing to admit. But that is unavoidable, since no thought takes place in a vacuum. Early modern thought carries over a great deal from pre-modern thought—at least in the way of shared language and themes—yet it still represents a break with the past. The same will surely be true of the early moments of any genuine postmodernity, if and when we see it.

Finally, central to my argument is the understanding that any consistently postmodern position must try to stand beyond the highest manifestations of modern thought: metaphysical freedom and History. My suggestion is that, freed from metaphysical freedom, *praxis* could emerge from the ever-tightening theoretical constraints under which it has operated in modernity. I will argue that this emancipation of *praxis* is a key to any genuinely postmodern political and moral understanding and is what both Nietzsche and Heidegger aimed at. Further, once philosophy is freed from the modern necessity of dictating to both

---

is still necessary for us to take cognizance of that has not been articulated in either Kant or Hegel. With the worldwide collapse of Marxist communism as a political force, it is doubtful that intellectuals will still feel obliged to fight out their differences under the umbrella of Marxism. And it is equally doubtful that Marxism will get another chance to fly its flag over a new world-historical nation.

But it is perfectly predictable that late modernity will continue to recycle the concept of metaphysical freedom on which the early Marx took his stand. We have seen post-Hegelian permutations of that idea in various forms of neo-Marxism, in Sartre's existentialism, in the work of the Frankfurt School—especially Adorno and Marcuse—and in recent defenders of modernity like Ferry and Renaut. My argument is that this is where late modernity seems to be forced to make its stand. The unavoidability of this stand points to the closure of modernity. Any genuine postmodernity would have to stand beyond metaphysical freedom.

praxis and *physis,* a new vision of philosophy becomes possible. Nietzsche designated that new philosophy "the philosophy of the future"; the later Heidegger captured it in the term *Gelassenheit.* Any genuine postmodernity would require a unique vision of both *praxis* and philosophy. Nietzsche and Heidegger attempted to be the midwives for both, and in the process were pallbearers for the respective modern alternatives.

PART TWO

Nietzsche's Critique of Modernity:
Modernity Intensified

6

The Protean Nietzsche

In what follows I will argue that Nietzsche carries the key modern ideas discussed above to their most extreme formulations to date while simultaneously sounding the first notes of a postmodern alternative. Like Socrates, who Nietzsche chooses as his great antagonist, Nietzsche is a prism between past and future. He neither completely extricates himself from the past nor paints a future with more than the broadest brush strokes. He is an author who stands between eternities. Nonetheless, profound changes are set in motion by disinterring fundamental presuppositions and bringing them into the light. And that is precisely what Nietzsche does.

There are few authors more difficult to interpret than Nietzsche. His published works are often polemical, hyperbolic and overheated. He experiments with different modes of speech, is a master of catchword phrases, and is altogether explicit in announcing that he does not desire to be understood by all.[1] Nietzsche did, however, desire to be widely read and to have a concrete influence on human affairs. Despite all his discussions of rank and subtlety, of the esoteric and the exoteric, no one who wrote as Nietzsche did could be said to intend his work as a privileged diary, to be read only by the initiated. *He wished to be heard and construed by all.* Hence with Nietzsche, of all authors, we must not lose contact with the surface and seek the subtle and secret before giving the obvious its due. I will argue that the web of words Nietzsche weaves on the surface of his writings, and the spells it was intended to cast, is central to his project.

We also must not lose sight of the rift between the "hard" Nietzscheans, including the Nazi apologists—who find in Nietzsche a

---

1. See for example Nietzsche, *The Will to Power,* #980, 512, and *Beyond Good and Evil,* #30, 42; #290, 229. *Beyond Good and Evil* henceforth designated in the text as *BG,* followed by a page number or aphorism number (distinguished by use of the number sign "#").

spokesman for great politics, great wars, the unification of Europe into a people, "breeding," the virtues of hardness, suffering, and cruelty, and so on—and the "soft" Nietzscheans, who find a spokesman for the superiority of a retreat from the political into radically personal, artistic, poetic, and philosophic efforts, i.e., a call for the private, solitary existence of the creative individual.[2] Others combine the two and see Nietzsche calling out to a new generation of philosopher-kings who would rule through consciously willed myths. Still others, moved by the spiritual lightning of various isolated gems, but finding no way to link them, ultimately throw up their hands and proclaim that Nietzsche constantly contradicts himself, but that that is nothing to be held against a man of inspired insight. Many, like Foucault, are happy simply to "use" Nietzsche.[3] Nietzsche has evoked a greater variety of interpretations—and in a shorter period of time—then almost any author one can name. And there seems to be no common ground linking those interpretations.[4]

2. For the latter, see especially Kaufmann, *Nietzsche: Philosopher, Psychologist, Antichrist,* 123, 176, 248, 280–81, 412.

3. "I am tired of people studying [Nietzsche] only to produce the same kind of commentaries that are written of Hegel and Mallarmé. For myself, I prefer to utilize the writers I like. The only valid tribute to thought such as Nietzsche's is precisely to use it, to deform it, to make it groan and protest"; Foucault, "Prison Talk," in *Power/Knowledge,* 53–54. I will try to spare Nietzsche the posthumous need to groan and protest.

4. Within ten years of his death in 1900 Nietzsche's works had been broadly disseminated. One of his earliest influences was among poets and novelists—e.g., the Stefan George "circle," Thomas Mann, Hermann Hesse, and others. On Stefan George and George Kreis, see Kaufmann, *Nietzsche,* 9–16. Consider Mann's *Magic Mountain* and "Death in Venice," as depictions of decadence and civilizational decay, and Hesse's *Steppenwolf,* as a form of the "retranslation of man back into Nature," and *Glasperlenspiel,* as a vision of *Ubermenschen* in a posthistorical world separated from the masses.

It was not until the late 1920s and early 1930s that Nietzsche's work began to find its way into academic circles. Many initially focused on Nietzsche's mental illness and collapse, e.g., E. F. Podach, *Nietzsche's Zusammenbruch* (Heidelberg: N. Kampmann, 1930). Others like Julian Benda characterized him as one of the most important intellectuals to "betray" contemporary, bourgeois civilization; see Benda, *La Trahison des Clercs* (Paris: B. Grasset, 1927). Some, like Karl Jaspers, tried to present a "kinder, gentler" Nietzsche, but only by removing all the sharp political and moral edges and glossing over many of his philosophical insights; see Jaspers, *Nietzsche: Einführung in das Verstandnis Seines Philosophierenes,* 2d ed. (Berlin: DeGruyter, 1947), 261–76.

The general response was to attempt to neutralize or soften either Nietzsche's teaching or his influence. But almost simultaneously Nietzsche was transformed for use by National Socialism. The Nazis gave prominence to such themes as the superman, great wars, cruelty, and the importance of suffering and slavery, but also (and altogether mistakenly) to anti-Semitism and the glorification of the modern state; see A. Baumler, *Nietzsche der Philosoph und Politiker* (Leipzig: Philipp Reclam, 1931), and A. Haertle,

In the roughly ninety years during which Nietzsche's influence can be easily traced, there have been a variety of attempts to accentuate one or the other aspect of his teaching, stressing either the "hard" political and moral teaching or, more frequently, the "soft," allegedly individualistic teaching, either the "form" or, far less frequently, the "con-

Nietzsche und der Nationalsozialismos (Munich: F. Eher Nachfolger, 1937). For a valuable treatment focusing on Nietzsche's influence in Germany, See Steven Aschheim, _The Nietzsche Legacy in Germany_.

Nietzsche's introduction to the Anglo-American world was almost singlehandedly accomplished by Walter Kaufmann. Kaufmann showed the inadequacy of the Nazi interpretation, but portrayed Nietzsche as a primarily apolitical thinker who praises "artist, saint and philosopher." Ignoring politics and morals, Kaufmann accentuated Nietzsche's relation to the voluntaristic teaching of postwar existentialism. Kaufmann saw Nietzsche's philosophy as a religion of self-perfection, which he depicted as comparable to Hegel's discussion of Absolute Spirit; see Kaufmann, _Nietzsche_, 152, 175–76, 280–81, 363–69. Kaufmann also tried to translate Nietzsche's philosophy into the categories of Anglo-American academic thought, that is, into the mold of prior systematic philosophy, paving the way for two generations of such attempts. Cf. Schacht, _Nietzsche_, and my review of Schacht in _American Political Science Review;_ see also Arthur C. Danto, _Nietzsche as Philosopher_ (New York: Macmillan, 1965), and Lea, _The Tragic Philosopher_. As part of this undertaking, Kaufmann went so far as to dismiss as an ill-considered cosmological position the doctrine of eternal recurrence, which Nietzsche considered his central thought; Kaufmann, _Nietzsche_, 307–33.

The work of Martin Heidegger more than adequately counteracts Kaufmann's blind spot about the doctrine of eternal recurrence. Heidegger's Nietzsche lectures were given in the 1930s and 1940s and first published in 1961; Heidegger, _Nietzsche_, 2 vols. As I will show in greater detail below, Heidegger argued that the analysis of nihilism was the central element of Nietzsche's philosophy, and he tried to show that that nihilism was the product of past philosophy, which had shared a central error from Plato to Nietzsche. According to Heidegger, Nietzsche, contrary to his conscious intention, reproduced a central feature of past philosophy—which Heidegger reduced to reliance on the "metaphysics of presence." Therefore, Nietzsche could not transcend the nihilism he properly diagnosed. This understanding led Heidegger to the paradoxical conclusion that doctrines like the will to power and eternal recurrence were actually the final manifestations of Western metaphysics, which reached its culmination in Nietzsche's thought.

A number of recent efforts stress the literary qualities of Nietzsche's work. For Derrida, no text has a referent in reality or an "ultimate signified," and no author has or can master a conscious intention, which would assume that the author was an ultimate signified. Hence there is no referent other than the book itself in its effect on a specific reader. Style holds hegemony over content, both political and philosophic. In this way Nietzsche is saved from Nazism, but at the price of becoming an author who cannot master his own project or pursue a consciously calculated and predictable effect. See Derrida, _Eperons: Les Styles de Nietzsche/Spurs: Nietzsche's Styles_, 37–39, and _Writing and Difference;_ see also my "Cacophony or Silence." A similar, and less esoteric, presentation of what can be called the "literary" approach can be found in Nehamas, _Nietzsche: Life as Literature_. Literary approaches to Nietzsche's texts constitute their own genre. One work claims that Nietzsche is aiming at the creation of a future form of thought—

tent." There have been almost no attempts to confront Nietzsche as a whole, especially if that means attempting to show that his political and philosophic teachings, his style and content, are necessary parts of a whole. It is such a whole account that I will try to give.[5]

I will argue that a substantial number of the major Nietzsche interpretations are correct in some significant way, but that each represents only part of the whole. Nietzsche's very project required that he be read in different ways by different readers. I will argue that he consciously tried to set different readings in motion. He did not believe that either concrete political action or a simple change in philosophic understanding alone could bring about the profound transformation that was needed. To those who argue that no author can have a conscious intention and no reader could access it if he or she did, I offer the counterevidence of the variety of Nietzsche interpretations to date. Nietzsche consciously fostered the various partial readings we have seen as part of his project of transition beyond modernity.

----

heavily reliant on the form of presentation—that can "again" transcend the distinction between poetry and philosophy and thereby chart a course out of nihilism; see Gillespie and Strong, *Nietzsche's New Seas,* 1–17. I believe this understanding is closer to the mark than some others, but this position again abstracts from the surface content of Nietzsche's teaching, stressing *how* Nietzsche speaks, not *what* he says. It is what Nietzsche does to us as readers that is of primary importance.

Other recent efforts have attempted to restore the psychological and material referents of Nietzsche's work. In almost all cases, however, Nietzsche's surface political and moral teachings are rejected. In a sophisticated effort, Deleuze tries to establish a referent for Nietzsche's work, isolating his "psychological" teaching and the interplay of "active" and "reactive" forces; see Deleuze, *Nietzsche and Philosophy,* 39–72, esp. 39, 53, 64–65. The outcome is the fundamental Freudianization of Nietzsche, again conjoined with relative silence about moral and political themes.

There have been many attempts to separate Nietzsche's political and moral teaching from his philosophical understanding. One such attempt goes so far as to claim that if Nietzsche had had the wisdom about markets and bureaucracies of Marx and Weber respectively he would have deduced a thoroughly modern, progressivist politics from what is allegedly his equally modern, individualistic, "agent-oriented" philosophical teaching; see Warren, *Nietzsche and Political Thought,* ix, 208, 213–14, 245, 247. Such attempts to make Nietzsche serviceable in the pursuit of thoroughly modern political agendas abound. For a more textually substantial and intellectually satisfying version of the attempt to separate Nietzsche's philosophy from his political and moral teachings, see Schutte, *Beyond Nihilism: Nietzsche without Masks,* which at least acknowledges that Nietzsche's politics cannot be entirely divorced from his "other theories" (pp. 161–64). See also MacIntyre, who in *After Virtue* concludes that Nietzsche's "solutions," unlike his "critiques," are "frivolous" (p. 108).

5. Two notable exceptions are Pangle, "The 'Warrior Spirit' as an Inlet to the Political Thinking of Nietzsche's Zarathustra," and Eric Voegelin, "Nietzsche, the Crisis and the War." What follows will differ from both accounts.

Nietzsche resolutely pursued a fixed intention; this is true whether one takes the "early," "middle," or "late" works.[6] In the "early" works he articulated the problem and pointed to what needed to be done; in the "later" works he set about pursuing a solution. Nietzsche had simultaneously (1) to give a *critique* of a present problem and show how it evolved out of past choices, (2) to set in motion a *transition* to a novel future, and (3) to intimate the contours of a *future world* he hoped to stand toward as midwife. He had to overcome the past, rally men in the present through a protracted transition, and eventually speak to those closed within a uniquely configured future. Nietzsche saw himself as a destiny, a bridge to the future, yet despite his desire to transcend modernity and pursue a transition to the future, he was forced to reproduce a variety of modern maneuvers, not the least of which being an accentuation of the place of the Will and the equally modern granting of priority to the future.

As is well known, Nietzsche felt that the "rational" world depicted by Hegel was a manifestation of decay. He tried to convince his readers that any attempt to accommodate man to his late-modern fate would ultimately fail. Nietzsche knew as well as anyone that decadence had engulfed humanity previously in history—softness had arisen and belief in the gods declined—and mankind had survived, even if individual human beings had suffered. But he saw the contemporary decay as uniquely sinister and threatening. He summed up the problem with the now famous locution, "God is dead." For Nietzsche this statement implied substantially more than that the Christian God had ceased to be believable, and in writing it he intended to do more than simply observe the advent of public atheism. Nietzsche meant that it would no longer be possible for man to believe in anything that transcends the immanent, temporal world, that the bases of the values that had previously shielded and protected humanity were destroyed once and for all.[7] Now that man had come to see that all values emanated from man himself, even if they had not up to now been consciously produced, the transcendent realm was destroyed, never to be restored. No mere poetic will to obfuscation or self-conscious horizon giving could change this fact. Eternity was driven out completely, and therewith Being, to be replaced by the unrelenting reign of Becoming.

---

6. Nietzsche himself makes this clear when he says that the key to his later works is to be found in understanding the issues developed in the earlier ones. Nietzsche, *On the Genealogy of Morals*, Preface #8, 22. Henceforth designated in the text as *GM*, followed by a page number.

7. See for example, Nietzsche, *Will to Power*, #1, 7–8, esp. subsection 3. Henceforth designated in the text as *WP*, followed by a page number.

In Nietzsche's understanding, mere "values" are useless once it is clear that there is nothing intrinsically valuable. Nietzsche was far from believing that "antifoundationalism" was good news. When values cease to have a ground, they lose binding force; everything is permitted, nothing proscribed. Simultaneously, the closed horizons of the separate nations and peoples were exploded and seen to be nothing but historically contingent, passing accidents, mere parochial influences that divided humanity. Even this natural ground for value was soon to collapse. A way had to be found to revalue all values. In Nietzsche's understanding, human beings cannot live without values and cannot be wholeheartedly committed to values that they know are merely human constructions. Fear may hold men in line; but it will never provide the conviction to cement them together through real hardships. Nor will it ever give meaning to life. The late-modern problem was not that one set of gods was to be replaced by another, or that one set of values was giving way to another—which had happened before—but that *all* prior bases of valuation had been dissolved. That Hegel would try to deify the immanent world and thereby to give an ontological ground to extant law and morality is, given this circumstance, understandable. The problem for Nietzsche was that this implied the necessity of accepting the status quo, which represented a radical limitation of the full range of human possibilities.

The alternative to abject despair was to live without values, to go on as if the death of God presented no problems. And it is clear from *Thus Spoke Zarathustra* that for some, the "last men," this is entirely possible.[8] But as far as Nietzsche was concerned, it was tantamount to becoming subhuman. For Nietzsche the distinctive thing about man is that he is the "esteeming being." Hence the life of the last men, who laughed at and mocked everything, dabbled in much but mastered nothing, borrowed from all past cultures but created nothing unique— all as an alternative to recognizing that there remained no substantial ground for commitment to anything—was not distinguishable from the existence of animals. Nietzsche saw his task, the task of *present* philosophy, as one of trying to develop a means by which mankind could again esteem and revere *with a good conscience*. Skepticism might be possible for the few, but for most it leads to the nihilism of the last man, and by extension to the destruction of the few.

8. Nietzsche, *Thus Spoke Zarathustra*. Henceforth designated in the text as *Z*, followed by a page number.

7

The Critique: The Early Nietzsche

The Problem of Socrates

For Nietzsche, the prelude to any transition to the future was to understand how humanity had been led to the conclusion that God is dead, the epochal event that had somehow to be circumvented. He had to clarify how this altogether unprecedented decay had occurred. For if, as Nietzsche asserts, man is and always has been the source of all values in a cosmically indifferent universe, we must determine the root cause of our ceasing to believe and behave as we have always hitherto believed and behaved. A "no-saying," or critical task, had to precede the "yes-saying," or positive task. Nietzsche's work is characterized by this half-destructive, half-creative effort. For Nietzsche the origins of late-modern nihilism could be traced back to the twin sources of Western civilization, Socrates and Christ. Hence contemporary nihilism had been a long time in the making, only now becoming manifest. Ultimately Socrates and Christ are presented as examples of a similar problem, growths from a similar psychological seed. I will focus on Nietzsche's view of Socrates, and conclude with a few brief remarks about Christ and Christianity.

It is difficult to be completely clear as to what the nature of Socratism is for Nietzsche. For despite Nietzsche's presentation of Socrates as the root cause of contemporary nihilism, a symbol of what he opposes, his relation to Socrates is complicated and paradoxical. Beneath the hostile veneer there remains a fascination Nietzsche cannot dispel: What did this ugly, plebeian little man have that made him a prism between past and future? In Socrates' influence Nietzsche cannot help but see an immense power. Indeed, for Nietzsche Socrates is a model of what the philosopher who stands between eternities can accomplish. Nonetheless, for my present purposes, it is the no-saying or critical thrust of Nietzsche's presentation that is most important.[1]

Nietzsche says of Socrates that he is a classic exemplar of the wise man (*TW* 473–74). As with all wise men, Socrates perceived life as no good, as something wearisome to be quit as soon as possible. Needless to say, Socrates defined philosophy as a "preparing to die" and bodily existence generally as an alienation from that which is truly most lovable. Whether this was primarily to console his friends, for example, as they gathered on the day he drank the hemlock, or whether it represented his understanding of human existence is at least debatable—but not for Nietzsche.[2] Nietzsche asserts that all "sages" are manifestations of decline, decadent phenomena of late civilizations (*TW* 473–74). As with Hegel's owl of Minerva which spreads its wings at dusk, all wise men are said to be pessimists, representing the "raven that smells carrion." Wisdom comes on the scene late in the evolution of a culture, at a time when practical possibilities have become limited and less colorful. For purely physiological reasons—i.e., not self-consciously—wise men adopt a negative attitude towards life. Christ merely reproduces the same physiological characteristics. But Nietzsche asserts that no longer may we talk pessimistically like sages; no longer may we judge life and denigrate it. To judge life must henceforth be seen as the epitome of unwisdom, at best a symptom of something pathological. Life must come to be the unquestioned standard of all thought, the supreme and highest good.

Socrates, the quintessential wise man, is also the very picture of the plebeian. He is ugly—which for a Greek is allegedly an indictment in itself—and of low, if not the lowest, class origins. He manifests a hypertrophy of the logical faculty and a "wantonness and anarchy of his instincts" (*TW* 475). This hypertrophy of the intellect leads Socrates to the bizarre equation of virtue, knowledge, and happiness. Socrates reached the conclusion, opposed to all the instincts of the Greeks, that Reason is the only means to virtue, which is in turn the only means to

---

1. There are two main places where Nietzsche thematically confronts what he calls "The Problem of Socrates": in the section of that name in *Twilight of the Idols* and in *The Birth of Tragedy*. *Twilight of the Idols* henceforth designated in the text as *TW*, *The Birth of Tragedy* as *BT*, in both cases followed by a page number. Despite the fact that one is a very early work and the other quite late, there is a significant agreement and overlap. That Nietzsche was later critical of *The Birth of Tragedy*, his first major work, is not significant for present purposes, for it was its Wagnerianism that he repudiated, not its view of Socrates. In what follows I will combine these two accounts.

2. See my "Dialogue and Dialectic in Plato's *Phaedo*: Plato as Metaphysician, Epistemologist, Ontologist and Political Philosopher."

happiness. He opposed this formula to the prerogatives of good birth, good breeding, fortuitous habituation, and "good form." But this plebeian alternative could only gain ascendancy because the "instincts" of the well-bred aristocrats were already in anarchy. Good breeding had broken down, and traditional education had collapsed. Into the moral vacuum caused by this chaos came Socrates, armed with dialectic. He forced the nobles, who in healthy times acted spontaneously on the basis of a unified and well-ordered self, to give a conscious account of themselves.[3] Consequently dialectic came to take the place of ancestral authority based on good bearing and good form (*TW* 475–76). But for Nietzsche, what must first be "proved" by dialectic is worth little and has no intrinsic value. And as dialectic replaces good breeding, plebeian taste replaces noble taste. The spontaneous noble *consciousness* is replaced by an increasingly *self-conscious* form of behavior based on a necessity to account for one's actions, ultimately even before one has acted.

For Socrates, only the examined life can be seen as the good life, only the life for which one can articulate clear principles of action is examined, and ultimately only principles that are universal can be clear and articulate. Therein lay the dynamite to destroy the morality of the noble few, based on "instinct" and habituation intrinsic to a particular class of people. In Socratic dialectic the seeds of cosmopolitanism and egalitarianism were sown. For Nietzsche, as for Hegel, the opening of self-consciousness is a slavish phenomenon; the unself-conscious noble individuals were no match for the plebeians armed with dialectic. With dialectic the plebeian sage had found a means of revenging himself on the aristocrats. Dialectic is nothing more than a mode of combat for those who have no other weapons, a means by which pathological instincts take hegemony over healthy ones (*TW* 476). Its aim is not to discover the truth, but to gain mastery and control. Certainly this is the modern notion of philosophy; knowledge is power. In Nietzsche's hands Socrates becomes a protomodern.

Armed with dialectic, Socrates avenges himself upon the noble few, those of good birth, good bearing, beautiful features, fortuitous habituation, and inherited means. Reason brings about the hegemony of the ignoble and slavish. The traditional world is vanquished, all beautiful myths and illusions destroyed. Faith in plebeian dialectic reigns su-

3. There are numerous occasions in the Platonic corpus where Socrates invites himself into a private assemblage, interrogates those present, and makes himself the center of attention (see *Protagoras, Gorgias*) or forces individuals to justify principles which, though inarticulate, could be the basis of perfectly decent and honorable lives (e.g., Polemarchus in the *Republic*).

preme. And with the victory of Reason comes ultimately the death of God; Reason cannot replace what only instinct, habit, and tradition can unconsciously build. But if this rather neat picture tells the whole story, why were the aristocrats so blind to what was happening and why did they fail to respond by simply killing all dialecticians; for that matter, why did it take Athens so long to attempt, halfheartedly at that, to silence Socrates? Even aristocrats with chaotic instincts should have been able to grasp their class interest.

Nietzsche's fall-back position is that, especially in Athens, there was a great love of contests *(agon)* and that Socrates fascinated his contemporaries because he had invented a new contest. Furthermore, Nietzsche admits that Socrates was a great erotic, and this was something with which the noble young could identify (*TW* 477–78). But this merely raises another problem: How can a great erotic be a hater of life, and how can a great lover of contests represent the antithesis of noble instinct? Furthermore, the giving of reasons for behavior preceded Socrates. The Sophists had spread self-consciousness and reason-giving throughout Greece, and were particularly popular in Athens. Indeed there are numerous occasions in the Platonic dialogues where Socrates, at least to some extent, defends the noble, traditional values against the Sophists. The defeat of Callicles is certainly a defense of traditional values and common sense accomplished by the use of dialectic.

Nietzsche seems not to be telling the whole story, indeed to be missing relatively obvious parts of it. One should first observe what emerges on the very surface: Nietzsche is at great pains to draw a clear distinction between the noble and "instinctive" aristocrats, who need no reasons for their actions, and the plebeian thinkers, who act "self-consciously" but with no other motive than the desire for revenge against those better endowed by Nature. "Instinct" is being opposed to "self-consciousness," a not altogether obvious dichotomy, *except for a post-Kantian like Nietzsche*. Put another way, the distinction Nietzsche is at pains to draw may apply more easily to modern than to Socratic rationalism.

But Nietzsche also explains the nature of what Socrates represented in an entirely different fashion. As in the previous account, the victory of dialectic is explained on the basis of the "anarchy" of the instincts displayed by the noble aristocrats. (We should stress that Nietzsche repeatedly brackets the word "instinct.") A decadence had already fallen over Athens. Old Athens was coming to an end because aristocrats had become "torn" by competing and conflicting impulses which could not be harmonized. With their instincts in anarchy it was necessary to find a new basis for spiritual unity. Rather than be tyrannized by anarchic instincts, they came to accept a countertyrant—Reason. In an atmosphere in which no one was master over himself, Socrates, despite the anarchy of his own plebeian instincts, was the only one who was in control, due to his tyrannical development of Reason. The ultimate outcome was obviously Socrates' victory, based not on weakness or the desire for revenge, but on strength and self-mastery.

What followed was an understanding that any concession to instinct, the unconscious and spontaneous, "leads *downward*" (*TW* 478). Thus to avoid chaos it was necessary for self-conscious Reason to suppress and control unself-conscious instinct. All of life had to be brought into "the most blinding daylight"; rationality, at all costs, had to be the ruler (*TW* 478–79).[4] This was the price for self-preservation. Thus Socrates became the savior of the decadent Greeks, short-circuiting an otherwise natural and healthy decay, thereby making a natural form of rebirth impossible. But finding now that Socrates is the great proponent of autonomous Reason rather than the unwitting dupe of a subconscious plebeian drive, we become unclear as to whether Socrates' "wisdom" is physiological, and thereby unconscious, or a self-conscious attempt to attain mastery. Did Socrates represent an alternate form of instinct or an attempt to *correct existence* through the use of self-conscious Reason? (*BT* 86–87). Offered these two possibilities, Nietzsche chooses the latter. But it is not obvious that this choice fits the facts either. Once again, one wonders if Nietzsche has not mistaken Socrates for Kant.

Nietzsche presents yet a third variation on his theme. For Nietzsche, the faith that self-conscious Reason could supply standards leads to a theoretical optimism about the prospects of overcoming the tragic nature of life. Again, this contradicts the observation that all sages are pessimists, haters of life. Nietzsche resolves this contradiction by saying that because of his pathological hatred of life, Socrates spun for

4. Nietzsche's reference to "blinding daylight" calls to mind the Socratic allegory of the cave presented in Plato's *Republic*. In that allegory the blinding light of day represents the world beyond the cave, the world where pure Reason can allegedly get in touch with the highest realities. But there is no indication in the *Republic* that the realm of light can replace the cave, or that the cave dwellers can be dragged out into the light en masse. In short, there is no indication that Socrates presented Reason as the solution to the human problem for every man, or even for himself, since he goes back into the cave. Nietzsche, however, asserts that Socrates wished to make values rest on self-consciously held principles—applicable to all regardless of birth, class, or nation (clearly at odds with the account in *The Republic*)—as opposed to the works of the poets, statesmen, and mystics whose "inspiration" welled up from some unconscious source. Socrates thereby delegitimized the vital wellsprings of inspiration and unleashed the phenomena that eventually killed them.

himself the illusion that Reason could "cure" the human condition, only to see at the end of his life that his faith in Reason was chimerical, and that life was unredeemable. Having destroyed the legitimacy of the instinctive bases for values, in the end Socrates' rationalist faith collapsed. Therein lies the real paradox and enigma of Socratism. Socrates destroyed the only true ground for order through a faith in Reason he came to see was an illusion. Socrates allegedly short-circuited the natural rhythms of growth and decay on the basis of an error, but this error, his real legacy, found its full flowering in ignoble modern science. Socrates' late wisdom leads to a skepticism with which Nietzsche is in fundamental agreement.

The real Socratic legacy is not his skepticism and pessimism, but his optimism and faith in the ability of Reason to correct and perfect existence (*BT* 86–93). Socrates became the father of the scientific faith that Reason can get to the core of Being, know the whole, modify it, correct it, and cure it. His famous assertion that he only had knowledge of his ignorance was apparently only his late wisdom, a wisdom that history has substantially dismissed. Hence Socrates is the symbol of, if not completely a manifestation of, the amusical, coldly rational individual, opposed to the intoxicated, spontaneous Dionysian.[5] According to Nietzsche, Socrates destroyed the basis of tragic, noble culture through his optimistic faith in Reason and science, and thereby destroyed belief in the unfathomable, impenetrable Dionysian core of Being. Science always destroys man's primordial openness to and longing for oneness with the mysterious core of Being. Further, science is always an escape from the pessimism that should follow from the correct understanding that one cannot penetrate the unfathomable core of Being. But the question that remains: Why is not optimism a greater sign of strength than pessimism? That Socratic optimism is based on an illusion should, from Nietzsche's perspective, be irrelevant, as illusion is necessary for life. But Nietzsche lines up pessimism, though not the hating of life, with strength and optimism with weakness. This issue is developed most sharply in the early work, *The Birth of Tragedy*.

Tragedy is said to be the "pessimism of strength," which died of the optimism of the theoretical man and his science (*BT* 17–27). The will to confront the frightful and unfathomable, which one finds in tragedy, comes from a great health and fullness. And the tragic sense, which sees the ground of Being as mysterious, or even ugly and horri-

---

5. To be fair, one cannot say much for the poetic capacities of a man who, when approaching certain death, remembers a divine injunction to be poetic, and can respond only by putting Aesop's *Fables* into verse.

fying, leads to the restlessness out of which creativity is born. Scientific optimism, on the other hand, leads only to rationalism, cosmopolitanism, and utilitarianism (*BT* 20–22). To the optimistic rationalist who sees the highest end of life in self-conscious utilitarianism, Nietzsche opposes the intoxicated Dionysian who creates unconsciously. Further, to be caught in Dionysian frenzy is allegedly to draw with the draft of Being itself, to become one with a force more comprehensive than that of the individual. (Nietzsche returns to this idea with his doctrine of the Will to Power.) Health requires that one cease striving to be a self-willed individual. But just as the distinction between unconscious instinct and self-conscious Reason blurs when pushed, the Dionysian core of Being, which here looks like a substantive given, becomes a product of art itself; one must act "as if" there were a mysterious Dionysian core of Being. Nonetheless, in this early presentation one cannot help but have visions of an erratic Hegelian *Weltgeist* trying to externalize itself and find concrete manifestation in the realm of appearance.

> Insofar as the subject is the artist, however, he has already been released from his individual will, and has become, as it were, the medium through which the *one* truly existent subject celebrates his release in appearance. . . . We may assume that we are merely images and artistic projections for the true author, and that we have our highest dignity in our significance as works of art. . . . As knowing beings we are not one and identical with that being which, as the sole author and spectator of this comedy of art, prepares a perpetual entertainment for itself. (*BT* 52; emphasis mine)

> The world—at every moment the *attained* salvation of God, as the eternally changing, eternally new vision of the most deeply afflicted, discordant, and contradictory being who can find salvation only in *appearance*. (*BT* 22)

One should never underestimate the influence of Hegel, and more generally German idealism, on Nietzsche's thought.[6]

For Nietzsche, Aeschylus was the last Greek spokesman for the creative force that flows from openness to the Dionysian. After him comes Euripides, the student of Socrates, who proclaims that to create unconsciously is to "say what is wrong." By this new understanding, all prior statesmen, poets, orators, and artists "knew" nothing. Therefore, all

6. One should also not underestimate the link between Nietzsche's discussion of the Dionysian and Heidegger's discussion of *physis* as simultaneously self-presenting and self-concealing.

did something that was "wrong" (*BT* 87). Socrates and Euripides set out to challenge all the greats of the past. Where Nietzsche recognizes the inspired, unconscious "instincts" of those of the past as having created important things, Socrates' only influence is his no-saying *daimon*, who pulls him back rather than moving him to creative action. Socrates undermined the beautiful surface creators had put in place to cover the Dionysian core, and left man without a world of appearance in which to live. Appearance is questioned as *mere* appearance. Hence there is no need to create a beautifying veneer; those of the Socratic faith believe that the core of Being itself is orderly and beautiful. But by denigrating appearance, Socrates makes the ultimate error—he loses his grasp on what is most real, and he destroys the creativity that puts it in place. Therein Socrates threatens life. The attempt to reestablish the reality of appearance, especially in the face of modern philosophy, is at the heart of Nietzsche's project—and Heidegger's as well.

The Apollonian longing for beautiful appearances spins a web of inspiring illusions to cover reality's ugly core, a surface based on myth. But Apollo and Dionysus can only exist together (*BT* 46). Only in response to the ugly is the beautiful called forth. To see the world itself as rational and orderly, or to try to remake it according to the universal dictates of Reason, is to destroy the ground of the Apollonian, of myth, of beautiful illusion, of appearance, in short, of a "world." To succumb completely to the Dionysian, to remain immersed, is to lose all individuation, all will and remembrance of personal ends, and be swallowed in an oblivion that destroys all action (*BT* 59). Man needs the Apollonian to be a proper "self"; the Dionysian must never reign victorious as it does, for example, in Eastern religion. Simple self-forgetting is not conducive to life. One must experience, but then leave behind, the boundless, Dionysian state: "For Apollo wants to grant repose to *individual* beings precisely by drawing boundaries between them and by again and again calling these to mind as the most sacred laws of the world, with his demands for self-knowledge and measure" (*BT* 72; emphasis mine). Apollo must give form and measure (*peras*) and become the ground of differentiation and individuation, because the possibility of difference is not a cosmic given. Apollo is the ground of difference. Difference rests on art, not Nature. Nietzsche, along with Heidegger, is the father of the "philosophy of difference," which eventually finds various diluted manifestations in contemporary postmodernism.

The Apollonian comes into being as a counter to the otherwise destructive Dionysian. But according to Nietzsche, the Dionysian is also a created thing, not the real core of existence (which apparently is either totally unfathomable or constantly tending toward stasis). According to Nietzsche, the Dionysian was born and created out of the fullness and strength of the tragic Greeks, who took it on themselves, in the height of their strength. Indeed, Nietzsche states explicitly that the tragic art form itself is in no way a testimony to the *fact* that life is tragic. For contrary to the classical tradition, art is *not* an imitation of the reality of Nature (*BT* 140). Art overcomes Nature; it does not imitate it. Even the Dionysian obscures and covers a still deeper reality—which, I will argue, is an even more destructive, entropic nothingness.

In Nietzsche's view, tragic art differs from dialectic in that it does not try to overcome tension and contradiction; that is tragic art's higher wisdom. Philosophy assumes that there is in fact something called "Nature" or "Being" that it penetrates at least to some extent; the tragic artist never makes that assumption. It is almost as if, for the tragic artist, there need not be any underlying substratum. Instead myth is superimposed over mystery or formless nothingness. We have a web of speech attached ultimately to Nothing—the Derridean resonance should be clear. Hence the artist that Nietzsche describes seems to stand in midair; at least he need not know where he stands. What is important is that he speaks. Nietzsche, the artist, speaks volumes. Thereby one can make a something out of a nothing. The ultimate impasse of the rationalist urge is that it allegedly finds itself without limits. For all limits are of human origin, born of a distinct culture, rooted in *indigenous* myths (*BT* 135–36). This is why it is far better that limits be unconsciously created than consciously sought. Nietzsche's paradoxical conclusion is that by proceeding "as if" the core of Being were Dionysian it was possible to achieve a limit. In this understanding, modernity's antinature animus has been raised to its highest power—Nature dissolves completely, no longer being even a foil. By comparison, Heidegger will argue that the ultimate source *is* a mysterious Nothing, openness to which brings *nomos* and *peras*.

Alienated from a sense of the Dionysian, the theoretical man merely lives off the accumulated capital of those of the past who have paid the price required to have artists, become rooted, and have traditions. The theoretical man becomes increasingly rootless by continually demonstrating the paradoxes of those traditions. In the process rationalism leads to the secularization of a people whereby they can no longer see the "stamp of the eternal" pressed upon their existence.

And any people—just as, incidentally, also any individual—is worth only as much as it is able to press upon its experiences the stamp of the eternal; [otherwise] it is, as it were, desecularized and

shows its unconscious inward convictions of the relativity of time
and of the true, that is metaphysical, significance of life. (*BT* 137)

And this is what must be avoided. *To link man again to eternity is the aim
of Nietzsche's project:*

> To impose upon becoming the character of being—that is the
> supreme will to power.
> Twofold falsification, on the part of the senses and of the spirit,
> to preserve a world of that which is, which abides, which is
> equivalent, etc. (*WP* 330)

Nietzsche asserts that to attempt to exorcise the tragic, i.e., all mystery,
pain, suffering, and contradiction, from *consciousness* is ultimately to
destroy the ground for the sense of being linked to eternity, which is
the cause of the rootedness which makes life possible. The hegemony
of Reason and dialectic destroys this possibility. Socrates wished to live
the most wakeful, self-conscious existence, whereas for Nietzsche it is
better to live in the twilight of unconsciously created illusion, and
thereby be rooted and have limits.[7] What Socrates set in motion was a
process that destroyed the basis for the *creation* of distinctions like those
between the noble and the common, the beautiful and the ugly, the
good and the bad, in favor of the universal pursuit of the easy and the
comfortable. By this understanding, Socrates' real vice was that he was
a utilitarian who refused to accept limits.

For Nietzsche, the basis of Plato's superior nobility vis-à-vis Socrates was that he, in seemingly Apollonian fashion, "invents" a realm of
beauty and goodness in itself that transcends common utility. But in
doing so he transported eternity to a transcendent realm, thereby radically calling into question the realm of appearance, the surface where
art and creativity must dwell. Thus in trying to overcome Socratic ig-
nobility and utilitarianism the noble Plato destroys commitment to the
meaningfulness of *this* world. He undermines the necessary faith in the
solidity and truth of the realm of appearance. This is what inspired poets avoid. Poets dwell in the realm of appearance. Plato's noble attempt
to moderate Socrates' plebeian rationalism merely paved the way for
Christianity, the great opponent of life. Noble as it was, Plato's work
was ultimately destructive. Hence in the name of life, Nietzsche con-

---

7. Nietzsche has created a distinctively modern either/or choice. In part 4 I will
argue that the postmodern must get beyond these artificial choices—reason/instinct,
reason/poetry, self-conscious/unconscious, reality/appearance, Being/becoming,
reason/tradition, and so on.

tinually announces his antagonism to Platonism and Christianity, although he realizes that Plato himself was too noble for either.

In this light, the critique of Christianity (which must be kept separate from Nietzsche's views about Christ, whom he considered to be of a noble power that eventually would have matured) adds only a few distinctive features. In general, Christianity is a manifestation of the further denigration of the world of appearance. It too destroys art; it too promises an orderly and beautiful world, if only the next one. In giving precedence to Being over Becoming, Christianity, like Platonism, transfers the locus of eternity from this world where we must live to another, and in so doing destroys commitment to action in this world. Nietzsche is clear that healthy action requires a sense of eternity. His radical espousal of Becoming, like his commitment to the Dionysian, is but a means to the recovery of a sense of eternity and the ability to act with a good conscience. This becomes clear in *Thus Spoke Zarathustra,* which represents the transition from the "no-saying" part of Nietzsche's project to the "yes-saying." It is in *Zarathustra* that Nietzsche proposes an alternative to the nontragic, rationalist civilization that he felt had reached its *reductio ad absurdum* in late modernity, especially as codified in the philosophy of Hegel.

By way of summation we must ask again what Nietzsche saw as the real "Problem of Socrates." In the last analysis, it was not his alleged weakness, decadence, or even utilitarianism and rationalism. The real problem of Socrates is that he helped pave the way for the *transference of eternity from the realm of appearance to another realm.* Nietzsche's "revaluation" attempts to reverse that transference and find a way to reenthrone the realm of appearance.

Rationalism and Historicism

According to Nietzsche, it is historicism which is the ultimate outcome of Socratism, Platonism, and Christianity and their transference of the locus of eternity. This can be seen most clearly by reflecting on Nietzsche's early, "untimely" attack on the historicist nature of his age, in *On the Advantage and Disadvantage of History for Life.*[8]

Too much knowledge of history can bring a withering and degeneration of life, while some knowledge of history is necessary. But that knowledge must be judged in light of the fact that Nietzsche wishes to "have an effect on the age to the advantage, it is to be hoped, of a com-

---

8. Nietzsche, *On the Advantage and Disadvantage of History for Life,* Preface, 7. Henceforth designated in the text as *AD,* followed by a page number.

ing age" (*AD* 8). History is only possible for humans; animals live naively and "innocently" entirely in the present moment. Nietzsche proclaims his envy of the happiness of the animals, but says that happiness is impossible for man because he can never unburden himself of his past; he can never completely forget. Man's life is that of "an uninterrupted having-been, a thing which lives by denying itself, consuming itself, and contradicting itself." Man never frees himself from the past without simultaneously losing his present (i.e., in death). But happiness requires the capacity to forget, if only for short periods: "With the smallest as with the greatest happiness, however, there is always one thing which makes it happiness: being able to forget or, to express it in a more learned fashion, the capacity to live *unhistorically* while it endures" (*AD* 9). What this means is that it is impossible to ever simply put Socratism, Platonism, Christianity, modernity, or anything else, behind us and return to some primordial moment. But we can come to remember the past in a way that is useful to human life—for example, as a twenty-five-hundred-year error, as the slow growth of nihilism, and so forth.

Nietzsche points toward a future *praxis* that can return to being unhistorical. One of Nietzsche's central intuitions is that *praxis* requires "innocence and forgetting," and that the possibility of that innocence and forgetting must be consciously projected by someone who continually remembers. Only by proper forgetting can most individuals live within the present moment *(Augenblick)*. And it is only in the present that we can engage in a *praxis* we can take seriously and nonironically. Practical action and the full grasp of the truth are incompatible. Indeed "without forgetting it is quite impossible to *live* at all" (*AD* 9–10). But total forgetting is out of the question as well. Only the really strong can benefit from an undiluted knowledge of history; only the greatest nature could remain unharmed by a thoroughgoing historical sense. Indeed for Nietzsche, this would be a way to test a soul's strength: How much truth can one accept? But even for the few, "what such a nature cannot master it knows how to forget" because "every living thing can become healthy, strong and fruitful only within a horizon" (*AD* 10).

Nietzsche is absolutely unequivocal in stating that every great historical actor or artist must presume to be unique and deserving of more admiration than is in fact the case. In looking back and contemplating such naive and unhistorical individuals and their actions, one elevates oneself to the "superhistorical standpoint." However, from the superhistorical standpoint, one sees only the blind, accidental nature of all great deeds. Having adopted that stance one "could no longer be tempted at all to continue to live and cooperate in making history" (*AD*

12). The superhistorical individuals have only wisdom and nausea; having seen the blindness that is required to act, they refrain from action. Eventually the superhistorical individual sees the past as showing all the possibilities that could be, finished and complete for all time. The past, present, and future become one, having eternally the same meaning; we reach the end of history. In this way the superhistorical individual silently becomes "unhistorical," living in the present alone. By Nietzsche's own definition, therefore, one becomes like the animals. By contrast, properly historical individuals look at history not for the sake of pure knowledge as with the superhistorical, but to serve life. Only the historical are open to the future as holding something new, and only they can learn something useful for life from the past. Still, "they do not know how unhistorically they think and act" even in this (*AD* 13).

For Nietzsche, what was most needed at the end of the modern age was not the wisdom of the superhistorical, but the "unwisdom" of historical men. More or less agreeing with Hegel, Nietzsche admits that the superhistorical do in fact have the truth, while the historical are unclear. But since life stands higher as a value than truth, and historical individuals serve life, one must choose unwisdom. One must not will clarity above the "mania, the injustice, the blind passion, and in general the whole earthly darkened horizon" of the truly great historical actor (*AD* 14). *Praxis* with a good conscience is more important for life than knowing the truth. Like Rousseau, Nietzsche draws a sharp line between the knower and the actor. The knower in the highest sense and the actor in the purest sense need to be kept separate. But the knower in the highest sense is needed. Nietzsche is a man with superhistorical wisdom who tries to serve life. *Praxis* must be supported by true knowers who are just offstage. The modern elitism I have discussed above recurs in Nietzsche's thought. The late-modern philosopher again becomes the manipulative legislator.

The properly historical individual requires cleverly manipulated doses of three different kinds of history, each in different proportions at different times: monumental, antiquarian, and critical.[9] It is only the superhistorical knower who can supply these and properly balance them. Monumental history gives great models, teachers, and comforters that are not available among one's contemporaries. They are frequently exemplary individuals who originally acted in a totally un-

---

9. This Nietzschean maneuver is thoroughly modern. We have a new version of writing History "as if." Only the nature of the "as if" has changed; the hegemony of the hypothetical remains.

historical fashion. Monumental history aids man by providing incentives to equal and try to surpass the great deeds of others, the reward for this being fame, honor, and glory to match that of those who went before in the eyes of those who follow. For such lovers of honor, great moments in the lives of previous individuals "form a chain, that in them the high points of humanity are linked throughout millennia, that what is highest in such a moment of the distant past be . . . still alive, bright and great" (AD 15). It is this belief in the repeatability of great possibilities that makes life seem a sweet and grand affair. This love of fame *links humanity with eternity*: "Fame is more than the most delicious morsel of our self-love, as Schopenhauer called it; it is the belief in the affinity and continuity of the great of all ages, it is a protest against the change of generations and transitoriness" (AD 15, 16).[10]

According to the early Nietzsche, a great culture can be raised upon the shoulders of only one hundred lovers of immortal fame and honor. Monumental history is always a reminder and encouragement to such individuals that they are rare and not defective, a necessary reminder in the posthistorical world. But to accomplish a repetition of past greatness the past must be distorted and distinct particulars forced into general categories: The "sharp edges and lines [must be] broken for the sake of agreement, if the comparison is to have [a] powerful effect" (AD 16). This should be considered in light of the later doctrine of the eternal recurrence, which seems to imply that the past can be simply repeated. Nietzsche here admits that there is no exact recurrence, *no metaphysically grounded eternal recurrence*; otherwise monumental history would not be required (AD 16–17). Since there is no simple metaphysical recurrence, the past must be "reinterpreted according to aesthetic criteria and so brought closer to fiction." Monumental history damages the past; it deceives with analogies, whereby "the courageous are enticed to rashness, the enthusiastic to fanaticism" (AD 17). Presumably, this is an example of what Apollonian artists can accomplish.

The antiquarian and critical uses of history likewise do damage to the truth. Antiquarian history preserves what is created by monumental individuals. The individuals dominated by antiquarian history look beyond their individual life to the "we" of their city with its collective roots. The preserving and revering soul looks back to its origins and

10. It is clear that what Nietzsche has in mind are primarily the deeds of individuals like Caesar, Napoleon, Alexander, Lincoln, Churchill, and their closer destiny-mates. By this argument, love of honor is the means by which we are linked to eternity, a linkage that occurs on the plane of *praxis*. On the theoretical level there may be no eternity with which to attain oneness, except the eternity of Becoming—i.e., the eternal recurrence.

preserves the conditions that fostered it. In the process "the small and limited, the decayed and obsolete receives its dignity and inviolability" (*AD* 19). A tradition comes into existence, is preserved, and, for a while, is life enhancing. In the process it brings pleasure and contentment to "modest, coarse, even wretched conditions." Antiquarian history ties less favored generations to their homeland rather than giving them over to "a restless cosmopolitan choosing and searching for novelty and ever more novelty" (*AD* 20). During many ages this serves life. But again, history as pure truth suffers in the process. And eventually the time comes when antiquarian history serves past life to the disadvantage of new, higher life. Antiquarian history eventually paralyzes the will to action, rather than fostering and preserving it.

It is at this point, when tradition is venerated for no other reason than being old, that *critical* history is needed. There comes a need for the Will to shatter what has ossified to enable man to live, i.e., to again engage in genuine, historical *praxis*.

> Occasionally, however, the same life which needs forgetfulness demands the *temporary* destruction of this forgetfulness. . . . We implant a new habit, a new instinct, a second nature so that the first nature withers away. It is an attempt, as it were, *a posteriori* to give oneself a past from which one would like to be descended in opposition to the past from which one is descended:—*always a dangerous attempt because it is so difficult to find a limit in denying the past* and because second natures are mostly feebler than the first. (*AD* 22; emphases mine)

This dangerous period is clearly the one Nietzsche thought he occupied. Also to be noticed is Nietzsche's understanding of how our "nature" is an acquired trait, and how *nomos* continually renews and recreates our *physis*.[11] For this to occur, there is the eternal need for the clever manipulator of history, a very modern conception. Life requires *praxis,* but *praxis* is not a self-sufficient possibility, as it was, for example, for Aristotle. The philosopher must intervene and continually make adjustments so that life remains viable. In ages when this intervention is not necessary this author of *praxis* can withdraw. In discussing *Beyond Good and Evil* I will point out where this withdrawal takes one.

11. Contrary to the view in contemporary deconstructionism, critical history is to be "temporary." The function of critical history is to give us afresh the possibility of being historical, of seizing the present and doing in the present monumental acts, which will eventually occasion a new round of antiquarian history, which in turn will need to be washed away by critical history.

According to Nietzsche, we live in an historicist age, a time of the hypertrophy of the historical consciousness, in which life has ceased to be the master of history because of the demand that history be a science, a science of universal becoming. This incorrect (Hegelian) approach to history brings about a situation where the soul of modern man is the "belligerent household" of competing pasts. Modern man carries all of these indigestible conflicting bits of knowledge around with him; the result is "an inside to which no outside and an outside to which no inside corresponds." With pride modern man looks at this chaotic inner world and calls it his "inwardness" (*AD* 23, 24). Because of the hypertrophy of this inwardness, modern man has no culture, only knowledge about past cultures.[12] Nietzsche specifies five ramifications of our historicist excesses: (1) personality is weakened; (2) man comes to think he possesses justice to a higher degree than existed in any previous age; (3) the instincts of both peoples and individuals are impaired and hence never mature; (4) a belief in the old age of man is generated, i.e., a belief that we are epigones; and (5) a dangerous ennui which leads to cynicism and a clever egoism is fostered.[13] Our historicist age must be replaced by a nonhistoricist one in which individuals cease to be cynical, ironic, and detached and can again throw themselves into action with a good conscience.

The weakening of modern man's personality can be traced to Socrates, but was clearly exacerbated by Kant and abstract, formal, antinatural, modern morality: "It comes to this: he has annihilated and lost his instinct; . . . he can no longer let go the reins and trust in the 'divine animal.' So the individual becomes timid and unsure and may no longer believe in himself: he sinks into himself, into his inner being" (*AD* 28–29). As a result, "he fails to see something which is yet seen *by the child,* he fails to hear something which is yet heard *by the child.*" (*AD* 28; emphasis mine).[14] Having a "personality" requires a childlike,

12. Nietzsche makes it clear, by way of discussing the Germans, that the unification of "inside" and "outside" primarily presupposes a spiritual transformation: the city is but the soul writ large. The solution to this problem may ultimately have a political component—the monumental actor has the look of a political founder, or statesman—but initially one must reorder the spirit; only then will external order follow. Hence a "higher unity in the nature and soul of a people must be *remade,* that break between the inside and the outside must disappear *under the hammer blows of need*" (*AD* 27; emphasis mine). This is fostered by the philosopher who recreates "need" at the end of history.

13. The resulting ironic relation to life is what Nietzsche asserts must be transcended. Compare this with Rorty's praise of that ironic stance; see especially Rorty, *Contingency, Irony and Solidarity.*

14. This should be compared with the section "On the Three Metamorphoses" in *Zarathustra.*

unself-conscious, "instinctive" relation to life in which one leans on the realm of appearance as the locus of eternity. Without personality so conceived, the individual withdraws into internal chaos and accomplishes nothing. Highly self-conscious modern individuals cannot act in any genuinely historical, or history-making, fashion. Consequently, they cease to be "sincere" in relation to themselves and others. According to Nietzsche, an environment dominated by individuals of this kind will not be sympathetic to art and religion, the "true helpers" of culture, only to the uniform, general education that makes man into a "walking lie." And under the circumstances of modern, historicist reality, real philosophy is in danger of being banished (*AD* 29, 30).[15]

Enlightened modern men with their historical "objectivity" also consider themselves to be just to a higher degree than any previous men. And Nietzsche admits, contrary to the popular stereotype of his work, that the just individual deserves our respect, because in that one quality lies hidden the highest and rarest of virtues: "This places him upon a solitary height as the most *venerable* exemplar of the species man; for he wants truth but not only as cold knowledge without consequences, *rather as ordering and punishing judge*" (*AD* 33; emphasis mine). The "just man," as Nietzsche portrays him, sets the boundary markers for his contemporaries and is the source of the "last judgment." Many serve truth, but justice is found rarely, for few can push through to the definitive judgments that justice requires. It is clear that Nietzsche's just man is not to be confused with the philosopher who sits on the fringes of life and keeps the engine of history moving by his alternating use of monumental, antiquarian, and critical history. He is rather the one who brings concrete measure and limit to the world of *praxis*.

In contrast to Nietzsche's just man, contemporary man is a "reverberating passivity." He seldom pursues a course of action through to

---

15. This is one of the central reasons why Nietzsche is concerned about late modernity. When historical knowledge becomes public, genuine philosophy is in danger and *praxis* dissolves. As the philosopher qua artist is the only ground of historical *praxis*, philosophy must be saved, for it is the ultimate means by which life can be continually renewed. My argument, taken up thematically below, is that Nietzsche wishes to restore philosophy as a *way of life*—rather than as ideological or as a public weapon in the service of mass democracy and the rationalization of the given. Nietzsche thinks it is necessary for philosophy to withdraw from the stance adopted by modern philosophy, which he characterizes as a revengeful refusal to affirm life in all its difference. This ultimately means that to defend philosophy Nietzsche must create for it a new public persona. Unfortunately, in a time of *transition,* the task of philosophy remains a practical one; thus, in Nietzsche's later terminology, present philosophy remains trapped in the Spirit of Revenge.

judgment, and when he does he judges by the superhistorical standard of "objectivity," i.e., detachment from all personal interest. Detachment and objectivity lead to relativism. "Objectivity and justice have nothing to do with each other." Objectivity is primarily a "lack of pathos and moral strength [which] usually disguises itself as penetrating coolness of observation" (AD 34–36). Only the just, judging actor— the "master builder of the future"—can discern what is worthy of preserving (AD 38). Only the monumental individual can be truly just in this sense and the ultimate source of traditions. The true philosophic knower is limited to the judicious use of historical fictions to put in motion the process that leads to just men who can curb the "rank impulse" to analysis that lays waste to the present and makes spiritual calm, growth, and ripening all but impossible. Only by setting a future goal can we "forget . . . that [we] are epigoni" (AD 38). Only the involved actor can project a posthistorical, postmodern goal. The philosopher is limited to creating the conditions for his existence. Philosophy and *praxis*—which have increasingly merged in the modern age—*must be severed.*

Because of the unrestrained "objectivity" of historicist modern man, Nietzsche argues, the young are "whipped through all millennia," blinded by *"much too bright, much too sudden, much too changeable light"* (AD 41). As a result, they lose all sense of wonder, are surprised by nothing, and tolerate everything. The young are trained as early as possible to be maximally useful as laborers; to do otherwise would "withdraw a lot of strength from 'the labour market.'" Hence, for the sake of usefulness, all is ruined before it is ripe (AD 41, 42). The modern battle cry becomes "division of labor." Scholars too become narrow and specialized. This narrowness not only destroys genuine historical action, eventually it will destroy science. Even scientists and scholars come to sense their mediocrity; they live with a premonition of ruin and hence become indifferent and careless about their future and that of others (AD 43). Their irony leads to cynicism, which in turn leads to passivity.

According to Nietzsche, we must cease taking "the great mass drives to be the important and chief point of history and [regarding] all great men only as the clearest expression, the bubbles, as it were, which become visible on the flood." "The task of history is . . . again and again to provide the occasion for and lend strength to the production of greatness. No, the *goal of humanity* cannot lie at the end but only *in its highest specimens.*" We must no longer write history from the perspective of the mass—as did Marx, for example—and must instead begin to see great individuals as the only interesting nodes of human

history (*AD* 55).[16] Nietzsche ends his characterization of the problems
of our time—and the nature of a postmodern destiny—on what one
assumes is intended to be an encouraging note. He tells us that our situation is not unique. Something similar was encountered by the tragic,
pre-Socratic Greeks. Their culture too was a chaos of foreign cultures.
But they cast off their false needs and did not remain the epigones of the
Orient. As a result, their culture became "a new and improved nature,
without inside and outside, without dissimulation and convention, [a]
culture as the accord of life, thought, appearing and willing" (*AD* 64).
Modern man could achieve the same thing; he too could again become
whole, *become natural*. What emerges with great clarity is the extent to
which, in Nietzsche's eyes, we stand locked between eternities, in the
decay of the old, incapable of entering the new. No romantic longing
to go back remained possible. Only the movement to a unique future
held promise. Modern, abstract, increasingly formalistic rationalism
and its enervating historical consciousness had to be transcended. It is
my contention, backed by Nietzsche's explicit statements, that this understanding of the problem never changed. Nietzsche's later work is an
attempt to effect a solution.

16. One is reminded of Tocqueville's discussion of the ways a democratic age will
write history; see Tocqueville, "Some Characteristics Peculiar to Historians in Democratic Centuries," in *Democracy in America,* 493–96. As the more mature Nietzsche came
to realize, more would be required than exhortations to a different mode of writing history. The return to the correct kind of existence required other prior efforts; in fact, it
required willing a self-imposed flood upon humanity. Nietzsche admits that the historically sick of his age will have to suffer from the antidote he proposes. During a necessary
interim period, individuals will "suffer from the malady and the antidote" simultaneously (*AD* 63).
Nietzsche asserts that in its heart of hearts, the modern age shares with Christianity
the thought that the end is near; it has the instinctive belief in the old age of mankind and
is "hostile toward all new planting" (*AD* 44). According to Nietzsche this belief, as in
Hegel, turns into a praise of the actual and eventually an idolatrous praise of success. In
opposition to this, Nietzsche says that the task for contemporary humanity is "not to
carry their generation to the grave but to found a new generation—that drives them
forward incessantly: and even if they are born as latecomers—*there is a way of living which
will erase this from memory*—the coming generations will only know them as first-
comers" (*AD* 49; emphasis mine). It is that *transition,* how to spark it, and how to endure
the interim that moves all of Nietzsche's later works. But if a novel future is to arrive,
the historical sense clearly must be overcome; a nonhistoricist age must follow. Likewise, the constant fragmentation and dissolution of everything into an "ever flowing
and dispersing becoming" must cease. A constancy and stability must come to pass.
"Being" must be reenthroned and eternity recovered. This time, however, it must be
the eternity *of the realm of appearance*. Only then would the hegemony of what the young
Nietzsche calls the just man—later designated "noble"—over *praxis* again be possible.

8

The Transition: Zarathustra's Five Modes of Speech

> The more abstract the truth that one wishes to teach is,
> the more one must begin by seducing the *senses* to it.
>
> Heidegger, quoting Nietzsche in *Nietzsche*, 2:35

The Prologue: The First Mode of Speech

Of *Thus Spoke Zarathustra* Martin Heidegger has written, "This work constitutes the center of Nietzsche's philosophy. . . . We emphasize the fact that this work is the highest peak attained by Nietzsche's thinking."[1] I am in agreement with Heidegger to this extent: *Zarathustra* is the central weapon in Nietzsche's publicly deployed arsenal. But I want to present a different picture of *Zarathustra* than Heidegger does. I will argue that *Zarathustra* is Nietzsche's central reflection on how to accomplish a *transition* from present to future. *Zarathustra* is a grand reflection on the nature of philosophic speech, its possibilities, and its relation to the various audiences it may encounter. It is a reflection on how philosophy can have an effect.

Following Nietzsche's explicit guidance, I have already suggested that in early works such as *The Birth of Tragedy* and *Untimely Meditations*—but also *Dawn* and *Human All Too Human*—Nietzsche articulates and traces the origins of the problem he confronts. He gives a critique of presently constituted humanity, making clear the need to move toward a transformed future humanity. In *Zarathustra,* the poetic symbol for the man of the present is the "last man," that for the future man, who can exist only after a great metamorphosis, is the "overman." *Zarathustra* represents a reflection on what is required to make a *transition* from last man to overman; Zarathustra himself is symbolic of the central figure in the transition. In what follows I make no attempt to give a comprehensive interpretation of *Zarathustra.*[2] I will discuss the status of the major Nietzschean themes that appear in *Zarathustra,* but my main

---

1. Heidegger, *Nietzsche*, 2:36. Henceforth designated in the text as *N*, followed by the volume and page number.

2. The most thorough interpretation of *Zarathustra* to date is to be found in Laurence Lampert's *Nietzsche's Teaching: An Interpretation of Thus Spoke Zarathustra.*

concern is to show what I think is the dramatic key to the work. That key is to be found in the various audiences to which Zarathustra's speeches are explicitly addressed. Nietzsche's major themes—Will to Power, Eternal Recurrence, Spirit of Revenge, and so on—are addressed to different audiences. Only after having seen how these themes emerge is it possible to discuss their significance. I have already suggested that Nietzsche consciously fosters most of the kinds of interpretations we have seen since his death. But one should not conclude from this that there is a little something for every taste in Nietzsche's work. I believe Nietzsche makes clear for what audience each speech is intended and how that audience fits into a transition to the future.[3]

3. I will try to show where some of the more important partial interpretations fit into Nietzsche's longed-for transition. A further note on method is also in order. Throughout my interpretation of Nietzsche I remain in close contact with the *published* works, eschewing reliance on the material contained in the *Nachlass*. Heidegger's important interpretative approach, to which I will give thematic attention below, takes the opposite tack and concludes that one is better served by sticking to the material in the *Nachlass*, which it considers "more contemplative" and measured, and more capable of being reduced to a systematic philosophical statement. In his analysis of Nietzsche, Heidegger draws primarily from the material collected in *The Will to Power* for his central discussions of nihilism, Will to Power, and Eternal Recurrence. Using this material allows Heidegger to conclude that Will to Power and Eternal Recurrence are metaphysical and ontological doctrines, and that *The Will to Power* was intended to be Nietzsche's main systematic philosophic statement. See especially Heidegger, *Nietzsche*, vol. 3, pt. 2, 159–84.
    I believe focusing on the *Nachlass* material, particularly that contained in *The Will to Power*, is a mistake and very misleading. First, it is clear if we compare the initial notebook materials and the versions of those notes eventually used in published texts that Nietzsche polished his aphorisms with considerable care. The transformations that Nietzsche's notes went through before surfacing in the written works is frequently significant. Second, Nietzsche's published works are clearly not composed of random thoughts strung together. The order of ideas, even in the most aphoristic works, is of crucial importance. Consequently, we have no idea how the material in Nietzsche's notebooks would have been polished and arranged, that is, what its import was intended to be. The material collected in *The Will to Power* is particularly misleading, in that the selection, arrangement, and chapter headings are not the work of Nietzsche. Furthermore, contrary to Heidegger, and the Kaufmann school, the entire thrust of Nietzsche's work is opposed to the understanding of philosophy as systematic and system building. Nietzsche explicitly attacked that vision of philosophy with a passion.
    Finally, and this is especially important in light of my project, it is the published works, not random aphorisms, that have had a concrete historical impact. One can endlessly marshal contradictory quotes from the *Nachlass*, an effort that is fundamentally fruitless. Nietzsche intended to have a *public effect*, not just an effect on the isolated scholar, and it is the published works that have made that effect possible. They are primarily responsible for Nietzsche's massive influence to date. Hence, with rare exceptions—and then only to support a point integral to a text—I have not focused on the *Nachlass* material.

Zarathustra begins rather abruptly. Nietzsche tells us nothing of who Zarathustra is, or of his life before he was thirty. At the age of thirty, like Christ, Zarathustra left his homeland and his friends, although he made an ascent into the mountains rather than a descent into the desert. For ten years he enjoys his "spirit and solitude." During this time, his only companions are a serpent (wisdom) and an eagle (pride and spiritedness). When we first encounter Zarathustra he is ascending from his cave to reflect upon the sun.[4]

At the end of ten years a change overtakes Zarathustra; like the creative sun, to which he compares himself, he feels the need to "shine" on those he has left behind in the valley (*Z* 9). He must go *down* to them. His own happiness depends on this going down. Zarathustra is overfull; he has become weary of his wisdom and must give it away, distributing it so that *the wise* may "find joy once again in their folly, and the poor in their riches" (*Z* 10). It is not clear yet if this is the necessary lot of wisdom per se, or only of the kind of wisdom with which Zarathustra is burdened. Perhaps this weariness comes only to those with "superhistorical" wisdom, although the early Nietzsche had argued that *all* wise men are sick and unhappy with life. What is clear is that a psychological imperative forces *this* wise man to attempt to share and indeed actualize his wisdom. Zarathustra has a need; it may even be called a sickness.

This sickness is a manifestation of the Spirit of Revenge. Zarathustra can affirm neither his present nor the past that led up to it so instead must take his revenge against it and try to transform it. Zarathustra wishes to quit his status as a wise, revengeful god, to step down from his wisdom by bringing everyone else up to his own level; only in that way can he quit his solitude without dissembling. He also longs to "go under" *(untergehen)*, to be forgotten as well as to accomplish a therapeutic forgetting. Hence Zarathustra leaves his mountain heights. Initially, he will attempt a version of the Enlightenment.

Zarathustra wanders down and eventually into a nearby town, Motley Cow (cows being herd animals who continually rechew the old),

---

4. The allusion to the Platonic doctrine of the cave—which occurs repeatedly in Nietzsche's works—is as clear as the repeated comparisons with Christ. The allusions to the twin wellsprings of Western civilization continue throughout *Zarathustra*. The ramifications of these allusions could fill volumes; I simply cannot pursue the issue at present. I would, however, point out one fact: Contrary to what one might expect, in *Zarathustra* there *is* a sun outside the cave. In light of the Platonic allegory this represents a significant concession, which bears on the nature of philosophy as it exists for the few, true philosophers in their *solitary* undertakings; regardless of Nietzsche's surface rhetoric there is a truth to reflect upon.

and into a crowd of people gathered to see the spectacle of a tightrope walker.[5] Zarathustra launches immediately into his gift-giving mission: "*I teach you the overman.* Man is something that shall be overcome. What have you done to overcome him?" (Z 12). Zarathustra exhorts the crowd to follow all past humanity in creating something which stands beyond themselves, and states that for them that something is the overman, the symbol of what will distinguish the future from the past. The alternative is to become indistinguishable from the beasts. At this point Zarathustra parodies Darwin and says that man will be the same laughingstock and embarrassment to the overman that the ape is to man.[6] It is not, however, natural selection that Zarathustra sees as the engine of evolution, but conscious human manipulation. In modern fashion, he declares the distinctively human to be a product of man's art, not of Nature. Zarathustra continues his unannounced, and unwelcome, lecture: "The overman is the meaning of the earth." A mere possibility not yet actualized is all that stands between man and the abyss of total meaninglessness. One must *"remain faithful to the earth,"* faithful to this world and its immanent possibilities, and not chase otherworldly hopes. This earth and what can be made of it is all the meaning that is left. To sin against the earth is now a greater sin than to sin against God (Z 13). The hegemony of immanence reminds one of Hegel.

Zarathustra tells his involuntary auditors that man has arrived at "the hour of the great contempt," when the pursuit of universal, com-

---

5. In descending he has earlier encountered an old saint who had left his seminary ("holy cottage") to look for "roots" in a return to or oneness with nature. The old man scornfully tells Zarathustra that he too once loved man, but gave it up because man is too imperfect. Now he loves only God. Zarathustra responds, "I bring men a gift." The old man tells him to keep his gift, to give only alms and a helping hand. But Zarathustra refuses to engage in such "pitying" and "despising" behavior: "For that I am not poor enough" (Z 11). He would rather redeem mankind with his gift of wisdom. Zarathustra leaves this saintly man, seeing no promise in his response to his world. Zarathustra agrees with Hegel and the rest of modern thought: Nature by itself provides no roots, a romantic return to primary nature no solution; a truly human existence is to be found outside the natural world. Further, the old saint's solitude is based on a hatred of the world rather than upon his own fullness and affirmation of life. He too suffers from what Zarathustra will shortly designate the Spirit of Revenge. Zarathustra leaves without telling the man of his gift, the news that God is dead, because he refuses to rob the old saint of the one solace he has left. Nonetheless, he cannot believe that the saint has heard nothing of this momentous occurrence.

6. Zarathustra parodies Darwin even further in saying, "And even now, too, man is more ape than any ape" (Z 12). Apes are famous for imitating and copying the actions they see, but men too can become what they would aspire to or imitate. In this Zarathustra reminds us of Rousseau's *Second Discourse,* 105–6.

fortable self-preservation and the modern understandings of reason and virtue must arouse contempt and disgust. The present, despite its soft charm and easy pleasures, must be quit in order to pursue a future that can justify existence itself. Otherwise, all past existence will have been meaningless, a mere accident which has led to nothing. Zarathustra becomes increasingly frenzied as he talks, but upon finishing is greeted with the flippant disdain of those assembled; he is told they have heard enough of this tedious harangue and want the show to begin (Z 13–14). Gentle amusement and novel spectacles are what the audience desires, "wretched contentment" and mindless diversion from their daily routine.

Zarathustra, in a display of composure, takes advantage of the stage that is set before him and responds, "Man is a rope, tied between beast and overman—a rope over an abyss. A dangerous across, a dangerous on-the-way, a dangerous looking-back, a dangerous shuddering and stopping" (Z 14). Present man is not an end, merely a bridge from something lower to something higher, a pregnant possibility hovering over nothingness. As such it is impossible for him to contemplate coming to rest in the present. For present man there is no firm ground, no immediate actuality, only potentiality. Like the tightrope walker, humanity must eventually reach firm ground or perish. Mankind must make it to the new eternity. Combined with what we have already seen in Nietzsche's early writings, this must mean that a nonhistoricist age needs to replace the present superhistorical age. Until then, contemporary man stands miraculously suspended over nothingness. At some point this ontological groundlessness must be replaced by a firm ground that holds fast; nothingness must be replaced by Being. But man cannot attain an ontological foundation by going back to the fixed, determinate ground of his animality: the return to premodernity is impossible. To reach firm ground man must be seized by a longing to reach the overman.

After his second attempt at persuasion, Zarathustra realizes his folly. Those listening have no idea what he is talking about. The citizens of this city have heard nothing of the momentous portents Zarathustra announces, and hence cannot regard them as important. They are all "educated"—products of the mass education Nietzsche had ridiculed and derided in the second of the Untimely Meditations—and their education has become the basis of a haughty pride. None of Zarathustra's words have any efficacy in convincing his listeners of their exposed position. But he concludes that perhaps he can convince them of something else. Instead of the overman he tries to tell the assembled people (Volk) of his antithesis, the "last man." For Zarathustra this is the most despicable man, the man who can no longer despise himself. He no longer aspires to anything or esteems anything. The last man mimics the philosopher by asking various banal questions in a manner completely devoid of passion—What is love? What is creation? What is longing?—and sleepily "blinks" in admiration of his own wit. He makes everything small; he has left behind the "regions where it was hard to live," for he is past caring for hardship and travail. He works only for amusement; he is neither poor nor rich—either would be too hard. He wishes neither to rule nor to obey; to do either is likewise too hard. He is clever and knows everything that has ever happened, but creates and builds nothing. Hence he has only derision for all who presume to the possibility of novelty and true creation. He has many small pleasures, but no strength for great ones: "'We have invented happiness,' say the last men, and they blink" (Z 17).

The last men are clearly suffering from the symptoms of the historical disease Nietzsche had diagnosed earlier. Zarathustra characterizes their world as a great herd with no shepherd, everyone the same and desiring to be so; anyone who is not "goes voluntarily into a madhouse" (Z 18). They are the inhabitants of the universal society of free, equal, and prosperous individuals, a state that for Zarathustra is worthy only of contempt. The last man is Nietzsche's characterization of the Hegelian posthistorical man, the classless man of a posthistorical mass society, longing for nothing higher than comfortable self-preservation. To go higher requires a quantum leap to something generically different, the overman. The legacy of the past must be quit, an entire eternity must be traded in to open up the possibility of something new. Zarathustra calls on the assembled *Volk* to quit the last man before it is too late, for he maintains that otherwise the time will shortly come when the last man will have become a totally universal, global phenomenon; then there will be no room left for those who could create something higher. There must remain a tension in the soul if it is to be possible to transcend the sleepy comfort of the last man: "I say unto you: one must still have chaos in oneself to be able to give birth to a dancing star" (Z 17).

Zarathustra again fails to move his listeners. He cannot raise contempt in their souls any more than he could arouse longing. They cry with mocking delight: "Give us this last man. . . . Turn us into these last men!" (Z 18). For the first time, Zarathustra recognizes the full depth of the problem, and herein ends his "first speech." His attempt to raise modern man to his level of wisdom has failed. Enlightenment has failed. He will not proceed in this fashion again.

By now the regularly scheduled performance had begun. The tightrope walker had come out on the rope stretched over the marketplace and the people. That is the real abyss, not the Dionysian abyss, which does not really exist. The herd of last men are the nothingness, i.e., the lack of differentiation over which the possibility of future humanity hovers. When the tightrope walker had reached the middle of his journey, a jester walked out after him, yelling, "You block the way for one better than yourself." With a devilish cry the jester jumped over the tightrope walker. The other, seeing he had been surpassed, "went under," and fell headlong into the marketplace, where no one attempted to break his fall. He landed right next to Zarathustra, who did not run, but likewise did not try to catch him. Zarathustra concludes that contemporary man is the great between, between beast and what could constitute future humanity. The danger is that dabblers like the jester could make man stumble and fall, thereby destroying the only vehicle of transition. In his first speech Zarathustra was just such a jester, attempting to rush humanity across to the overman. The tightrope walker's fall is the symbol of what Zarathustra must avoid. He must rein in his own need for the sake of his ultimate project. Zarathustra will never know satisfaction; *his* distress is the engine of transition.[7]

The people grow weary of the spectacle, their "idle curiosity" wanes, and they leave Zarathustra with the corpse and his reflections on times so uncanny that "a jester can become man's fatality" (Z 20). Finally Zarathustra takes the corpse to bury it, realizing that while he had played the jester that day, he had had the good fortune to be merely ridiculed. As he leaves town he is warned by the original jester that he should not return, for the "good and the just" hate him as their enemy and the true believers see him as a danger. He was saved because most of his listeners only laughed and because his stooping for the dead body was taken as a sign of pity (Z 21). Zarathustra carries the body and eventually puts it into a hollow tree, to keep the wolves away from something that has gone under but deserves respect even now. He concludes that he will no longer carry the dead past, and that he will talk only to a few companions and disciples.

The Prologue ends with a chastened Zarathustra who will no longer talk directly to the people: "An insight has come to me: Let Zarathustra speak no more to the people but to companions. Zarathustra shall not become the shepherd and dog of a herd." Zarathustra will instead try several other modes of speech aimed at different audiences in an at-

---

7. As with Hegel, it is a psychological need that moves history. Hegel tried to accommodate the few to the given; Nietzsche tries to harness their distress, in fact to heighten it.

tempt to set his transition to the future in motion. Zarathustra had come down from his mountain to drain himself of his heavy and grave wisdom. But it was a wisdom no one was willing or able to take from him. Hence he failed to minister to his own need. That is what drives him on to alternate modes of speech. Now pride and wisdom, his companions from his years of solitude, return. The serpent is wrapped around the neck of the eagle, for the spirited and proud do not prey upon the wise even though they could (Z 25). This is indicative of the solution Zarathustra is forced to pursue once he realizes that exhortation directed to the many will not work. Spirited pride must be unleashed and put in the service of those who know; only the eagle is capable of carrying wisdom aloft so that it may gain a noble and comprehensive vision of the whole. Philosophy is safer in the company of the spirited, honor-loving few rather than the *demos*. I will argue that Nietzsche's future solution requires precisely this conjunction of wisdom and pride, *albeit not their mere convergence*.

From *Volk* to Epigones: The Second Mode of Speech

Zarathustra's second attempt to foster a transition to the future begins with an allegory, "On the Three Metamorphoses." Zarathustra asserts that the spirit of man has changed historically from an unspecified beginning, perhaps as a mere animal being, first into a camel, then into a lion; with luck, in the future, it can be transformed into a child. The camel represents a strong, reverent being that can carry great burdens, endure great restraint, and accept a total humbling of its haughtiness (Z 26). In assuming the burden of traditional morality—the traditional virtues and the heritage of Platonic, and especially Judeo-Christian, civilization—man is transformed into something human. Eventually this camel enters its "loneliest desert." Now the spirit, wishing to become "master in his own desert," seeks out its last master and its last god in order to vanquish them. Thus a second metamorphosis occurs, from camel to lion. The lion opposes its "I will" to the "Thou shalt" of the camel, which speaks for values thousands of years old, but sees no need to create new values. With the lion, the antiquarian impulse gives way to the critical. The lion must overcome the beast of burden, say No to all past duty, and create the transitional anarchy that will insure the possibility of a new dawn.

But this is but a prelude to a yet unaccomplished metamorphosis. For while the lion can destroy, *it cannot create new values*. The lion is a no-sayer incapable of being a yes-sayer (Z 26–27). Fundamentally critical, late modernity is nihilistic, as is its hegemony of the Will. It is incapable of creating anything but negative values. To the extent that Nietzsche himself primarily engages in "critical history" we must conclude that he is primarily an exemplar of the lion. The lion's primary task is to destroy the spirit of reverence that blocks new creations. A new creation must come from another source and create a new *basis* for values, different from all past bases. Only after a future creation of new values will it be possible to circumvent the last man. But for that to happen the preying lion must give way to the third metamorphosis, the child. The lion will not occupy the new kingdom. The nihilistic phase must be transcended by the unhistorical child. The child represents "innocence and forgetting, a new beginning, a game, a *self-propelled wheel*, a first movement, a sacred 'Yes'" (*Z* 27; emphasis mine). He who remembers the past, both camel and lion phases, is barred from creating. The critical, destructive, no-saying age of the lion is necessary but becomes a great danger if it does not lead to the emergence of an unhistorical naivete. Deconstruction must lead to reconstruction.

Everything is dependent upon how one accomplishes a future innocence and forgetting, what Nietzsche in *Beyond Good and Evil* will call the "translation of man back into Nature" (*BG* 161).[8] The philosopher of the present cannot openly will values, but he can will innocence and forgetting. Zarathustra now realizes the error of his first speech; he must create the possibility of naivete, not transfer knowledge to the last men. Zarathustra's first speech had remained all too modern.

The architectonic metaphor about the three metamorphoses comes forth while Zarathustra still sojourns in the vicinity of Motley Cow. He now speaks in parables aimed at a few "disciples." They are the *means* to his future children. In this second mode of speech, Zarathustra becomes far more circumspect. He must calculate how his words will affect his disciples and how their diluted renditions will affect the many—i.e., he is concerned with the issues of "dissemination" and "deferral." Zarathustra now repeats themes sounded in the Prologue. The new audience and the new intention account for both the repetition of themes and the different messages. I will limit myself to a few examples.

Agreeing with Marx, Zarathustra observes that the old camel virtues—and their contemporary extensions—were no more than opiates that fostered good sleep. Zarathustra speaks of a sage who is

8. I will argue that the spontaneous, unself-conscious child is the symbol for "Nature" throughout Nietzsche's thought. For Nietzsche, it is possible for man to *become* natural only at the *end* of History. The future will be "natural" and beyond the self-conscious Will.

honored and rewarded highly for saying "honor sleep and be bashful before it—that first of all" (Z 28). This sage's wisdom is that good sleep requires exorcising all striving, longing, thirsting, and tension from the soul. One must reconcile oneself to everything, overcome bitterness, never covet, lie, or commit adultery, for these will destroy good sleep. One must avoid honors and jewels, obey even crooked magistrates, tell the poor of spirit they are right, and above all, reconcile oneself with God. Of this sage's wisdom Zarathustra observes, "And verily, if life had no sense and I had to choose nonsense, then I too should consider this the most sensible nonsense" (Z 30). But there is a higher meaning to life than that which the old sages of sleep have offered for thousands of years. It is a harder and sterner wisdom that is needed: "Contentment" and "adjustment" will not be the aims of the next age of humanity.

Likewise, all otherworldly religions must be overthrown. The "afterworldly" make *this* world seem like a fiction, colored smoke, the dream of a tortured god. Concurring with Hegel, Zarathustra asserts that it was suffering and incapacity that created all afterworlds, a weariness that did not want to want any more (Z 30–31). Zarathustra now adds that it was the despair of the suffering *body* which invented all soul-stuff. In the future man must bear freely this earth and the limitations of the body. This is the only way remaining to create new values. This is surely an *anti*modern note, i.e., it is opposed to metaphysical freedom. The essence of man must come to be seen as resting in the body and its subconscious "instincts." According to Zarathustra (remembering always that since his first failed attempt he has adopted the mode of indirect speech), it is the healthy body alone that speaks of the meaning of the earth.[9] While Zarathustra does say that behind everything lies the "self," which is the "unknown ruler," it is nonetheless true that "in your body he dwells; he is your body." The self-conscious "I" merely thinks it escapes the control of this self/body; but it cannot. It is always the self/body that makes the ego think or sense. According to this critical, no-saying teaching the unconscious, "instinctive" self has hegemony over the self-conscious ego, which is never autono-

9. "The awakened and knowing say: body am I entirely, and nothing else; and soul is only a word for something about the body." What is also interesting to note is that the *child* says, "Body am I, *and* soul" (Z 34; emphasis mine). Apparently the childlike future will bring about a return to a previous understanding; after the no-saying which is still taking place, there may be no further need to speak publicly in favor of the monism of body. The transitional teaching, however, is that *the body is the great reason,* and "spirit," "thought," and the "I" are just other words for that great reason.

mous.[10] The parallel with Freudianism is clear. All Freudianizations of Nietzsche have a foundation in his work, but only in a specific rhetorical part of the whole. Faith in "instinct," the body and its effects, the subconscious, and so on is needed for a transition to the future.

In his new mode of speech, Zarathustra further asserts that the fervent unconscious wish of the self is to create beyond itself. Only those who despise the body—who are unable to create beyond themselves because their bodies are sick—will the existence of the soul and afterworlds. It should be noted that there is no simple, inert materialism in what Zarathustra is preaching here. This self/body is not a fixed, determined, inert, material thing; it is able to craft something unique of itself (Z 34–35). It changes over time in response to a variety of causes—at least that is what Zarathustra would like his epigones to believe. Where once the "self" was the battleground of passions, and of virtues opposed to those passions, now there is only the battle of different virtues, the residue of the victorious fight against the "passions."[11] Inner war and battle are absolutely healthy, but in the end modern men came to pursue only one virtue—sleep and "wretched contentment," and with it their "instincts" withered. Thereby the basis of motion in the self is exhausted (Z 36–40, passim).

Man's primordial, malleable self is entropic; it tends toward rest. In the past, necessity staved off that entropy. Henceforth, only the philosopher, using pregnant fictions, can oppose this entropy. The good news seems to be that since our bodies are constructs, we can, as great philosophic artists, create and re-create our species, as was true for Rousseau. At the deepest level, man is a nothing that must be constituted and reconstituted as a work of art, a notion that is nothing but an advanced form of the modern antinature animus.

After talking about the need to overcome the last man and his pale virtue by means of a "red judge"—that is, in a harsh and bloody fashion[12]—Zarathustra seems to sense that his parables have become

10. This monistic materialism implies the existence of a dogmatic given that Nietzsche will later explicitly reject. But this is no contradiction if we note that this materialism is elaborated as part of the second mode of speech.

11. For Nietzsche, "instincts" and "passions" come and go: "Once you suffered passions and called them evil. But now you have only your virtues left. . . . In the end all your passions became virtues and all your devils, angels. Once you had wild dogs in your cellar, but in the end they turned into birds and lovely singers" (Z 36–37). In this regard, the work of Foucault should come immediately to mind. See chap. 22, n. 4.

12. To the straightforward nature of this bloodiness, one must juxtapose that which Zarathustra must endure. "Whoever writes in blood and aphorisms does not want to be read but to be learned by heart" (Z 40). Zarathustra is more than willing to accept the ambiguity between these different kinds of bloodiness. While he is not squeamish about

too heavy and grave and is caught in a dilemma: His wisdom cuts him off from the majority of his contemporaries and makes him seem like a criminal; this in turn makes him grave and melancholy. But he recognizes the necessity of being light, that health and laughter go together. No-sayers, while necessary, cannot easily be light. They are still caught in the Spirit of Revenge, for they cannot accept their present or past. That Zarathustra falls continually into the Spirit of Gravity is a sign that he cannot heal himself, that transitional individuals like him can find no solution.[13]

After spreading his parables, Zarathustra again leaves the city and wanders alone in the surrounding mountains. He reflects that the more humanity strives for the heights and for lightness of spirit, the more mankind's roots must be struck down into the earth, the dark, the deep, and the evil (Z 42). As a metaphor, the earth so construed bears significant resemblance to the Dionysian.[14] Rootedness requires a nonself-conscious immersion in a dark, incomprehensible substratum. Lightness of spirit requires the closed, parochial, and indigenous, not the universal. The pursuit of the universal leads to the Spirit of Revenge. One needs "rootedness," not "autonomy."

The possibility of the overman is indeed tenuous, resting as it does on Zarathustra and his paradoxical relation to his epigones. He needs them for he has seen that he cannot talk directly to the people. But they represent a danger to his teaching. They will at best dilute it. And at best they will endure a great spiritual torture, but like Moses never enter the new kingdom or even fully understand what it looks like. Hence Zarathustra says to his epigones, "My brothers in war, I love you thoroughly; I am and I was of your kind. And I am also your best enemy." Furthermore, "I know of the hatred and envy of your hearts. You are not great enough not to know hatred and envy. . . . If you cannot be saints of knowledge, at least be its warriors." It is *for them* that

---

the need for things like red judges, he realizes that "not by wrath [alone] does one kill but by laughter." In another parable, Zarathustra relates that "I would believe only in a god who could dance." It is the devil who is serious (Z 41).

13. Likewise, it is important to recall that Zarathustra continually adjourns to his solitude yet longs to "shine" on and be with his fellow human beings. These tensions, which Zarathustra's wisdom and his position between past and future make inevitable, are the ground of the energy that drives him on to be a bridge to the future. Need, not benevolence, is what propels Zarathustra. Like the Socrates of Nietzsche's early presentation, Zarathustra represents something pathological. Future, affirmative philosophy must be freed from this pathology born of the Spirit of Revenge and the Spirit of Gravity.

14. Heidegger uses the metaphor "earth" in a very similar fashion. I will return to this theme in part 3.

Zarathustra observes, "It is the good war that hallows any cause" (*Z* 46–47). Zarathustra relies on many such double-edged swords.

We have yet to receive any concrete word about what is to be created in the future except that it is symbolized by the overman. The yes-saying part of the task has not become evident. This is perhaps not sur-prising, for the lion stage which Zarathustra represents precedes the in-nocent and forgetful child of the future. But shortly we find that what creators should create is "peoples." It is by creating a people that one preserves life. It is the modern bureaucratic state that has killed peoples. The state presents itself as the embodiment of the will of the people. But Zarathustra asserts that it is nothing but an association of the weak (*Z* 48–49). In establishing itself the state sins against custom and pre-scriptive rights. A genuine people always has its own language of cus-toms, its own tongue of good and evil which it does not share with its neighbors. But the modern state mixes many tablets and languages in one, borrowing from everywhere while creating nothing new. It rep-resents a great confusion of tongues of good and evil—i.e., eclectic openness and indiscriminate toleration replace fervent commitment. In the process, the state is the breeding ground of superfluous numbers of individuals, the "all-too-many." The rapid modern increase in popula-tion reinforces the state because the state is needed to minister to the needs of those who can no longer be self-sufficient. In the process, this "new idol" makes great individuals impossible, for they would endan-ger the "all-too-many."[15]

The future overman must grow from the soil of a people rooted in its own distinct traditions. Precisely because man is a nothing, he must be immersed in a people with a shared tablet of good and evil. Nietzsche's "antifoundationalism" points toward community, not the self-legislating individualism and pluralism—or praise of an-archy—of contemporary postmodernism. To flee the modern state is by no means to flee the "political," quite the contrary—except for a rare few "Free Spirits." In the last analysis, the true individuals can only live far from the marketplace, either in solitude or rooted within a people.[16]

15. For Nietzsche, the state is identical to the Hegelian state which presents itself as a God: "On earth there is nothing greater than I: the ordering finger of God am I" (*Z* 49). To this Zarathustra responds, "Only where the State ends, there begins the human be-ing who is not superfluous" (*Z* 51). Only where the state ends is there the bridge to the overman. This is not a praise of the private and the idiosyncratic. Nietzsche is praising the rule of unwritten custom and immersion in a distinctive "community."

16. For Nietzsche, true solitude is never possible in the marketplace of the modern state, where the primary actors are likened to unwitting jesters. Not one of them is great

Throughout this discussion, and elsewhere in his work, Nietzsche praises peoples as the locus of greatness. In his second mode of speech this is also elaborated upon in the discussion of friendship. It is no accident that a discussion of friendship follows Nietzsche's discussion of peoples and the modern state.

Being part of a people allows friendship as a basis for community, rather than simple Hobbesian coercion or Hegelian bureaucratic control. Like Aristotle, Nietzsche sees friendship as a subject that goes hand in hand with politics. A community needs not only justice but friendship. As Aristotle observed, friendships are only possible among equals. According to Zarathustra, equality emerges because friends *make* themselves equal in a process that is mutual and reciprocal—as if in "a rough and imperfect mirror" (Z 56). In the process they create a ground for community that transcends that of the modern state and its marketplace of isolated, competing atoms.

Perhaps most important of all, friends must esteem the same things to be friends. It is necessary to esteem in groups. And to preserve itself a community must esteem in a manner different from that of its neighbors. One cannot be friends, as defined here, with all of humanity. Zarathustra asserts that never has one people understood another; good for one was evil and wickedness for the other. The shared esteemings of a people are eventually written into their bodies. Furthermore, what a people praises as good is always what it deems difficult. Tablets of good and evil are always menus of a people's "overcomings," a sign of their collective Will to Power. At first, peoples created their tablets collectively; only later were they created by individuals (Z 58–59). They created their tablets for the preservation of the group, for "delight in the herd is more ancient than the delight in the ego." But regardless of who gives the tablets, through esteeming alone is existence given meaning, for *"without esteeming, the nut of existence would be hollow"* (Z 59).

Zarathustra has asserted that it is esteeming that makes man different from the animals: Man *is* the esteemer. But a major difficulty arises here. The fundamental problem is not that the last man no longer esteems anything, which is true. And it is not even that the ground for esteeming can no longer be attached to the transcendent, which is also true. Something more substantial is announced:

---

enough to do any real harm, but in great numbers they are like "swarms of flies." Zarathustra's pride will not allow him to strike back, but like flies they will bite, and become an extreme nuisance and distraction. Hence he longs to flee the marketplace and the state which defends it (Z 51–54).

A thousand goals have there been so far, for there have been a thousand peoples. Only the yoke for the thousand necks is still lacking: the one goal is lacking. Humanity still has no goal.

But tell me, my brothers, if humanity still lacks a goal—is humanity itself not still lacking too? (*Z* 60)

A single goal for all of humanity is needed. But we have just been told that a people always needs to define itself in opposition to another people. There is no contradiction, for the one *goal* is attachment to the possibility of the future existence of the overman. A people must be constituted upon the opinion (as if) they are the necessary means to the overman. Different peoples having different visions of what the overman is would be possible. Each people would, however, think it was pursuing a *universal* goal. [17]

Having asserted that humanity needs a single goal, Zarathustra confronts Christianity, which had already presented a universal goal, but of a categorically different kind. He argues, for example, that death can be transcended *only* by choosing it at one's own time. Biological death is a mere physical accident, and one should not let his existence be ruled by accidents. Nor should one see death as the *summum malum*. One can overcome Chance if one acts at the right time—for the sake of one's goal and one's heirs, i.e., for the future (*Z* 71). Endless prolongation of life gives no example to others. Only when one chooses death, not in the belief that one will rise victorious over it to life everlasting in some afterworld, but because one wants it and knows it is final, does one's death stand as a monument for one's heirs. To desire to live forever is to live a slow death, as much for those who attempt to accomplish it in the manner of Descartes as for followers of Christ. Death must be a spur and promise to the survivors.

Socrates' death was such a rallying cry to his followers and certainly did much to advance his influence and the life for which he stood. But Christ's death has had an even greater relation to his influence than that of Socrates. Nonetheless, Zarathustra concludes that Christ's death came at an inappropriate time, because it changed what his influence would have been. Zarathustra would have us believe that not even Christ would be a Christian had he had more time to reflect upon it. Hence Christ gave a meaning to this earth that puts it in a radically deficient light vis-à-vis another world. Zarathustra is intent on giving the highest meaning to the here and now. He longs to "restore" man to this

---

17. It should be noted that it would be counterproductive if humanity ever actually reached or actualized the overman. The overman would have to remain, like a Kantian "regulative idea," constantly receding at the same pace at which one approaches.

earth, to accommodate him to it and to make him take it seriously as his only real ground. For this reason Christianity must be vanquished as a future. It is an indigenously rooted people, esteeming and pursuing an immanent yet future goal, the overman, that gives a new basis for esteeming.[18]

Zarathustra ends his second mode of speech by again remarking upon his "gift-giving virtue." This occurs in a final discussion with his disciples, after he has said farewell for the last time to the marketplace of the modern state. His disciples have followed him to a crossroads, at which point he says he wishes to walk alone. They give him a staff with a serpent wound around a sun. This time wisdom is linked with a symbol for the source of the life-giving (the ground of presence) rather than with spiritedness. Before turning to go, Zarathustra preaches that the greatest gift and highest virtue is to sacrifice oneself to the future, to hold the future more dear than oneself, to sacrifice for others unborn rather than say "everything for me." Zarathustra advises his followers to remain faithful to the earth, not to fly beyond it to some god: "Give the earth a meaning, a human meaning," and in doing so you will create the men of the future, *and they will create new values (Z* 76–77). He exhorts his disciples to be willing to give themselves up so that man may come to be the result of a conscious plan, even if not *their* conscious plan. In the transition, they must be willing to go under. Like Machiavelli, Zarathustra aims to conquer Chance, a modern undertaking. And in modern fashion, Zarathustra once again projects the priority of the future.

Now Zarathustra prepares to go back to his solitude, assuming that his task is complete and that he has left in place those who will get the project under way. He seems confident that in his second mode of speech he has succeeded where he had failed in his first attempt. But his last words before leaving are, "I bid you lose me and find yourselves; and only when you have all denied me will I return to you" (*Z* 78). When this forgetting is accomplished Zarathustra could return with a good conscience a *third* time, at the "noon" between beast and overman. Man as he presently exists still is not even halfway to the goal: *"Dead are all gods: now we want the overman to live*—on that great noon,

---

18. But if Zarathustra is serious about his doctrine of freely choosing death, one might ask why he remains so long after sowing his seeds. Indeed we will never be given an example of Zarathustra choosing a free death. He has given his heirs a goal, if not a very concrete one. He wants to see what they will do in fostering it; hence he asks forgiveness for lingering in curiosity. Shortly, he will conclude that his project has gone astray and requires readjustment. Had he hastened to a free death he would have been unable to supply the needed midcourse correction.

let this be our *last will.*" (*Z* 79; emphasis mine). Zarathustra means, not a last will and testament, but literally the *last act of Will.* At the noon of the overman, self-conscious willing will give way to a spontaneity of action, to "innocence and forgetting," to the hegemony of the unself-conscious flowing of the Will to Power. And at that great noon when man has become something that is not an accident, Zarathustra, and those like him, will be able to accept man as he is, and no longer desire that he be something else. For that to be possible, the modern transformation of Reason into Will must be brought to its highest manifestation. But the highest act of Will must will the overcoming of the Will. That is surely *anti*modern. It is not, however, in my sense, *post*modern.

Zarathustra returns to the mountains and his solitude, where he waits "like a sower who has scattered his seed" (*Z* 83). In the Prologue, Zarathustra was overly optimistic about the time needed for success. In his second attempt he has become more circumspect. By the time of his third coming, after a brief interlude on the "blessed isles," he is more circumspect still, speaking increasingly with an eye to individuals of the future. We should recall that the subtitle of *Zarathustra* is "A Book for All and None." It will be as a bible for all in the future. But Zarathustra increasingly sees that his words are for none who are now alive.

On the Blessed Isles: The Third Mode of Speech

Years pass and Zarathustra becomes impatient. He still has the "shame" of a giver; i.e., he still has his own need to cure. But he still holds back his most abysmal thought—even from himself. He hopes not to have to deploy it. He is "overripe" again and can endure his solitude no longer. He cannot wait like the perfect husbandman for his seeds to mature; he realizes that his teaching, and hence his potential health, is in danger: "My enemies have grown powerful and have distorted my teaching till those dearest to me must be ashamed of the gifts I gave them. I have lost my friends; the hour has come to seek my lost ones." To lose his epigones is to lose the battle, for they are the means to his success.[19] He had hoped to use their passion, and their misunderstanding, to set in motion a transition to the future. He longs for the "blessed isles" where he will rediscover and be safe with his friends (*Z* 83–84). They have withdrawn, or been forced to withdraw from the

19. Zarathustra realizes these things are true when he looks into a mirror held by a child, symbolizing the child in the three metamorphoses. Instead of his reflection he sees a devil's grimace, which he takes as symbolic of the fact that his enemies have stigmatized his teaching as the epitome of evil.

environs of the modern state. They too have sought solace in solitude. With his third coming Zarathustra adopts a third mode of speech: "New ways I go, a new speech comes to me; weary I grow, like all creators, of the old tongues. My spirit no longer wants to walk on worn soles" (*Z* 84).

Zarathustra's third mode of speech centers explicitly on the issue of the Spirit of Revenge and leads up to announcing the doctrine of Eternal Recurrence. But, before articulating his most abysmal thought, Zarathustra engages in what I will argue are his most open and least rhetorical speeches. He is now alone with an enclave of disciples who have withdrawn to the peace of an epicurean garden. They can be of no further use to him as epigones. Hence Zarathustra articulates not parables but skeptical ruminations that will be sustenance for the truly philosophical of both the present and the future. Again I will limit myself to a few examples.

In his initial, public teaching Zarathustra used the memorable phrase "God is dead." To his disciples, safely secluded on the blessed isles, he says, "God is a conjecture" (*Z* 85–86). The phrase "God is dead" is a popular teaching, chosen for its rhetorical overkill. The many could not understand the skeptical observation that "God is a conjecture," which in effect means that it cannot be known whether He is dead or alive; His existence or nonexistence is beyond human knowing. One of Nietzsche's central public teachings is that beliefs about God have always been the product of human willing. But the simple assertion of atheism is a dogmatism Nietzsche also rejects. As Zarathustra now presents the matter, the real problem with willing the existence of God is that it has been counterproductive, for it was directed to an object beyond the capacity of human willing. One cannot really will a God. It is possible to actualize the overman if only men rein in their Will and attach their striving to something immanent and concrete.

Another reason God must remain unthinkable *for present man* is that, if there were gods, the creative Will of man could not endure not being godlike. That leads to the hubristic, revengeful stance of modern man. This is what Zarathustra tells those followers who remain. There cannot be gods, for then the creator could not endure his purely *human* task: "But let me reveal my heart to you entirely, my friends: *if* there were gods, how could I endure not to be a god! *Hence* there are no gods. Though I drew this conclusion, now it draws me" (*Z* 86–87). Zarathustra would have men proceed "as if" there were no God. This is a much more subtle reflection than that contained in the rhetorically more stunning "God is dead."

Zarathustra now discloses that there is yet another problem: The idea of God is always linked with the idea of the "One . . . and the Un-moved and the Sated and the Permanent." But, Zarathustra asserts, the poets of the present must now speak of Time and Becoming: "It is of Time and Becoming that the best parables should speak: let them be a praise and a justification of all impermanence" (Z 86–87).[20] Belief in the hegemony of Becoming is the condition for creativity, much as the Dionysian is the condition for the Apollonian. Of course, the hegem-ony of Becoming must be asserted for the same reason as the fact that God is dead—because it is *rhetorically useful*. Zarathustra does not at-tempt to prove or assert as true that all is Becoming rather than Being; his statement regards what must be said if the overman is to come into being. As I have argued above, Nietzsche attributes something very similar to the tragic Greeks. Out of their strength they consciously gave themselves the dread of the Dionysian in order to call forth the creative wellsprings of the Apollonian. In similar fashion, the poets of the present, for the sake of creativity, must induce in themselves the nausea that comes from the consciousness of the abyss—understood now not as the marketplace of the last men but as the hegemony of godless Becoming. The last man, in his wish to esteem and value no more, falls into a nothingness tantamount to rest—for it is esteeming which makes a something of man—not of chaos and Becoming. There is both a fruitful and a destructive nothingness.

Poets and artists must confront the abyss and help create values for a people. The philosophers are incapable of willing values because they are too superhistorical and self-conscious. Hence Zarathustra *wills* the abyss; he does not discover it. "To say it more honestly: this very destiny —my will wills" (Z 86–87). Nietzsche's abyss is an "as if," a hypo-thetical construction—an altogether modern maneuver. Zarathustra now openly admits that, in willing the abyss to help set in motion a transition to the future, he will cause much distress. It moves him to pity, and overcoming that pity becomes a major undertaking for him. But men must come to feel better joys than the ones they feel in pitying others. So far, humanity has felt too little joy and too much pity. Ac-cording to Zarathustra, that is man's original sin. To pity is to trans-gress against another's pride. Great indebtedness does not make men grateful, only vengeful. Zarathustra observes that if one did not forget his debts, charity would always turn into resentment.[21]

---

20. Heidegger is one of Nietzsche's closest followers here. For Heidegger, Being is no longer one and self-identical; it is mysterious and self-concealing.

21. In similar fashion, Aristotle's "great-souled" man forgets the good deeds done for him, remembering only his own great deeds for others. This is the attitude that must

ZARATHUSTRA'S FIVE MODES OF SPEECH

In the same vein, Zarathustra storms against those who are termed "virtuous," taking up the subject for a third time. Zarathustra now argues that the virtuous, as they have been until now, always wanted to be paid, always wanted a reward, whether now or later. They wanted more than the previously announced "good sleep." Zarathustra says the virtuous are mad at him because he teaches that there is no reward for virtue, and even that virtue is not its own reward. Reward and punishment were lies. And those lies have become the basis of men's selves: "Your virtue is your self and not something foreign, a skin, a cloak, that is the truth from the foundation of your souls" (Z 94). Humanity should consider itself too "pure" for the words "pity," "revenge," "punishment," "reward," and "retribution," which have been at the core of past virtue. Zarathustra would emancipate men from past versions of virtue, but certainly not so that like the last men they esteem nothing. His is an emancipation that points forward to a new discipline. Zarathustra wishes to strip men of their present virtues but will give them "new toys" to replace the lost ones (Z 96).

Zarathustra has now seen that the soft, "liberating" part of his teaching has been accepted, while the part that carries the need for self-restraint and a new discipline has been dropped. Nonetheless, he continues to stress the liberation over the discipline in an attempt to overcome those habits shaped by ignoble virtues. Only when emancipated from past conceptions of virtue can joy become a part of life on earth, perhaps for the first time. But to achieve that joy humanity must also be emancipated from both its hatred and its pity of the low. Both destroy the joy of which humanity is capable. Although it is a bitter pill to swallow, Zarathustra now admits that the existence of the low is always an absolute necessity. One must not will its extinction, merely its subservience: "Once I asked, and I was almost choked by my question: What? does life require even the rabble?" (Z 96–97). His answer is an unequivocal yes. For Zarathustra, what is unflatteringly called "the rabble" is defined not by its social or economic conditions but by its living without a sense of honor or pride, burdened with vengeance and resentment. One must overcome the nausea that follows from the realization that the low and base cannot be overcome. That realization requires overcoming the modern dream that everything unacceptable to our Will can be pro-

---

be adopted by all creators. Creators must be willing to sacrifice themselves and others, but not on the cross of pity, which is simply fruitless. Zarathustra and his disciples must avoid falling into the trap of pity and vengeance. This is his private advice to them. Zarathustra now begins to reveal the importance of overcoming pity and the Spirit of Revenge.

gressively done away with through modern science, the conquest of scarcity, mass Enlightenment, and a universalistic ethics. We must learn to affirm life in *all* its diversity and difference. Shortly Zarathustra realizes that his present emancipation from nausea rests upon his abstraction from the existence of the rabble, which does not exist on the blessed isles, rather than upon an affirmation of it. He, like his disciples, has deluded himself into thinking that the few can find their joy beyond the necessity of sharing anything with the rabble (*Z* 98–99). But the purely epicurean solution is not available to Zarathustra. He quickly becomes disillusioned and leaves the blessed isles.

The Spirit of Revenge now emerges as *the* central theme for Zarathustra. The bridge to the overman requires deliverance from this spirit, and deliverance requires that the few cease to feel guilty about proposing a solution that cannot be universalized and that affirms, rather than attempting to transform, reality. Zarathustra asserts that the resentful will to equality qua identity stands behind the present vision of virtue and justice. Indeed, Zarathustra says, until now *no one* has been free from the Spirit of Revenge. The impulse to punish is powerful because reality is intransigent; it repeatedly casts forth inequality (difference) rather than equality (identity). Zarathustra does not want his "doctrine of life" confused with assaults on traditional virtue undertaken in the name of radical equality, which, according to him, manifest a hatred of life.[22] Agreeing with Marx, Zarathustra argues that all past philosophers have been nothing but ideologists, not for the ruling class, as Marx would argue, but for the rabble. That, according to Zarathustra, is why they have been tolerated. To this extent philosophers have never really served truth and never been "Free Spirits." The powerful among the rabble want to have a famous wise man going before them to make the way safe, but they will not tolerate a serious

22. He now reconsiders the subject previously discussed under the rubric "Flies in the Marketplace," asserting that he does not want to be confused with the teachers of equality, whom he likens to tarantulas. The tarantula is poisoned by his Spirit of Revenge, and with that poison he stings others and ruins all of life (*Z* 99). The love of total equality qua identity is nothing but a manifestation of the Spirit of Revenge. Zarathustra realizes, however, that his teaching *will* be confused with that of the tarantulas, and even used by them. And he realizes that this has political ramifications.

Zarathustra asserts that war and conflict, and parties and factions, are necessary, because life is contradiction and present life must overcome itself again and again: "Struggle and inequality are present even in beauty, and also war for power and more power." This is by no means a metaphorical argument; Zarathustra discusses it in what he calls the "plainest parable." Since struggle is necessary for life, "let us strive against one another like gods" (*Z* 101–2). Competition, opposition, and contradiction are good.

openness to the truth. Genuine philosophic openness is hateful to the rabble. In the future, true philosophy must be emancipated from this ideological impulse (*Z* 102–5). But that will require a different political universe than the one ruled by the last man and his apologists.

Having articulated the central concept of his third mode of speech—the Spirit of Revenge—Zarathustra launches into three consecutive "songs."[23] He falls into introspection and reflects on himself, life, and his disciples. It becomes clear to Zarathustra that he has again failed. The epicurean retreat on the blessed isles is not at present a feasible means to the end he seeks. He apologizes to his disciples for the fact that evening has come and has brought the time when wisdom could wonder "why life at all." What an evil stroke of luck to have been born during the great night. The soul must rise out of the abyss of this tomb of nausea. But Zarathustra recognizes that "only where there are tombs are there resurrections." Only by passing into and through this great night can one rise again. Only by Will, and Will alone, can Zarathustra rise out of this tomb now that he realizes that his past speeches have failed to accomplish anything but the seclusion of a few on an island that will become increasingly less blessed. By Will alone he will rise up to his fourth and most abysmal speech, the Eternal Recurrence (*Z* 112–13).

It is at this point—as part of his third and most straightforward mode of speech—that Zarathustra thematically introduces the doctrine of the Will to Power. If I am correct, one cannot lose sight of the setting and the audience if one is to understand its meaning. Having decided that everything stands or falls by his own Will and having seen his previous efforts fail, Zarathustra comes forward with a doctrine that is a form of the poetry of Becoming he has previously praised, which opti-

---

23. Philosophy, Zarathustra asserts, must become a king of song and again merge with poetry. Neither the poets nor the philosophers of the past have been adequate. Philosophers have been agents of the Spirit of Revenge, and poets thoughtlessly superficial, speaking primarily of such trivial subjects as lust and boredom. When they have gone beyond this, they have been unclear and presented nothing but "muddy waters" (*Z* 127–28). New poets are needed for a new cultural education. Future poetry must serve a high purpose. Future philosophy must become poetic and erotic. Doctrines like the Will to Power and Eternal Recurrence attempt to support a public amalgamation of philosophy and poetry, wherein one can cease to be grave and resentful in the face of a world that cannot be changed and mastered. Out of recognition of intransigent mysteriousness will come joy, laughter, and dancing. Therein the great confrontation between philosophy and poetry will be resolved. For only the poet can truly "sink into the unfathomable," the changeable and stubbornly opaque core of Being and not will to transform it.

mistically asserts the eternality of Becoming in the face of the potential end of history in the "timeless tombs of death."[24]

The early doctrine of the Dionysian and the later doctrine of the Will to Power are quite similar, and both have to be willed. My primary point is that the doctrine of the Will to Power is *not* a doctrine about the Being of beings, as Heidegger will assert when he tries to translate Nietzsche's thought into his own idiom. As Nietzsche makes explicit in *Beyond Good and Evil*, it is a hypothetical assumption. If one could get future men to act "as if" reality was fundamentally driven by Will to Power—and in line with its necessary adjunct, Eternal Recurrence—one could overcome the Spirit of Revenge and the Spirit of Gravity. That is Zarathustra's "experiment," which rests on Will—i.e., clever rhetoric qua erotic poetry; a poetry of Becoming.

It is in this vein that Zarathustra asserts that wherever there is life there is this Will to Power, which can manifest itself in a variety of ways (*Z* 113–14). The Will to Power should not, however, as with Hobbes, be seen as a mere drive for self-preservation. The desire for self-preservation imparts a teleology the Will to Power does not. The Will to Power is the drive to impose Being upon Becoming, even at the expense of one's own life: its imperative is either the enhancement of individual strength for its own sake or, in the larger scheme of things, the preservation of the species rather than the individual. Contrary to the protomoderns, Zarathustra asserts that there is much that life esteems more than the mere continuation of life. Life must always overcome itself, must repeatedly destroy and rebuild. For this fundamental reason a code of good and evil which is intransitory cannot exist. Of course, that understanding is superhistorical and hence potentially destructive of life if universalized.

If popularly accepted, the doctrine of the Will to Power is a means by which one can impress some semblance of Being on the river of Becoming. One can posit the eternality of Becoming in all its diversity both high and low and can ground faith in the earth and the body. With

---

24. Zarathustra gained great clarity about this subject after he "flew too far into the future" and dread overtook him, for when he looked around, "time was [his] sole contemporary" (*Z* 119). All men were gone; nothing was left; humanity had been abolished. He attributes this outcome to those who objectively and detachedly watch life, the "educated." As Nietzsche observed in *On the Advantage and Disadvantage of History for Life,* in place of the cultivated or cultured individual we now are left with educated individuals who wear the past painted all over them; they are but an eclectic combination of past thoughts: "Motley, all ages and peoples peek out of your veils; motley, all customs and faiths speak out of your gestures" (*Z* 119–20). Inside they have nothing that is truly their own. Their reality is but a vapor, which can blow away leaving only time and its endless uniform passing, as in Zarathustra's dream.

this hope Zarathustra finds a way of overcoming his melancholy and redeeming himself. Thereby he gains the strength to carry on toward his fourth speech, which redeems History itself and thereby all of history past and present through the highest act of Will—*willing* the Eternal Recurrence.

Will to Power and Eternal Recurrence must be seen as responses to a specific need at a specific time. Zarathustra has concluded that if one is to ground possible future values mankind must believe either that there is no fixed core of things or that it lies in such concealment that it can never be articulated. As a *ground,* the Will to Power is an ever restless, self-concealing principle, and thereby a guarantee that History will never end. So understood, it is quite similar to Heidegger's conception of Being as *physis.* If the Will to Power is popularly accepted, all individual wills could be presented as particular manifestations of the universal Will to Power. The Will to Power could be presented in such a way that an individual like Zarathustra could be seen as a prime conduit for its welling forth, and all History could be read as the mysterious saga of the Will to Power manifesting or "outering" itself in a diversity of ways—or in Heideggerian terms, in a diversity of epochs or dispensations of Being.[25]

Zarathustra immediately asserts that the doctrine of the Will to Power implies that wherever there is life there is commanding and obeying (*Z* 114).[26] All must either command or obey, and he who cannot com-

---

25. Actually, the doctrine of the Will to Power serves several rhetorical functions: (1) as a ground—a new, self-concealing *Weltgeist* beyond total nothingness which is still not reducible to the traditional conception of static Being; (2) as a ground and justification for "inspiration" and unself-conscious, willful action and poetic creation; (3) as a psychological solace for those, like Zarathustra, in dark times and in the midst of the last man; and (4) as a limitation and ground for the Will beyond mere self-indulgent *laissez-aller.* Nietzsche uses the Will to Power in a variety of different rhetorical fashions, depending on the circumstance. But what must not be lost sight of is the point at which the doctrine emerges—when Zarathustra struggles with nausea and the thought of the inefficacy of his isolated disciples, and in conjunction with a discussion that juxtaposes the superiority of poetic creativity to detached contemplation (*Z* 117). As Nietzsche argues in *On the Advantage and Disadvantage of History for Life,* future humanity must quit the stance of detached objectivity. More generally, one must turn away from a preoccupation with what lies either *inside* the self or *beyond* our world, for it must be true of future man that "his happiness should smell of the earth [and thereby, body] and not of contempt for the earth" (*Z* 117). In short, one must live unhistorically and unself-consciously and act with an innocent, naive good conscience.

26. Given that the imperative of those operating under belief in the hegemony of the Will to Power is to enhance their power—and that can only be judged relationally—it is unlikely that such a doctrine can be given a *consistent* egalitarian interpretation. In his discussion of the tarantulas, Zarathustra makes clear his disappointment that his *previous*

mand himself must obey; but only a few can command. Zarathustra appeals to a few self-selected individuals to act "willfully"—i.e., instinctively and unself-consciously—with a good conscience. The Will to Power is a rallying cry for the few that provides them, at least rhetorically, with an ontological support, a support indeed which can fortify them in an egalitarian age and justify them in a future aristocratic age. Despite the hegemony of the last man, there remains the possibility of a few individuals remaining immune to the last man's leveling influence, if only they can rally themselves, recognize each other, and see the need to destroy and create. Zarathustra's disciples have by now proven that they are not such individuals. He will wait for "laughing lions."

But if the Will to Power really existed as an ontological fact, the last man and the present darkness would present no real problem for Zarathustra. In due course, the Will to Power itself would move humanity beyond its contemporary situation; all that was required would be patience; the decay would eventually pass. Precisely because it does not exist, it must be willed; the Will to Power has the status of an "as if." This said, if taken ontologically, the Will to Power comes close to being a nonlinear, nonprogressive, nonself-conscious *Weltgeist;* a *Weltgeist* with no inner logic of development, yet with the ongoing necessity of self-manifestation. The debt owed to Hegel is significant.

The Eternal Recurrence of the Same: The Fourth Mode of Speech

Zarathustra now abandons the more prosaic teaching and returns to the use of parables. He has more discussions with himself than with others. This leads up to his articulating a fourth mode of speech, which makes sense only because of a transformation that has occurred in response to his previous efforts. In "On Great Events" we are given a picture of a ship that sends a crew ashore to shoot rabbits. It is said that Zarathustra is known and loved by all of the sailors, but not by the captain: i.e., the *Volk* now know and love him; the captain (what passes for a leader) is unaware he exists. Things have changed. The disciples have had some effect after all. Zarathustra's ideas have been disseminated.[27]

---

speeches had been usurped by the egalitarian doctrines he was attempting to counter. This new rhetoric cannot be so easily co-opted.

27. Apparently one of the teachings that has taken hold is the praise of earth and body, in which Zarathustra attempts to ground the future *Volk*. His message to those who are watching is that the earth and what spills forth from it are good: there is no Hades; love the earth and that in you which is earthlike. In concrete terms, this involves a praise of the passions, "instincts," "emotions," and so on, i.e., the superiority of un-

Zarathustra, like Nietzsche, has become a household name; he now casts a long shadow. And that shadow is far more revolutionary than the great egalitarian rabbit shoot—that is, the French Revolution. The sailors see Zarathustra's shadow descend into the earth. When he returns he relates a conversation with a "fire hound" he met there that represents the spirit of the French Revolution. To that hellhound Zarathustra's shadow proclaims, "Freedom is what all of you like best to bellow; but I have outgrown the belief in 'great events' wherever there is much bellowing and smoke. Believe me, friend Hellishnoise: the greatest events—they are not our loudest but our stillest hours." It is not political revolutions and noisy, boisterous movements—all of which he likens to mere rabbit shoots—but intellectual transformations that bring the greatest change (Z 131).

Having somehow had his teaching sink down to the level of the *Volk,* Zarathustra must craft a new mode of speech for the *Volk* of the future. He now sees that in the fullness of time his efforts will in fact have a practical impact. Yet his first attempt to talk directly to the *Volk* was unsuccessful. He must take that into account in the new mode of speech. *Thus Spoke Zarathustra* is a great, ongoing reflection on theory and practice, on speech and how it can have a concrete effect and bring about change. Zarathustra's various attempts show the limitations and possibilities open to philosophic speech. They show the various audiences to which the philosopher can speak and the necessity of not addressing all audiences in the same fashion. *Thus Spoke Zarathustra* is a great reflection on how to talk to different audiences, knowing that *direct* persuasion is impossible and immediate political action as trivial as a rabbit shoot, in an attempt to accomplish something indirectly.

Zarathustra's disciples show they can no longer be of use, for they are much taken by the noise and smoke he has refuted. They have hardly listened to him; they wish instead to tell him of the ship, the rabbits, and other trivial affairs. Zarathustra shakes his head and wonders: "What shall I think of that?" (Z 133). He now seems to recognize that a very long twilight will come and cannot be bypassed or quickly

---

conscious forces over self-conscious ones, forces unreflectively operative *in everyone.* The doctrine of the Eternal Recurrence will reinforce Zarathustra's earlier success in this regard.

It is hard at this point not to be reminded of the myth of the metals in Plato's *Republic* and its argument that men grow directly out of the soil of their motherland. That was one of the components of the "noble lie." The other component—that there is a natural hierarchy of human types—is also part of Nietzsche's teaching for the future. We should also look forward to Heidegger's discussion of "the Fourfold," in which there is likewise a significant overlap with the noble lie.

short-circuited, neither politically nor through disciples. Zarathustra must consider how he is to preserve his teaching through this long period of sadness, enervation, and eventual chaos—"For it shall be a light for *distant* worlds and even more *distant* nights" (*Z* 133–34; emphasis mine)—so that it will be available when the next great cycle begins its upswing and eventually, necessarily, its decline.

Zarathustra is torn from his pessimistic dreams of a future where he has failed and nothing is left but dusty tombs, where "time . . . crawled, if time still existed" (*Z* 134–35), to a dream of regeneration when he hears the noise of someone "carrying his ashes up the mountain," much as Zarathustra had once done. A shrill whistling wind tears open the gates of his nightmare castle of death and throws open a coffin from which laughter flows at his feet. The disciple he loves most rises to interpret this dream. He says that it is Zarathustra who tears open these gates, that the dream is autobiographical. It is Zarathustra, he continues, who is the advocate of life that laughs at the possible cessation of time. But Zarathustra shakes his head, for this is not the correct interpretation. Zarathustra can be a midwife but no more. To redeem the future, Zarathustra must also redeem the present and the past. Others will have to fill in the future.

But Zarathustra finds the "now" and the "past" unendurable precisely because they are the products of contingency and accident: "To redeem those who lived in the past and to recreate all 'it was' into a 'thus I willed it'—that alone should I call redemption" (*Z* 138–39). Redemption is possible only when the Will has been liberated from the Spirit of Revenge against time and its "it was" (*Z* 139). The Will must cease to be an angry avenger against everything that escapes its power.[28]

In transcending the great accident of the past, one must not, in the mode of modern ethics, science, and technology, will the overcoming of "cripples" or the transcendence of the rabble. The redemption of the Will from its Spirit of Revenge requires that one will the Eternal Recurrence, which implies that one must accept the past as just as one would have wanted it and as one would want it to repeat itself. Thus is the Will liberated from the Spirit of Revenge, redemption assured, and a future with more than tombs and dusty, timeless emptiness, at best populated by a few curators, guaranteed. This is how one wills a commitment to the earth, to the body, and to the primacy of the realm of Becoming

---

28. Who in our time has not seen this anger manifested in one movement after another that condemns and dismisses all of the past? This anger seems far from having played itself out. It is the *modern* anger and resentment carried to its logical and so far most extreme manifestation.

and appearance. One must take the entirety of reality—body, earth, and appearance—as a fecund necessity in its infinite circling.

Zarathustra's is not an emancipatory redemption *from* temporal existence, as was longed for by Platonism and Christianity, but an acceptance of the eternal flux of Becoming, of the mysterious cauldron of the Will to Power, as if it were necessary and just as one would want it, both backward and forward. The Eternal Recurrence is the capstone of Zarathustra's fourth experiment in speech. To argue that it has no historical or scientific basis is to miss the point as completely as if one argued that it was a metaphysical doctrine. It is poetry. It must be willed as a means to overcoming the Spirit of Revenge.[29] To fail to be emancipated from the Spirit of Revenge, which refuses to accept the past and present—or time and its inexorable "it was"—is to continue the angry attempt to change everything that is and has been. It is here that we find the pivot point of Nietzsche's *post*modernity.

According to Zarathustra, only when the Will finally redeems itself from the Spirit of Revenge will man become innocent and childlike again. The proper redemption of the Will from the Spirit of Revenge ultimately implies its emancipation from autonomous, self-conscious willing: "This is what is eternal in the punishment called existence, that existence must eternally become deed and guilt again. *Unless the will should at last redeem itself, and willing should become not willing.*" "All 'it was' is a fragment, a riddle, a dreadful accident—until the creative will says to it, 'But thus I willed it.' Until the creative will says to it, 'But thus I will it; thus shall I will it'" (*Z* 140–41; emphasis mine). One must will not to will. This is a modern means to a postmodern end. An affirmative innocence, understood as an openness to a spontaneous immediacy that accepts the realm of appearance as a given and does not try to fly beyond it, is Nietzsche's vision for a redeemed future. It is what Nietzsche means by the "natural" as it plays itself out in human existence.

Zarathustra admits that he has up to now led his disciples away from the doctrine of the Eternal Return by teaching them that the autonomous Will is a creator (*Z* 141). The accentuation of autonomous creativity was a *partial truth,* an *interim teaching* necessary to the destructive no-saying work of the lion stage. That was the focus of a previous mode of speech that Zarathustra has now transcended. The early, will-

---

29. The doctrine of the Eternal Recurrence, understood as the ontological necessity of a cyclical history, is very old news. But Zarathustra does not posit it as an ontological fact. For the Eternal Recurrence to be willed is a different matter altogether. One must will a different future relation to reality that is no longer revengeful.

ful teaching is insufficient when it comes time for the transition to the innocent, yes-saying future. What Zarathustra has taught so far is itself part of the Spirit of Revenge. The famed Nietzschean voluntarism must give way to its opposite if there is to be a future that avoids the timeless tombs of death. Having been a no-sayer, Zarathustra must now engage in his highest act of affirmation. More concrete forms of affirmation—more concrete *nomoi*—would have to wait for the innocence of others. Zarathustra's highest affirmation or yes-saying, is willing the doctrine of the Eternal Recurrence. Since we can never be freed from the past but must cease to be enervated by it, we must come to see its necessity as something we would have willed, the perfect compromise. This compromise, of course, will only be understood by a few, but they are the ones for whom the problem is most psychologically acute. By solving their problem, one can obtain a much more complete innocence and forgetting for the rest of humanity.

Zarathustra has seen his teaching finally sink down to the *Volk;* now even cripples are his followers and his disciples misinterpret him. He has planted many seeds, spread many doctrines, but things are still not going as he had hoped. Once one disseminates ideas they take on a life of their own. His "stillest hour" arrives and the ground gives way under his feet. Nothingness threatens to encompass him again. He would like to bring his crowning doctrine to speech, but still cannot. He is spoken to by a dream without voice, a "silent call": "What do you matter, Zarathustra? Speak your word and break!" (*Z* 145–46). Zarathustra says that he cannot; he awaits the "worthier one." He despairs: "As yet my words have not moved mountains, and what I said did not reach men. Indeed, I have gone to men, but as yet I have not arrived." The speechless voice comes to him again and tells him that this restraint is his weakness, saying, "This is what is most unforgivable in you: you have the power, and you do not want to rule. . . . O Zarathustra, you shall go as a shadow of that which must come: thus you will command and, commanding, lead the way" (*Z* 146–47). And Zarathustra is ashamed. He has not become the child that could shed shame; innocence and forgetting remain impossible for him. He cannot participate in the solution towards which he points. He is caught between eternities.

The opening of part 3 of *Thus Spoke Zarathustra* finds Zarathustra wandering alone in the mountains again. His solitude is again a temporary solace, but he realizes he is destined to remain a wanderer among mountains. There will be no solution for him, or for others of his level of clarity. He now stands before his "final peak," having begun his "loneliest walk." There is no longer any path left behind; his previous speeches have made going back impossible (*Z* 152–53). He reaches a ridge and sees the new coast, the new eternity, stretched out before him. Zarathustra goes down to the sea and boards a ship, along with another man from the blessed isles. But after boarding, he remains silent for two days and merely listens to his shipmates. Around him are men who refuse to live without danger and like to travel far, and Zarathustra sees them as comrades. Hence he tells them what he calls a "riddle," the "vision of the loneliest." He tells of how his soul had fought upward against the Spirit of Gravity that drew it downward toward pessimism and the abyss. And this grave and pessimistic weight, in the persona of a dwarf, tells him that no matter how high he casts his philosopher's stone, "every stone that is thrown must fall." All philosophic projects must fail. To this Zarathustra responds, "Dwarf! It is you or I!" (*Z* 156–57). Zarathustra, like Sisyphus, must ignore this kind of wisdom. The dwarf jumps from Zarathustra's shoulder and they both stand before a gateway. It is a gateway between eternities, between the road to the future and that to the past. The gateway is called "moment" *(Augenblick)*. Zarathustra says:

> Behold this gateway, dwarf! . . . It has two faces. Two paths meet here; *no one has yet followed either to its end* [emphasis mine]. This long lane stretches back for an eternity. And the long lane out there, that is another eternity. They contradict each other. . . .
>
> . . . Must not whatever *can* walk have walked on this lane before? Must not whatever *can* happen have happened, have been done, have passed by before? . . . Must not this gateway too have been there before? (*Z* 157–58)[30]

We have arrived at the exhaustion of a particular eternity. We will return to this moment of exhaustion at the end of each successive eternity, each cycle of human existence. In that respect, History is circular, not linear and progressive, but only if Nietzsche is successful and if someone at some time in the future again stands at this gate and wills yet another new eternity.

All of a sudden the dwarf, the gateway, and everything else is gone. Willing the Eternal Recurrence is a possibility that is evanescent. One must seize precisely the right moment, a moment of despair and distress. Zarathustra tells this riddle to his fellow wanderers

30. There is a suggestion that the past has not been exhausted. Nietzsche chooses to explore only the future, for all the reasons we have been discussing, the most significant being that the past harbors the Spirit of Revenge, but apparently there are options, perhaps even the possibility of a "second beginning."

out on the uncharted seas. Then, he reports having seen something of which he *"had never seen the like."* He saw "a young shepherd . . . writhing, gagging, in spasms, his face distorted, and a heavy black snake hung out of his mouth. [Never had he] seen such nausea" (*Z* 159; emphasis mine). There is no recurrence here; this is entirely novel. Zarathustra yells to the shepherd to bite off the snake's head. And he bids those who are bold and who would sail on "unexplored seas" (a journey of *discovery, not recovery*) to guess the meaning of this second riddle. The shepherd bites the head off the snake, spits it far away, and jumps up, laughing in a way about which it can be said, "Never yet on earth has a human being laughed as he laughed," no longer a shepherd, *no longer even human* (*Z* 160). It is this victory of laughter over nausea that makes the Eternal Recurrence possible for the *first* time. Only by passing through and overcoming the great nausea can one make the greatest joy possible. Mankind had to arrive at nihilism before it was possible to truly inherit the earth for the first time. All of the past must be seen as a necessary prelude to this possibility. In his fourth mode of speech, Zarathustra presents two riddles and then asks, who is the shepherd still to come—it is not Zarathustra—who will bite the head off the great Spirit of Gravity and overcome the great pessimism? Who will make the Eternal Recurrence a concrete possibility and thereby launch the future? Riddles purposely invite multiple interpretations.

The remainder of part 3 of *Zarathustra* is a chronicle of his psychological torture and drifting (*Z* 163). His no-saying has been completed; he has succeeded in calling forth a thoroughgoing nihilism. And he has made his great affirmation, his great yes-saying, willing acceptance of the necessity of the accidental past. Before the arrival of the future, which will be signaled by "laughing lions," mankind must experience nihilism in all its depths. On the other side of that nihilism will come the restoration of Chance: " 'By Chance,'—that is the most ancient nobility of the world, and this I restored to all things: I delivered them from their bondage under Purpose" (*Z* 166). Zarathustra has willed the reversal of the modern attempt to conquer Chance: "O heaven over me, pure and high! That is what your purity is to me now, that there is *no* eternal spider or spider web of Reason, that you are to me *a dance floor for divine accidents,* that you are to me a divine table for divine dice and dice players" (*Z* 166; emphasis mine).[31] Willing the Eternal Recurrence means willing the

---

31. Nietzsche here alludes to the metaphor he used when he first articulated the doctrine of the Eternal Recurrence in *The Gay Science,* aphorism 341.

reign of the mysterious and incalculable; it stands in opposition to the modern desire to manipulate, control, and transform reality. One must affirm everything that is cast up by eternal Becoming.

Under the sway of the doctrine of Eternal Recurrence, future philosophers would be freed from their modern desire to transform reality, and hence freed from the need to proceed hypothetically. That modern approach is only interesting if one wishes to manipulate and dominate. The paradox is that this is to be accomplished in perfectly modern fashion by hypothetically positing doctrines like the Will to Power and the Eternal Recurrence in the mode of an "as if." But what Nietzsche aims at in using these modern tools is nothing less than the reversal of the modern transformation of the philosopher into an angry, resentful legislator. The great legislator Zarathustra legislates the end of conscious legislation and opens the way to a new vision of philosophy.

Solitude and Silence; The Long Wait and the Lonely Vigil: The Fifth Mode of Speech

Zarathustra returns to land and wishes to find out what has happened to man since he posited the Eternal Recurrence. He learns, before returning to his mountain and his cave for the final time, that "everything has become smaller!" (*Z* 167). In the interim, the few who have remained faithful have become more nauseated. Zarathustra finally realizes that it is of no use to speak "where nobody has [his] ears." He decides to wait for the great "fire" that must wash this all away (*Z* 170–72). "Woe unto this great city! And I wish I already saw the pillar of fire in which it will be burned. For such pillars of fire must precede the great noon. But this has its own time and its own destiny" (*Z* 178). On the basis of what he had done before—his no-saying activities—Zarathustra believes the holocaust is already fated. An apocalypse will have to precede the hegemony of the eternity signified by the Eternal Recurrence. Again, Zarathustra will have to rein in his pity, for he is all too well aware of what he has willed: "great wars" the like of which have never been seen. While "great events" can *create* nothing, the phoenix presupposes the ashes.

Zarathustra finally arrives at his mountain and regains his solitude, his *public* no-saying and yes-saying completed. He claims he again feels clean, alone with his "happy silence." Bringing the truth to speech is the greatest of trials. Having enunciated the doctrine of Eternal Return, he need not return to the *Volk*. What he has unleashed will have a life of its own. He sits "surrounded by broken old tablets and new tablets half covered with writing," and engages in what seems to be a grand summary of his teaching—a remembrance of where his soul has been and how he arrived where he is. This recapitulation—as well as the rest of the fifth mode of speech—takes the form of a silent discussion with himself. Yet in this seeming recapitulation there are some significant additions—or, more to the point, clarifications. Zarathustra is clearer now about his own deeds, although he remains a "convalescent." He now realizes that as a "firstling" he will be sacrificed and forgotten (Z 200). In the future, each successive generation will reinterpret everything that has been a bridge to itself.

As one example, Zarathustra now explicitly states that contemporary rootlessness and nihilism are a breeding ground for tyrants. He points toward only one alternative to such despotism:

> Therefore, my brothers, a *new nobility* is needed to be the adversary of all rabble and of all that is despotic and to write anew upon new tablets the word "noble."
>
> For many who are noble are needed, and noble men *of many kinds* [emphasis mine], that there may be a nobility. Or as I once said in a parable: "Precisely this is godlike that there are gods, but no God." (Z 202)[32]

With none of his previous audiences had Zarathustra discussed his new nobility so openly. Nor had he given so clear an intimation of what might be meant by the ambiguous term overman. But for Zarathustra's new nobility to exist, a "people," not a state based on the consent of "shopkeepers," is needed as its soil. "Community" is required, and it is not based on consent:

> Human society is a trial: thus I teach it—a long trial; and what it tries to find is the commander. A trial, O my brothers, and *not* a "contract." Break, break this word of the softhearted and half-and-half! (Z 211–12)

Zarathustra has also finally realized that for some, like himself, innocence and forgetting will never again be possible; some will never be cured:

---

32. Below, in my discussion of *Beyond Good and Evil,* I will return to the issue of "nobility." The new aristocrats Zarathustra hopes will come into existence are the ones who will complete the half-filled tablets, not someone still caught in the Spirit of Revenge, or like Zarathustra longing for solitude. Those who will write the noble doctrine are *part* of what is intended by the generic concept of the overman. But *many* kinds of nobles will be needed: The overman is a catch-all symbol for different kinds of individuals, and, as becomes clear in *Beyond Good and Evil,* it masks various incompatible characteristics.

Once you are awake, you shall remain awake eternally. It is not my way to awaken great-grandmothers from their sleep to bid them sleep on!

. . . I, Zarathustra, the advocate of life, the advocate of suffering, the advocate of the circle; I summon you, my most abysmal thought! (*Z* 215–16)

He faints from the thought and falls as if dead. When he awakens, his animals relate for him, in their own words, their version of the Eternal Recurrence—that there is joy in the world because as *cosmological fact* all eternity rolls back into itself. Everything *necessarily* repeats. They have misunderstood, and Zarathustra smiles at them. This misinterpretation shows that for some forgetting will be possible. Zarathustra's words, a great weight for him, have become for them a refreshing, beautiful folly.

In general, Zarathustra's fifth mode of speech is not only an addendum and a series of clarifications, but a series of striking phrases that can be quoted by those who come in the future, much as the Bible is quoted. Zarathustra's frequently repeated benediction can be taken as an example: "For I love you, O eternity!" (*Z* 228). It highlights one of the ramifications of willing the Eternal Recurrence, while simultaneously offering a memorable phrase for future readers. Only in eternity can man find any joy. Zarathustra longs for eternity, even if it is only the eternity of Becoming, the eternity of the Eternal Recurrence. The well-being of humanity requires the recovery of a relation to eternity.

For all practical purposes *Thus Spoke Zarathustra* comes to completion and closure at the end of part 3. Part 4, then, presents us with a problem. It was written later, after the intense period that produced the first three parts. It was not initially part of the book, and it is not clear what Nietzsche's intentions for it were. There is evidence that Nietzsche tried to retrieve the copies that had been circulated privately and that he did not wish part 4 published. It was published by his "friends" after he was in no position to stop them. Nevertheless, Nietzsche did write part 4, and from my perspective it fits well as an Afterword to the understanding I have been advancing. Part 4 represents Zarathustra's prediction of the kinds of misunderstandings that would follow from his teaching.

Zarathustra has returned to his mountain and the companionship of his animals. He has become ripe and sweet; the chaos in his soul has dissipated; he can no longer be a bridge. He can wait in patience, for now he knows that "one day it must yet come and may not pass." Humanity has entered the realm of his willed necessity, an unavoidable destiny. Zarathustra waits for "our great distant human kingdom, the Zarathustra kingdom of a thousand years" (Z 239–40). But the wait is not entirely pleasant. His solitude is invaded by a series of "higher men" who are products of his previous speeches. Each is a stunted growth who has focused on only a part of Zarathustra's teaching. They flee to Zarathustra because "there [are no] blessed isles any more," no places to hide, no epicurean gardens for the few (Z 244).

Two kings come who were stirred by such speeches as "You shall love peace as a means to new wars. . . . It is the good war that hallows any cause" (Z 247–48). They have been moved by the martial spirit of Zarathustra's previous speeches, an indication of how spirited men will interpret his maxims. He then meets a man—the "conscientious of spirit"—who has become an expert on the brain of the leech. He took Zarathustra's speeches about pursuing truth unmercifully far too strictly, and, in coming to know a great deal about a very narrow subject, has found a way to avoid nausea and the abyss. Zarathustra also meets an "ascetic of spirit" who succumbed to his nausea, wearied and gave in to the ironic life that Zarathustra—and the early Nietzsche—had decried. He meets the "last pope," who, having finally realized that God is dead, comes to find Zarathustra, "the most pious of all those who do not believe in God." He wants a new master, something Zarathustra does not wish to be (Z 258–60). And the "ugliest man" comes, the one who killed God. His arrival freezes Zarathustra (Z 263–66).

Zarathustra also finds a peaceful man sitting on the ground among the cows urging them not to fear him; he is giving them a "sermon on the mount." Zarathustra asks what he seeks, and the man responds, "The same thing you are seeking, you disturber of the peace: happiness on Earth" (Z 268–69). From unhistorical cows this man hopes to learn how to be rid of nausea and be happy. He longs for unhistorical forgetfulness. He kisses Zarathustra's hand as a man without nausea. It is the defeat of nausea that he sees as the highest end, regardless of what eventuates from that victory. This preacher is the "voluntary beggar," who threw away great riches and fled to the poor. He became a "social worker," but his clients did not accept him, so he went to the cows. The mob had become rebellious and arrogant. When the overrich try to give to those in the mob, the recipients are outraged rather than thankful; they demand their rights rather than alms (Z 270). Zarathustra sees this beggar as one who has turned his teaching toward the pacification of existence, precisely what must be overcome when one wills the Eternal Recurrence. As the beggar leaves, Zarathustra's shadow speaks to him. He

has cast such a long shadow that all manner of men now think themselves his disciples. The shadow asks, "Must I always be *on my way?*"
(*Z* 273; emphasis mine). He longs for rest from this wandering; he
longs for the cessation of Becoming and the promised Being and eternity. He longs for the end of the transition and the return of "that
mendacious innocence that [he] once possessed, the innocence of
the good and their noble lies" (*Z* 274). He realizes that his solitude has
been destroyed, and that he now needs even higher mountains. And
Zarathustra tries to outrun the shadow of influence he has cast.

One by one those who have taken too literally one part of Zarathustra's
teaching come to him, and he sends them to his cave for solace. They
wonder why the overman has not come. That prospect alone has made it
possible for them to continue to live and to maintain "the *great* hope."
Zarathustra responds that his guests are not high enough or strong
enough, for they stand on sick and weak legs. They are mere bridges for
higher men to stride over. He flees in search of fresh air and silence. On
returning to his cave he sees that the "higher men" are all praying to a new
god—the ass—for in braying, "Yea-Yuh," he always says "yes" to the
world. Hence he must be the great yes-sayer of the future, the one who
will affirm all that is. Zarathustra takes the ass festival as a sign of their
convalescence and bids them to celebrate it again in remembrance of him
(*Z* 310–17). The higher men leave the cave, and the ugliest man proclaims that finally he is satisfied that he has lived his whole life. He loves
the Earth, and he proclaims, "Was *that* life? . . . Well then! Once more!
. . . For Zarathustra's sake! Well then! Once more!" (*Z* 318–19). He has
accepted the Eternal Recurrence.

At the sight of these higher men, Zarathustra realizes again that even
his own past speeches must be overcome. And he says to his heart, "I still
lack the right men" (*Z* 325). Then a flock of doves flies around
Zarathustra; his ark must be nearing firm ground. A sign comes to him;
the laughing lion has also arrived. It is the sign Zarathustra looks for, that
"My children are near, my children" (*Z* 326). He cries profusely, and the lion
licks up the tears. Genuine spiritedness does not prey on wisdom. But
the lion roars savagely at the higher men, and they flee back within
Zarathustra's cave for safety. And Zarathustra denounces his pity for the
higher men, for he is not "concerned with *happiness*—[he is] concerned
with [his] *work*" (*Z* 327). And he realizes he must find even higher mountains to regain his solitude, and even more subtle masks.

9

Zarathustra and the Dynamic of Transition:
Epigones and Interpretations

In *Thus Spoke Zarathustra,* all the major themes of Nietzsche's thought are to be found. How these themes fit into the whole depends on their point of deployment. If I am right that there are five modes of speech, the third or central mode has a certain priority. In that third mode of speech the central concept is the Spirit of Revenge. That concept is the pivot point of Nietzsche's thought, not the rhetorically more stunning themes that usually occupy center stage: God is dead, last man and overman, love of earth and body, praise of war and hardness. I have purposely left out of this list the two doctrines I believe are indicative of Nietzsche's projected poetry of the future: Will to Power and Eternal Recurrence. To put the matter succinctly: Most of the rhetorically most famous Nietzscheanisms are found in the first two modes of speech, addressed to either the last men or the disciples that Zarathustra eventually repudiates. After the central reflections on the Spirit of Revenge, Zarathustra becomes introspective, has silent dialogues with himself, tries to bring himself to articulate his most abysmal thought, and then to cure himself of the pity occasioned by willing the Eternal Recurrence.

In the concept of the Spirit of Revenge Nietzsche encapsulates his critique of modern thought. The desire for the conquest of Chance—whether by political, ethical, economic, scientific or technological means—is at the heart of the modern longing. Modern man refuses to accept the world as it is given—with its suffering, inequality, and contingency—and wills to transform it. By late modernity that project approaches its telos: Nature, both human and nonhuman, has been significantly transformed. But there remain many examples of intransigence. Contingencies based on the inequality of ability, industriousness, appearance, birth, and so on still determine human life. Those "accidents" occasion intensified manifestations of the Spirit of Revenge. Likewise, external Nature recoils as the conquest of Nature leaves behind noxious residues, pollution, dwindling resources, and frightening imbalances. The response to this intransigence by thoroughgoing moderns is the call for a redoubling of efforts: More sophisticated technologies aimed at external Nature, greater bureaucratic control and economic rationalization, and more massive moral and political assaults on difference as it manifests itself in human nature.

Nietzsche's prediction was that as this modern Spirit of Revenge reached its highest point an ever increasing Spirit of Gravity, humorlessness, and intolerance of everything playful, joyful, and spontaneous, and every manifestation of difference would occur. He would not have had long to wait. The mass butcheries and human torture of the twentieth century would be traced by Nietzsche to the Spirit of Revenge and the associated Spirit of Gravity. Nazism, for example, proved him right with its invention of the idea of group guilt, an idea that has had a variety of incarnations: we look to isolate the group that intransigently opposes the unlimited desires of the late modern Will— Jews, the bourgeoisie, white males, etc., etc., etc. For Nietzsche, the move to the future required a victory over this Spirit of Revenge. That victory required an affirmation of life—present and past. *Zarathustra* is a reflection on how to foster a transition beyond a completed modernity that culminates in the highest manifestation of the Spirit of Revenge.

The primary poetic *symbol* of the future that is freed from the Spirit of Revenge is found in the idea of Eternal Recurrence. It is presented as a "vision and a riddle," as poetry, not cosmology or ontology. The poetic doctrine of Eternal Recurrence goes hand in hand with quitting the desire to transform the world on the basis of a self-consciously projected plan, with the acceptance of spontaneously occurring outcomes. It involves loving the earth and what is earthlike in us: i.e., our bodies, subconscious drives, passions, and "instincts," in short, difference. It involves an acceptance of the unavoidability of the recurrence of all manifestations of contingency and difference—high and low, pacific and bellicose—*despite* the transformative power of modern science and technology and their cousins political science, administration, economics, and ethics. It requires accepting the past as having been just as we would have wanted it, rather than revengefully dismissing it as hopelessly this-centric or that-phobic.

Eternal Recurrence, along with its necessary adjunct the Will to Power, are poetic symbols posited in the hope of establishing a future belief that would ground a world that could overcome the Spirit of Revenge and the Spirit of Gravity. They are not truths about reality, they are *illusions* that might support life. The philosophers of the future will know they are not "true." They are not indicative of Zarathustra's or Nietzsche's true ontological understandings but must be *willed*. That act of Will must be the *last* act of Will by late-modern man. Future man must be freed from the Will. Belief in Eternal Recurrence and Will to Power will convince men of the future that life is moved by an un-fathomable and impenetrable source which is nonetheless a fecund basis for life—an eternal Becoming. The Socratic—at least as Nietz-sche presents the matter—and modern scientific belief in the penetra-bility, understandability, and ultimate perfectibility of Being is a faith that has to be reversed—replaced by a counterfaith—for the sake of life. Nietzsche wills a faith in an unfathomable *Abgrund* that inevitably and repeatedly returns us to our beginnings: innocence and forgetting are necessary, recurring parts of Being.

In the process, Nietzsche hoped to emancipate man from the nihilis-tic hypertrophy of self-consciousness which manifests itself in the he-gemony of the self-grounding, self-legislating ego qua Will, which ultimately will accept nothing else in reality but itself. Belief in Eternal Recurrence puts the stamp of Eternity on the river of Becoming, which endlessly circles back on itself. It justifies and grounds the repeated re-turn to "immediate" or "natural" consciousness. That in turn makes it possible to again take the realm of appearance seriously. Nietzsche is as aware as Hegel that the outcome will be tragic. But for Nietzsche, the tragic is good for life.

As Zarathustra makes clear, the *ground* of these myths is perfectly modern: "Thus *my* Will wills it." As poetic symbols for the future, Will to Power and Eternal Recurrence must be given concrete manifestation by someone *of the future* who has become freed from the Spirit of Re-venge and the Spirit of Gravity. Transitional individuals like Zarathustra —and Nietzsche—are aware that they are still sick and too burdened with resentment against time and its "it was" to complete the half-filled tablets they project. Nietzsche, like his Zarathustra, is lim-ited to willing the speeches that he hopes will set in motion a *transition* to the future. He can will the general contours of that future but can do no more. Future *nomoi* must come from future "children," putting an end to philosophy's resentful efforts at willing *nomoi*. Only in that fash-ion can philosophy cure itself, transcend the Spirit of Revenge, and avoid the repeated devaluation of all values. For now, philosophy can only will the overcoming of the Will—a modern means to a *post*-modern end.

If what I have suggested is correct, the famous Nietzschean willful-ness, voluntarism, and subjectivism are all foreground. The *initial* rhetoric is just that, far from the last word. To foster a transition Zarathustra experiments with various modes of speech addressed to various audiences. The aim of those speeches is to foster a certain kind of action—and interpretation—that will cause a breakdown of the old tablets and a transition to a time when new tablets can be filled in. That transition requires projecting calculated partial understandings—and even misunderstandings. And it requires an intervening chaos. As the action of *Zarathustra* shows, the attempt to "enlighten" the *Volk* fails. Eventually Zarathustra's disciples fail him as well. But by the end of the book we see that a newly constituted *Volk* have heard of Zarathustra and love him. His teaching has been disseminated and sunk down to their level. On one level, his rhetoric has succeeded—even though it eventuates in various stunted "higher men." At that point, all he can do is wait.

Thus Spoke Zarathustra is an almost unrivaled case study of the nature of philosophic persuasion and the relation between theory and practice. A student of the sociology of knowledge, of the dissemination and deferred ramifications of thought, could do worse than to study and reflect upon *Thus Spoke Zarathustra* and the multiple, conflicting, partial interpretations that have followed it. It shows that to have a practical effect, the philosopher must rely on elements of rhetorical misdirection and the resultant misinformed action. It develops what follows from the loss of faith in general enlightenment. Those with the clearest understanding are *not* those who are most useful in bringing about change. Further, *Zarathustra* makes clear that at some point, and in some fashion, the philosopher must sway the *Volk*.

Zarathustra makes clear throughout that no one, from his disciples to his animals to the "higher men," has correctly grasped what he understands and intends. But through them, his thought has consequences in a variety of indirect, labyrinthine ways. Multiple failures come as well. Having consciously to foster failures is repugnant to Zarathustra and causes him to experience profound pity, but he must harden himself not to pity the failures. Zarathustra realizes that he is a destiny and that the possibility of a transition to a novel future rests entirely upon him. If he fails, the future will be lived out in dusty tombs where time has ceased. His Will must will an intricate web of words, which in turn must occasion another diluted web of words, and so on. That this process takes time is indicated by Zarathustra's increasing clarity that the period of transition will be protracted.

Seen in this light, the various interpretations of Nietzsche's words we have seen since his death are, by and large, precisely the ones he intended to foster, together with the undesirable ones he predicted.[1] However, the vast majority of interpretations of Nietzsche have focused on the rhetoric of *transition,* missing the centrality of overcoming the Spirit of Revenge and the Spirit of Gravity. Let me give a few examples of what I have in mind; others will no doubt be fairly obvious. The voluntarism and groundless willing of existentialism is clearly present in Nietzsche's rhetoric. The modern, all too modern, stress on "creators" and "legislators" is also clearly present. But both can only be manifestations of the Spirit of Revenge. They can only be transitional. But, as the discussion of "tarantulas" shows, Nietzsche fostered these partial interpretations even though he was aware that this voluntaristic teaching would be co-opted by egalitarian and progressive thinkers—a point reinforced in the discussion of false versus genuine "Free Spirits" in *Beyond Good and Evil.*

Those egalitarian and progressive arguments, which rely on metaphysical freedom for their foundation, are almost always completely at odds with the praise of the earth and the earthlike in us, as well as the entire Nietzschean attack on self-consciousness and subjectivity in the name of instinct and a return to Nature. Nietzsche clearly invites the Freudian interpretation of his thought. He invites the exploration of the unconscious as grounded in the body and its "drives and effects."[2] He encourages a movement beyond faith in autonomous "egos" or "subjects." But for Nietzsche, the great problem is that there is no unchanging natural substratum to human existence. Nietzsche clearly takes over and radicalizes modernity's antinature animus. Man's being is evanescent and must be re-created and reinvented over and over again, forged in the crucible of hardship, striving, and new collective tablets of esteeming.

The praise of the martial spirit is all too clear in Nietzsche's work. The National Socialist apologists who tried to use his work were not dreaming this up out of thin air. They were clearly attuned to part of Nietzsche's argument, even though they missed the most significant parts, as is obvious from reflection on sections like "On Great Events." The present political environment accounts for why this aspect of the whole is now seldom discussed. But it does not guarantee that this element of Nietzsche's thought will not rise to prominence again unless it is adequately deflected. And it does not prove that Nietzsche's al-

---

1. As I have tried to indicate, Nietzsche gives explicit indications throughout the book of the kinds of misinterpretations he expects. Part 4 of *Zarathustra* is almost entirely a reflection on some of those misunderstandings.

2. Cf. Deleuze, *Nietzsche and Philosophy.*

legedly "emancipatory," antifoundationalist philosophic critique can be easily severed from the political and moral ramifications he predicted—"red judges."

Nietzsche's stern political and moral teaching easily links up with that interpretation of the doctrine of the Will to Power which openly accepts the inevitability of power politics. In the late-modern world power politics, emancipated from traditional moral restraints, can only eventuate in fragmentation and chaos unless other consistent deflections are made. Nietzsche makes explicit his expectation that great wars and general chaos, some cleansing apocalyptic flood, would be needed for there to be a transition to a novel future, that they were inevitable in the wake of the decline of faith in Western rationalism he helped foster. He did not think that political and moral acts *alone* would ever get humanity beyond the Spirit of Revenge; but neither would a philosophic critique.

Throughout his work Nietzsche openly asserts that what passes for understanding is in fact interpretation. Authors like Derrida raise this part of the teaching to primacy. Derrida goes even further: There is no ultimate referent for speech. Consequently, there is no self-identical author who can master a consciously posited project. The configuration of the future is as unpredictable as knowledge of the past is impossible. All is a flux of interpretation and reinterpretation. A better basis for "innocence and forgetting" one could not wish.[3] But, if I am correct, Nietzsche differs from this view in believing that he can calculate the effects of his speeches, at least in general terms. This implies that there is a reality that is not entirely evanescent and that on some level is knowable. Nonetheless, from Nietzsche's perspective, deconstructionism would be a useful transitional phenomenon, part of the necessary period of chaos.

The message of the withdrawal of the few into solitude and artistic, aesthetic, and philosophic monasteries of one kind or another, unsullied by the mass culture outside, can also be found in Nietzsche. But Nietzsche, through the figure of Zarathustra, makes clear that this freedom and solitude are not presently available in any serious sense. They

3. Several late-modern (self-described as postmodern) thinkers have seen fostering forgetting as a conscious part of their undertaking. This has usually been manifested in attempts to subvert traditional texts and their authority, thereby closing off any return to tradition—and hence any creative addition to it as well. The subverted texts would be expunged from the public record as much as possible. But this effort is clearly a manifestation of the Spirit of Revenge and the Spirit of Gravity, i.e., a refusal to affirm the past as having been exactly as one would have wished it. Such affirmation requires remembering the past, and in very considerable detail.

will be available for the genuine Free Spirits only in the future, after thought is freed from the Spirit of Revenge. One cannot yet playfully, innocently, and detachedly skip across the anthills of late-modern civilization. As part 4 of *Zarathustra* makes clear, the crowd will follow ever higher up the solitary's mountain. One's epicurean retreat will be invaded. If Nietzsche is correct, one cannot now remain in a form of sophisticated detachment. The prelude to such a possibility requires the intervention of the "laughing lions."[4]

One could extend this list, but it should be clear that the prominent themes that form the basis of most partial interpretations were posited by Nietzsche himself as means of effecting a process of transition beyond the late-modern sickness designated by the idea Spirit of Revenge. As I will try to show more clearly in the next chapter, Nietzsche is in fact attempting to get philosophy out of the modern role of legislator, manipulator, and master over *praxis*. Philosophy itself must come to be seen in a new light. It must cease its vengeful attempt to transform *praxis,* and thereby return to *praxis* its own spontaneity and autonomous rhythms. Future philosophers will have to *choose* such a stance if they hope to be emancipated from the Spirit of Revenge. I will argue that this, and the search for a new, revenge-free thinking, are among the genuinely *post*modern element in Nietzsche's thought.

---

4. The one interpretative attempt that has no foundation in Nietzsche's thought is the desire to compartmentalize and reduce his teaching to the categories of past, dogmatic, system-building philosophy. That is what Nietzsche most openly tried to avoid. For Nietzsche the will to system-building was always seen as a form of weakness and self-delusion. This interpretation is now reasonably dormant in the face of contemporary postmodernism.

10

The Future Possibility: After the Metamorphosis

Philosophy Past and Present

Having sketched the dynamics of a hoped-for transition from the past to the future in *Thus Spoke Zarathustra*, Nietzsche needed to give a more concrete glimpse of the future he anticipated. That future is presented most clearly—at least as clearly as it is ever presented—in *Beyond Good and Evil*. Like *Zarathustra*, *Beyond Good and Evil* is highly rhetorical, with a loud, shrill foreground or surface and more guarded interiors. In many ways, it is a more difficult book to penetrate than *Zarathustra*, less forthcoming, offering fewer glimpses of the inside, emphasizing the foreground. The foreground is symbolized by the intentionally shrill title. Needless to say, the sharpest edges are removed when we find that the author's intention is not to promote rampant amorality; in trying to transcend past distinctions between good and evil, he does not intend that we should project ourselves beyond "good and *bad.*"[1] More indicative of Nietzsche's intention is the subtitle of the work, "Prelude to a Philosophy of the Future."

It is important to attend to Nietzsche's own characterization of *Beyond Good and Evil* in *Ecce Homo:* "This book (1886) is in all essentials a *critique of modernity,* not excluding the modern sciences, modern arts, and even modern politics along with pointers *to a contrary type* [emphasis mine] that is as little modern as possible—a noble, Yes-saying type. In the latter sense, the book is a school for the *gentilhomme.*"[2] He also says, "The revaluation of our values so far, the great war—conjuring up a day of decision. This included the slow search for those *related* to me, those who, prompted by strength, would offer me their

1. This becomes even clearer in *On the Genealogy of Morals,* where Nietzsche shows he wishes to plot a course toward a future noble morality.
2. Nietzsche, *Ecce Homo,* "Beyond Good and Evil," 310. Henceforth designated in the text as *EH,* followed by a page number.

hands for *destroying*" (*EH* 310; emphasis mine). Nietzsche goes on to talk about the narrowing of vision and perspective in *Beyond Good and Evil*: a "*deliberate* turning away from the instincts that had made possible a Zarathustra" (*EH* 311).

Beyond Good and Evil is a book for "nobles" or "gentlemen" which is also intended as a *prelude* to a philosophy of the future. Nietzsche tried to put an end to all past philosophy, which had been sullied by the Spirit of Revenge, and to sketch a vision of a future philosophy freed from that *ressentiment*. He concluded that the existence of that new, revenge-free philosophy presupposed the *prior* existence of "noble" individuals. There must be a "long ladder of an order of rank" in a society.[3] At the bottom are the ignoble, at the top the "Free Spirits," with qualitatively different rungs in between. The *gentilhomme* occupies a middle rung, yet one prerequisite to the existence of the higher rungs, helping foster the "pathos of distance" that makes revenge-free thinking possible.

Beyond Good and Evil can be divided into two parts separated by the stylistically different "Epigrams and Interludes."[4] The first three chapters are respectively on philosophy, past, present, and future. The last five are on morals and politics, culminating in a discussion of nobility. Hence we are confronted thematically with the issue that perplexes many of Nietzsche's commentators, the allegedly contradictory relation between his philosophical prescriptions and his political and moral teaching. In *Beyond Good and Evil* these themes are juxtaposed as necessary parts of a whole.[5]

"Supposing truth is a woman—what then?" (*BG* 2). What if, in other words, truth is changeable and evanescent, in need of being beguiled and won, yet fecund and pregnant with possibilities? If that is the nature of truth, Nietzsche asserts that all past attempts to woo truth—i.e., all past systematic philosophical dogmatisms—were a

3. Nietzsche, *Beyond Good and Evil*, aphorism 257.
4. On the order of *Beyond Good and Evil*, consider Leo Strauss's "Note on the Plan of Nietzsche's *Beyond Good and Evil*."
5. Nietzsche presents an exhilarating new vision of philosophy, one that transcends the modern academic straitjacket that reduces philosophy to epistemology. He extends the modern attack on metaphysics and theology and undermines the premises that ground the liberal, capitalist state and modern science. To some, therefore, he seems philosophically to advance progressive ends. By contrast his political teaching seems reactionary; but these two teachings necessarily go together. It is a mistake to believe that one can pick and choose among the parts of Nietzsche's teaching in the manner of postmodernist pastiches. To avoid the dangers implicit in what Nietzsche has helped unleash, we must get to the essence of what he has spoken and deflect it in a far more consistent fashion.

sign that philosophers did not understand its nature. But their day has come to an end; dogmatic systems are no longer believable. In the future, philosophy must have a different *public persona* and proceed according to a different idiom.[6] In the service of that end, Nietzsche begins by exposing the shortcomings and "prejudices" of all past philosophers, only to then engage in the same maneuvers he has attacked.

Nietzsche asserts that all philosophies are the personal confessions of their authors. Every philosophy has a physiological foundation, which for Nietzsche is to say, a moral basis. Behind every theory are valuations that help preserve a certain kind of life. It is therefore absurd to believe in the possibility of objectivity, detachment, and disinterestedness. Furthermore, every philosophy has its origin in hunches and "inspirations." Philosophers do not arrive at their *archai* by strict dialectic or logic. It allegedly follows, therefore, that thinking is not the opposite of instinct, but rather one instinct among many; philosophy has a source in the unconscious, inspired, and "instinctive." Nietzsche further asserts that, like all instincts, philosophy is a manifestation of the Will to Power; it is the most subtle form of the Will to Power (*BG #*9). If this is true, philosophy is not categorically different from politics, art, religion, poetry, or any other activity. The difference is one of "subtlety" alone. Nietzsche draws the inevitable conclusion and asserts what has become the dogma of our time: All is interpretation, even modern science (*BG #*14). Consequently, we can no more read the text Nature than we can live "according to" Nature (*BG #*9) or believe that Nature in all instances conforms to uniform laws (*BG #*22). This is democratic, egalitarian interpretation—that is, prejudice—not text.

According to Nietzsche, even in physics there is no reason to interpret in ignoble ways once one realizes the true relationship between explanation and interpretation. In a democratic age physicists try to interpret nature in a fashion compatible with democratic tastes, but the same text can be read in a variety of ways—e.g., as showing hierarchy, relentless claims to power, and the Will to Power. Nietzsche asks whether "this also is only interpretation," and comments, "well, so much the better." He encourages us to have a consciously perspectival physics, and by extension, psychology or biology,[7] but asserts that the

6. Rorty reaches a similar conclusion, that philosophy must adopt a new persona. He believes "epistemology" must now be replaced by "hermeneutics"—in his somewhat idiosyncratic sense. But Rorty's attempt would be seen by Nietzsche as just another modern manifestation of the Spirit of Revenge. See Rorty, *Philosophy and the Mirror of Nature.*

7. One might expect, for example, a biology of native American women, feminist physics, white male geology, and so on.

perspective should be nondemocratic and nonegalitarian, and should implicate unpredictability and contingency.[8] Since all "explanation" has a moral basis, it may as well enthrone "noble" values. Nietzsche here reasserts one of his earliest themes, that the will to truth should not be the highest will. The will to life should be the highest will; and life requires illusions. All past philosophies have been illusions, but past myths, especially modern ones, have been egalitarian and ignoble. The age of *noble* lies is at hand. A "new species of philosophers" is coming, who will inscribe something different onto Nature and even onto the basic text *homo natura* (*BG* #2).

With "our" belief that all is determined by the Will to Power, "we" philosophers *of the present* lose our easygoing faith that the first cause is pure and unsullied. The temporal is not grounded in the timeless, the good is not the cause of all goodness. In fact, Nietzsche argues that we should *experiment* with the belief that things originate in their opposites—the selfless in the selfish, the pure in lust, the high in the low, the good in evil, and so on—a perfectly modern maneuver. New "psychologists" should engage in a variety of such experiments, should "risk it," despite the fact that it will make mankind "sick." Nietzsche advises the many to "stay away" from such ideas. Nevertheless, "we" psychologists of the present will experiment with the idea that hatred, envy, covetousness, lust, and the like are needed in "the general economy of life" (*BG* #23).

The other major line of argument in part 1 asserts that there are no immediate certainties. Hence to believe in either "I think" or "I will" requires blind faith (*BG* #16). To believe in the ego as cause or, for that matter, in cause and effect generally, is a mere prejudice and conventional fiction. We do not cause our thoughts anymore than we are the autonomous causes of our actions. Thoughts come when *they* wish, not at the beck and call of our ego (*BG* #17). There is no *causa sui*. Free will is a myth. To believe otherwise is to believe we "pull [ourselves] up into existence by the hair, out of the swamps of nothingness" (*BG* #21).[9] The opposite side of this coin is that it is equally false to believe

8. Shortly after Nietzsche's death, modern physics itself arrived at the premise of cosmic unpredictability and indeterminacy. The import of that conclusion has not yet manifested itself as fully and radically as it will in time.

9. Nietzsche asserts that willing is a complex phenomenon. One element is found in sensation, the attraction "toward" and repulsion "away from." Second, there is always an element of consciousness involved, a "ruling thought" that dominates consciousness at the moment we experience attraction and repulsion. Finally there is the "effect" those who succeed in commanding think they have over those who are forced to obey. This "effect" finally translates itself back into "feelings" which give the sensation of a "com-

in the unfreedom of the Will. There is no way to prove the operation of Necessity: "It is *we* alone who have devised cause, sequence, for-each-other, relativity, constraint, number, law, freedom, motive, and purpose. . . . The 'unfree will' is mythology; in real life it is only a matter of *strong* and *weak* wills" (*BG* #21).

Reliance on the idea of an unfree Will is a moral trick of those who do not wish to be answerable for anything or personally blamed; due to their own weak wills, they want to lay blame somewhere else. What dominates life is not Necessity, or cause and effect, but a contingent phenomenon like language, especially grammar. And, like all things, Nietzsche asserts that grammar finds it foundation in the physiological valuations and the social conditions of a people (*BG* #20). In the final aphorism of part 1, Nietzsche concludes that philosophy must yield "again" to psychology as "the queen of the sciences." Psychology is the path to the fundamental problems, if not to enduring answers. This is apparently the key to the great escape from the present, not so much through the mere understanding of psychology as through a practice of psychology freed from moral prejudices so that it can recognize itself as "morphology and *the doctrine of the development of the will to power*" (*BG* #23). The psychologist must become a manipulative, modern legislator.

What occurs in part 1—the critique of past philosophy—is a string of mere assertions that serve to foster tensions that tighten the contemporary human bow by promoting total intellectual fragmentation. Public discussion would become impossible; each is encouraged to assert his or her "physiological" difference. A public cacophony of voices is the only conceivable outcome of the assertions in part 1.[10] The picture of philosophy one is left with when one is emancipated from all the alleged prejudices of part 1 is a philosophy in which anyone can participate. It requires no rigor, no learning, no genius, merely simple self-assertiveness, that is, democratic politics with a cap and gown. At best this kind of "prejudice-free" thinking can be critical, pointing out the

---

plex state of delight" (*BG* #19). We have the certainty that an effect does and should ensue from causes we initiated. But faith in such causality is pure myth. Nothing is changed in those instances where we conceive of ourselves as both the one who commands and obeys. The sense of being the ego that commands *and* the matter that is constrained or compelled does not prove the existence of a *causa sui*.

10. If I am correct, that is precisely what Nietzsche intended. All of the initial assertions in part 1 of *Beyond Good and Evil* are foreground, rhetorical attempts to move the half-clear and the never to be clear to perfectly predictable responses: "Every time a beginning that is *calculated* to mislead: cool, scientific, even ironic, deliberately foreground, deliberately holding off" (*EH* 312).

"errors" or naivete of any systematic philosophy that takes itself seriously.

The assertions of part 1 will primarily breed a herd of "philosophers" who can lend their hands to Nietzsche for destroying.[11] They are dynamite; they can create nothing. That such a philosophy is not the last word becomes clear in the remainder of Beyond Good and Evil. But after Nietzsche's death, literal armies have fanned out and adopted the *assertions* of part 1—e.g., "all is interpretation"—as dogma never again to be questioned. That is surely not the genuine Nietzschean spirit. And endless deconstruction was not Nietzsche's *end*. It was rather a *prelude*.[12] Real philosophers, true "Free Spirits," will avoid such *public* posturing. And they will not write.[13]

Future Philosophy, Religion, and Free Spiritedness

After his polemical refutation of the pretensions of past philosophy, Nietzsche turns to a thematic discussion of Free Spirits. According to Nietzsche, the true Free Spirit should not be a "martyr for the truth," adopting the public pose of being its protector. Instead the Free Spirits should flee into concealment, protecting and shielding themselves with various subterfuges and consciously projected "masks."[14] Genuine

11. "One day my name will be associated with the memory of something tremendous—a crisis without equal on earth. . . . I am no man, I am dynamite. . . . When truth enters into a fight with the lies of a millennium, we shall have upheavals, a convulsion of earthquakes. . . . All power structures of the old society will have been exploded: . . . there will be wars the like of which have never yet been seen on earth" (EH 326–27).

12. The surface teaching in part 1 of Beyond Good and Evil must also be read in light of the clear distinction Nietzsche makes between "esoteric" and "exoteric." He asserts that the use of exoteric and esoteric speech is a sign that "one believe[s] in an order of rank." "Our highest insights must—and should—sound like follies and sometimes like crimes when they are heard without permission by those who are not predisposed to them and predestined for them" (BG #30).

13. "Books for all the world are always foul-smelling books" (BG #30). The writing of a book is a political act; real philosophers—the free spirits of the future—will eschew such acts, and private speech among equals will take priority over writing. Nietzsche ultimately agrees with the Socrates of Plato's Phaedrus—writing and the truth do not go well together. In this vein, consider: " 'Let's talk *seriously* about such and such a thing.' As if that were possible! As if 'talking' were something that could done with ultimate radical seriousness and not with the pained conscience of someone performing a farce! If one truly wishes to do something *seriously* the first injunction is to keep quiet. *True knowledge, as we shall methodically see, is silence and reserve.*" José Ortega y Gasset, The Origin of Philosophy, trans. Toby Talbot (New York: W. W. Norton, 1967), 59.

14. "Rather, go away. Flee into concealment. And have your masks and subtlety, that you may be mistaken for what you are not, or feared a little. *And don't forget the*

philosophic Free Spirits must flee into an epicurean garden, quit the public posture of past philosophy, but do it freely, for it is not healthy to be "compulsory recluses [like] the Spinozas or Giordano Brunos," who always turn into "sophisticated vengeance-seekers" (*BG* #25). Only on the basis of a consciously chosen solitude can the Free Spirit allow himself a philosophical sense of humor, rather than moral indignation, which always degenerates into the Spirit of Revenge characteristic of all past philosophy. This withdrawal into privacy is good for both the Free Spirit and others, because only on the basis of illusion, myth, error, and ignorance can a political community be maintained for the nonphilosophic.

Nietzsche asserts that even the edifice of scientific knowledge is constructed upon a foundation of initial illusion—that mathematics, for example, always falsifies. Neither modern science nor modern politics are proper activities for the Free Spirits, who should instead instinctively question the solidity of received ignorance and undermine the necessarily mythical edifices erected upon that ignorance. And no Free Spirit could bring himself to will myths or be taken in by them. The Free Spirits of the future, who will have no inclination to be dogmatists or system builders, will have no need to pursue a public vocation, or give themselves a public manifestation in written words. They can cease to be legislators. They can, and should, remain separate from the community "below" and its doings. What they do in their private gardens purposely remains unclear, although we must keep in mind that at the beginning of *Zarathustra* there *is* a sun outside the cave. Mankind as a whole, requires this separation between those who *know* and those who *do*.

As *Zarathustra* makes clear, this solitary and revenge-free purity is not presently available. Philosophers in the present must still will the future—a form of the Spirit of Revenge. But true Free Spirits must gain independence from common opinion and political life—they must not "remain stuck to a fatherland" (*BG* #41), but must continually test themselves, and demand of themselves independence and self-command. They must be the great "attempters." The Free Spirits of the future will be "curious to a vice, investigators to the point of cruelty" (*BG* #42, 44), and not merely no-sayers and destroyers. But they are not really yes-sayers or creators either (for that would entail creating dogmas). Their existence presupposes the prior existence of moral

---

garden, [emphasis mine] the garden with golden trelliswork. . . . Choose the *good* solitude, the free, playful, light solitude that gives you, too, the right to remain good in some sense" (*BG* #25).

communities, but they will never really be part of any moral or political community except at the very fringes.

There is one force, however, that always pulls the genuine Free Spirit back to the *Volk*: a sense of curiosity and wonder (*BG #26*). The many and their doings are one of the main objects of philosophic curiosity. This is apparently Nietzsche's way of explaining what Plato does not—why the philosopher continually reenters the cave, yet is never at home when he does so. But upon going down to nonphilosophic man, the Free Spirit must build for himself a defense; simultaneously he radicalizes the journey within, into an exploration of the self: "And he would go *down,* and above all, he would go 'inside'" (*BG #26*). The Free Spirit remains distant from others while nonetheless among them and drawn to them. This explains Zarathustra's inner tension. To be too much with the nonphilosophic is to fall prey to martyrdom or sophisticated vengeance, yet curiosity continually tempts, much as a flame tempts a moth. But in a way, this curiosity saves the Free Spirit from a journey into the self that might be altogether tragic (*BG #29*).

Nietzsche explicitly forces us to reflect on the fundamental relationship between the Free Spirits (i.e., the true philosophers) and the nonphilosophic communities in which they must exist. This reflection forces him into a discussion of the nature of public speech and philosophic silence. Obviously the Free Spirit cannot and should not simply speak his mind. The true Free Spirit will understand the need for esoteric speech. Like Plato, Nietzsche never gives us a picture of what real philosophy is. Real philosophy—revengeless, free spiritedness—certainly would consist of more than the merely assertive, no-saying, and the self-invalidating platitudes of part 1. Nietzsche brings us to the realization that all writing is political and moral in nature, and in principle a form of the Spirit of Revenge. The real philosophers do not write and leave no trace, which is why History was determined by the vengeful who did write.

It is in light of this distinction between the philosophic and the nonphilosophic, and between esoteric and exoteric speech, that one must approach what is, for all intents and purposes, Nietzsche's sketch of the stages of human history, a discussion enlarged upon in the *Genealogy of Morals*. He observes that prior to the "Socratic turn," back in prehistoric times, the value of an action was judged by its consequences, not by its origin. This was the "premoral" period when "know thyself" was not yet a moral dictate. In the Socratic age, self-consciousness became the only legitimate origin of action. Only the *intentionality* of a self-conscious actor conferred value. This age clearly culminates in the Kantian victory of self-conscious Will over "natural" impulsion and the turn of ethics toward the centrality of intentionality. In the future another reversal is required. The future perspective must become "extramoral," which for Nietzsche implies that what is *unintentional* in an act is what is valuable.

It is as part of the discussion of the postmoral age that Nietzsche gives his clearest statement of the ontological status of the doctrine of the Will to Power. He asserts that it is a "supposition," a hypothesis, a strategic "as if." Nietzsche's moral teaching is constructed upon no other bedrock or substratum than the poetic speech of "we" Free Spirits of the present: "*Suppose* nothing else were 'given' as real except our world of desires and passions, and we could not get down, or up, to any other 'reality' besides the reality of our drives" (*BG #36*; emphasis mine). Nietzsche asks us to proceed "as if" everything "lies contained in a powerful unity before it undergoes ramifications and developments in the organic process (and, as is only fair, also becomes tenderer and weaker)—as a kind of instinctive life in which all organic functions are still synthetically intertwined along with self-regulation, assimilation, nourishment, excretion, and metabolism—as a *pre-form* of life" (*BG #36*). He says the "conscience of *method*" demands this *experiment* from us.

We should not, as with Aristotle, presume the necessity of four causes to explain the world, but instead see if we can make do with one—efficient causality. We must "make the experiment of positing the causality of the will hypothetically as the only one" (*BG #36*). Of course, we should recall that Nietzsche has already told us that causality is only a convenience or fiction. But we should proceed "as if" everything were determined by the Will to Power as the fundamental efficient cause, contrary, for example, to Kant, who would have us proceed "as if" there were a realm of freedom which emancipates us from the realm of necessity, understood as efficient causality. Nietzsche's implication is that we should act "as if" there were only a realm of necessity and no realm of freedom. Nietzsche asserts that this does not imply that "God is refuted, but the devil is not. . . . On the contrary!" (*BG #37*). While there is no transcendent God, there is the new, posited Will to Power. This can be postulated as the ontological foundation for the unself-conscious, postmoral period of the future. If we proceed "as if" this were true, potentially the same thing will happen that happened with the French Revolution— *"the text finally disappeared under the interpretation."* (*BG #38*). Indeed Nietzsche tells us that we are the posterity or deferred ramification of such an interpretation.

Along with the new morality will come the overcoming of the morality of self-denial, which pretends to be devoid of interest. One will cease to stress doing for others but not for oneself. Instead individuals will pursue whatever "desire" wells up from "below," and follow it with a good conscience. We must drop the moral fiction of autonomous intentionality in the service of secularized Christian self-denial and disinterestedness. The future approach shares with the moral, Socratic period the search for the *origin* as the source of value, but it will be a subconscious rather than self-conscious origin that takes precedence.[15] This morality is clearly *not* a prescription for the Free Spirits, for their task is the self-conscious, and primarily solitary, plumbing of their own labyrinthine depths and awestruck perusal of the world around them. From the perspective of the Free Spirit, all of these changes of *moral* perspective are no more than a "moral prejudice," something to be avoided. But the two discussions are linked. Nietzsche has concluded that free-spiritedness presupposes a particular moral environment.

After discussing the Free Spirits, and the new moral horizon that need not implicate them as legislators, Nietzsche turns to a discussion of what might be translated as the "religious essence," or perhaps, and far less literally, the nature of the religious experience per se.[16] Herein we get a discussion of what he calls the "philosophers of the future." They will not be as free as the future Free Spirits but can, properly trained, be the Free Spirit's "well-trained hounds" and "servants" (*BG* #45). They will believe many things the Free Spirits never would, and they probably will write.

Nietzsche observes that the theistic satisfaction of the past is dead but "the religious instinct is indeed in the process of growing powerfully" (*BG* #53). The true psychologist of the present will make use of this. The future will be a-theistic, but not a-religious. As Nietzsche puts the matter, we must "sacrifice God" and pray to the No-thing (*BG* #55). That "God is dead" means that the religious instinct can no longer be linked to a transcendent being, but it can live as openness to an intoxicated Dionysian submission to the No-thing, understood as the eternally circling Will to Power. The religious experience can be revived as a relation to the immanent, mysterious, self-concealing

15. The problem for Nietzsche is that the hegemony of the subconscious has to be willed. Nietzsche is much closer to Rousseau than Freud, in that he considers the real problem to be that man does not have a fixed natural substratum. It is a mistake to Freudianize Nietzsche, although Freud is a manifestation of what Nietzsche hoped to posit. The Freudianization of Nietzsche is indicative of an inability to see the rhetorical nature of Nietzsche's work, and the "problem of nature" that calls it into existence. See for example, Deleuze, *Nietzsche and Philosophy,* chapter 2, "Active and Reactive," esp. 52–53. I will return to the issue of the "problem of nature" in part 4.

16. Kaufmann translates the title of part 3 as "What Is Religious."

ground of existence. There can be a religion that is "high spirited, alive and world affirming," that accepts "whatever was and is . . . [that] wants to have *what was and is* repeated to all eternity." Worshiping God as *"circulus vitiosus deus"* will bring with it greater "space around man," a world "more profound; ever new stars, ever new riddles and images become visible" (*BG* #56, 57). In the future the religious experience will be demanding rather than a solace. It will require the strength of a Pascal, the Will to Power of the Saint, the "gratitude" and "nobility" of Greek religion, the stern grandeur of the Old Testament (*BG* #45, 51, 49, 52). The "philosophers of the future" will be implicated as priests in this new religiosity.

The key to any religiosity, Nietzsche asserts, is psychological cruelty. That cruelty has taken many forms. At one time we sacrificed to God the possession most loved, e.g., a son or the first born. Then in the moral period we sacrificed our own strongest instincts, or "Nature," in ascetic self-denial. In the future, that necessary cruelty will take the form of sacrificing God himself—i.e., "whatever is comforting, holy, healing; all hope, all faith in hidden harmony, in future blisses and justices." This leaves one to "worship the stone, stupidity, gravity, fate, the nothing" (one should stress here the *No-thing*)—the indeterminate and mysterious, the Dionysian, the unself-conscious Weltgeist: "To sacrifice God for the nothing—this paradoxical mystery of the final cruelty was reserved for the generation that is now coming up: all of us already know something of this" (*BG* #55). As I have argued above, it is Heidegger who explores the ontological ramifications of this notion most deeply. The destruction of Christianity and theism leads to the regeneration of the religious—albeit without the instinct for fasting, sexual abstinence, and the like. Never again must religion "invert all love of the earthly and of dominion over the earth into hatred of the earth and the earthly" (*BG* #62). And unlike especially Protestant Christianity, such a religion can help support the leisure class that every noble society requires, and which is altogether necessary for the existence of nonrevengeful Free Spirits.[17]

Nietzsche asserts that the religious instinct is destroyed by anything that destroys leisure. To preach atheism is a way to overcome the increasing indifference to the religious experience of an industrious, modern race. It is intended to help delegitimize the commercial industriousness that seems so intimately tied to Protestant Christianity. Un-

17. "Genuinely religious life . . . requires a leisure class . . . with a good conscience. . . . Our modern, noisy, time-consuming industriousness . . . prepares people, more than anything else does, precisely for 'unbelief'" (*BG* #58).

like Christian priests, the priests of the future will not take revenge against the world which supports their leisure. And if freed from the grips of the Spirit of Revenge future religion need not hate earth and body. "We" psychologists and still revengeful Free Spirits of the present understand that "the philosopher as *we* understand him, . . . as the man of the most comprehensive responsibility who has the conscience for the over-all development of man—*this philosopher* will make use of religions for his project of cultivation and education" (*BG* #61; emphasis mine). This means the "philosophers of the future," the priests of the Dionysian Will to Power, will remain subservient to the legislator of the present—i.e., the Nietzsche who wills the Eternal Recurrence. And their existence will help shelter the true Free Spirits who are still to come.[18] Nietzsche was not pointing forward to a race of voluntarist philosopher-kings who would rule day-to-day affairs, quite the contrary. Such philosopher-kings would still be locked in the Spirit of Revenge; they would not have the leisure or solitude for which the true Free Spirit longs. The true Free Spirits of the future will "rule" with only an occasionally applied, extremely light hand.

Religion has other uses as well. Politically it can be used to foster mastery and self-control among rising classes, to spiritualize them through "asceticism and puritanism [which] are almost indispensable," while it also affords rulers a means for overcoming resistance by creating a bond between them and their subjects; indeed it brings contentment to those who must exist for service and nothing else (*GS*61). Religion justifies suffering, and that will not change in Nietzsche's hoped-for future. But religion must always remain subservient to philosophy. It should never be sovereign and independent of the philosopher's hand, as a tool for his educating and cultivating. And humanity, lacking a fixed Nature—"the *as yet undetermined animal,* the rare exception"—will continually have to be cultivated, to be made and remade. Given man's essential malleability, it is little wonder that Nietzsche says that the "*excess* of [human] cases . . . [do] not turn out right" (*BG* #62). But for Nietzsche it is important that the failures not be preserved; one must not have an autonomous religion that administers

18. "And if a few individuals of such noble descent are inclined through lofty spirituality to prefer a more withdrawn and contemplative life and reserve for themselves only the most subtle type of rule (over selected disciples or brothers in some order), then religion can even be used as a means for obtaining peace from the noise and exertion of *cruder* forms of government, and purity from the *necessary* dirt of all politics. That is how the Brahmins, for example, understood things: by means of a religious organization they gave themselves the power of nominating the kings of the people while they themselves kept and felt apart and outside, as men of higher and supra-royal tasks" (*BG* #61).

primarily to the suffering of the failures, but rather one that justifies the strong, and makes possible the solitude and leisure of the few.

The Problem of Nature: The Place of Ethics and the Political

In part 5, entitled "Natural History of Morals," Nietzsche turns to a discussion of politics and morality. The title, with its assertion that moral codes, like geology, have a natural history, was intended to be paradoxical. Moralities are no more based on self-conscious Reason than is the movement of glaciers. Nietzsche asserts that any "science of morals" offends "good taste." He points instead to the moral importance of a shared *ethos,* which is always an inarticulate background phenomenon.[19] "Genealogists" realize that it is no longer possible to take seriously any "*rational foundation* for morality" (*BG* #186). Attempts at rational moralities tell us about the author and what he desires more than anything else; they are a "sign language of the affects" (*BG* #187). Past moralists have been weak, frightened, and revengeful. They wished for peace and security. According to Nietzsche, rational moralities are always universalistic, egalitarian, hedonistic, and pacifist. What Nietzsche desires is an aristocratic morality. But why choose an aristocratic moral code over a democratic one? Is this not a matter of self-interest as well? Yes, Nietzsche has concluded that the only genuine individuality is philosophic and that the prerequisite for the existence of genuine, revenge-free Free Spirits is an aristocratic *ethos.*

Nietzsche's new genealogical approach changes our entire perspective on morality. For example, rather than take seriously the substance of a moral teaching, the new approach deflects attention to its origin

19. In discussing morality and politics, Aristotle makes the famous observation that one should not expect more precision from a science than the subject matter allows. Morality, for example, can never have the precision of geometry. In this sense there can never be a "science" of morals, at least not when science is understood as an apodictic, deductive enterprise. For Aristotle, virtue is based on habit which is in turn rooted in the habit background of a distinctive *ethos.* Hence instead of offering a metaphysics of morals, Aristotle observes that virtue is a mean and offers such moral rules of thumb as advising that individuals aim in the direction of the vice opposite their natural inclinations, thereby maximizing the likelihood of hitting the mean. Nietzsche's discussion of morality can be viewed in the same light.

In general terms, Nietzsche analyzes the vice he sees as peculiar to the present and rhetorically aims at the opposite vice. The moral vice of late modernity, as he sees it, is found in the drive to find a rational, universal, apodictic foundation for morality, which culminates in the attempt to transform morality into a deductive, ethical science. In his eyes, such a morality can only be egalitarian, utilitarian, and hedonistic. To such a "science of morals" Nietzsche opposes his "genealogy of morals," which is intended to deflect ethical discussion in a different direction.

and history. This simultaneously deflects attention in at least two different directions. As one disinters the inarticulate roots of present moral codes one fosters detachment from action and thereby undermines passionate commitment. On the other hand, one focuses attention on the kinds of originary experiences that make a shared *ethos* possible—rather than the appropriate logic of rule derivation that takes precedence in most post-Kantian discussions. While disinterring the roots of past moral presumptions is presently popular—Foucault's use of the similar "archaeological" method being one of the more interesting—rarely do contemporary genealogists consider the origins of countervalues. Most often genealogical dynamite is used to destroy the last scraggly remnants of traditional morality, in the service of a modern, egalitarian, utilitarian, democratistic anarchism.

But Nietzsche asserts that despite their different physiological and historical conditions every morality is a form of tyranny. The essence of any moral code is that it constitutes the basis for a long period of compulsion. This compulsion forms man's "Nature." Any morality of *laissez-aller* undoes the possibility of man having a "Nature" or any higher spirituality. What is essential is "that there should be *obedience* over a long period of time and in a *single* direction." From this always develops distinctive forms of "virtue, art, music, dance, reason, spirituality—something transfiguring, subtle, mad, and divine" (*BG* #188). The spirit is turned onto the path of everything great and distinctive through enforced behavior which becomes habitual. On this level, Nietzsche is obviously not the spokesman for moral idiosyncrasy, individual self-creation, or freedom from external determination. That way of life makes sense when applied to genuine Free Spirits, but they are a microscopic part of the whole. Others need to have form impressed upon them from without.[20]

In *Beyond Good and Evil,* Nietzsche gives only a brief intimation of a moral genealogy. Other genealogies can be found elsewhere in his corpus. At times of danger, he asserts, when fear arising from external

20. The need for a long compulsion is part of Nietzsche's understanding of the place of "sublimation." Our "drives" are sharpened and heightened by their suppression. In a more thoroughgoing sense than even Rousseau, Nietzsche questions whether man has any primary instincts or "Nature"; at least he questions whether we have them any more. "Instincts" are born out of habits and acts of sublimation that rest on one form or another of tyranny. Remove the counterpressure and they dissolve. This is the "problem of nature" in Nietzsche's thought. Since morality can be in accordance neither with Nature nor with Reason, Nietzsche concludes that its basis must be "unreason," which puts the matter in the most rhetorically memorable fashion. But this is not the same as saying that the existence of morality is unreasonable. It rather points to the importance of habit.

causes—from neighbors—is heightened, the need for preservation of the community—the unity of the herd—takes moral precedence. Threatening circumstances, which create the need for powerful individuals and leaders, are the basis of one set of moral virtues. In more sanguine times, powerful individuals are feared more than neighbors; everything that elevates an individual above the group then becomes a vice. The group becomes so timid that even just punishment seems unfair. New values are created in an attempt to abolish fear (*BG* #201). But even in ages of disintegration, dominated by "herd timidity," powerful individuals still arise, individuals of "multiple origins," made possible by a mixing of "instincts" and "races" as neighbors become less threatening and intermingle. Various drives and values fight each other externally and internally. The majority wants wars to end, but the same wars lead a few to greatness (*BG* #201). The homogenization of modern man is simultaneously an "involuntary arrangement for the cultivation of tyrants" (*BG* #242). "The frightening danger that they might fail to appear or that they might turn out badly or degenerate—these are *our* real worries and gloom" (*BG* #203). With their emergence, the cycle is complete and the return to the harsher origins is assured. Another reversal of values will occur. The implication is clear: The collapse of traditional values (aided by late-modern antifoundationalism) will eventuate in a bourgeois, egalitarian outcome for only a brief moment.

Like Kant, and contrary to Aristotle, Nietzsche denigrates any morality that has "happiness" as its highest end, because such a morality for him is nothing but a recipe for the destruction of our "instincts." Happiness as a moral end points toward "resting, . . . not being disturbed, . . . satiety, . . . finally attained unity, as 'sabbath of sabbaths'" (*BG* #200). One must have no dropping of the reins. The desire for happiness is the desire for tranquilization, for the overcoming of all tension. In the modern environment, the resultant immediate gratification of desires leads to their *weakening* and eventual nonexistence. Only if harshly restrained do the "passions" remain alive. And since rarely will one exact that harshness upon oneself—at best only a few truly distinctive beings will—it is necessary that the hardness be imposed from without by harsh circumstances and powerful individual wills. That man is a nothing points toward the need for discipline, not toward an "agent-oriented," or an-archic morality.

Throughout the central chapters on morality, Nietzsche uses the pronouns "us," "we," and "our" to refer to the Free Spirits or psychologists of the present. He differentiates "us" from a variety of other groups: the "philosophers of the future," future "commanders," "scholars," "scientists" (objective spirits), and "nobles," and especially *future* Free Spirits. Nietzsche asserts that "we" Free Spirits can at best provide the stimuli to the others. We have "partly to create and partly to exploit" the conditions for the "new types of philosophers *and* commanders" that will be necessary in the future (*BG* #203; emphasis mine). Those in the present who are capable of the "comprehensive look" must assume architectonic control. The general reduction of philosophy to "theory of knowledge," the hegemony of modern science, the autonomy of scholars and countless other similar phenomena are signs of architectonic abdication in the face of previous modern projections. The late-modern emancipation of scientific practitioners, scholars, and others from architectonic genius means they plod on endlessly without direction. This is one of the more refined effects of democracy, which is hardly surprising since for Nietzsche contemporary scientists and scholars merely support democratic tastes. Their autonomy was first set in motion when modern philosophy took precedence over theology, which in turn had taken precedence over original philosophy. Modern science and scholarship eventually emancipated themselves from modern philosophy. Hence came an autonomy and supremacy of the "specialist and nook dweller."[21]

Recalling a theme from the early works, Nietzsche asserts that we

---

21. According to Nietzsche, the great modern emancipation of science and scholarship from architectonic vision takes on a certain legitimacy because of the wretchedness of recent philosophy. Furthermore, modern science has come to flourish and has a good conscience because of its extreme utility. In this environment, philosophy becomes at best a handmaiden. Contemporary philosophy limits its pretensions to the mere clarification of problems generated elsewhere. This is not the noble, architectonic philosophy that is the queen of the sciences. Hence in the modern world the scholar who aims at disinterested knowledge has no guidance or leadership; he pursues his craft with at best a disinterested aimlessness, at worst in the grips of the Spirit of Revenge. His "dangerous unconcern" says "neither Yes nor No." Nothing in existence is affirmed. For Nietzsche, the task is, therefore, to find a way to reassert the supremacy of the higher over the lower, of those of vision over scholars, scientists, future philosophical laborers, theologians, "commanders," nobles, and so on.

Having castigated the scholars for thinking they could be free from philosophy— and after assigning even Kant and Hegel to the lower rank of "philosophical laborers" who merely work out the premises embedded in someone else's "legislation"— Nietzsche seems to conclude that those with a truly architectonic standpoint are so rare they may include only Socrates and himself. Be that as it may, the "philosophers of the future" will not have such a view. That is left to a few rare, epochal individuals like Nietzsche, who can create the broad horizon within which others, as his heirs and instruments, will fill in the details. The others include statesmen, scholars, scientists, poets, prophets, nobles, the "philosophers of the future," and probably even the solitary Free Spirits of the future.

Free Spirits of the present—those capable of the architectonic vision—are still burdened with the superhistorical sense, an ignoble sense that has a taste for everything: "*Measure* is alien to us; let us own it; our thrill is the thrill of the infinite, the unmeasured" (*BG* #224). Our virtue is "honesty." Our desire to know runs contrary to the "natural" desire for the superficial, the apparent, the surface (*BG* #229). The truly noble are horrified by this lively curiosity. Every noble culture is self-sufficient; it "naturally" loves what is its own and narrows its possibilities. But *we* can appreciate every possibility, unlike those in more noble ages which have a very definite yes and no. Nonetheless, Nietzsche goes on to call this historical sense our greatest virtue. We make a virtue of that which is a vice for a noble culture. Hence we Free Spirits of the present are assuredly ignoble, or at least the inevitable products of an ignoble culture. We cannot create the necessary noble, non-historical, cultured horizon.

It is against this backdrop that Nietzsche presents the central concept of *Beyond Good and Evil*. He asserts that the task which confronts the present is to "translate man back into nature; to became master over the many vain and overly enthusiastic interpretations and connotations that have so far been scrawled and painted over that eternal basic text of *homo natura*. . . . That may be a strange and insane task, but it is a *task*—who would deny that?" (*BG* #230). Late-modern man must come to stand before himself as modern man has stood before the rest of Nature up to now, as creator, and must *make of himself* a natural being. "Nature" is Nietzsche's solution to the problem of nihilism. But Nature is itself an immense problem. Primary Nature has been overcome, but according to Nietzsche, History should have Nature as its terminus at both ends. After a long movement, History must dissolve back into Nature—that is, into the rule of non-sense, Chance, fate, destiny, *fortuna,* the contingent and the unpredictable, "instinct" and appearance, the hegemony of the surface. Only those of superhistorical knowledge, capable of a comprehensive vision, who can subsume others under their projects, can make this possible.

The problem of Nature is highlighted by Nietzsche's discussion of women, which follows immediately. That Nietzsche should now turn to the subject of women seems, to be generous, non-sequitous. It is all too easy to accuse him of misogyny. But readers who recognize the rhetorical overkill and misdirection of Nietzsche's mode of writing elsewhere seem to forget that insight completely when it comes to this subject. On the surface, Nietzsche's remarks about women seem to range from gratuitous to outrageous. One must bear in mind, however, that Nietzsche puts woman forward as the paradigm of what is natural; read with this understanding, his discussion of women sheds light on the status of any potential recovery of *homo natura*.

Nietzsche asserts that "what inspires respect for woman, and often enough even fear, is her *nature,* which is more 'natural' than man's" (*BG* #239). Nietzsche's women care about beauty and appearance more than truth. They take the surface seriously. This ability to remain on the surface, in contact with the world of appearance, is something women possess "naturally." To be natural requires the "will to mere appearance, to simplification, to masks, to cloaks, in short, to the surface—for every surface is a cloak" (*BG* #230). To accept the surface of things (the realm of the *eide)* is to accept the differences that exist in the realm of appearance. Difference is a phenomenon of the surface; it exists only in relation to some Other. Hence the attempt to enlighten and emancipate women, which Nietzsche sees as an attempt to make women the same as men, destroys difference and threatens the reign of identity and nothingness. Given that there is no real natural substratum underlying human existence, uniformity is entirely possible (*BG* #239).[22] The distinction between male and female is one of the last remaining distinctions that *seem* to have their basis in primary Nature. In previous ages the rule of Necessity made various appearances harden into reality. But the distinctions that harsher times impose under the demands of necessity are eventually overcome, especially in a democratic age supported by modern technology. For Nietzsche this leads to a situation where one must will difference precisely because it does not exist by Nature. To that end, one must will opposition.[23]

As Marx saw, one of the things that follows from the modern con-

22. Nietzsche's philosophy of difference reduces to this: Difference rests on otherness. Otherness is contingent. Universal identity is as possible as difference. But total reduction to identity brings on the nihilistic reign of nothingness. Hence, otherness must be willed.

23. Consequently, one must not "go wrong on the fundamental problem of 'man and woman' [and] deny the most abysmal antagonism between them and the necessity of an eternal hostile tension" (*BG* #238). Further, "when the *man* in man is no longer desired and cultivated . . . woman degenerates. . . . Wherever the industrial spirit has triumphed over the military and aristocratic spirit, woman now aspires to the economic and legal self-reliance of a clerk . . . *woman is retrogressing*" (*BG* #239). When that happens, man necessarily retrogresses as well. If we wish the continued existence of the "Eternally-and-Necessarily-Feminine" as the counterpoise to a newly reinvigorated Eternally Masculine, it must be willed. All manner of other forms of difference must be willed as well by willing their preconditions. For Nietzsche, the recovery of difference is the prerequisite for the "retranslation" of man into Nature, because "Nature" is a mask, an Apollonian surface stretched over what is at best a mysterious, evanescent, malleable, and probably entropic core.

quest of Nature is the possibility of overcoming almost all manifestations of difference, from the differences between nations, classes, and town and country to the distinctions between male and female, young and old, healthy and normal, noble and ignoble, beautiful and ugly, and so on. But the maintenance or recovery of difference is central to Nietzsche's recovery of Nature. In the absence of primary Nature it becomes necessary to rely on Culture as the basis of difference. And Culture and race turn out to be related phenomena in Nietzsche's lexicon. A race is shaped by sharing a specific cultural space. New races are shaped by the coming together and mingling of the previously separate individuals in a new shared cultural space. Nietzsche observes that the democratization of Europe has brought about the mingling of previously separate peoples and classes. As a result Europeans have become more and more similar to each other; they simultaneously become less attached to the conditions under which previous racial distinctions originated, independent of any determining milieu, climate, place, or class. A supranational, nomadic, cosmopolitan type thus develops, which Nietzsche hopes will open up the possibility of forming a united European people capable of the task of global mastery.

It is for these reasons that Nietzsche is a proponent of "fatherlands," albeit not of modern nationalism. Nationalism for Nietzsche implies petty, atavistic, tribal politics. He has nothing but scorn for that petty nationalism, especially German nationalism. He looks to the formation of a *new* entity that could take a leading place in the "great politics" of the future. Nietzsche predicted that only large empires would be capable of acting politically in the age of global politics at the culmination of modernity. Hence, he asserts that "reason" dictates the emergence of a new people based on a shared, extended discipline, not the "fatherlandishness" of Bismarck or Wagner, which presumed preexisting "natural" differences. He asserts that all the important cultural phenomena of the recent past have favored the formation of "good Euroeans" and must be supported. Napoleon, Goethe, Beethoven, Stendhal, Heine, Schopenhauer, Delacroix—all unconsciously had the synthesis of Europe at heart. That synthesis moved inarticulately through their work, though they did not realize it: "Geniuses of [this] type rarely have the right to understand themselves." Instead they necessarily act in an unconscious fashion, they are "born enemies of logic," they are "inspired" (*BG* #256). Such inspiration helps form a people. The one Europe surges mysteriously through the inspired, unbeknownst even to them. They are moved silently by a spirit they cannot articulate, one Nietzsche wishes to channel and use because the Free Spirits of the present cannot form a people by simply willing it. To be natural again man

must be returned to the surface: the realm of poets, artists, and musi-
cians, types allegedly more likely to create a noble culture than are dialecticians.

Consequently Nietzsche, in his discussion of fatherlands, talks primarily not of statesmen or political leaders but of art and artists. Artists
are more important in the formation of the lasting character of fatherlands or "communities" than anyone else. Shared tastes silently determine a people; there is a prearticulate rhythm that is indicative of and
binds together any people. It manifests itself in, and is formed especially by, music. Nietzsche points to precisely the same phenomena as
does Socrates in his discussion of music in the *Republic*. Nietzsche also
has his own version of hardness or gymnastic. The prearticulate education of a people must simultaneously inculcate hardness and softness,
toughness and rhythm, taste and the martial spirit. Balance is required.
This is the basis of Nietzsche's praise of poets and artists. But they
should be no more autonomous than scientists or scholars.

Nietzsche asserts that "the 'European problem' as I understand it,
[is] the cultivation of a new caste that will rule Europe" (*BG* #251). He
surely did not mean a caste made up only of artists and composers, and
certainly not of solitary Free Spirits. Nietzsche wished to foster the reconstruction of Europe as a cultural entity, led by a new aristocracy,
shaped by indigenous artists and poets, which could assume global
leadership in the age of great politics that he predicted. He hoped that
the new European culture would transcend narrow nationalism and accomplish a mingling of many old races and stocks; he singles out especially the Jews, which he calls the strongest, toughest race in Europe. In
Nietzsche's vision, the Jews were to be amalgamated into Europe; the
Russians were to be Europe's great "Other" (*BG* #251).[24]

24. Nietzsche also praises the character of France and indicts that of England: "European *noblesse*—of feeling, of taste, of manners, taking the word, in short, in every
higher sense—is the work and invention of *France;* European vulgarity, the plebeianism
of modern ideas, that of *England*" (*BG* #253). Nietzsche's Englishmen are not philosophic, and they are likewise amusical (*BG* #252–53). It is not by accident, he asserts,
that the English are the home of modern science, particularly that of Darwin. No truly
noble spirit would grovel in "small and common facts," which requires "narrowness,
aridity, and industrious diligence" (*BG* #253). Nietzsche asserts that the true German
rises in disgust against these English ideas. But Germany is too "northern," it is dominated by "the gruesome northern gray on gray and the sunless concept-spooking and
anemia." It is the French who show the way by combining northern profundity and the
southern finesse and sensuousness. The future European culture must be light and gay,
and as we have seen before, must embody joy and dancing; a lively "tempo" will be of
major importance, something, we are told, which is impossible for Germans (*BG* #254).

Nobility and Difference

Nietzsche concludes *Beyond Good and Evil* with a discussion of nobility.[25] He asserts that "every enhancement of the type 'man' has so far been the work of an aristocratic society," and goes on to stress that we are to understand this in a quite straightforward sense. Every higher culture is begun by men of prey with a lust for power. From a harsh, predatory beginning a beautiful edifice can eventually be constructed, but one must pay a price to get from the amusical, superhistorical present to a cultured future: "In the beginning, the noble caste was always the barbarian caste: their predominance did not lie mainly in physical strength but in strength of the soul—they were more *whole* human beings (which also means, at every level, 'more whole beasts')" (*BG* #257). Such founders are "natural" in the sense of being untorn, unself-conscious, unified, and unidirectional in their impulses. The discussion recalls the aristocrats Socrates vanquished with dialectic in Nietzsche's earlier account. Such noble individuals not only stand at the *beginning* of a people, but justify the eventual emergence of the *pathos of distance* that makes other, higher types of individuals possible:

> Every enhancement of the type "man" has so far been the work of . . . a society that believes in the long ladder of an order of rank and differences in value between man and man, and that needs slavery in some sense or other. Without that *pathos of distance* which grows out of the ingrained difference between strata— when the ruling caste constantly looks afar and looks down upon subjects and instruments and just as constantly practices obedience and command, keeping down and keeping at a distance— that other, more mysterious pathos could not have grown up either—the craving for an ever new widening of distances *within the soul itself,* [emphasis mine] the development of ever higher, rarer, more remote, further-stretching, more comprehensive states. (*BG* #257)

A healthy aristocracy must wholeheartedly experience itself as the "*meaning* and highest justification" of all that exists. While it is only the Free Spirit who is the real justification of all that is, the aristocrats of the future must not know this; they must act with a good conscience free from a consciousness of having to follow theoretical projects posited

25. It should be noted that the word usually translated as "noble" is *vornehm*. *Vornehm* includes such ideas as "extraction," "origin," and "fortuitous birth."

by others. A healthy aristocracy also accepts with a good conscience that all other human beings are instruments provided for its sake (*BG* #258). Hence the true, noble aristocrat never concludes that what is necessary is to refrain mutually from injury, violence, and exploitation by placing one's will on a par with all others. Life requires limits. Someone must impose form on reality, and force others to accept *their* forms. On this level, the idea of the Will to Power gives ontological support to the forms imposed unself-consciously by the few. The new aristocrats must believe that their "will" is but a manifestation of a deep, ontological source.

One who senses himself as noble and masterful considers that his "proud states" of soul confer distinction and determine rank. It is always masters who initially posit the public value of things; slaves have only what value is attached to them by others (*BG* #260). The slavish additions to moral systems are always appendages to tablets that originate in aristocratic "instinct"—a theme developed more fully, and in a rhetorically more shrill fashion, in *On the Genealogy of Morals*. Nietzsche admits that for all practical purposes, all moralities are mixtures of the two (*BG* #260). Given that almost all moral codes are hybrids, drawing from what amount to contradictory sources, there will always be tensions and contradictions within any living moral system. A totally rational morality—which is both alive and legitimate—is impossible. To disturb healthy conventions to attain total rationality is always an error.

The noble individual forms his own opinion of himself and wishes others to conceive of him precisely as he conceives of himself. Nobles have no trouble determining who or what they are, are happy with themselves as they are, and never calculate or search for a persona that will publicly portray them as anything different from the way they are or conceive themselves to be (*BG* #261). This is as it should be: "Truly high respect one can have only for those who do not *seek* themselves" (*BG* #266).[26] Nietzsche asserts that the ignoble individual always waits for an opinion of himself and is delighted by every good opinion that he hears. Hence the ignoble are prone to vanity, for they want others to have a higher opinion of them than they have of themselves. This vanity strikes the noble as being in bad taste and showing a lack of self-respect; it is a kind of mask wearing that nobles disdain and eschew (*BG* #261). The noble individual is self-assertive without being vain. The conscious mask wearing of the Free Spirit would be seen as ignoble and vain by such a being, if he were to understand it.

26. Nietzsche is approvingly quoting Goethe to Rat Schlosser.

Master morality necessarily looks down and despises what is non-noble. In this type of morality, good and bad are indistinguishable from noble and contemptible. Further, "it is obvious that moral designations were everywhere first applied to *human beings* and only later, derivatively, to actions." The noble type of being experiences itself as determining values by merely following its unreflective inclinations. The noble individual judges that "what is harmful to me is harmful in itself; it knows itself to be that which first accords honor to things. . . . Such a morality is self-glorification" (*BG* #260).

Nonetheless, noble morality also leads to a reverence for age and tradition. The horizon of temporality that predominates for the noble consciousness is the past, unlike ignoble moderns for whom the future takes hegemony. The preference for the future corresponds with the modern belief in progress, and brings with it a lack of respect for the past. It is the respect for tradition and the past upon which law rests for those generations of nobles who come after the "founding": "All law rests on [a] double reverence—the faith and prejudice in favor of ancestors and disfavor of those yet to come are typical of the morality of the powerful" (*BG* #260). The hegemony of the noble individual leads in the direction of traditionalism rather than legalism. On the other hand, slave morality is based on a pessimistic suspicion about the whole condition of mankind. It leads up to virtues such as pity, a warm heart, patience, industry, humility, and friendliness—in short, virtues that ease the existence of those who suffer—because of a concern that one may eventually suffer and need such care in return. This is the origin of the opposition *good* and *evil*. The good is seen as that which is non-dangerous and unthreatening; evil is all power and strength and anything which inspires fear. In slave morality the *bonhomme* with his lack of striving and the lack of tension in his soul becomes the standard and the norm (*BG* #260).

When the noble confers value on things, that imposition of value then becomes the basis of a *nomos*. Future generations come to venerate that *nomos* and venerate those who brought it forth. As a result a tradition emerges and is maintained. The movement Nietzsche presents is from barbarism to a traditional *ethos*. Nietzsche can praise this noble dialectic not because he thinks it represents the highest of human possibilities, but because he thinks it is the prerequisite for the mode of existence he does find highest. He is explicit in stating that the fact that he can praise the noble is not the same as saying he thinks it is the most choice-worthy life: "'He praises me: *hence* he thinks I am right'—this asinine inference spoils half our life for us hermits, for it leads asses to seek our neighborhood and friendship" (*BG* #283). In many ways the aristocrat that Nietzsche describes is put forward as a simple datum of Nature, but given Nietzsche's understanding of the "problem of Nature," this simply cannot be. In fact, the existence of the aristocratic noble and his "hardness, uniformity and simplicity of form" rest primarily on a response to difficult conditions—i.e., "through the long fight with essentially constant *unfavorable* conditions. . . . In this way a type with few but very strong traits, a species of severe, warlike, prudently taciturn men . . . is fixed beyond the changing generations."

But eventually "conditions become more fortunate and the tremendous tension decreases" (*BG* #262). The basis of the old discipline collapses; it remains, if it does, only as a matter of taste, no longer due to necessity. It is then that less "unified" types become prevalent. At this point in the evolution of an aristocratic age "variations" emerge, either as something higher and more subtle or as monstrosities. The "individual" comes forth and dares to be individual and different, to transcend tradition in favor of individual idiosyncrasies. No longer is there limit or restraint; the old morality slackens, is shaken, and dissolves, to be replaced by mass idiosyncrasy which leads inevitably toward homogeneity. In this fashion, the victory of the non-noble is assured. By a necessary dialectic, this victory brings with it the unbending of the human bow. But when this state of affairs holds sway, the pathos of distance, which makes possible the only genuine, philosophic kind of individuality, is threatened. The instinct for reverence collapses and the sense of high rank, the "height of a soul" *(meglopsychia),* decays.

Simultaneously, there is a loss of reverence for those great documents that form a ladder of veneration. Eventually everyone traipses about in the "great books" and they are "figured out" and lose their moral function (*BG* #263). The loss of a sense of reverence is a sign of the decline of the sense of nobility.[27] Everything militates against the

27. There are other reasons why nobility is always a fragile growth. Different races or peoples are shaped by different recurring, shared inner experiences. It would be impossible for the entire species to have had the same experiences. In time, Nietzsche asserts, concepts are developed as signs for these shared inner experiences. Over time, the process of abbreviation continues, which is the necessary course of any language (*BG* #268). Need and danger bring together human beings who must be able to suggest to each other similar meanings in a short time. But this process of abbreviation levels off the nuances of experience, and leaves only its most common aspect. By its very nature, language is ignoble; it makes everything common. Language, while a necessity, is always a problem—i.e., a political and moral problem that brings commonness and decay. This is all the more reason why *nomos* must grow up from some inarticulate, prelinguistic source and rest on a basis that is not penetrable by speech. For this same reason, real philosophy should exist in silence, not speech. Contrary to Derrida, for

existence of the noble, especially when need and danger decrease. The higher human being is always in the greatest danger. The ruination of higher souls is the rule.

Our time, at least for Nietzsche, is a time of superabundance and ease. It is this more than anything else which makes it deficient in noble *consciousnesses*. One must re-create threatening circumstances to recover noble morality; that is part of what willing the Eternal Recurrence implies. For Nietzsche nobility is primarily a phenomenon of consciousness, not of primary Nature. A noble consciousness requires an ignoble consciousness as its Other. A strong Hegelian element survives in this understanding. That in turn means that a strong modern element remains. For Nietzsche there are different levels of "nobility," but all are based on the consciousness of height, distance, and distinctiveness. The ladder of nobility is discontinuous; between the higher and lower rungs there is a radical incommensurability.[28] For example, suffering is another way in which rank is determined: "Profound suffering makes noble; it separates." But the deep suffering of those "elect of knowledge" forces upon them masks and disguises, which is to say they want to be judged by others differently than they judge themselves (*BG* #270). This is certainly a different kind of nobility than that of the aristocratic individual who assigns values to all things. The desire of the "true psychologist and Free Spirit" to be misunderstood takes many forms, from casualness to cheerfulness to superficiality; "occasionally even foolishness is the mask for an unblessed all-too-certain knowledge." This is all necessary for any of those of the tribe of "free, insolent spirits who would like to conceal and deny that they are broken, proud, incurable hearts" (*BG* #270). Free Spiritedness is a burden as much as a joy. For Nietzsche, philosophy is no longer the simple, pure pleasure of Greek *theoria*. The Free Spirits must

---

Nietzsche words have experiential referents. They are more than signs endlessly signifying only other signs. Nonetheless, as Derrida asserts is true of all Western writing, Nietzschean writing is at a second remove from the origins, with speech being closer to the source. Words are auditory signs for shared experiences, and written words are but signs for the primary auditory signs.

28. Nietzsche is at some rhetorical pains to leave this incommensurability ambiguous so that these different types of noble spirits will be able to sense that which they share rather than that in which they are incommensurable. Again, on the one hand we have the politically involved, proud individual and on the other, the solitary "saint" whose pity "is pity with the *dirt* of what is human, all too human" (*BG* #271). Those not capable of the highest peaks are necessary: "To condescend to them, for a few hours; to *seat* oneself on them as on a horse, often as on an ass—for one must know *how to make use of* [emphasis mine] their stupidity as much as of their fire" (*BG* #284).

"[invent] the good conscience to enjoy their souls for once as *simple;* and the whole of morality is a long undismayed forgery which alone makes it at all possible to enjoy the sight of the soul. From this point of view much more may belong in the concept of 'art' than is generally believed" (*BG* #291).

11

Nietzsche's Vision of the Postmodern Future

> Philosophy forms . . . a sanctuary apart, and those
> who serve constitute an isolated order of priests, who
> must not mix with the world, and whose work is to
> protect the possessions of Truth.
>
> Hegel, *Lectures on the Philosophy of Religion*, 3:151

In Nietzsche's "philosophy" we see the simultaneous intensification and disintegration of modern thought. The Will attains hegemony, but the modern faith in the desirability of the conquest of Chance (Nature) is reversed. I have bracketed "philosophy" because as Rousseau remarked about his "legislators," Nietzsche was in no position to use either simple persuasion or presently constituted power to accomplish his ends (*SC* 151). Despite the fact that for Nietzsche Western philosophy was the ultimate cause of nihilism, a new philosophy could not undo the problem through a transformation of understanding alone. A political and moral project was also required.[1] Nietzsche hoped that future *praxis,* if freed from revengeful modern theory, might regain a degree of autonomy, moving in response to its own laws and rhythms. To protect such a *praxis,* future free-spirited philosophy had to be reconstituted to avoid the Spirit of Revenge. To do so it would have to refrain from revengefully imposing theoretical projects upon *praxis.* In the process, several *post*modern notes are sounded.

All of modern thought had diverted philosophy into a form of practical activity, and *praxis* eventually became fully, self-consciously informed by theory. For Nietzsche, that amalgamation of philosophy and *praxis* was central to the nihilism he wished to transcend. The key to Nietzsche's postmodernity is his attempt to sever theory and practice. This was the prerequisite for the revaluation of values.[2] Only because of the need for a *transition* to a novel future did Nietzsche see a

---

1. I say this despite Nietzsche's protestations that he is antipolitical, by which he means antinationalist, antistate, anti-Bismarck, and so on. He was anti–*modern* politics, but he understood the place of the closed horizon of a distinctive moral *ethos* in human affairs.

2. This means that, contrary to Hegel, the free-spirited philosopher of the future would eschew public "recognition." Real wise men, as opposed to the "Famous Wise Men" of *Zarathustra,* would cease to see honor before the majority as their highest end.

need for philosophy to project one last public teaching upon the world. But it was a teaching that aimed at overcoming itself.

Nietzsche believed that without values that were believable—i.e., seen as intrinsically valuable—man would remain in the squalid enervation of the "last man," at a time when planetary rule was his destiny. The smallest man would walk the earth when the greatest of men were required. Long-range planning in the use of immense new forces was needed; but the will to long-range perseverance was missing. Values had to seem to be grounded in something bigger than man, beyond man's individual will. This possibility rested on illusions; remythologization was required. But myths are only useful when they are taken as true. The poet who begins by explaining that his or her images are illusions is as inept as the magician who begins by explaining the forthcoming trick—unless the real trick lies at a still deeper level. Thus philosophers could not simply will myths and hope that suspicious late-modern individuals would accept them as truths.

In an attempt to overcome an impending impasse, Nietzsche had to accomplish several things: (1) accelerate and bring to a climax the decay of the old values, which were no longer believable but were inhibiting new growth; (2) as a means to so doing, heighten the self-conscious awareness that man alone is the source of all valuation, thereby setting in motion fragmentation and eventual chaos; and (3) eventually get the vast majority of humanity to forget the past and the life-destroying truths that stand at the basis of human existence—i.e., take up the rope of transition and destroy it. The problem was that the first two necessities required the heightening of the self-consciousness of modern man, while the latter required its overcoming. Of necessity, any public teaching had to be paradoxical. Nietzsche had to say different things to different people—that is, to philosophic and nonphilosophic humanity[3] —and different things to present and future man, and to say them all simultaneously. His distinctive mode of writing was adopted in response to these requirements.

According to Nietzsche, man had reached this impasse—"the de-

---

3. "The hermit does not believe that any philosopher—assuming that every philosopher was first of all a hermit—ever expressed his real and ultimate opinions in books: does one not write books precisely to conceal what one harbors? . . . Every philosophy is a foreground philosophy" (*BG* #289). "Every profound thinker is more afraid of being understood than of being misunderstood. The latter may hurt his vanity, but the former his heart, his sympathy, which always says: 'Alas, why do *you* want to have as hard a time as I did?'" (*BG* #290). In the last analysis, Nietzsche presupposes one fundamental kind of natural difference, that between the philosophic and the nonphilosophic. This distinction might be a form of "spiritual elitism"; or it might be an empirical fact.

valuation of all values"—because he had launched so radically into the exploration of the "self" begun by Socrates, deepened by Christianity, and brought to a peak by modern philosophy. In the self all man had found was the increasingly abstract, self-grounding Will. The only remaining guidance for the Will was the abstract universal, which promised the destruction of all difference and the reduction of humanity to the identity of the last man. Humanity had to be emancipated from groundless, self-legislating subjectivity, radical self-consciousness, and revengeful theoretical projecting. This emancipation of *praxis* pointed toward immersion in groups with their own distinctive "Cultures." Precisely because man does not have a Nature, a Culture, i.e., a "second nature," was necessary. In Nietzsche's understanding, the solution to the problem of late-modern nihilism was not the universalization of the radical individualism that is possible only for the few self-disciplined Free Spirits. Nietzsche's project points toward both community and radical individualism, but limits the latter to only a few Free Spirits who would exist in conjunction with a genuine community. Further, Nietzsche thought the basis of community in a very resolute fashion. Postmodern communities would require a basis in an inarticulate *ethos,* the origin of which, Nietzsche thought—following Machiavelli—would be inevitably harsh.

Philosophers of the present cannot will cultures *ex nihilo.* A culture must grow up *spontaneously* from indigenous sources. But the late modern world threatens and delegitimizes those sources. The job of the philosophers of the present was to create the conditions for indigenous spontaneity and to legitimize its products. That required "innocence and forgetting," a return to the surface, a respect for the realm of appearance, and an acceptance of the earth both as external given and as it rises up unconsciously within us. In other words, man had to *become* "natural" again. But for Nietzsche, Nature is a problem, something into which man must be "retranslated." Man needed to recover a sense of otherness. For that to be possible, one must transcend "metaphysical freedom." Nietzsche's response to modern nihilism was to will the "flight *from* the self," which had to be made to look like a "flight *back* to Nature." For Nietzsche this was a willing of a return to that which modern man initially willed to quit (GS #109, 167–69). Hence Nietzsche *wills* the existence of a "natural" humanity, even though he admits there has never really been a natural humanity (*WP* 73; *Z* 552).

If Nietzsche thought that self-consciousness had been merely appended to *homo natura* like a surface or skin obscuring a deeper reality, sublimating and suppressing it—e.g., in Freudian fashion—his task would have been much simpler and his writings less complicated. Then his only task would be to destroy the hegemony of democratic, bourgeois, secularized Christendom, remove the moral restraints of the past, step back, and let Nature reassert itself, as the jungle quickly reclaims the asphalt and mortar. For Nietzsche, however, the problem of man's *re*integration into Nature is complicated by the fact that once one strips through the surface that is modern self-consciousness, one confronts not a wild animal but something more "shameful"—a fundamentally indeterminate being—a shameful nakedness at its worst.[4] The body "is" primarily what the spirit attaches itself to: "Even the determination of what is healthy for your *body* depends on your goal, your horizon, your energies, your impulses, your errors, and above all on the ideals and phantasms of your soul" (*GS* #120, 177). For Nietzsche the great danger posed by late-modern man's fundamental indeterminacy is the "last man" who reveres nothing, and thereby falls into a complete abyss of nothingness. According to Nietzsche, in late modernity, what is left is a dispirited mass that flees its emptiness into a mindless gratification that makes order and leadership impossible. Great technological sophistication comes at a time when man no longer has any high purposes to guide and master it.

For Nietzsche, man becomes human by being the Other of the nonhuman; he becomes male by being the Other of woman, master by being the Other of a slave, European by being the Other of the non-European, and so on, with all manner of distinctions. These distinctions are needed but are not fundamentally natural. This veneer, or surface, born of the contingent nexus of difference needs to be defended. Future humanity would have to be determined by accepting a variety of differential roles beyond which it would not seek to interrogate further (*BG* 215; *GS* 38). Man would have to act "as if" he were determined by instinct, without delving into the self in search of rules for action (*GS* #354, #356, 297–300, 302–3). Difference had to appear natural or all action would be ironic, detached, uncommitted. Nietzsche did not long for an ironic civilization. For the sake of life, it was necessary to posit in such a way as to create the ground for the reemergence of difference and intense action with a good conscience.

Future individuals would not be simply equal when robbed of self-consciousness. The unreflective "instinct" of one or a few would be

---

4. "A naked human being is generally a shameful sight. I am speaking of us Europeans (and not even of female Europeans!). . . . I am not suggesting that all this is meant to mask human malice and villainy—the wild animal in us; my idea is, on the contrary, that it is precisely as *tame animals* that we are a shameful sight and in need of the moral disguise" (*GS* #352, 295).

predominant. Whatever those willful ones "desired" would be seen by them as cosmically *good*; what countered their desire would be seen as *bad* (*BG* 204–5). Those individuals would feel no qualms about using others to pursue their own good as they see it (*BG* 202, 205). Some would unreflectively "will"; others would obey. Action would take on the look of being instinctive, for it would not proceed from self-conscious calculation. "Be thyself" would replace "know thyself" as an oracular maxim. Out of modern homogeneity, difference would be re-created, first through the difference of *strata* and the resultant differentiation of consciousnesses. And the mass of individuals would again find values "outside" of themselves, not be exhorted to look for them within.

Over time, very long periods of time, cultural patterns would ossify as bodily traits. One could come to have a "Nature" eventually, as long as one avoided the constant cultural vacillation and aimless flux of the last man, who flits from one fad to another, at best living off the cultural heritage of the past but never creating any new *nomoi* which could in time become the basis of a new *physis*. But the *nomoi* must appear to grow up from the soil along with the rest of the flora and fauna, from the core of Being understood as Will to Power. *Nomos* must also appear to flow from "inspiration," which in turn must be perceived to have an ontological foundation (*EH* 300–1). Nietzsche has *willed* both aspects of Socrates' noble lie: political and moral hierarchy has an ontological basis, and human beings are rooted in the soil of a native place. The problem is that all of this rests on perfectly modern, predatory, Machiavellian beginnings and the modern hegemony of the Will.

For Nietzsche, our only possibility of transcending nihilism in the future lies in allowing traditions to reemerge, and revering and nurturing them (*BG* 205–6). His attack on the old, moribund traditions is not an attack on traditionalism per se. It is, in fact, just the opposite.[5] Locked in a cultural horizon, future humanity could have a present that it would not revengefully try to quit in endless pursuit of a categorically different future. Only by finding joy in the present can we transcend the Spirit of Revenge and affirm life. In a future present moment, individuals would turn more to the past than to the future to de-

---

5. "*First proposition of civilisation.*—Among barbarous peoples there exists a species of customs whose purpose appears to be custom in general: minute and fundamentally superfluous stipulations . . . which, however, keep continually *in the consciousness* [emphasis mine] the constant proximity of custom, the perpetual compulsion to practise customs: so as to strengthen the mighty proposition with which civilisation *begins* [emphasis mine]: any custom is better than no custom" Friedrich Nietzsche, *Daybreak*, aphorism 16, 15.

fine themselves—to their "having-been." According to Nietzsche, the past is more consistent with the possibility of having a present—and the unhistoricality that makes life possible—than the priority of the future, which takes hegemony in modern thought.[6] But we are still *in transition* to the future, even if in that future we hope to escape the modern need to be endlessly in transition.

Our confusion in understanding Nietzsche grows from the fact that his new aristocrats, the ground of the new *nomoi,* are lumped ambiguously under such catch-all rubrics as noble and overman. On the one hand, the overman/aristocrat is the "instinctive," vital, active man who will not be torn, and who will act with a single will. The overman is a Dionysian, a warrior, committed to earth and body, who will not see self-interestedness, lust, and despotic rule as vices. But Nietzsche says repeatedly that the overman/Free Spirit will pursue truth unmercifully. He will be a solitary who subjects himself to immense psychological cruelty and self-restraint (*BG* 41, 49–50). In the presentation of the overman/noble we seemingly have the combination of the active and the solitary, cruel restraint and "instinctive," "inspired" outpouring. The overman/noble looks like the merging of the traditional active and theoretical men, a perception capped by Nietzsche's observation that the overman represents "Caesar with the soul of Christ." But nobility ("magnanimity") is especially incompatible with the pursuit of truth, as much for Nietzsche as it was for Aristotle. As one sees in Nietzsche's discussion "What Is Noble," the noble, magnanimous man is clearly not philosophic and requires linkage with a distinct people. It is beyond all such cultural wholes that the true philosopher is to be found (*WP* 514–15). Why does Nietzsche leave his idea of the overman/noble so ambiguous and loaded with incompatible characteristics?[7] It is not because he wishes—in modern fashion—to see

6. Nietzsche's destructive work aims at clearing the field for the emergence of a noble, aristocratic *consciousnesses.* The praise of willfulness, hardness, and the desire to rule justifies the rule of those "great-souled" men. New aristocrats would bring into being what is the primary practical value—permanence: "Duration is a first-rate value on earth" (*GS* #356, 302–3). And permanence is what is impossible under the rule of vacillating last men. The ability to persevere is what is most required if man is to accomplish global mastery without destroying his species or reducing it to animality. The future could be made safe only on the basis of a profound aristocratic reverence for the past, which could carry forth a tradition into the future.

7. This ambiguity is reminiscent of Plato's conscious blurring of the distinction between the philosopher and the gentleman, with its resultant lack of a clear distinction between intellectual and moral virtue. Plato did this so that the gentleman could believe that the peak of the active life represented the peak of existence, and from the other side,

praxis and thinking merge. It is for precisely the opposite reason. Nietzsche wishes to reverse the modern amalgamation of thinking and *praxis,* returning autonomy to *praxis* and epicureanizing thinking. Nietzsche constructs a long ladder of rank and hierarchy with the true philosopher at the peak. But he is at pains rhetorically not to differentiate the rungs of the ladder too clearly.

At the top of the ladder of rank stands the true philosopher qua Free Spirit: "The new philosopher can arise only in conjunction with a ruling caste, as its highest spiritualization" (*WP* 512). Nietzsche has concluded that in the future true philosophy will be safest in an aristocratic society. The question of what regime best defends philosophy is a venerable one. One should recall how Plato depicts the fascination of the aristocratic young with Socrates, and his singular lack of success with the *demos.* Yet it was a democracy that allowed Socrates to practice philosophy *in the open* of the marketplace until he was in his seventies. But this is precisely what Nietzsche does not want his future breed of philosophers to do—practice in the open. This is not only for the sake of keeping the philosophers from the fatal mistake of trying revengefully to transform the world; it is also to shield the practical world from their life-destroying truths. The true Free Spirit would not have to rule except on millennial occasions, which would be a check on his desire to intrude and invent "ideals" and change the world, thereby succumbing to the Spirit of Revenge and falling into the trap of all past philosophy.

If Nietzsche's willing is successful, he hopes humanity will be thrust onto a historically unique and safe plane, becoming "again" part of the ebb and flow of natural forces. Humanity would revert to a situation like that of its beginnings. But this "recurrence" to the beginnings cannot be complete. There is no simple metaphysical recurrence of the same; if there were, there would be no need for Nietzsche to *will* his project. Indeed Nietzsche says of the doctrine of the Eternal Recurrence that it stands in history as a "mid-point," and that at some point it will be necessary to "dispose" of it (*WP* 544–45). As a midpoint it is clearly an illusion, *useful* at that point. While not the final metaphysical wisdom or the correct word for all epochs and times, it will be *the* word for the next epoch. Manipulated innocence and forgetting will be required at intervals. New poems will be needed. Repeated returns to the "beginnings" must be willed because Nature does not accomplish this alone.

---

to show the true philosopher in the least radical light, allowing him to withdraw to a degree of solitude. Nietzsche's practical project requires a comparable, although not identical, ambiguity.

Nietzsche tried, at a time when genuine *praxis* was in danger of being replaced by the administration of things or the "invisible hand's" autonomous determination of merely economic man, to give *praxis* a new dignity and autonomy. At a time when philosophy seemed at an end, he sought to restore the possibility of philosophy as a way of life rather than something always eventuating in dogmatic systems and the Spirit of Revenge. At a time when the work ethic had evolved into a commitment to production and consumption as ends in themselves, he posited the basis for a leisure class and a vision of the dignity of leisure as the highest kind of activity. In the face of ever-encroaching uniformity, Nietzsche tried to radically rethink the basis for the reemergence of significant diversity and difference. In a time of constant change and the hegemony of idiosyncrasy, he sought a basis for something that could stand the test of time, for duty, obligation, and cross-generational respect.

In many ways, Nietzsche tried to find his way back. Like other modern thinkers before him, he attempted to recover at least surrogates of past possibilities; but he did so while retaining and heightening the modern commitment to the Will, together with the notion that all difference is a contingent phenomenon primarily of consciousness. To get to the future "recovery" it was necessary for man to pass through yet another modern transition, in this case an extended period of moral, philosophical, political, and psychological crisis. Even if the things Nietzsche tried to recover are desirable, it remains unclear whether his teaching could ever get humanity beyond the chaos of the *transition* to the future to which he dedicated his life's work. No doubt it is the desire for recovery, together with the refusal to reject the core principles of modern philosophy, that led him to pose the contemporary problem in such a radical fashion. In the process, Nietzsche helped leave generations of contemporary individuals with no present in which to live, and with rapidly diminishing hope for the future.

With Nietzsche, one is left with the hegemony of the self-grounding, modern Will. If that is our only ground, why may not one will the universal, cosmopolitan society of free, equal, and prosperous individuals, supported by modern science and technology and consummated on a bed of democratic anarchism, as do so many "left Nietzscheans" (a.k.a. postmodernists)? The answer hinges on an empirical judgment. Will the collapse of age-old philosophic, moral, and political beliefs—which Nietzsche both sees happening and exacerbates—lead in a cosmopolitan, democratic direction or in the parochial, hierarchical direction

Nietzsche both predicts and wills? In part 4 I will suggest there is evidence that Nietzsche's empirical prediction has significant force.

Another question is unavoidable. Is Nietzsche on solid ground in attempting to reverse modernity with modern means? Heidegger will argue that the answer is no. As I will argue in part 3, Heidegger tries to fashion other tools. But Nietzsche uses almost entirely modern tools in his attempt to transcend modernity. In perfectly modern fashion, he still sees the world as our projection. Nietzsche radicalizes the core Cartesian premise—the world is not in any serious sense *self*-presenting—and announces explicitly what was implicit from the beginning of modernity: in positing the world, Will engages in an act of *poiesis*. In Nietzsche, modern Reason, now freed entirely from Nature and History, is autonomous as self-grounding Will, and poetry is finally freed from mathematical and epistemological limitations; it is unlimited in the forms it may impose.

Nietzschean philosophy, like all earlier modern philosophy, is still hypothetical, proceeding on the basis of the ubiquitous modern "as if." We must proceed as if there was one mode of causality, the efficient causality of Will to Power, as if all reality constantly circled back on itself, as if everything is caught in the grips of Eternal Recurrence—thereby attempting to overcome the modern linear conception of Time. Nietzsche proceeds as if Will to Power and Eternal Recurrence were true, in the hopes that behavior will be transformed and change ensue—a change that in some sense he thought could be predicted.[8] In perfectly modern fashion Nietzsche still gives primacy to the future and projects the need for yet another transitional period. All of modernity has been "on the way," incapable of occupying its present with a good conscience. And in conjunction with the need for a transition, the elitism of the philosopher manipulating reality from the wings returns, at least until the transition is complete. The philosopher *of the present* is still primarily a "legislator."

Many of the things Nietzsche posits for the future are fundamentally *anti*modern. He tries to move man back to the surface, to convince late modernity to take the realm of appearance seriously and accept it with a good conscience, and to give the realm of appearance an ontological foundation.[9] But Hegel, to give but one example, had attempted that

---

8. Nietzsche cannot be a thoroughgoing "poststructuralist"; otherwise prediction would be impossible. The world is, in some fashion, still a predictable place for Nietzsche despite what he posits.

9. It is frequently claimed that Nietzsche's return to the surface merely brings about

before him. [10] Nietzsche attacks modern philosophy's subjectivism and faith in autonomous self-consciousness. He argues against the possibility of radical individual autonomy—only to turn around and grant that possibility to Free Spirits—and asserts instead the necessity of participation in a community. Again Hegel had made the same attempt to establish the importance of "ethical substance." But as Heidegger will observe, the conscious willing or positing of a "we" or "community" is but another manifestation of modern subjectivism.

In similar fashion, Nietzsche wills a return to "spiritedness" and "great-souledness." He tries to reestablish the legitimacy of honor and nobility, which prior modernity had fixed as at the heart of what had to be transcended. Nietzsche wills us back to "Nature," understood as a move back to a nonself-conscious acceptance of appearance and the surface, primary Nature having dissolved, and he wills the future hegemony of Chance. He wills the move beyond metaphysical freedom toward the reenthronement of contingency—one must affirm life by loving Fate. But in doing so, he retains the central, altogether modern premise that Nature does not exist in any self-subsistent way. "Nature" must be willed as a myth. Further, Nietzsche relies on the key element of Hegel's phenomenological codification of modernity: Different consciousnesses are constituted primarily in relation to each other. This list could be expanded, but the point I am making should be clear: Most of Nietzsche's positing is *anti*modern, but even in willing the antimodern his means are consistently modern.

The distinctively *post*modern in Nietzsche's thought has as its basis the critique of the Spirit of Revenge which points toward the need for a new revenge-free philosophy. A postmodern thinking, understood as free-spirited, would have to take itself out of the business of legislation, manipulation, change, and control. To be free of the Spirit of Revenge, the postmodern thinker would have to rein himself in. A change of attitude on the part of the philosophers launched modernity; another change of attitude would be required to transcend it. A philosophy freed from the Spirit of Revenge would have to affirm life as it presents *itself.* This might require retiring frequently to private conversation

---

an inversion of the Platon*ism* which had given priority to the realm of disembodied ideas. We should not forget, however, that the Platonic forms are *eide;* they draw their very being from the surface "look" of things. Hence Plato's "metaphysics" is not as far removed from the realm of appearance as some claim, and he is not as far from Nietzsche as some believe.

10. In Nietzsche's eyes Hegel had failed, for the task cannot be accomplished *theoretically.* It has to be accomplished poetically, and that implies a moral/political component.

with a few friends. But I will argue that it does not require the complete, longed-for Nietzschean epicureanization of thought. There are other ways to maintain an ongoing victory over the Spirit of Revenge. Still, the vision of a new, revenge-free philosophy represents one postmodern element in Nietzsche's thought.

The opposite side of this coin is the need for a recovery of a *praxis* that is autonomous to the extent that it is not in the service of *theoretical* projects. That requires reflection on how *nomoi* can be generated "internally," from out of life itself. In part 4, I will call this attempted recovery of autonomy for *praxis* the "recovery of the political." I do not believe it requires that we deliver ourselves over to predatory nobles or idiosyncratically inspired poets and artists. And I do not believe that a postmodern *praxis* has to be at odds with limited, constitutional government.

PART THREE

Heidegger's Critique
of Modernity and the
Postmodern Future

12

Recovering Heidegger

Heidegger simultaneously attacks the modern elements in Nietzsche's thought and expands and ontologically deepens the potentially postmodern elements—a new vision of thinking freed from the Spirit of Revenge, and a newly autonomous *praxis*—in a way that makes him Nietzsche's most profound student. Heidegger's emendation of Nietzsche yields valuable new weapons that can be added to a *post*modern arsenal. But before it is possible to see the ways in which this is true, it is necessary to free Heidegger's thought from the misleading interpretative orthodoxies that have grown up around it.

In his discussion of Free Spirits, Nietzsche observes that all great thinkers require masks, and around their work masks are always growing. A variety of such masks have already grown up around the thought of Heidegger, principally surrounding his involvement in National Socialism. Needless to say, as reflection on his posthumously published "Nur Noch Ein Gott Kann Uns Retten" will show, Heidegger is responsible for projecting some of those masks himself. The orthodox dogma regarding the Heideggerian "turn" *(Kehre)* or "reversal" was just such a mask projected to insulate Heidegger from criticism. But in the aftermath of the affair surrounding the publication of Victor Farías's *Heidegger and Nazism,* it will be difficult to return to this approach.[1]

---

1. Farías, *Heidegger and Nazism;* for an extended discussion of this issue see my "Heidegger's Postmodern Politics?" Given its philosophical merits, the Farías volume has already been overcommented upon, and I will not extensively reconsider it here. It can be said that it is simultaneously useful and disappointing. Farías refers us to pertinent documents that have only recently become readily available in the English-speaking world, but he seldom quotes pertinent, primary texts, and when he does it is at times in questionable ways. Farías presents us with a tour through the young Heidegger's family life, provincial hometown, early church affiliations, and gymnasium environment; an exegesis of the philosophical ruminations of Frau Elfride Heidegger-Petri

According to what was becoming an almost universal interpretative picture prior to Farías, the allegedly still modern voluntarism, subjectivism, and "metaphysical" tendencies of the early Heidegger's thought, especially as expressed in *Being and Time,* made the Nazi "mistake" possible; but the later Heidegger turned away from this understanding—he reversed his thinking. According to this interpretation, if one jettisons the "early" Heidegger and turns instead to the "later" work, the Nazi issue disappears.[2] I will try to show that while Heidegger frequently changed his *mode of speech,* he thought one central, ontological thought and pursued an unchanging vision through-

---

(in such works as "Thoughts of a Mother on the Higher Education of the Young"); and the extraordinary argument that one of the central thinkers in Heidegger's life was Abraham a Sancta Clara (pp. 228–34). Along the way we get a look at the pivotal years 1933–35. Throughout we are introduced to seemingly everyone who eventually received a NSDAP card and was ever in the vicinity of Heidegger from the time of his infancy. The result is either an in-depth proof that no one lives and thinks in a vacuum or a thoroughgoing demonstration of the plausibility of guilt by association. The philosophical trivialities of this account detract from making the obvious case: Heidegger thought National Socialism somehow advanced at least some of the ends he desired. A far more substantial account has now been published by the Freiburg historian Hugo Ott in his *Martin Heidegger: A Political Life.*

Nonetheless, beyond the annoying fascination with the tawdry and the human, all too human, we get a picture that cannot be dismissed and should provide our point of departure. Heidegger miscalculated grossly, was stubborn to the point of indecency, and was so coolly detached as to be unable to differentiate between mechanized modern agriculture and extermination camps. A picture emerges of a stern and generally humorless man who because of frequent moral waffling on occasions when resolute courage was called for, had at best an ambiguous character that, at least retrospectively and from the outside, makes him appear to be a very unappealing person. It is now clear, as it should have been from the beginning to any attentive reader, that Heidegger's association with National Socialism was not an accident on the part of a politically naive thinker. Nor was it a momentary infatuation. The attempt to disseminate this picture by French apologists like Jean Beaufret and his student Francois Fedier should have been seen though from the beginning. We now hear from Derrida that he knew long ago that this story was fanciful, yet refrained from unmasking it. See Neske and Kettering, *Martin Heidegger and National Socialism,* 145–48. Derrida was not alone in his silence. That Heidegger's support of National Socialism was not an aberration was clear enough without Farías's *Heidegger and Nazism.* As Gadamer has observed, everyone in Germany knew from the beginning what Farías presumed to have "uncovered." See Neske and Kettering, *Martin Heidegger and National Socialism,* 141.

2. Unlike the reversal theorists, I will argue that it is necessary to begin with the fact of Heidegger's association with National Socialism, even though it is noteworthy that Heidegger's thought, unlike Nietzsche's writings, was never co-opted by Nazi propagandists. One must understand how Heidegger's thought could lead to both his involvement with and rejection of National Socialism. That has seldom been done in any straightforward way. The Farías flap has certainly not advanced understanding of the latter.

out his work. In what follows I will try to reintegrate Heidegger's early work, especially *Being and Time,* into his corpus as a whole. When that is done I think it becomes clear that Heidegger's collaboration with National Socialism was not a mistake.[3] This does not, however, imply that the genuinely *post*modern elements in Heidegger's thought are intrinsically fascist.[4]

Another frequently encountered, and equally misleading, maneuver is performed by postmodernists like Rorty and Derrida, who try to abstract one part of Heidegger's teaching and use it to dismiss the remaining, far greater part of his work. In the process, that which is essential to the task Heidegger explicitly undertakes is jettisoned. Such postmodernists have focused on Heidegger's deconstruction of Western philosophy and his unpacking of the metaphysical tradition—which culminates in the unique view that metaphysics rests on the doctrine of Being as presence. This critique of metaphysics is then turned against the rest of Heidegger's thought in an attempt to dismiss any discussion with a substantive content. In this way Heidegger's central ontological passion is dismissed and his longing for a postmetaphysical mode of thought transformed into a longing for a postfoundationalist thought

3. Heidegger was a National Socialist, though in his own eyes only he, Heidegger, remained true to the "inner truth and greatness of National Socialism," as opposed to revisionists like Hitler, Goebbels, Bauemler, Krieck, and Rosenberg. Heidegger signaled his dismay with orthodox National Socialism as early as 1935, when he observed that the Nazis were fishing in the "troubled waters of 'values' and totalities.'" When in 1953 Heidegger finally published, under the title *Introduction to Metaphysics,* his remarks about the "inner truth and greatness of" National Socialism, the complete statement referred to above read as follows: "The works that are being peddled about nowadays as the philosophy of National Socialism but have nothing whatever to do with the inner truth and greatness of this movement (namely the encounter between global technology and modern man)—have all been written by men fishing in the troubled waters of 'values' and 'totalities.'" Heidegger, *An Introduction to Metaphysics,* 199; henceforth designated in the text as *IM,* followed by a page number. The volume contains reworked lectures from 1935, first published in a corrected text in 1953. Given the gap between inception and publication, this work spans the period of the alleged "reversal" in Heidegger's thought.

This infamous statement is clearly an indictment of mainstream National Socialism. Nevertheless, National Socialism was seen by Heidegger as better equipped to respond to the rootless nihilism of technological modernity than any other available modern political dispensation. Heidegger was always a proponent of the virtues of an involved, rooted, populist "community." For a time, National Socialism was viewed as a basis for resolute action with and for a people in search of renewal and a new beginning in the face of rootless, urban, bourgeois cosmopolitanism.

4. Intellectual conscience alone should convince us that it is time to tear up this overused trump card. Its use seldom accomplishes anything other than insulating us from the need to engage in serious, substantive discussion.

that could serve as the linchpin for an age that is, for example, irre-trievably an-archic (Schurmann and others), totally pluralistic (Schurmann, Vattimo), or liberally ethnocentric (Rorty), or that engages in ongoing, endless critique (Derrida).[5] But all of those efforts remain thoroughly modern.

Subjected to maneuvers like this, the Heidegger who never ceased to discuss Being—the "essence of" this, the "foundation of" that, the "ground of" yet something else—is silenced and dismissed, as is the Heidegger who opened himself passionately toward the mysterious ground. On those occasions when it is admitted that these issues were at the heart of Heidegger's quest, they are dismissed as a form of atavistic reaction on his part, a metaphysical relapse not to be tolerated by a deconstructionism that seems to have no eye to reconstruction. I would argue that in this way, and in a variety of others, Heidegger's thought has been eclectically co-opted in the service of constructing a perfectly modern, postfoundationalist, self-legislating, bourgeois pluralism.[6]

We should discard one other common maneuver. Many have simply concluded, especially in the aftermath of the Farías fracas: So, Heidegger was a Nazi; good, then we no longer need to read him. But for better or worse, Heidegger's thought will not go away that easily. Heidegger's relation to National Socialism needs to be confronted rather than covered up or used to summarily dismiss his work. Furthermore, fairness should lead us to recall that Heidegger does not stand alone in modern thought in longing for a new beginning to be followed, it was hoped, by the emergence of a shining new city on the hill. As Lacoue-Labarthe says, "Who in this century, in the face of the unprecedented world historical transformations that have taken place, and in face of the apparent radicalism, whether of 'right' or 'left' of the various revolutionary projects, has not been duped?"[7] Let us go further in our honesty, Heidegger was not alone in his willingness to consider —at least at one point in his life—the necessity of an apocalypse as the cleansing means to a transition to a novel future. Marx, and an army of neo-Marxists, as well as Nietzsche and many post-Nietzscheans—to

5. See Schurmann, *Heidegger on Being and Acting;* Vattimo, *The Transparent Society* and *The End of Modernity;* and Rorty, *Contingency, Irony, and Solidarity* and *Philosophy and the Mirror of Nature.* See also my "Cacophony or Silence" and "Heidegger's Postmodern Politics?"

6. In openly admitting this, I think Rorty is by far the most honest of Heidegger's postmodernist descendants.

7. Lacoue-Labarthe, *Heidegger, Art and Politics,* 21.

say nothing about Machiavelli and many other good moderns—are among the many who reached the same conclusion.[8]

I want to argue that the various masks that have already grown up around Heidegger's thought keep us from traveling the path that Heidegger himself traveled. Likewise they make it impossible to find the genuinely postmodern elements in his thought. It is far too late to ignore, dismiss, or simply reverse Heidegger's influence. What is required is to understand it and *deflect* it in a fashion consistent with the general thrust or essence of Heidegger's ideas. To accomplish that it is necessary to see the extent to which Heidegger's thought represents a consistent whole, which first requires, as I have already noted, reinserting Heidegger's "early" work into his corpus, and again taking seriously his magnum opus *Being and Time*. I have argued that there are always a great variety of ways in which the thought of a great thinker might be deflected. But ultimately, I do not believe that the deflections of postmodernists Rorty, Derrida, Vattimo, and Schurmann—to say nothing of the reversal theorists—are consistent with the essence of what Heidegger has put into speech. Heidegger's thought, however, will continue to work its way into the intellectual landscape of the late-modern world through a myriad of sources, and its logic will, I believe, transcend the inconsistent deflections seen to date.

Right down to his posthumous *Der Spiegel* article, Heidegger made it clear that he did not believe that vacillating, unleadable consumer democracies were capable of answering the challenge presented by the world that was coming. He saw nothing intrinsically different in

---

8. As I will stress below, a recurrent theme in Heidegger's thought is that one can hope for the "saving grace" of a move beyond the nihilism of completed modernity only by first getting in step with the present revelation of Being, in all its myriad ramifications. Like Nietzsche, Heidegger felt we must enter into late-modern nihilism, exacerbate it, and live through it, not simply ignore it or merely adopt a negative stance to it. If the essence of the West can, as Heidegger thought, be traced back to an origin in the allegedly productionist metaphysics of Plato, then modern global, technological totalitarianism is, for Heidegger, completed metaphysics. According to Heidegger, the complete devastation of man and earth were the fated destiny of the metaphysical West. National Socialism was seen as the necessary culmination, qua closure, of that destiny. Heidegger did not think it was possible to stand outside this completed destiny; it must be entered into fully and without reservation. To do otherwise is to reproduce the essential technological will to domination. Using a distinction characteristic of *What Is Called Thinking?*, the present "devastation" blocks all new growth. One must enter that devastation completely to get to the "destruction" that levels the ground for a new growth in the future. In other words, the situation must be exacerbated, taken to its extreme, brought to a head, and so forth. In this way, one prepares for a cleansing apocalypse and a future rebirth.

Marxist collectivism. Heidegger was no friend of any of the available modern moral and political dispensations; since he was unwilling to build upon any of the available late-modern dispensations, he set about leveling them all and hoping that a phoenix would rise from the ashes.[9] Those delighted by the collapse of foundationalism usually assume they can retain the moral and political principles of the Enlightenment without its encumbering metaphysical foundations. This eclecticism rests on a misplaced faith in the inevitability of modern political and moral inertia—i.e., a hidden faith in the end of history. Heidegger had no such faith. Remove the cornerstone and the entire edifice falls. He was both clear-sighted and stern enough to face up to hard realities, and not the least bit squeamish.[10]

Contrary to contemporary postmodernism, Heidegger was intent upon the recovery of what for the moment I will loosely call the "political."[11] For Heidegger this required the distinctive historical action of a unique people. The alternative would be the endless repetition of the monotony of modern technological civilization, accomplished through the replacement of political action by technical decision making. In Heidegger's thought, the possibility of genuine, unique historical action always presupposed the recovery of certain primordial experiences, like those endured by the Greeks, presented to them by their thinkers and poets—a possibility obliterated by the monolithic revelation of reality of techno-modernity. In agreement with Nietzsche, Heidegger concluded that *praxis* requires peoples and is constituted as art,[12] a thought that led him to see the Greeks and Germans

9. The antifoundationalist deflections of Heidegger's work take off from this point. They stress the an-archic (i.e., without *archē*, or first principles) nature of Heidegger's thought. By this understanding, contemporary anarchy culminates in the decline and decay of all past Western principles and the beginning of a world where *praxis* is without foundational guidance. When *praxis* is deprived of *archē*, it is simultaneously separated from *theoria*. *Praxis* stands autonomous, supposedly opening up the possibility of a plurality of different forms of action. Hence the postfoundationalist world is projected as a pluralist world. But there is a great deal of wishful thinking here, to which Heidegger was not prone. Heidegger expected (hoped?) an anarchic antifoundationalism would lead to a cleansing, leveling chaos from which something new could grow. Heidegger did not believe in the simple fecundity of ongoing antifoundationalist flux. Nor did he revel in the collapse of Enlightenment—or more generally Western—foundationalism; he instead announced the inevitability of its arrival and characterized it as "devastation." See Heidegger, *What is Called Thinking?* 28–32.

10. He was anything but the muddled, apolitical professor of the—hopefully now defunct—orthodox myth of the "turn."

11. For a similar understanding see Lacoue-Labarthe, *Heidegger, Art and Politics.* One might also consider the work of Carl Schmidt; see Schmidt, *The Concept of the Political.*

12. If the core notion that moved Heidegger toward National Socialism was the be-

bound in a spiritual alliance against the rest of Europe, dominated as it
is by the Latin influence. It is this understanding that led Heidegger to
see the centrality of Germany in the revitalization of the West. A revi-
talized Germany would require its neighbors likewise to seek their
roots and accede to their own unique history.[13]

Throughout his work, Heidegger makes clear that everything great
so far in human history has required rootedness in a specific place and
an indigenous tradition. National Socialism was for a while generally,
though erroneously, viewed as the *means* to the regeneration of sheltering traditions, albeit absolutely not the simple, reactionary recovery of
old traditions. "The inner truth and greatness" of National Socialism
was not to be found in reactionary positions—like those of Junger, for
example[14]—but in a hope that it could be instrumental in getting beyond what Heidegger saw as the alienation and nihilism inherent in the
uprooting, globalizing, totalizing tendencies of the ever-encroaching
global, technological civilization. Heidegger had no faith in the autonomous choices of abstract, universal, modern "subjects." From beginning to end, he remained committed to the need for the reemergence of
rootedness in tradition-dominated communities, which would eventually become confronted by a plurality of similarly constituted communities. He came to see that actual National Socialism would eventuate in nothing of the kind, being in fact just another extreme manifestation of the modern, technological longing for the domination of man
and earth.

Heidegger reopens long closed discussions about the nature of the
ethical and political—even though his work never explicitly takes the

---

lief that the political is formed by art and that he could be the central artist, then Heidegger certainly miscalculated grossly. Far more interesting is the realization that if this is
the notion that moved Heidegger, once again, he hardly stands alone in modern
thought. From Machiavelli's desire to conquer chance to Rousseau's invention of
"metaphysical freedom" to the eleventh of Marx's *Theses on Feuerbach* to Nietzsche's
public rendition of a new breed of "philosopher-kings" we see the modern faith in the
fundamental malleability and shapability of man, with the political being a principle
tool for that shaping. The debate is over how that shaping should occur, who should do
it, how consciously it can be done, and what should emerge as an outcome. If there is a
postmodern element in Heidegger's thought it will not be found in this. See in this regard Lacoue-Labarthe, *Heidegger, Art and Politics,* 17–25, 61–104.

13. Presumably, this would bring a return to a situation comparable to that when the
Greeks had their Homer, the Romans their Virgil, the English their Shakespeare, the
Germans their Goethe, and so on, with none of the cosmopolitanizing homogenization
that leads to such phenomena as uprooted "world literature." Unlike the Nietzsche who
longed to fashion a united Europe, Heidegger longed for smaller political entities.

14. For the opposite view cf. Zimmerman, *Heidegger's Confrontation with Modernity.*

form of ethics or political philosophy. Lacoue-Labarthe provides a useful observation:

> Heidegger reopened philosophically, in the wake of Nietzsche and Romanticism, questions which the Marxist *vulgate* that prevailed in Europe during the first twenty years after the war (the years of the antifascist consensus) regarded as completely obsolete, but which we can today see to be unavoidable: these are the questions of peoples (or nations), languages, and religions.[15]

For Heidegger, a properly rooted existence—rooted in primordial experiences—is one of the ways that Being makes itself manifest—admittedly a "derivative" manifestation. That said, it is nonetheless true that for Heidegger Being manifests itself more substantially directly through the thoughts of the great thinkers.

Like Nietzsche, Heidegger tried to open a path to a future thinking, freed from the Spirit of Revenge. In Heidegger's case it is a thinking that relates itself to thinking the mysterious *Abgrund*, which grounds by staying away. For Heidegger both a properly rooted *praxis* and an open, pious, awestruck thinking had to be recovered. If we are to find the genuinely postmodern elements in Heidegger's thought it will be in this newly grounded *praxis* and thinking. Beyond the obfuscation of the reversal theorists and the modern, all too modern, deflections of the postmodernists, we need to relate ourselves to the Heidegger who, like Nietzsche, longs for the autonomy of a genuine *praxis* and a new thinking which no longer has the conquest of Chance as its primary end. For Heidegger, genuine *praxis* and thinking so conceived were the only authentic conduits for Being into the world. Without them, Being withdraws and nihilism is assured.

15. Lacoue-Labarthe, *Heidegger, Art and Politics,* 115.

13

The "Early" Heidegger: Recovery and Deconstruction

For my purposes, Heidegger's "early" period takes him from his gymnasium days to the lectures in *An Introduction to Metaphysics* and includes such works as *What is Metaphysics, Vom Wesen des Grundes,* and the *Rectoratsrede*. But the defining work of this period is clearly *Being and Time*. During this time Heidegger went through a search for a philosophical metier, moving from a concern for ancient (primarily Aristotle) and medieval (e.g., Scotus) metaphysics to an attempt to provide a metaphysics of metaphysics to phenomenology to his own unique version of "hermeneutic phenomenology" to "fundamental ontology." The changing metiers are not as important as the central themes that never ceased to move Heidegger's thought. In what follows, I will focus primarily on *An Introduction to Metaphysics* and *Being and Time*. Unlike the customary readings, I will not ignore the clearly deployed political and ethical themes. Those elements are not peripheral—although the term "political" must be taken in an architectonic, nonreductionist sense and ethics must be linked with the general notion of having an *ethos*.[1]

Further, throughout all his writings Heidegger claims that it is ontology or the question of Being that is at the center of his thought. More specifically, he claims that his main intention is to bring about a reawakening or recovery of fundamental questioning concerning Being, and thereby a recovery of our primordial relation to Being. It is instructive, therefore, that the relatively early series of lectures, *An Introduction to Metaphysics,* where this reawakening is thematically dis-

1. We should keep in mind throughout that Heidegger repeatedly asserts that every "sense of Being" implies an *ethos,* and every *ethos* points toward a distinct sense of Being. The relation is unavoidably mutual and reciprocal; to transform one is to transform the other. I will return thematically to these issues in part 4.

cussed, turns out to be one of Heidegger's most clearly and openly political works.[2]

"Why are there essents [existent *things*] rather than nothing?" (*IM* 1).
That, Heidegger asserts, is the "fundamental question" of philosophy.
Philosophy is born of an awe and wonder *(thaumazein)* that there is
anything at all. This fundamental awe strikes man in full force only in
moments of great despair, rejoicing, boredom, and like moods, and
then fades away. Consumed by such moods we give up all previous
security and attachment to everyday life and radically question our
concretely achieved mode of existence. According to Heidegger, our
age does not recognize this kind of fundamental questioning as a primordial human force; it is perceived as unessential and irrelevant. But if
fundamental questioning always brackets its own time, why should
any age be open to this fundamental philosophic questioning? Like
Nietzsche, Heidegger admits that philosophy is always essentially "untimely" (*IM* 8, 9). Hence it is to be expected that it will always be
viewed with some suspicion. But given the reigning indifference to
fundamental questioning, philosophy is in danger of extinction because of its alienation from Being, the only genuine "object" of philosophic awe. As a result, modern man is locked in the "forgetfulness of
Being"; concrete things lose their force and weight for us: banality
reigns.

Heidegger clearly believes that the great danger to be expected from
this alienation from fundamental questioning is that—despite the fact
that it can have "no immediate echo" in its own epoch—philosophy is
always "intimately bound up with a nation's profound historical development, and can even anticipate it." Indeed, "philosophy is one of the
few autonomous creative possibilities and at times necessities of man's
historical being-there" (*IM* 8, 9). If genuine questioning ceases to be,
man cannot hope to have any genuine historical existence. Yet philosophy can never simply be a political and ethical efficient cause:

> Philosophy can never *directly* [Heidegger's emphasis] supply the
> energies and create the opportunities and methods that bring
> about a historical change; for one thing, because philosophy is al-

2. One might want to position this work—initially given as a series of lectures in
1935—at the beginning of a middle or transitional period. It comes after Heidegger
leaves his position as rector and ends his active participation in Nazi activities, after the
Rectoratsrede and before the Nietzsche lectures. But its themes are entirely consistent
with those of *Being and Time, Rectoratsrede, Vom Wesen des Grundes, What Is Metaphysics*
and other early works. Further, this work provides a valuable point of entrance to
Heidegger's thought by showing clearly the few key ideas that never change despite his
ongoing, often neologistic, experimentation with language.

ways the concern of the few. Which few? *The creators,* those who
initiate profound transformations. [Nonetheless], it spreads . . .
indirectly, by devious paths that can never be laid out in advance,
until at last, at some future date, it sinks to the level of a commonplace. . . .

What philosophy essentially can and must be is this: a thinking
that breaks the paths and opens the perspectives of the knowledge
that sets the *norms and hierarchies,* of the knowledge in which and
by which *a people fulfills itself historically and culturally,* the knowledge that kindles and necessitates all inquiries and thereby
threatens all values. (*IM* 10; emphasis mine)

Genuine questioning cannot predict where its efforts will lead. Others
are required: Poets, prophets, statesmen, artists, and so on. Nonetheless, ontology always points toward ethics—i.e., a specific *ethos*—and
having an *ethos* is the ground of the political.[3]
Heidegger asserts that the possibility of a genuine "historical destiny" for nations—and the nation, not autonomous individuals, always
remains the unit of analysis for Heidegger—arises only when there is
an authentic relation to *things,* and this requires that things be grounded
in Being. This is the issue of "ontological difference" for Heidegger,
i.e., the difference between, yet relatedness of, Being and beings. In
our time the relation between Being and beings has been sundered. For
Heidegger, when beings have no foundation in Being, our practical life
decays. As a propaedeutic, philosophy must call into question the
reigning, familiar relation to *things* in order to make possible another
more authentically open and intense historical relation. Contemporary
men and nations are in "decline" because they have "fallen out of Being." The result is that Western man finds himself in the midst of an
immense spiritual decline where *"time as history* has vanished from the
lives of all *peoples"* (*IM* 37–38; emphasis mine). According to Heidegger, contemporary man is locked in the cultivation and domination of
present "essents," rather than the "uncovering" of unique future ones.
As a result we experience time merely as "velocity," a succession of
nows, which pass ever more quickly as one races to experience—albeit
superficially—all things (*IM* 38). Thus we have arrived at the "darkening of the world" wherein one confronts "the flight of the gods, the
destruction of the earth, the transformation of men into a mass, the hatred and suspicion of everything free and creative" (*IM* 38, see also 45).

As a result of this spiritual decay, Heidegger sees Europe caught between the twin pincers of Russia and America, which he asserts are

3. For a discussion of this issue see Vattimo, *The Transparent Society,* 105–20.

metaphysically equal in their mass bureaucratic organization and technological frenzy. In the environment dominated by Moscow and Washington, "the spiritual decline of the earth is so far advanced that the nations are in danger of losing the last bit of spiritual energy that makes it possible to see the decline" (*IM* 38). Modern man requires new energies so that his existence can be restored to the "domain of history." Heidegger joins Nietzsche in asserting that because of his spiritual decay, contemporary man has ceased to strive for excellence, or to act in conformity with any rank ordering. Consequently, mere quantitative considerations have gained hegemony over qualitative ones, and all life becomes a business equation, which both presupposes and fosters humanity's reduction to a uniform mass. With this onslaught against the *qualitative,* every world-creating impulse is destroyed by the mass which is ruled over by a cross section of its own. Spirit is reinterpreted as "intelligence," understood as the mere calculating cleverness that examines all things with an eye to changing, manipulating, and dominating them, destroying poetry, art, statesmanship, and religion—indeed all spiritual forces—giving everything over to "*conscious* cultivation and planning" (*IM* 45–48). All spiritual forces come under the hegemony of a utilitarian intelligence, a mere cleverness in manipulation, regulation, and organization. Simultaneously arises the victory of routinization. In this picture we see the same concern as Nietzsche's about the destructive ramifications of an increasingly global, technological, utilitarian mass society organized for no other purpose than the domination of Nature in the service of comfortable consumption.

For Heidegger, in the process of this great technological march our alienation from Being has accelerated. We have fallen away from the question of Being and what the word says and for the moment cannot find our way back. The way forward to new possibilities must be preceded by opening the way back into the question of Being, so that we may understand how that word became an evanescent vapor and ultimately almost a nothing. For Heidegger, the regeneration of a serious historical *praxis* requires a philosophical propaedeutic, an undertaking, however, always guided in advance by awareness of a practical problem—Heidegger is repeatedly explicit about this relationship. Not only is he *concerned* with political and moral problems; his project is entirely motivated by these concerns from beginning to end.[4]

---

4. It is entirely disingenuous to turn Heidegger into an apolitical thinker. His ontological reflections are in the service of confronting the practical problem that results from late-modern nihilism. For Heidegger, genuine thinking and genuine historical ac-

We must go back, disinter the roots of the Western tradition of thought, and inspect them. This is what Heidegger means by the "destruction" of the Western tradition. We sort through the sedimented layers of the Western tradition to uncover the origins. We uncover the origins in hopes of making a "second beginning." Heidegger asserts that it was the question of Being that provided the stimulus for the researches of the pre-Socratics, Plato, and Aristotle, but no sooner had that question been opened as an issue than it faded as a theme for actual investigation. From that point on there came into existence a series of dogmas which have led inexorably to the neglect of the question of Being, and ultimately to the destruction of genuine, historical *praxis*. Hence for Heidegger, the history of the West *(Abendland)* has been the slow going down or setting of the light of Being; it is the history of nihilism.

In *An Introduction to Metaphysics* Heidegger approaches the unpacking of the Western tradition—*his* deconstructive method—by engaging in some of his more famous (or infamous) etymological analyses. Heidegger explicitly states that his etymological analyses have the practical intention "of demolishing a world that has grown old and of *rebuilding it authentically anew*" (*IM* 126; emphasis mine). To a certain extent, then, it misses the point to recognize how bizarre and idiosyncratic some of these analyses are from a conventional point of view. Heidegger's etymological analyses illuminate, in a fairly concrete way, what it is that he is attempting to "recover." I will focus specifically on his interpretations of such key Greek terms as *physis, ousia, alētheia, logos, nomos, eidos, idea, doxa, polemos,* and *noein.* But the central thought that ruled all of Heidegger's thinking is found in his presentation of what he asserts is the primary Greek experience of Being as *physis* (customarily translated as "nature").

Heidegger claims that in the decisive and greatest moment of Greek thought—in the age of Parmenides, Heraclitus, Pindar, and Sophocles —the Greeks understood Being as the *emerging power* that "issues from concealment" through a "spontaneous unfolding that lingers" (*IM* 61). *Physis* is a "standing-in-the-light," a "coming to shine," a generated permanence, not in the sense of eternality, but as an avoidance of complete evanescence (*IM* 101). *Physis* and appearance are intrinsically linked, because *physis* is that "power" *(dynamis)* that is always pushing

---

tion have an unavoidable relation. And both must be recovered. *This does not change in the later works.*

toward the surface, sometimes unfolding out into the light as presence, at other times falling back into some mysterious, impenetrable, and unfathomable abode, into concealment and absence. Being, so understood, implies presence, but not fixed and eternal presence. As a result, Being positively requires man; Being must appear for someone or, put another way, through someone; otherwise it would remain No-thing, hidden, concealed. Appearing and No-thingness are different manifestations of the same mysterious power. When *physis* succeeds in lingering out in the open, it is present as *ousia*—the standing presence that lingers. So understood, becoming, like appearance, is not the antithesis of Being, but belongs to it. Contrary to the understanding that allegedly emanates from Plato and Aristotle, for Heidegger Being is not that which has left behind and emancipated itself from all appearing and becoming; the "overpowering" power of *physis* positively requires that it bring itself to the surface, over and over again, ever achieving unique appearances. Heidegger says that when becoming and appearance are "degraded" to the status of mere epiphenomena, the original conception of Being as *physis* has been lost, to be replaced by Being as *ousia,* now understood as eternally and permanently self-identical presence, *substantia, hypokeimenon,* Absolute Spirit, and so on.

When detached from the concept of *physis, ousia* is misunderstood and misconceived as permanent, eternal presence, as a self-subsistent thing that has escaped "absence" once and forever and is no longer in danger of falling back behind itself. To accomplish this, that which counts as Being was first moved from the sensible realm to a supersensible realm, and all becoming and appearing were degraded to not-Being. In the process (1) one becomes alienated from asking the question about what it is that *allows* the emerging power to linger, and (2) one is thereby emancipated from the necessity of engaging in the acts that *make* that lingering possible. According to Heidegger, in the original conception of Being as *physis,* the process of coming to appearance cannot help but take primacy. And in the original understanding, the Being of a thing is linked to the "empirical intuition" which the face or facade of a thing shows: i.e., its *eidos.* Eventually *eidos* is linked with *idea,* and Being is transformed into a nonappearing idea. Plato is allegedly responsible for this move.[5] According to Heidegger, the Being of a thing, or of things as a whole, was initially linked with the *surface,*

---

5. Heidegger's Plato is indistinguishable from conventional Platon*ism.* Heidegger seems incapable, or unwilling, of making the distinction between the two that Nietzsche does. There is little indication that he considers Plato too noble for Platonism.

the way things show themselves to everyone. Plato transformed Being into an idea beyond *(meta)* the surface.[6]

Heidegger asserts that to come to stand erect and stable in the light, to attain presence, requires that the overpowering power achieve a limit, *peras* (*IM* 60).[7] "It" must be brought to appearance by bringing form or limit out of chaos. Heidegger asserts that for the early Greeks, "limit" was understood in the sense of reaching fulfillment, as an end, *telos*. But since there is no fixed *telos*, no transcendent model or permanently present underlying substratum that determines the end or limit, *physis* was seen as incapable of reaching a limit or end without the intervention of poets, philosophers, thinkers, and statesmen (*IM* 62). They "wrest" limit out of No-thingness and chaos. It is *through* them that the overpowering makes itself manifest. The process by which the original chaos and limitlessness is transcended and brought to order— i.e., by which the dispersed and indeterminate is gathered, collected, and thereby given form—is through *logos,* understood in the "original" sense as that which allows Being qua *physis* to come to presence as truth, or *alētheia*. *Logos* is the "permanent gathering" principle. Heidegger asserts that in its original Greek meaning, *logos* is linked with the *happening* of Being, not primarily with language, discourse, or statement (*IM* 128, 129). Without *logos* so understood, Being and truth could not occur. Without "creators"—poets, philosophers, prophets, and statesmen are Heidegger's examples—*logos* does not occur. They all seem to do the same thing as the "phenomenologists" Heidegger discusses in the introduction to *Being and Time*.[8]

Hand in hand with Heidegger's distinctive depiction ("recovery") of Being as *physis* goes his understanding of truth. The overpowering power that issues from concealment, from absence into unconcealment and presence, is truth understood as *alētheia* (*IM* 61). Hence by extension, falsity, absence, not-Being, and concealedness are all equivalent.

6. In this regard we should recall Nietzsche's attempt to return men to the surface. Heidegger, in his own way, tries to return man to the surface and give Being back to appearance.

7. The ambiguity in Heidegger's early conception of Being should now be noted. Being is used synonymously with that overpowering power that both shines forth into presence and holds itself back in absence, but it is also used as a term for that half of the grand whole which shows itself—i.e., as synonymous with *presence* alone. The later Heidegger will attempt to transcend this ambiguity by substituting a variety of locutions for the traditional term for Being. But the core ontological intuition, or "sense of Being," never changes.

8. Heidegger, *Being and Time;* henceforth designated in the text as *BAT,* followed by a page number.

Truth requires appearance for its happening; it is a form of appearing. Yet truth can be covered over and concealed by "semblance" as well as by the "withdrawal" of the limitless Overpowering back into concealment. Everything that appears does not have Being in the same proportion. Being and truth are terms of distinction. There are things that are uncovered (present) in their true essential nature, and other appearances that are mere semblance or subjective viewpoints imposed on things by autonomous individuals acting without the overpowering power coursing through them. When man merely imposes a look, perspective, or "view" *(Weltanschauung)* on things, these views cover over the possibility of a thing showing itself as it truly is. Semblance takes the place of truth and Being. Things so encountered are without Being, albeit they are in their own way present. As murky as this distinction is, the point seems to be that one cannot give a true limit through an act of autonomous Will. In Heidegger's account, the complication is that the overpowering power of the limitless No-thing does not simply and in an unmediated fashion bring itself to appearance, to essential unconcealedness; it always requires the mediation of man, who is simultaneously one of the main causes of semblance. The relationship between man and Being is a complicated one, but throughout his work Heidegger tries to assign priority to Being itself. The nuances of the account do change, but not enough to be seen as a radical turn or reversal.

Being and not-Being, revealing and concealing, presence and absence necessarily interpenetrate each other; all that surrounds us is rife with contradiction, untruth, and No-thingness. Contrary to Hegel, in the Heideggerian account contradiction and untruth can never be overcome; the Overpowering can never bring itself to total, self-identical presence. The Being of things must repeatedly be won back through a battle against semblance *(BAT 51–55)*. *Physis* can never be completely secured or eternally frozen into permanence as, for example, given, present-to-hand objects, whether they be things, buildings, ethical theories, religious texts, or constitutions. It must continually be wrested and rewon. It is *doxa* that accomplishes this. *Doxa,* originally understood as "glory," helps grant permanence, albeit not eternal permanence. The glorious act gives permanence. *Doxa* is not to be understood as mere opinion. It too goes with Being as intrinsically as appearing. Hence there is no intrinsic antimony between *doxa* and *alētheia.*

With his conception of Being as *physis* also comes Heidegger's unique understanding of alienation. The primary foundation of alienation is the alienation of man from that limitless overpowering power *(physis* qua *dynamis)* which needs him to manifest itself. This alienation eventuates in a lostness among those things that are the leftovers from previous presencings, things which have since fallen into mere semblance.[9] When this occurs men and nations lose their way, fall into a groundless situation, and are expelled from History and genuine historical action. All decay, decline, and decadence are traceable to the fall "out of Being" *(IM* 37). When this occurs, when a nation's relation to Being is severed, language itself comes to be "worn out and used up" *(IM* 51). Hence language becomes another of those merely present things which cover the emergence of the Overpowering. And as the "world turns away" man loses all his spiritual possibilities.

The return to a healthy *praxis* requires the amazed, awestruck openness to the overpowering power that eventuates in *logos, doxa, peras,* and *nomos.* It does not require, in Nietzschean fashion, the conscious willing of untruth, or of illusions. Further, *logos*—that which gathers, brings together, and gives permanence to the otherwise indeterminate and absent primordial source of all fecundity—is not accomplished by negating all tension and conflict, but positively requires a "conflict of the opposites." Indeed that conflict *is* genuine *logos (IM* 131). One must not use *logos* to overcome difference, which provides a barrier against the overwhelming chaos of the complete sway of limitless differencelessness. There is no doubt that Heidegger joins Nietzsche in founding the philosophy of difference that becomes so important for contemporary postmodernism. But for Heidegger, difference is never primarily a *human* contrivance, even though it changes.

By authentically giving limit to primordial chaos a "world" comes to pass, not understood as Nature, or the whole of what is concretely given, but as a spiritual or cultural realm. Without world there would be the reign of limitless No-thingness, the destruction of difference *(IM* 61–62). One of the clearest concrete intimations of what is implied by the early Heidegger's destructive recovery comes when he asserts that the *nomos* of the *polis* is an example of a limit-giving, primordial *logos.* What is required is a "*nomos* for the *polis,* the statute that constitutes or puts together, the inner structure of the *polis,* not a universal, not something that hovers over all and touches none, but the original unifying unity of what tends apart" *(IM* 131)[10] The founding of a dis-

9. A concrete example of this might be the remains of a Greek temple, which has lost the meaning and significance it had for its originators.
10. Heidegger is discussing Heraclitus' fragment 114.

tinct, individual *polis* is an event of truth; it does not require consciously willed Nietzschean illusions, but it does require a founding
that accomplishes a rank ordering, just as it requires opposition.[11] A
genuine *nomos* never produces a reduction to identity, an abolition of
tension and hierarchical difference.

According to Heidegger, there can be no "Being," no limit, where
all contradictions, differences, and orders of rank and hierarchy have
been overcome (*IM* 133–34). Man "is" man precisely because he is not
a god; the noble "is" noble precisely because it is not the base, the ignoble, or the slavelike, and so on.[12] Heidegger says that primordially
understood, *logos,* in its manifestation as *nomos,* need not be spoken or
articulated in an explicit discourse; it can come to pass as an unspoken
ethos. Indeed, given its nature, the true as *logos* can never be reduced to a
set of formulas that everyone can grasp; to some it will not show itself
at all (*IM* 132). Not only does genuine historical existence require the
transcendence of contradiction-free uniformity, it also requires transcendence of belief in the superiority of legalism—i.e., an explicitly articulated, totally present, rational, legal or moral code. Unspoken
tradition *(ethos)* can bind better than written law. These are the things
that Heidegger asserts the pre-Socratic Greeks knew, which we must
recover if we are to recover our relation to Being and thereby find a
ground for our daily existence. But they also remind one of Aristotle's
preference for custom over written law as the basis of the *hexis* necessary for moral virtue.[13]

Logos is best manifested as the *nomos* that grounds an *ethos* for a distinct community, because in the same way that appearance is always

11. "Because being as *logos* is basic gathering, not mass and turmoil in which everything has as much or as little value as everything else, rank and domination are implicit
in being" (*IM* 133; emphasis mine). Heidegger is summarizing Heraclitus' fragment 54.

12. In one of his more imaginative translations, Heidegger asserts that "Heraclitus
says (Fragment 53): 'Conflict is for all (that is present) the creator that causes to emerge,
but (also) for all the dominant preserver. For it makes some to appear as gods, others as
men; it creates (shows) some as slaves, others as freemen'" (*IM* 61–62).

13. Heidegger's debt to Aristotle is immense and has not been adequately appreci-
ated. It is hard to decide whether he owes more to Aristotle or Nietzsche. Contrary to
MacIntyre, who tells us that an either/or choice must be made between Aristotle and
Nietzsche, I believe Heidegger has found a way to synthesize them. See MacIntyre, *After Virtue*. It by no means misses the mark to say that Heidegger points toward the rule of
custom over a specific community, rather than the rule of a rational legal code over a
modern nation-state. Again, the correspondence with Nietzsche on this point is significant. I will try to show that this understanding remained constant throughout Heidegger's thought, despite all the interpretive obfuscation that has tried to prove almost the
opposite: i.e., that Heidegger aims at a peopleless, democratic an-archism.

prone to semblance, *logos* is prone to being locked into a fixed and present discourse and language, which can then be dissected until it loses its original force and Being withdraws. It then becomes mere opinion or semblance to which all have access, destroying all conflict, tension, and *polemos*. As such it is used up and covers the Truth and becomes a part of the process of concealing. In concrete terms, we might say that whenever the *nomos* becomes too well articulated and concretely scrutinized it will cease to have the binding force and authority it initially had. Communal life is endangered when custom becomes reduced to a code of law, action is reduced to mere rule-following behavior, and both are dissected endlessly. Then, according to Heidegger, the reigning *nomos* must be overthrown and replaced by a new *logos* which brings the limitless into unconcealment anew (*IM* 62). Man must continually break out of what has devolved into the familiar and trivialized, act "violently" against the already accomplished reality that has devolved into mere givenness, and allow *physis* to break to the surface anew (*IM* 162).

But Heidegger is at pains to make clear that it is not man by himself, as a meager "subject" striking out idiosyncratically against an intransigent "object," who willfully performs acts of violence against the already attained *logos, nomos,* and *alētheia:* "Being itself hurls man into this breaking-away, which drives him beyond himself to venture forth toward being, to accomplish being, to stabilize it in the work, and so hold open the essent as a whole" (*IM* 163).[14] The ever-renewed struggle to bring both openness and limit must be informed, indeed moved by, the limitless Overpowering itself, whether it is designated as Being, "It," or "that which regions." It is only through riding the crest of the primordial overpowering source that man brings a genuine, new *logos* into existence and allows *physis* to manifest itself and give meaning to essents and purpose to historical man. Man must always let the Overpowering flow through him in the manner of "inspiration."[15] This theme is repeated in later discussions including "The Origin of the Work of Art," "Building, Dwelling, Thinking," and other essays that originally appeared in *Holzwege* and *Vörtrage und Aufsätze.*

Heidegger deepens the attack on self-consciousness and subjectivity

14. Notice the two senses of the term "Being." See note 7 above.

15. "The violence of poetic speech, of thinking projection, of building configuration, of *the action that creates states* is not a function of the faculties that man has, but a taming and ordering of powers by virtue of which the essent opens up as such when man moves into it. This disclosure of the essent is the power that man must master in order to become himself amid the essent, i.e. in order to be historical" (*IM* 157; emphasis mine).

begun by Nietzsche by trying to give unself-conscious inspiration a deeper ontological exploration. Heidegger even asserts that man's openness to the Overpowering is what was originally meant by "thinking" in the sense of *noein*. Originally, *noein* implied a receptive stance—albeit not a passive one. Heidegger claims that only in this sense of *noein* can Parmenides state that Being and thinking are the same. Being is *achieved* through wondrous, awe-inspired openness to and longing for oneness with the limitless, which occurs in receptive *noein*. After announcing the "end of philosophy" and the "end of metaphysics" in his "middle" works, Heidegger returns to this understanding of thinking in his discussion of *Gelassenheit*. Thinking becomes "openness to the mystery."

This "early" account I have sketched claims to be a recovery of the original, pre-Socratic, Western relation to Being. But having arrived at this point, we cannot help but draw a parallel with the Hegelian account. The empty, abstract Hegelian *Geist* initially hurled itself into Nature, into a concrete manifestation which was at the same time an immense spiritual alienation for the previously pure, if empty and unselfconscious One. Simultaneously the empty, abstract One hurled itself into dispersion and multiplicity, such that it could not be manifest to itself as what it essentially was, i.e., Spirit. The initially empty spiritual One, after alienating itself into Nature, works through men, and to a far lesser extent Nature, to make itself manifest to itself. Through the use of opposition, it drives on until eventually it has spiritualized and re-created the initially dead matter within which it was immersed. Ultimately, it gains a permanent, eternal presence, present for itself and for any particular consciousness that can achieve oneness with it through Absolute consciousness. Having attained Absolute self-consciousness, the Hegelian Absolute need never fall into "absence" or "concealedness" again. It achieves oneness with its concretely achieved reality, and consciousness of itself. It need no longer set man in opposition to man or to Nature, or state in opposition to state. All tension, opposition, and contradiction were phenomena that could be overcome. To the extent that Being no longer needs man at all, man becomes something of an expended residue left over from the process of the concretion of Spirit and the spiritualization of the dead otherness into which Spirit initially threw itself.

By comparison, in Heidegger's account, what corresponds with the Hegelian Spirit is the overpowering *physis*. Both Being and not-Being, presence and absence, concealing and unconcealing, granting and withholding are eternally parts of its essence. It is incapable of final concretion; it thereby remains eternally restless, unlike Hegel's Absolute Spirit. Heidegger's *physis* must continually use man to achieve presence; it can never overcome or do without man. Furthermore, it can be thwarted by man in his turning away toward a preoccupation with present beings. Through man, *physis* achieves presence while simultaneously assuring absence through the things and traditions that *eventually* obscure more than they reveal. This relationship is never capable of being transcended. Heidegger's ontological source can never come to rest. Nonetheless, we must ask if the core insight Heidegger presents is primarily pre-Socratic or a reworking of the Hegelian ontological intuition minus completion, stasis, fruition, total self-identical presence, and so on. Or would one have to go back to at least Leibniz and Spinoza in search of the origins of Heidegger's original ontological "sense"? Or would that inevitably lead to Parmenides? Unfortunately, this issue, which should be pursued, cannot be pursued here. But it seems to me that there are reasons to believe that Heidegger's key ontological intuition is more modern than pre-Socratic.

Be that as it may, for Heidegger, when man becomes alienated from openness to Being qua *physis* he becomes lost in the reigning essent, cultivating, manipulating, organizing, and attempting to dominate what already is present, but revealing nothing new. In the process, he ceases to be a historical being, loses the capacity to truly act, becomes incapable of breaking out of the familiar and orderly, and refuses to risk disorder and No-thingness. He spends his time trying to preserve old traditions, *nomoi,* art forms, and religions, which have ever-decreasing force or meaning for day-to-day life. Or he thinks this alienation will be overcome by a romantic return to primary "Nature," again a previous concrete manifestation of the emerging power. Alienated, contemporary man is given to *ennui,* boredom, and despair—or to mindless violence and destruction for its own sake—because there ceases to be any ontological ground for his existence. It is a return to openness to the Overpowering itself that is necessary. Heidegger spent a lifetime trying to bring that newly opened relationship to speech in a way that would not reproduce the problem he was trying to confront.

Heidegger's assertion is that we must gain clarity about the nihilistic path Western thinking took away from its beginning if our alienation is to be overcome. We must recover the sense of Being we had at the origin of the West. When we do, we will see that the falling away from the beginning grew out of the *original* conception of Being itself. The original conception of Being is itself implicated in the forgetting of Being. Because of its necessary relationship to appearance, Being was always in danger of being confused with mere semblance. Hence an immense fight had to be fought to try to save Being from semblance. This was accomplished by taking the "look" *(eidos)* of the thing, its "what," and differentiating it from the "thatness" of the thing. The whatness alone became the Being of the essent, and its thatness was degraded to error or not-Being. As a result, the Being of essents was abstracted from their empirical thatness. The Being of essents became *idea* qua ideal, while the appearing essent itself became a mere copy of that ideal. One could no longer take the appearance of the thing seriously; hence there was no reason to engage in the primordial battle to bring about a "true" appearing. All this allegedly took place in the work of Plato. In the process the "that" of Being, the *happening* of *presencing* itself withdrew as an object for thought. Abstract thinking about ideas took priority over all other manifestations of Truth in *praxis,* art, *poiesis,* and so on. The multifaceted nature of truth was lost.

Eventually the truth "shifts its abode" from the realm of appearing to *statements* about the correspondence between the ideal and its copies (*IM* 186). Aristotle codified this shift by proclaiming that it is *only* statements that can be true and false, not things or appearances. Thereby Being became a permanent, tranquil given which could be exhausted and held constant by a set of "categories." Contradiction was expelled from Being and its qualities became finite.[16] Thought eventually becomes that which dictates to essents what can be said about them, and thereby it dictates the Being of any possible beings. Increasingly this dictating of the Being of beings takes place within a "subject" that dictates the terms of Being to external "objects" (Descartes). At that point one is but a few steps from the hegemony of the autonomous, subjective human Will, which wills illusions and destroys the need for openness to anything other than and beyond the logical, rational, or willful projecting self.

As soon as truth shifted its abode, finding the ground of the "ought" became an immense problem. Plato was the first to give manifestation to this problem. In Plato the Idea of the Good, the source of value, the first potency, the model of the models, is beyond Being; hence it is not-Being. The ought was stripped of having an ontological ground at the very beginning of metaphysics. This is carried to its logical conclusion in Kant when the categorical imperative, a projection of thought, is opposed to Being understood as permanently present Nature—the realm that can be understood in mathematical, representational thinking.

---

16. Eventually, even the preconcrete Hegelian *Geist* could be articulated on the basis of finite, pure abstract concepts, waiting for concretion. As a result, Hegelian logic took the place of true awestruck wonder and openness, making *poiesis, nomos,* and primordial *logos* ontologically irrelevant. See Hegel, *The Science of Logic,* esp. 28, 30, 156, 165.

The ought is now not only divorced from any ground in Being, it is *opposed* to Being. The status of the ought is now reduced to that of a mere "value," which as ontologically groundless is in principle valueless. As priority passed increasingly to the "objective" essent, for it had Being, the ought had to find some other ground for its justification. In an attempt to give substance to the ought, History became the ground of value. History, as opposed to Nature, was regarded as the arena of the realization of values. In Hegel, as in Kant, the realm of freedom is opposed to that of necessity, with History providing the reconciliation if not victory of the one over the other. But when History is stripped of any ontological ground, as occurs in Nietzsche, values have no ontological ground; God is dead. Once severed from Being and emancipated from the categorical imperative, values become increasingly the product of an autonomous Will. This, allegedly, is the ultimate outcome of defining Being as *idea* qua ideal, rather than as *physis,* the emerging power. Following the Platonic deflection of pre-Socratic thought, Western History was inevitable.

14

Being and Time

The Existential Analysis of Everydayness:
The Priority of the Lifeworld

I will argue that *Being and Time* consistently displays the central themes that dominated all of Heidegger's thought, even in its "late" manifestation.[1] I especially want to point out several aspects of *Being and Time* which are either pushed to the periphery or simply missed by most readings. For example, in the second part of the published material, by weaving in and out of such distinctions as ontic/ontological, death/demise, anticipation/resoluteness, Heidegger gains a rhetorical purchase which allows him to articulate a version of the fundamental chasm in his thought that is never bridged. In the later works, that split manifests itself in the two components of *Gelassenheit*, "openness to the *mystery*" and "releasement toward *things*," but the same bifurcation can be found in *Being and Time*.

Other significant later positions can be seen in *Being and Time* as well. Throughout the book, as throughout all his work, Heidegger showed his trademark concern for reawakening the fundamental question about Being. He repeatedly argues that ancient ontology, by transforming Being into Nature—that is, constant, totally in view presence-at-hand—paved the way for modern technological civilization, and he seeks to reverse the hegemony of that understanding. In *Being and*

---

1. In the process I will try to pin Heidegger down to something concrete to avoid the mountains of neologisms that often pass for interpretation of this difficult author. I am unconcerned that this approach might land me in the lap of "metaphysics," for I have no interest in playing the fashionable game of nonmetaphysical one-upmanship. I do not care which Heideggerian text is least metaphysical any more than I care which author at the end of modernity is least metaphysical. *Heidegger intended his work to have an effect.* One cannot have an effect that has no concrete manifestation. If philosophy becomes metaphysical anytime it approaches a concrete discussion, then so be it. Let us live with being metaphysical.

Time, he argues that Western metaphysics cannot, therefore, deal with concrete, factical, historical life because factical, historical life cannot be brought to the standstill that the Western metaphysical tradition imposes on Being. By starting from everyday Dasein to illuminate Being Heidegger has from the beginning presupposed the end, which is that Being itself is historical. This is not explicitly developed in *Being and Time* as it will be in what I will call Heidegger's "middle" or "transitional" period, but the idea is controlling.

In *Being and Time,* Heidegger explicitly admits that *all* analyses are moved in advance by a "sense of Being," and that every sense of Being has concrete ramifications. That understanding of a reciprocal relation between an ontology and an *ethos* never changes. More to the point, the fundamental ontological intuition or sense of Being never changes in Heidegger's thought, nor does the longing to ground a genuine *ethos* toward which it points.

According to Heidegger, traditional metaphysics fixes truth as correct correspondence between a statement and some presumed fixed reality. Throughout his work, Heidegger's response is that truth makes itself manifest in a *variety* of ways: as art, poetry, *technē,* authentic, historical *praxis,* the thoughts of the great thinkers, and so on. In *Being and Time* authentic, historical *praxis* takes priority in the discussion. Authentic *praxis,* as *a* mode of truth, is presented as a disclosive event, part of the presencing of Being. This analysis forms a part of Heidegger's critique of the reduction of the locus of truth to statement and logic as well as part of his critique of representational thinking and all correspondence theories of truth. Throughout his corpus Heidegger argues that primary events of truth precede all detached theoretical staring, all representational thinking, all correspondence theories. In *Being and Time,* this is presented in the analysis that tries to show the fundamentally practical nature of our prior, "everyday" relation to reality, which authentic *praxis* makes possible by keeping a "world" in place. In the later works there is no repudiation of authentic historical *praxis* as a mode of truth; we simply see a change of emphasis from, for example, statesmen or prophets to poets and thinkers as conduits for Being.

For Heidegger, the theoretical relation to the world—which includes everything from traditional metaphysics, to Christian theology, to the transcendental subject legislating to man and Nature, to modern physics and modern technology—is always derivative from a more immediate, lived experience. All theory takes off from rootedness in a distinct world, a world kept in place by authentic, disclosive activity. Consequently, no theoretical activity is morally, politically, or ontologically neutral. This is tantamount to saying that the political (understood as unique historical action in a world) is architectonic precisely as Aristotle argues.[2] In *Being and Time,* the rootlessness and nihilism of the late-modern world is related to the hegemony of the theoretical consciousness, especially in its modern mode of positing subjectivity. Heidegger holds out the possibility that one can eventually reverse that hegemony. Somehow, resolutely locked within an authentic world, man might in the future recover, in a transformed manifestation, a future rootedness and again live in the nearness of Being *and* beings. Only then could mankind be safe on the far side of the constant, revolutionizing rootlessness of a runaway, modern technological existence. The analysis of man's (Dasein's) "everydayness" in part 1 of *Being and Time* is explicitly said to be part of the attempt to work out *"the idea of a 'natural conception of the world'"* (*BAT* 76), which is not to be confused with a description of primitive Dasein. Everydayness is always a mode of Dasein's Being, especially in an active and "highly developed and differentiated culture—*and precisely then,"* whereas primitive Dasein has a mode of everydayness *"of its own"* (*BAT* 76; emphasis mine). Even in modern, highly differentiated, industrialized, mass societies, one can arrive at a "natural conception of the world." One can recover the natural without going back to the primitive.[3] An intimation of what this means is found in Heidegger's observation that in attempting to recover a natural conception of the world, he is also attempting to recover a "primordial *absorption in* 'phenomena'" on the plane of a highly differentiated modern civilization (*BAT* 76; emphasis mine). "Natural" man is open to "phenomena" which are *self*-presencing, that is, open to *physis* in

2. I cannot explore this here—and it has not been explored adequately, although Gadamer has done by far the most valuable work—but *Being and Time* goes a long way toward attacking traditional metaphysics in the name of Aristotle's practical philosophy and psychology. See Gadamer, *Reason in the Age of Science* and *Philosophical Hermeneutics.* Understanding the political architectonically should be opposed to the modern reductionist understanding in which politics is only concerned with the ultimate use of force by the state for defense, or to accomplish the authoritative allocation of valuable, useful things, or is simply derivative from the subpolitical. In the architectonic sense of the political, one must grasp the intimate relation between *polis* and *ethos* precisely as Heidegger argues in *Introduction to Metaphysics.*

3. Heidegger is not making some trivial observation about recovering some prior, primary natural state, reveling in the consciousness of aborigines, or praying again to Zeus. What is at stake in "recovering" a "natural consciousness" is finding a new relation to Nature, ourselves, and other human beings, one that is different from the modern stance that sees the world as *our* projection rather than as *self*-presencing. What is involved is to see Nature—and the natural in us—as self-subsistent and "other" than our self-grounded projection.

Heidegger's distinctive sense. "Natural" consciousness stands before the world in a stance other than modern, projecting hubris.

The primary, existential structure of everydayness that Heidegger develops is "Being-in-the-World." In discussing this concept, Heidegger engages in another characteristic, yet intriguing, etymological derivation. He traces the origin of the "in" to archaic German words that allegedly mean "to reside," "to dwell," "to be accustomed to," "to be familiar with," "to look after." This leads him to themes that preoccupy him in later works: to be in-the-world is to dwell, to be rooted, to be at home, to reside with a good—that is, nonironic—conscience. Furthermore, "I" am always the being who "dwells"; the "I am" *(Ich bin)* allegedly relates etymologically to words that mean "'I reside,' or 'dwell alongside' the World, as that which is familiar to me" *(BAT* 80). Hence Being-in implies residing alongside things in the world and being *absorbed* in them *(Besorgen).* Hence the fundamental, existential Being of man is Care *(Sorge).*

Everyday Dasein is always already a Being-in-the-world and hence is always *already alongside* entities. Dasein's primordial essence is to be "externalized" in this fashion.[4] Any theoretical knowing presupposes this prior, externalized alongsideness of Being-in.[5] Primordial Dasein is always already "outside" in a certain oneness with what it helps reveal or disclose. And it is in turn constituted by what it discloses—mutually disclosing and revealing—a conception quite similar to one found in Aristotle's *De Anima.* According to Heidegger, there is no need to prove the existence of the external world or how it is known by a subject. The "scandal of philosophy" is that the attempt to bridge the gap between man and the outside world is raised over and over again *(BAT* 249). There simply is not, except derivatively, a worldless subject unsure of its world *(BAT* 250).[6] Being-in is not a situation in which a knower qua subject caught within itself succeeds in getting "outside"

4. Note that Heidegger does not prove this; he merely asserts it. Heidegger's method throughout his corpus is one of assertion. This implies that one either grasps its fundamental truth or not; there is no way to work up to it in steps. As is true with Aristotle, one must simply grasp the *arche* directly before any other efforts are possible.

5. To become locked within oneself in a Cartesian dream of subjective isolation is not man's primordial or natural state but a derivative way of being that needs to be explained. What Descartes took as an unencumbered beginning point already carries with it a great deal of prior ontological, moral, and political baggage.

6. Nevertheless, Heidegger claims that traditional philosophical realism is incorrect to the extent that it tries to explain "reality" *ontically* as a constellation of self-subsistent things present-at-hand. Traditional idealism is wrong to the extent it becomes "psychological idealism" and tries to explain that Being and reality are only "in consciousness" and not in the things at all *(BAT* 251–52).

of itself to reach an accommodation with some external ensemble of "objects." This *theoretical* understanding of one entity's "knowing" another external entity has come to take priority in our understanding of Being-in. This establishes a theoretical relationship to the world that then becomes the standard by which all other activity is judged. In the process the real phenomena, which show *themselves,* get covered over.

It is only when we cease being involved, fascinated, and actively engaged with things that we encounter them as mere external objects and as purely present-at-hand to be contemplated theoretically. For Heidegger, it is the possibility of *pretheoretical* familiarity that is at issue. When we have a primordial—by which Heidegger means naive, natural, pretheoretical—relationship to entities, we encounter them as "ready-to-hand," as use objects or equipment. We always start from the kind of Being entities have in those dealings that most concern us. In "circumspection" *(Umsicht)* things are unveiled as what they *essentially are (BAT* 98). Primordial man is primarily an active, practical being, not a contemplative one. We are primordially confronted with and are familiar with the *pragmata* of our *praxis,* which we grasp in a pretheoretical fashion in using them and interacting with them.[7]

The second component of Being-in-the-world, "world," is likewise not something merely present-at-hand; hence it cannot be the sum total of entities.[8] The world is that background phenomenon that makes it possible for entities to be present for us. There is always an involvement in some task: e.g., one needs a chalice *for* communion, a sword *for* battle, a constitution *for* a *polis,* vows *for* a marriage, and so forth. These involvements in turn are always linked together into a totality, which precedes the possibility of encountering individual things. What a thing "is" is determined by what it is for, which is determined by a nexus of "references," or "assignments," linked together by an ultimate "toward-which" or "in-order-to." The ground of this architectonic ordering principle is the world.

Heidegger is loath to connect this ultimate end with any natural characteristics or determinate essence of man that must be fulfilled or completed *(BAT* 119). The in-order-to is not fixed but is beyond our control. The world is the *a priori* that lets things be encountered for the first time, and thereby have Being. World grants the possibility of pres-

7. Compare this with Marx, "Theses on Feuerbach," 121–23, esp. thesis 1, 121.

8. The world is also not to be confused with Nature *(BAT* 92). Nature is merely one of the things discovered within the world. Since there is more than one possible world, there is more than one way to relate to Nature.

ence, while itself remaining absent. Once it becomes totally present for theoretical inspection it ceases to operate as a world. At extreme moments Dasein's involvements recede to such an extent that the world's existence is seen as a problem, and all action, indeed all Being, becomes problematic. Then we are worldless and nihilism ensues. According to Heidegger, we live in such a time.

If metaphysics is a form of humanism grounded in a voluntaristic anthropology, then *Being and Time* is *not* metaphysical.[9] Heidegger attempts to return *praxis* to its primordial, ecstatic immediacy, to dethrone self-consciousness, to undermine atomistic individualism, and to show the necessity of fidelity to one's shared destiny with others.[10] Even in *Being and Time* it is clear that man cannot master the ground which grounds by staying away, self-concealing, in its abysmal grounding qua *Abgrund*.

Heidegger claims that a primordial, "ontological" spatiality, which precedes the possibility of any ontic spatiality, follows from his understanding of world. Man's essential spatiality is *not* that of the insideness of one extended, ontic entity within another; it is the spatiality of "deseverance." Man is the kind of Being who brings things close, severing the distance between himself and things by having a concerned interest. Using different terminology, it is man who "lights things up," who gives them a "site" for their existence. And any time that we have "de-severed" an ensemble of objects, we have a "directionality"; we are directed toward and *already outside, alongside* a certain region and its things. Our primordial spatiality is always the space inside *a* world, and within *a* specific region within that world toward which we are directed.[11] Being itself grants this ontological spatiality and thereby

9. Heidegger argues that his account does not dissolve into mere voluntarism, for the reference structure with its "toward-which" and "in-order-to" can never be consciously posited, it is always already *there*. But "we" (as theoretical onlookers) cannot help but want to fathom the mystery of how the world comes to be *there*, for it is the world that grants the Being of things. If Heidegger is to avoid Nietzschean voluntarism, he must argue that Being qua *physis* uses the world to accomplish presence; "It" puts the world in place by using poets, thinkers and statesmen. According to Heidegger, Western metaphysics devalues the mysterious No-thing; Heidegger would recover it from oblivion. According to the early Heidegger, what worlds in the world is No-thing, acting through man as a site.

10. Heidegger tries to show that man transcends his authentic historicality in only two directions: (1) in openness to the abysmal ground, the No-thing that is mysteriously responsible for all presence, and (2) in mere theoretical staring at already revealed present-at-hand things.

11. As an example, man can bring a beloved child close in circumspect concern, much closer than the eyeglasses through which the child is viewed. This is not an "ob-

opens distinct places through man. When we are concerned with the
ready-to-hand, things have a "closeness" for us; they are in some "region" of "inconspicuous familiarity" (*BAT* 136–37). Primordial space
is split up into these regions, linked into a unity by the *a priori* phenomenon world.

Contrary to the modern understanding that begins in Cartesian subjectivism and reaches a logical extension in Lockean individualism, we
always exist in groups and are codetermined by being part of a shared
revelation of things. Hence, in everydayness the "who" of concernful
"being-with" others is the "they-self." Put another way, "community"
is part of Dasein's Being, not something to be consciously constructed
after the fact. As much as Heidegger tries to avoid talking in this fashion, in more traditional terms, his analysis means that everyday Dasein
is fundamentally "social," in a very deep ontological sense. Atomistic
individualism would always be a derivative way of existing. In its basic
constitution, Dasein is very much an externalized, unselfconscious,
other-related, active, social Being.

But while Dasein might to some degree be "social," it also tends toward an indifferent form of concern and solicitude, which is comparable to disinterested theoretical staring at things merely present-to-
hand (*BAT* 163). When this happens, Dasein's Being is determined by
others, but rarely by definite others. There is frequently an inconspicuous codetermination by indistinct others. The "who" of *everyday*
Being-with is the indefinite "They" *(das Man)*. While dominated by
the They, every Dasein becomes the same as the next. This averageness
of the They leads to a "leveling down" of all possibilities. Heidegger
will argue that there is a more essential mode of Being-with others and
Being-toward things. While Dasein's "publicness" always determines
it, it need not be "insensitive to every difference of level and of genuine-
ness" (*BAT* 164–65). Unfortunately, Heidegger's account of everydayness leaves him with the great difficulty of trying to explain how any
public existence beyond a leveled-off averageness can be possible.

In inappropriate absorption in the They, Heidegger asserts that it

---

jective," quantifiable, ontic distance but a distance based on involvement, concern, and
solicitude (*BAT* 141–42). Only because space has already been opened up in this prior,
ontological, discontinuous, qualitative fashion can we stand back and view space as
quantifiably uniform, a derivative understanding. All ontic relations to things presuppose the prior ontological opening of space. One consequence is that all ontic sciences—
which require quantitatively uniform space—presuppose a prior prescientific relation
to things. *No ontic study is without ontological presuppositions.* Hence no ontic study is or
can be autonomous. Every ontic study is determined by *a* world.

seems that no one at all is consciously responsible for what comes to pass. Things happen without any conscious design; historical drift reigns. In the process Dasein is disburdened of responsibility for anything that happens (*BAT* 165). If all is beyond Dasein's control, it might as well float along, without efficacy, and without taking responsibility. This makes Dasein's life easy, albeit vacuous and meaningless. Dasein seems caught in the grip of forces over which no one has control. It seems manipulated, but there is no real manipulator. Dasein is totally out of control, floating along on a tide nobody ordained. All is accident; nothing is even worthy of anger. At best resignation is all that can be mustered. Dasein surrenders, but to no one in particular.[12] Heidegger terms this way of Being "inauthentic."[13]

Heidegger asserts that only in "authenticity" can things reveal themselves as they are "in-themselves," as genuine "phenomena." This revelation presents itself only to actively involved participants, *not* detached observers. Becoming an authentic self is not to be confused with a Platonic emancipation from the cave, for *"authentic Being-one's-Self does not rest upon an exceptional condition of the subject, a condition that has been detached from the 'they'; it is rather an existentiell modification of the 'they'"* (*BAT* 168). Authenticity requires a new way of relating to one's shared publicness, a trade of one mode of publicness for another. Authenticity implies a form of concernfully absorbed action, shaped by a pregiven *ethos* that eventuates in something like Aristotelian *phronesis*.

Heidegger asserts that our primordial relation to life always rests on a "thrownness" into a world with a specific tradition; a "having-been" delivered over to a particular set of circumstances, disclosed in a certain way. Dasein's Being as thrown is also *pathetic*. In the *pathos* of moods, with all their variety, the world is primordially disclosed for Dasein, space is opened, and entities become present (*BAT* 172–76). The premodern dream of an atemporal, contemplative detachment is a chimera. No detachment—Platonic, Christian, or Cartesian—can cast off the effects of this necessary pretheoretical relation to reality. And from the primacy and unavoidability of moods follows the fact that ontically the best way to "persuade" and move individuals is not through theoretical discourse, but on the more fundamental level of moving

---

12. A similar analysis, wherein there is domination without a visible dominator, is developed by Heidegger's student Herbert Marcuse and other writers of the Frankfurt School. See especially Marcuse, *One Dimensional Man*.

13. Heidegger's dreaded inauthenticity is the ideal most postmodernism fosters and endorses.

them into and out of different moods. Heidegger points us toward Aristotle's *Rhetoric,* which he calls the first systematic treatment of Dasein's fundamental everydayness:

> Contrary to the traditional orientation, according to which rhetoric is conceived as the kind of thing we 'learn in school,' this work of Aristotle must be taken as the first systematic hermeneutic of the everydayness of Being with one another. Publicness, as the kind of Being which belongs to the "they" . . . not only has in general its own way of having a mood, but *needs moods and 'makes' them for itself.* It is into such a mood and out of such a mood that the orator speaks. He must understand the possibilities of moods *in order to rouse them and guide them aright. (BAT* 178; emphasis mine)

It seems reasonable to assume that Heidegger (the authentic actor qua author) is doing more than giving a theoretically detached string of analytical propositions. He too moves his audience into and out of moods, and this is true throughout his work.

Dasein is always pathetically thrown into a world with its distinctive past and projected, either actively or by inaction, toward viable future possibilities (*BAT* 184–87). When indifference and inaction dominate everyday existence, "Dasein drifts along toward an ever-increasing groundlessness as it floats, the uncanniness of this floating remains hidden from it under [the] protecting shelter [of the They]" (*BAT* 214).[14] At best one project follows another without anything being carried to completion. Nowhere is there any staying power. There is a constant, fast-paced flux, many "happenings," but nothing serious occurs, and one opportunity after another is snatched away (*BAT* 212). This inability to be a truly disclosive There, to reveal or disclose one's surroundings and oneself in a "primordial" manner, is what it means to be "uprooted" as that term is used in *Being and Time.*

But since in Heidegger's sense, everyday, social Dasein is always falling away from and uprooted from a direct relatedness to Being, any

---

14. The inaction of *contemporary* inauthenticity is dominated by an "idle talk" that chatters endlessly about all things without getting to anything essential. Likewise it is carried along by a "curiosity" that never genuinely understands what it sees; i.e., it is not actively involved with things. In this curiosity we move from one thing to another in search of repeated novelty, a restless excitement in changing encounters. We are constantly distracted, such that there never develops any ongoing, circumspective concern; we find ourselves in the state of *"never dwelling anywhere"* (*BAT* 217). Dasein is ambiguously "everywhere yet nowhere," hence it becomes impossible for Dasein to be a There in the primordial disclosive sense. In "ambiguity," taking action and carrying a project through becomes impossible.

simple nationalism or romantic longing to return to the soil can never by itself solve the problem of man's rootlessness. Man must initially sink his roots into something more primary than a nation, a people, a class, indigenous things, language, and so on. True rootedness implies an ontological foundation, which is only possible through transcendence of the reigning They-self. Dasein requires openness to Being itself. Yet since Dasein is necessarily a social being, there must also be a more primordial relation *to entities* that can exist within the realm of publicness. As Heidegger puts the matter in *Vom Wesen des Grundes,* there are *two* categories of primary revealedness or truth: "ontological truth," which comes from openness to Being, and "ontic truth," which comes from openness to properly disclosed beings. But in the last analysis, ontological truth somehow enables ontic truth. This duality of direct openness to Being and proper openness to beings is found throughout Heidegger's work. In *Being and Time* one aspect of the duality is stressed; in later works, the priority changes.

Everyday absorption in things is all-pervasive because of its "tranquilizing" effects; each repeatedly succeeds in convincing all others that they are leading a full and genuine life, and hence they all leave well enough alone. But this is the tranquillity of ambiguous hustle and bustle and its constant monotonous motion and changeability. As a result, one is alienated from one's "ownmost potentiality-for-Being" and one's "ownmost self," but is presumably quite happy because Dasein has no determinate "Nature" that will assert itself and cause a sense of being unfulfilled and dissatisfied. This tranquilized falling convinces itself that it has experienced and secured all possibilities and becomes self-satisfied, much like those who mockingly demand of Zarathustra that the last man is what they want. To retain its tranquillity, Dasein "levels off" all substantial differences which might intrude upon the well-beaten path. What follows "is at the same time *alienating*" (*BAT* 222). Heidegger asserts that this alienation from one's ownmost possibilities is not an ontic alienation from another part of oneself, which would drive one into an account like that of Freud; nor is it a Marxian alienation from one's "species' Being," which for Heidegger could only mean an alienation from the They-self. It is an alienation from, openness to, and oneness with Being, or *alternately,* an alienation from the possibility of immersion in authentically disclosed things as they are "in themselves," as *phenomena* in Heidegger's technical sense.

Heidegger discusses one distinctive way of transcending alienation. Unlike the great majority of moods which bring Dasein into an absorptive understanding of the world and the things disclosed in it, anxiety turns us away from the totality of beings in the world. As

Heidegger expresses the matter in "What Is Metaphysics?," an essay from roughly the same period, anxiety provides for the possibility of "transcendence," the possibility of transcending the falling absorption within the world of the They which makes one inauthentic.[15] In anxiety we experience the possibility of the impossibility of Being-in-the-world. What anxiety does is to allow Dasein to come in contact with the phenomenon world, bracket it, and reflect upon its mysterious status.

The very possibility of the world is that in the face of which we have anxiety (BAT 231). In anxiety we are projected out beyond Being-in-the-world into No-thingness as individualized for our "ownmost" Being-toward our individualized possibilities. In the process, all familiarity collapses, all tranquillity dissolves, and everyday "dwelling" becomes impossible.[16] Dasein eventually flees the uncanny tension which it experiences in anxiety and falls back into absorption in the familiar things in its world, and thereby anxiety gets dimmed down. Heidegger asserts that to break out of the tranquilized present and project authentic future, *ontic* possibilities, then some concrete, ontic modalization of anxiety is required (BAT 239–40). Somehow, *transcendence toward the ground* and action *in the world* must be linked. That linkage is far more problematic than is recognized in most interpretations; it involves the *rhetorical* modalization of "anticipation" and "resoluteness."

The New Thinking and the Recovery of *Praxis*

At the beginning of part 2 of *Being and Time,* Heidegger admits that what he presented before in working out the constitution of everydayness was only a discussion of the "*concrete* constitution of existence" (BAT 274; emphasis mine). What remains is to show how a being like man, who is not essentially a present-to-hand being, can achieve totality. The problem of totality exists for any being determined by a Not. When ontic Dasein achieves totality it ceases to be There in a very straightforward sense: it reaches its own demise. Hence, Heidegger asserts, ontically Dasein can never be experienced as a whole without

15. Martin Heidegger, "What Is Metaphysics?" 325–61.

16. In "What Is Metaphysics?" Heidegger explicitly observes that anxiety or dread "necessitates changing man into his *Da-sein,*" and says further that "*Da-sein* means *being projected into* Nothing. . . . Projecting into Nothing, *Da-sein* is already beyond what-is-in-totality. This 'being beyond' . . . what-is we call Transcendence" (pp. 337, 339). In this transcendence one becomes a potential site for the presencing of the No-thing, the Overpowering, and thereby, the coming to pass of Being. One should notice how Heidegger differentiates Da-sein as projection toward the *Abgrund* from more generic, everyday Dasein. I will retain this device in what follows.

ceasing to be (*BAT* 280). But it is an ontological totality for which Heidegger is searching. In this discussion, perhaps more than anywhere else, Heidegger consciously uses his distinction between ontic and ontological to his rhetorical advantage; it is only "Being-toward-death" that allows Dasein to be a whole, not ontic "Being-toward-demise." To die in the ontological sense is to transcend the world. What one achieves is a projection out into the No-thing, the abysmal ground, the source. What occurs in the ontological phenomenon of dying is not "Being-*at*-an-end," but "Being-*toward*-the-end." Death, in the sense in which a certain ontological totality or wholeness is attested, is a way *to be*; it is a phenomenon of life (*BAT* 289–90).

Being-toward-death is a distinctive possibility, which one cannot call forth at one's own discretion. So conceived, death is the possibility of the absolute impossibility of Being-in-the-world, of being a There in the sense of being the place or location where things are revealed or come to presence (*BAT* 294). As long as Dasein exists it is always confronted by the possibility of this transcendence, but most individuals never experience death so understood. They will never know it because they flee from it into a falling absorption with things in the world of concern; they fall into the They's tranquilized quietude. Being-toward-death is a Being-toward the question "Why is there something rather than nothing at all?" It is a projection out into the No-thingness that mysteriously grounds all that is, into which all that is constantly threatens to dissolve except for some mysterious perseverance and semipermanence. Being-toward-death is thinking in its purest sense. This is the new thinking the later Heidegger will discuss thematically. Its possibility is already attested in *Being and Time*. As such, philosophy is a form of preparing to die.

If Heidegger is to prove that the ontological phenomenon of death is interesting to the concrete realm of everydayness, he must argue that it has an ontic, *existentiell* manifestation as well; there must also be a possibility of an *existentiell*, ontic Being-a-whole.

. . . If Being-toward-death belongs primordially and essentially to Dasein's Being, then it must also be exhibitable in everydayness, *even if proximally in a way which is inauthentic* [emphasis mine]. And if Being-toward-the-end should afford the existential possibility of an existentiell Being-a-whole for Dasein, then this would give phenomenal confirmation for the thesis that "care" is the ontological term for the totality of Dasein's structural whole. *If, however,* [emphasis mine] we are to provide a full phenomenal justification for this principle, a *preliminary sketch* of the connection between Being-toward-death and care is not sufficient. We must be able to see this connection above all in that *concretion* which lies closest to Dasein—its everydayness. (*BAT* 296)

What follows proves only that a concrete, *existentiell approximation* of Being-toward-death falls within everydayness—no more and no less. But that means that Being-toward-*demise* is what falls under care, a Being-toward-demise vouched for in fear, before something present-to-hand, which is by definition inauthentic.[17] Heidegger goes to considerable rhetorical lengths to blur the distinction between the truly philosophic individual ("thinker")—who has his foundation in the anxiety-induced awe of Being-toward-death—and the nonphilosophic person incapable of transcendence, just as Nietzsche did. We should be reminded of Heidegger's comments about Aristotle and rhetoric quoted above as well as his explicit observations about how philosophy must always present its case in subtle and indirect ways:

> Is there not, however, a definite *ontical* way of taking authentic existence, a factical ideal of Dasein, underlying our *ontological* Interpretation of Dasein's existence? That is so indeed. But not only is this Fact one which must not be denied and which we are forced to grant; it must also be conceived in its *positive necessity* [Heidegger's emphasis], in terms of the object which we have taken as the theme of our investigation. Philosophy will never seek to deny its 'presuppositions,' but neither may it simply admit them. It conceives them, and it unfolds with more and more penetration both the presuppositions themselves and *that for which* they are presuppositions. (*BAT* 358; emphasis mine)

17. Heidegger's primary discussion focuses on average, everyday Being-toward-demise as it is interpreted in idle talk. The They knows death only as a mishap that befalls others; it "is encountered as a well-known event occurring within-the-World" (*BAT* 297). Everyday Dasein experiences only a present-at-hand event that happens to present-at-hand beings which have biological life. The They only experiences death as demise, never as an authentic, philosophic Being-toward-No-thingness, an almost religious transcendence that projects out into the mystery. (One should notice how close this experience in Being-toward-death is to Nietzsche's discussion of Being-toward the Dionysian.) Everyone vaguely recognizes that "one dies," but it is not "me"; others can represent me in this indefinite possibility. The They transforms anxiety in the face of the impossibility of Being-in-the-World into fear of an oncoming event, then consoles Dasein by showing the indefiniteness of that event. Finally, the They argues that thinking about death is morbid and cowardly; only indifferent tranquillity is noble and fitting. The They accomplishes a fleeing in the face of demise and will not permit the courage for the anxiety that makes transcendence possible. This would appear especially true of modern, bourgeois Theyness.

As a factical, ontic, *existentiell* Being, Dasein is always falling away from the fundamental disclosure of the truth, which has its ground in Being-toward-death; it is always falling into untruth and ceasing to be disclosive: "Primordially 'truth' means the same as 'Being-disclosive,' as a way in which Dasein behaves. From this comes *the derivative signification:* 'the uncoveredness of entities'" (*BAT* 300; emphasis mine). *Being open to the uncoveredness of entities is always secondary, and derivative; yet essential.* First one must be open to the abysmal ground, the No-thing. Derivative from that comes the proper disclosedness of entities. The truth fundamentally manifests itself in a form of direct, unmediated apprehension accomplished in thinking, not primarily through the mediation of things or speeches about things. Genuine ontological grounding is achieved through an unmediated openness to the mysterious source of presence. The mediated relation to Being through things is always, as Heidegger says explicitly, secondary. Consequently, Heidegger rejects what Socrates in the *Phaedo* calls his "second sailing," and opts for the first sailing, the direct approach to the abysmal ground.

Heidegger asserts that Dasein must be open to Being-toward-death by being ready for anxiety if it is to become its ownmost self. This state is reached in what Heidegger calls "anticipation" (*Vorlaufen*). In anticipation Dasein (qua Da-sein) is "liberated" from those possibilities and entities into which it is thrown. It is liberated from the They-self so that it can pursue its "*ownmost* potentiality-for-[oneness with]-Being" (*BAT* 307). Furthermore, "anticipation discloses to existence that its uttermost possibility lies in giving itself up, and thus it shatters all one's tenaciousness to whatever existence one has reached" (*BAT* 308). One must give up one's commitment to present entities to make it possible to open up and reveal new ones. But the person who does so is always *apolis*.

In anticipation, Dasein is in the truth; qua a concernfully absorbed self within the domination of the They, it lies in untruth. As open to authentically uncovered entities it is in the truth in a *derivative* sense. Since the species as a whole never transcends the They-self and its everydayness en masse, it can never achieve total enlightenment or self-conscious "transparency." Dasein, understood as the species, will always remain in truth and untruth simultaneously (assuming philosophic openness remains possible or something authentic gets revealed; otherwise, it will exist entirely in untruth). The Hegelian account of the complete actualization of the truth, which implies the closure of unique historical possibilities, should be impossible as long as we reappropriate genuine Being-disclosive as a way of being.

As a result of anticipation, "the possibility of Dasein's having an authentic potentiality-for-Being-a-whole emerges, *but only as an ontological possibility.*" How this translates itself into authentic action immersed
in properly revealed entities remains a question.

> This existentially "possible" Being-toward-death remains, from
> the existentiell point of view, a fantastical exaction. The fact that
> an authentic potentiality-for-Being-a-whole is ontologically pos-
> sible for Dasein, signifies nothing, so long as a corresponding on-
> tical potentiality-for-Being has not been demonstrated in Dasein
> itself. (*BAT* 311)

In anxiety, "Dasein finds itself *face to face* with the 'nothing' of the possible impossibility of its existence *[Existenz]*," but this in no way dem-
onstrates how one must act within the *existentiell* world of concern
(*BAT* 310). Indeed the question remains "as to *whether the Anticipation
of . . . death, which we have hitherto projected only in its* **ontological** *possibility, has an essential connection with that authentic potentiality-for-Being
which has been* **attested**" in everydayness (*BAT* 311).

We are told there is a form of authenticity within the structure of
care. Authenticity within the ontic world of everyday concern "takes
the definite form of an *existentiell modification of the 'they'*" (*BAT* 312;
emphasis mine). *Existentiell* authenticity requires a transformation of
the dominant public self, a concrete modification of the public way of
seeing, talking, interpreting, and understanding. In the highest sense,
that kind of change would be what is accomplished by what would customarily be called a founder, whether understood as a statesman, a poet
of the rank of a Homer, or a great prophet. The *existentiell* possibility of
authenticity rests on a mode of existence that is a far cry from the quiet,
solitary reticence of anticipation, where one has been radically stripped
of all objects of concern. The *existentiell* possibility of authenticity requires commitment to concernfully absorbed action. How does this
relate to the awestruck wonder and anxiety that raises the question of
why something exists rather than nothing at all? Far from transcending
the world and the They, an authenticity that is implicated in an *existentiell* modification of They merely calls one into an immersion in a
newly opened world and the unique publicness of its newly constituted
They (*BAT* 312–13).

The possibility of there being an *existentiell manifestation* of Being-
toward-death rests on what Heidegger designates the "call of conscience." The call of conscience brings Dasein out of its lostness in the
reigning publicness of the They, in which Dasein has been relieved of

its responsibility for choosing and acting.[18] Conscience calls Dasein out of that situation in which everything occurs because They did it, or They decided thus and such, where everyone assumes that someone is making conscious choices, but no one does. Conscience calls *concrete* Dasein out of the historical drift that destroys conscious choice and leadership. When this occurs, one is called to "resoluteness" *(Entschlossenheit).*

Heidegger asserts that in resoluteness Dasein breaks away from the They. Dasein is called to choosing for itself, interpreting for itself, seeing, listening, and discoursing for itself. This is not the "silent listening" of anticipation. Heidegger also says explicitly that resoluteness is not the willfulness of self-definition in the mode of an isolated, subjective self: "The appeal to the Self in the they-self does not force it inwards upon itself, so that it can close itself off from the 'external world.' The call passes over everything like this and disperses it, so as to appeal solely *to that Self which, notwithstanding, is in no other way than Being-in-the-world*" (*BAT* 318; emphasis mine). Dasein is not called into an isolated, worldless self-consciousness; it is called into the World in such a way that it causes an "existentiell modification of the They" to come to pass. In the call of conscience, Dasein is called to *praxis* in a perfectly Aristotelian sense. Resoluteness is a form of *praxis* tantamount to what the later Heidegger will call "building": "Resoluteness brings the Being of the 'there' into the existence of its Situation. . . . As resolute, Dasein is already *taking action*" (*BAT* 347).

> In Resoluteness the issue for Dasein is its ownmost potentiality-for-Being, which, as something thrown, can project itself *only upon definite factical possibilities.* Resolution does not withdraw itself from 'actuality,' but discovers first what is factically possible; and it does so by seizing upon it in whatever way is possible for it as its ownmost *potentiality-for-Being in the "they."* (*BAT* 346; emphasis mine)

But "who" is the caller in the call of conscience; who makes the indefinite call? Heidegger's answer is that it is the Dasein of anxiety (a.k.a. Da-sein), in the depths of the "uncanniness" of anticipation.

18. The call of conscience gives no specific information about worldly events; it makes no articulate assertion. It summons Dasein from lostness in the They, but tells it nothing specific about how to accomplish a victory over the hegemony of the They (*BAT* 318). This is not to be confused with the transcendence of genuine Being-toward-death, which brackets the possibility of Being-in-the-World. Conscience vouches for an *existentiell* phenomenon, an *existentiell* authenticity, and an *existentiell* form of totality.

And it is Dasein as constituted by the tranquilized They-self that is called to. Da-sein calls Dasein. But it is not the same Dasein that receives and sends the call. Heidegger makes the most of a consciously deployed ambiguity; nonetheless, he makes his point explicit: "*The caller is unfamiliar to the everyday they-self* [emphasis mine]; it is something like an *alien* voice. What could be more alien to the 'they,' lost in the manifold 'world' of its concern, than the Self which has been individualized down to itself in uncanniness and been thrown into the 'nothing'?" (*BAT* 321–22). Simultaneously, Heidegger flirts with a theme to which he will return later, that there is a mysterious "It" that gives the call *(es gibt),* the call of the Overpowering, and thereby grants Thereness, openness, and primordial spatiality.

Heidegger asserts that there are times when "'It' calls, against our expectations and even against our will. We are left with the assertion that the call of conscience is entirely immanent, silent, lacking in substantive content, is in no way a universal conscience, and like Socrates' *daimon* primarily warns and reproves; it is a 'no-sayer'" (*BAT* 324). While the call of conscience calls nothing that can be articulated, it nonetheless conveys a declaration of guilt. In so far as Dasein factically exists, it is guilty in the very essence of its being because of *"Being-the-basis of a nullity"* (*BAT* 326, 329). Dasein must never cease in its efforts at maintaining the openness of a world. The world has no eternally present ground, and we as individual beings have no eternally present being. Human existence is defined by a Not, a straightforward manifestation of the modern, antinature animus. Our guilt points toward the need to be the basis of this nullity. But we cannot accomplish that by being self-grounding, self-legislating egos. Whether resolutely taking over being the basis of a nullity is possible without a recurrence to the subjective modern ego remains an open question.

Because of the coprimordiality of the three fundamental structures of care—understanding projection (which is directed toward the future), facticity and thrownness (which immerses one in the past), and falling absorption in the They (which gives priority to the present)—Dasein can never be free to determine its own basis from the ground up. Resolute Dasein is ecstatically temporal, always dominated by a past over which it has no control, yet needing to project future possibilities. That past rests on the remains of a prior disclosedness, mindless acceptance of which always puts Dasein in danger of falling into nullity. That is why Dasein must relate to its past with an eye simultaneously to its future. Dasein must *in the present* draw up its past (tradition) and project a future on the basis of what is still possible rather than naively awaiting its arrival. The danger of falling into nullity is constant, as is the need for authentic projections, for there is no ideal which once attained can be stored away in some safe fashion. Legalism—in either law or ethics—can never replace a properly opened and continually reopened *ethos*.

Heidegger asserts that the possibility of morality follows from out of our nullity and essential Being-guilty, as a derivative, factical phenomenon (*BAT* 332). All morality must build upon the recognition of this fundamental guilt and the need it implies. We must *become* moral beings precisely because we are a nullity. In other words, because we have no eternal Nature that determines good and evil, we must become the basis of good and evil. But we cannot simply will a moral code, it must emerge out of an authentic disclosive *praxis* qua involved, ecstatic being-with.

Resoluteness immerses and absorbs Dasein in its historical world—its having-been—but in a way that does not drift along waiting for the They to choose and act for it. In doing so, resolute Dasein allows others to become themselves as well (*BAT* 344). Since being disclosively related to entities and to others is made possible by worldhood, it should be clear that the maintaining of worldhood is what is accomplished by resoluteness, while constantly recalling that for Heidegger resoluteness is not the willfulness of an isolated "I," and the world is not merely a humanly constructed horizon. Resolute Dasein makes an "*existentiell* modification" of the world so that others can remain related authentically to things and to each other.[19] In the process, however, the others do not become authentic; in fact, they merely become immersed in a newly modified They, a new publicness. But they will at least be immersed in properly revealed entities for a time.

By definition no concernful absorption in the world can take the place of hearing the silent call of anticipation or of being resolute. But the majority can become "open" to the truth by being related to entities that have been revealed as they are "in-themselves." Heidegger's resolute Dasein is foundational, by helping to keep entities properly revealed. Resolute Dasein remains emancipated from immersion in what for others is a shared work world, a world dominated by the primordial disclosure of things as ready-to-hand, and "others" as fellows engaged in shared projects. I offer a speculation: Following Aristotle, Heidegger seems to be preparing for the recovery of a theoretically autonomous *praxis* by grounding a *phronimos* who keeps open the pos-

19. Since by Heideggerian definition such authenticity precedes the possibility of morality, it is "beyond good and evil," by becoming the ground of good and evil for others.

sibility of an *ethos* and *polis* for others.[20] As I have stressed, and will
stress throughout, Aristotle's influence on Heidegger can hardly be
overestimated. While he is substantially tone-deaf to the dialogic character of Plato's thought, Heidegger penetrates deeply into the spirit of
Aristotle's. Indeed, at one time a book on Aristotle was projected. It
was replaced by *Being and Time*.[21]

In the phenomenon of anticipation, Heidegger grounds the possibility of something like an awe-inspired thinking, a thinking that neither makes anything nor engages in *praxis*. Thinking, *praxis*, and *technē*
cannot converge as they do, for example, in the work of Hegel. Instead
of *theoria* in the Greek sense, we get a thinking that is more like a re-

---

20. Heidegger tries to paint a picture of human beings as the most distinctive beings
in existence, with a privileged relationship to Being. Thereby he hopes to emancipate
humanity from the reductionism of modern science. He tries to accomplish this increase
in dignity without either (1) reinstating the distinction between body and soul, which he
believes leads to the view that man is primarily an extended object to which is appended,
almost as an afterthought, something incorporeal, or (2) linking man with a transcendent realm, whether that of the Platonic ideas, the Christian heaven, or the Kantian
transcendental subject. In *Being and Time*, not only does Heidegger attempt to emancipate practical, political life from theoretical domination, the hegemony of technology
and modern science, and subservience to the transcendent—he also tries to emancipate
primordial practical life from domination by absolutes, universals, and the *apodictic* in all
its forms.

In the face of Christian dogmatism, Kantian/Hegelian universalism, modern scientific reductionism, and liberal doctrinairism, Heidegger tries to return flexibility to human practice; he tries to open up again that realm in which something like Aristotelian
prudence *(phronesis)* could operate. He tries to allow room for the fluidity and flexibility
of discretion in an age increasingly dominated by rationalized administration, legalism,
and universalistic ethics. And he tries to overcome the nihilism of an ethics swamped by
the fact/value dichotomy by showing that facts never primordially appear as mere facts,
but emerge only because they are valuable. (Unfortunately, Heidegger does not equal-
ize the status of facts and values by showing the objectivity of values, but by historiciz-
ing facts.)

Heidegger likewise tries to free men from the constant motion and flux of styles and
fads, which makes relativism seem a way of life, by pointing to the ground for the reemergence of a sheltering *ethos*. On such a basis the early Heidegger thought it would be
possible for men to take over their fate and take responsibility for their existence at a
time when the species was armed with the greatest of powers and no serious moral or
political purpose. Finally, like Nietzsche, Heidegger tries to reinvigorate the notion of
the tragic—that man always "falls." "Progress" in the strong sense is not a possibility;
modern man is not at the peak or height of all history. History is not linear and unidirectional, and hence excellence must be recovered anew by each generation. No generation
is exempt from the need to struggle back to a point where it can repeat the openness,
insight, and virtue of previous ones. And this is as true for the thinker as it is for resolute
praxis.

21. In this regard, see Pöggeler, *Martin Heidegger's Path of Thinking*.

ligious awe in the face of a mysterious concealing and revealing Overpowering/No-thing that cannot be articulated in a final discourse. Thinking eventuates in silence, not *logos*. This is similar to Nietzsche's projection of a future philosophy as a form of religious pathos rather than a logical enterprise ultimately brought into the service of, and thereby subordinate to, *technē*. Thinking becomes a Dionysian openness to the mystery at the core of all that is which can never become totally present. In *Being and Time, praxis* gets redefined as disclosive, foundational activity that stands prior to any theoretical detachment. The new hierarchy runs from thinking qua anticipation to resolute disclosive *praxis* to authentic shared being-with to detached theoretical activity in the service of *technē*, which is always in the service of fostering a tranquilized way of life that is the most occlusive.

The nature of the new thinking, which is related to the No-thing, and how to name its object, is the preoccupation of the later Heidegger. It is not stressed in *Being and Time,* but it is announced. *Being and Time* primarily discusses and legitimizes that resoluteness that becomes the ground for *nomos,* for the circle of care—i.e., of a shared community with its own distinctive *ethos.* Heidegger tries to free *praxis* from *technē* and *theoria.* He tries to ground an autonomous, ecstatic *praxis.* But there is nonetheless an intimation of the new vision of thinking that will become thematic in the later works. Even in *Being and Time* that thinking is freed from the Spirit of Revenge, for it has no worldly function. It is a thinking that is openness to a self-presencing Other which is formless, nameless, without attributes, never totally present, limitless, No-thing. Such thinking eventuates in silence, it is solitary and *apolis* (*IM* 152–53).[22]

I have presented resoluteness as an immersed, engaged, disclosive form of *praxis.* And I have presented Being-toward-death, which is attested to in anticipation, as an awestruck openness to the mysterious *Abgrund.*[23] How are the two related? What can be made of Heidegger's

22. Throughout his work, Heidegger makes it clear that man is central to the event *(Ereignis)* of Being and truth. In the early works it might appear that what *man* does is as important as what is done by the absent source. The focus later shifts to the grace of the No-thing. In *Being and Time* Heidegger has merely looked at the issue from the perspective of man rather than that of Being/No-thing. Despite all the ground covered by the published portions of *Being and Time,* it stops short of explicitly dealing with the main issue it set out to clarify—the meaning of Being. Still, it becomes clear that man is the site or vortex at which absence and presence are linked. Some acts are disclosive of the abysmal ground, others occlusive. How Heidegger knows one from the other remains unclear and to my mind is clarified nowhere in his corpus. Nonetheless, even in *Being and Time,* the absent source has priority over man.

23. "An authentic potentiality-for-Being-a-whole on the part of Dasein has been

attempted combination of these two in "anticipatory resoluteness"? In his attempt to link these two ways of existing, Heidegger paradoxically begins by conceding what seems to vouch for the impossibility of his task:

> How are these two phenomena of anticipation and resoluteness to be brought together? Has not our ontological projection of the authentic potentiality-for-Being-a-whole led us into a dimension of Dasein which lies far from the phenomenon of resoluteness? What can death and the 'concrete Situation' of taking action have in common? In attempting to bring resoluteness and anticipation forcibly together, are we not seduced into an intolerable and quite unphenomenological construction, for which we can no longer claim that it has the character of an ontological projection, based upon the phenomena?
>
> Any superficial binding together of the two phenomena is ex- cluded. There still remains one way out, and this is the only pos- sible method: namely, to take as our point of departure the phenomenon of resoluteness, as attested in its existentiell possi- bility, and to ask: *"Does resoluteness, in its ownmost existentiell ten- dency of Being, point forward to anticipatory resoluteness as its ownmost authentic possibility?"* (BAT 349)

To the extent that the merger of anticipation and resoluteness remains questionable, so do the ontic possibility of Being-a-whole and the on- tological foundation of practical existence. That is the tension that ex- ists in *Being and Time*. That tension is not satisfactorily resolved, which Heidegger eventually realized.

At the basis of anticipatory resoluteness lies a perception of mortal- ity, finitude, and potential ontic nothingness, i.e., the consciousness of *demise*. Heidegger wishes to heighten this consciousness, that is, to heighten a specific mood or *pathē*, the *public* consciousness of nothing- ness, the abyss, and nihilism. He will make this theme explicit in *What Is Called Thinking?* and elsewhere in his later works, where he asserts there is a need for a "positive" relation to nihilism. Whereas Hobbes begins with the priority of consciousness of demise only to build a pro- ject that will soften or extirpate it—a movement also central to the

---

projected existentially. By analysing this phenomenon, we have revealed that authentic Being-toward-death is *anticipation*. Dasein's authentic potentiality-for-Being, in its *exis- tentiell attestation* [emphasis mine], has been exhibited, and at the same time existentially Interpreted, as *resoluteness*" (BAT 349).

thought of Hegel—Heidegger wishes to heighten awareness of Being-toward-demise. To put the matter in sharpest focus, whereas Hobbes and Hegel depict the bourgeoisification of humanity as necessary, Heidegger wishes to reverse it because the confrontation with certain primordial experiences puts us in closer contact with Being than would be possible if they were extirpated. Certain experiences are "disclosive." If they are in danger of being lost, so is our relationship to Being. Anticipatory resoluteness is built upon a consciousness of one's mortality, of Being-toward-demise, which Heidegger hopes to link with a desire for immortality through the doing of great deeds, i.e., "monumental," repeatable deeds that live far beyond the biological existence of the actor in the collective memory and *ethos* of a community.[24]

Resoluteness leads to accepting one's fated destiny within one's generation. In doing so, Dasein *"can, by handing down to itself the possibility it has inherited, take over its own thrownness and be* **in the moment of vision** *for 'its time'"* (*BAT* 437). The possibilities that are revealed in this way are *repeatable* possibilities: "The Resoluteness which comes back to itself and hands itself down, then becomes the *repetition* of a possibility of existence. . . . *Repeating is handing down explicitly*—that is to say, going back into the possibilities of the Dasein that has-been-there." This repetition allows Dasein to "choose its hero," making one "free for the struggle of loyally following in the footsteps of that which can be repeated" (*BAT* 437). This does not mean we simply copy the concrete action of predecessors with the aim of reactualizing the identical concrete outcome. Heidegger is not arguing for going back and simply, atavistically reliving some previous time, epoch, or age. To accuse him of that is to trivialize his thought. One can never simply reactualize the present-to-hand past. What is at issue is a formal repetition of a mode of existing, a way of being, a way of relating to life that has previously been attained. "Monumental possibilities," *in precisely the Nietzschean sense,* are what would be reactualized. We can repeat the experiences of great statesmen, poets, artists, and prophets, together

---

24. Heidegger explicitly co-opts the Nietzschean term "monumental." Anticipatory resoluteness provides the critical stance that is needed beyond the unworld of the present. In an age in which the world falls away and worldless man is left exposed, one now needs a resoluteness modalized by anticipation. In other ages this will not be necessary. Different times call for different things, just as for Nietzsche one needs critical, monumental, and antiquarian history at different times. It would not miss the mark to say that Heidegger has given ontological foundations to the core intuitions contained in Nietzsche's *Advantages and Disadvantages of History for Life*. Again, Heidegger's explicit invocation of the "monumental" is no accident.

with the solidarity of a community fatefully bound together. We cannot repeat the present-to-hand.[25]

On the basis of awareness of Being-toward-demise, one is convinced of the necessity for resolution, for the doing of great and immortal deeds. Historical drift and inauthenticity are the results of the universal bourgeoisification of man. "Anticipatory resoluteness" aims to reverse this bourgeoisification. *But it is only a rhetorical possibility,* an experiment Heidegger later gives up on.[26] While clear correlates to anticipation and resoluteness can be found in the later works, anticipatory resoluteness drops out completely for at least two reasons: (1) Heidegger's experience with Nazism, and (2) his experience with, and rejection of, popular existentialism, especially Sartre's version. These issues are addressed in *The Letter on Humanism,* to which I will return shortly.

Nietzsche too had seen the need for a unique kind of behavior based upon exacerbating and heightening the consciousness of nothingness, i.e., the need for a public teaching emphasizing the abyss. In the face of the fact that the enervated last man had so completely destroyed the ground for genuine historical action, the heightening of the sense of pain and need was necessary. Heidegger tries to do something comparable—not identical—in his discussion of anticipatory resoluteness. Nietzsche wished eventually to get beyond this preeminent awareness of the abyss; he wished to recover a naive, immediate consciousness, one that was more "natural" and "instinctive." Heidegger, in *Being and Time,* points to that possibility in his idea of pure resoluteness. But such

25. Further, monumental individuals and their deeds always belong to *a* distinct community; and without such deeds genuine communities cease to exist. In *Being and Time* I would argue that resoluteness, understood as something like a "great-souledness" armed with *phronesis,* takes primacy as a form of monumental action. In the later works, that primacy will shift to the poets and artists (*BAT* 444–49). Heidegger's biggest problem is that he fails to explain how to tell the difference between a Washington or Lincoln and a Hitler or Mussolini, or between Moses and Jim Jones. But that would lead him into a theoretical *logos* which he thinks would reproduce the problem he is trying to surmount.

26. Heidegger cannot posit any simple, natural, instinctive impulsion to resolute action, no natural core of Dasein that loves honor, no natural desire to be like or to replace the gods. Anticipatory resoluteness takes the place of such an instinctive basis for action; it represents a mode of understanding determined by the unique unworld of the present. In other words, it is based on *our* distinctive mode of thrownness and the possibilities it opens up. One must be convinced of the need to take action now rather than defer until later, i.e., to defer indefinitely to the They. For Heidegger, this is a concrete ground upon which action can stand outside of the hegemony of the reigning They. Needless to say, it is determined by its distinctive factical situation; Heidegger's own argument attests to that. In this respect, *Being and Time* is a form of anticipatorily resolute action.

resoluteness requires a prior reappropriation of an authentic relation to past, present, and future—i.e., an authentic, ecstatic temporality which presupposes an authentic *ethos* and the traditions that make it possible.[27]

The basis of anticipation apparently exists in and of itself in primordial anxiety, and that of resoluteness in man's essence as an active, practical, social being. Anticipation and resoluteness represent primordial ways to be. But before such primordial possibilities can be assured of repetition, an act of anticipatory resoluteness is required. Anticipatory resoluteness points toward our present position between eternities. In that regard, man has a primacy in the revelatory process in *Being and Time* that Heidegger will significantly downplay later. Nonetheless, even in *Being and Time,* the revelatory experience of anticipation retains priority: genuine Being-toward-death is where Dasein becomes the primary site for the presencing of the No-thing. It precedes the authentic revealedness of entities that is also required.

When Heidegger turns explicitly to the argument that temporality is the true horizon of man's being, he turns to a discussion of the authentic and inauthentic ways of being related to past, present, and future. The authentic mode of relating to temporality is that which is disclosed by resolute Dasein, locked authentically within the circle of care. Looking forward in a concerned fashion, with the eye, that is, of one responsible for the future's coming into being, is Dasein's authentic mode of Being toward the future. This is opposed to the inauthentic mode of mere "awaiting," in which one is prepared to take whatever comes—usually assuming it will be identical to what one has in the present: i.e., inauthentic awaiting assumes the end of history. Dasein must also always have some relation to its present, its facticity, that into which it is thrown and falling. One is authentically related to the present in the "moment of vision," the *Augenblick,* the resolute, ecstatic rapture in which Dasein is carried away to a vision of whatever possi-

---

27. In *Being and Time* pure resoluteness is presented as immersed, committed action, which shows one the factical situation of one's shared fate and destiny; i.e., it leads to a perception of one's place in the progression linking past and future. But when the present has lost its ecstatic relation to past and future, as has ours, such resoluteness is not immediately possible. The phenomenon at which we arrive when resoluteness is modalized by anticipation is that unusual form of action based on a heightening of the awareness of Being-toward-demise. It bears all the marks of an extraordinary basis for action, as is necessary in a time such as ours. In *Being and Time* there is no indication that gods will intervene or that a mysterious dispensation of the No-thing/Being will make man's anticipatory resoluteness irrelevant.

bilities are encountered in the current factical situation, as opposed to the inauthentic, passive contemplation of what is given as present-at-hand (*BAT* 376). The authentic relation to the past eventuates in the desire for the "repetition" of monumental possibilities, as opposed to the forgetting that always backs away from its "ownmost having-been," and from its distinctive tradition and the limitations it imposes. With his discussion of authentic, ecstatic temporality, Heidegger presents an "ontology of tradition," as opposed to an "ontology of freedom."[28]

Dasein is a temporal Being because it is always, in some fashion, whether authentically or inauthentically, caught in a nexus of past, present, and future, determined by its thrownness, immersed in its facticity, and with certain limited yet distinct future possibilities to project. Temporality so understood determines Dasein more than its ontic, present-at-hand makeup. The past is never simply the no-longer present; the future is never simply the not yet present. Past and future are always "present" and determine Dasein. This conclusion is the ultimate end toward which Heidegger's earlier attempt to lower the ontological status of "the real" or the "actual" aimed. Dasein's Being is dominated by something that is present for it in a way that is not present-at-hand, just as the thing closest in one's primordial concern can be someone or something at a great ontic distance. Put another way, the ontically absent can have more presence than the ontically present-at-hand. Indeed, resolute Dasein's authentic past and future would always be more present than the concrete things that surround it and into which it has fallen.

Dasein's temporality is fundamentally ecstatic or "outside itself," and projected beyond its presently attained ontic existence (*BAT* 376–77). Heidegger differentiates the ecstatic temporality that characterizes the Being of Dasein from the "ordinary" conception of temporality. According to Heidegger, to say that Dasein is fundamentally temporal is not to say that Dasein is a being "in time," but that it is a being determined by what is, what has been, and what still can be. According to Heidegger, the "ordinary" conception of time, which views time as a uniform succession of nows endured by present-at-hand entities, is only possible as a leveling off of authentic ecstatic temporality. This inauthentic within-timeness is based in turn on an inauthentic or derivative form of spatiality, the "being-within" of one present-at-hand entity in relation to another. By arguing that Dasein is temporal, although not an entity within time, Heidegger feels he avoids the

28. For the opposite view see Dallmayr, "Ontology of Freedom."

charge of historicism, which he claims relies on the ordinary conception of time.[29] In this fashion, Heidegger also presumes to avoid *Weltanschauungphilosophie,* perspectivism, or what he will later call the "Age of the World View." According to Heidegger, all prior Western metaphysics—and that includes Hegel—has missed the sense in which Dasein is temporal. Dasein *is* in its very being a social being with a tradition and a variety of limited possible futures. An authentic Dasein should neither forget the past nor be indifferent to the future. One should not aim at the "innocence and forgetting" that naively locks one in the present. In this regard, Heidegger provides a significant critique of Nietzsche. And in this emendation of Nietzsche, a *post*modern note is sounded.

On the basis of this resoluteness, Dasein chooses to accept the necessity of its concrete, factical situation, its fate and destiny. *Only* as resolute (not in pure anticipation or anticipatory resoluteness) is Dasein concretely historical and hence capable of unique historical action. As resolute, Dasein takes over its heritage, grasps its present, and projects a future from within the world.

> The resoluteness in which Dasein comes back to itself, discloses current factical possibilities of authentic existing, and discloses them *in terms of the heritage* which that resoluteness, as thrown, *takes over.* . . . This is how we designate Dasein's primordial historizing, which lies in authentic resoluteness and in which Dasein *hands* itself *down* to itself, free for death, in a possibility which it has inherited and yet has chosen. (*BAT* 435)[30]

---

29. Heidegger does not consider himself a historicist; like Nietzsche he considers historicism the problem that must be transcended. Heidegger's claim is that historicism is the product of a derivative mode of temporality, that of "within-time-ness," rather than one that is "ecstatic." Historicism only appears when one has ceased to be resolute, which happens when one stands back from life in theoretical detachment. In the process, one's world becomes an unworld. No authentically resolute Dasein would ever believe in historicism, or for that matter ever be confronted by it.

30. Heidegger asserts that while the three ecstases of temporality always authentically exist in a unity, nonetheless, in different existential structures, different ecstases take precedence. Understanding, which is projective, is fundamentally oriented toward the future. Moods, which relate one to their thrownness, are linked to one's having been. And falling brings one into the present (*BAT* 385, 390, 397). Likewise in anticipation, one is fundamentally related to the future, to one's ownmost being-toward-the-end. In anticipatory resoluteness the current factical situation is revealed, hence the present takes precedence. However, in pure resolution, one takes over and is related to one's thrownness; one preserves what has been handed down. Therefore, one's having-been takes precedence. This why it is primarily resoluteness that makes the *maintenance* of a tradition possible.

Dasein freely accepts its fate, yet looks for the possibilities latent in that over which it has no control. So understood, resoluteness is freed from the Spirit of Revenge.[31] In resoluteness Dasein accepts "Time and its it was," and gains a form of completeness within-the-world. Without shared, long-term projects, the lives of most individuals lack purpose and become fragmented. Dasein's (not Da-sein's) Being-a-whole is concretely possible only within a community (*BAT* 436). Yet that community *must also point beyond itself* toward Being—and hence also include genuine thinking—something orthodox National Socialism never even remotely considered.

When resolute individuals dominate *praxis,* they set the contours of the possibilities that will be present in the future; they help determine the future world. As the world conditions the primary disclosure of things, they would determine how all individuals would be related to things within the world. Put in Aristotelian terms, which is by no means misleading, Heidegger has tried to show the ontological presuppositions for the possibility that the regime or constitution of a community can be architectonic, determining the way of life and what arts and sciences will be seen as acceptable—since all theoretical activity presupposes a specific world. By attempting to regenerate the possibility of an autonomous *praxis,* Heidegger hopes he has provided the ground for generating a *logos* and *nomos* from *within* the structure of care, from *within* the world. Newly clear about its derivative status, theory would cease to dictate to practice: the modern priority would be reversed. Indeed, in the future, abstracting from a different world, different theoretical options ought to emerge.[32]

31. The new thinking is also freed from the Spirit of Revenge. Anticipation, as the new basis for thinking, does not lead to the detached theoretical attitude, which then tries to manipulate present-at-hand things, for it brackets all Being-in-the-World rather than standing back detachedly staring at things within-the-world. So conceived, a future thinking could eventuate at most in a theo-mythos, rather than in an "onto-theo-logos" or manipulative theoretical science. This transformation of philosophy would simultaneously help free *praxis* from the late-modern stranglehold of theory.

32. Heidegger has tried to accomplish the same things Nietzsche hoped for from the doctrine of the Eternal Recurrence. (Of course Heidegger would see Nietzsche's vision of eternal recurrence as resting on an inauthentic version of temporality, one based on the ontically uniform succession of nows where the only possibility of repetition was to will a return to the beginning.) He tried to find a way to return spontaneity and autonomy to *praxis,* free future thinking from the Spirit of Revenge, and make everything from scholarship to modern science properly subservient to genuinely architectonic activities. Realizing the architectonic status of resolute acts means that the possibility of a universal science, religion, economics, ethics, anthropology, psychology, or anything else, is entirely dependent upon whether a world comes into existence which is planet-wide. As the later Heidegger makes clear, that is a possibility, but not a sanguine one.

When one acts resolutely and repeats monumental possibilities, the effect is clearly to change the ontic world while preserving worldliness itself. This would concomitantly change the way present-to-hand entities are revealed, and that in turn would change the way they are thematically projected theoretically. Thus would be set in motion a change in everything from the workplace to the laboratory. Man's fascination with universal history would cease. The scientific debunking of religion and, more generally, *mythos* could conceivably be overcome since they stand closer to the pretheoretical disclosure of things than modern science or technology. Furthermore, the theoretical projection of things as objects, as opposed to knowing subjects, could be overcome, for it is derivative of one variant of the theoretical stance, which is determined by *one* specific world. The fact-value dichotomy would be overcome as it becomes clear things become primordial "facts" only because they have some value; otherwise they would remain undisclosed. The Heidegger of *Being and Time* hopes that everything that bedevils contemporary man and pushes him toward nihilism can be overturned by monumental, disclosive repetition.

The historical existence appropriate to Dasein is that of the ever recovered possibility of repeating certain revelatory and disclosive experiences and states of Being, which in turn lead to the creation of potentially unique concrete worlds. History could end only if those revelatory experiences could no longer be repeated. For Heidegger, one must not sit back and rationally calculate means to concrete ends, but must reappropriate various primordial ways to be and a "natural" relatedness to reality, regardless of where it leads concretely. In Kantian fashion, the form of action takes precedence over the substance of what concretely follows.[33] This is one reason why Heidegger could fall prey to the *form* of National Socialist resoluteness, while remaining indifferent to what it concretely implied. Heidegger eventually fell back in dismay—far too late and far too lamely—from the concrete acts of his erstwhile destiny-mates. That falling back led in the direction of a far more reticent rhetoric, and less faith in statesmen as the agents of truth.

In concluding his discussion of the possibility of authentic historicality and of the possibility of a science of history, Heidegger quotes Count Yorck approvingly:

33. It is true that in *Being and Time* we find more than a few Kantian, i.e., modern, elements. A veneer of the transcendental mode of analysis remains. And we have the reemergence of Kantian formalism, this time attached to a tragic vision of the course of human events, rather than Kantian optimism.

That a science can become practical is now, of course, the real
basis for its justification. But the mathematical *praxis* is not the
only one. The practical aim of our standpoint is one that is pedagogical in the broadest and deepest sense of the word. Such an
aim is the soul of all true philosophy, and the truth of Plato and
Aristotle. . . . *The only thing worthy of notice is what drives them to
come from physics to ethics.* (*BAT* 454; emphasis mine)

Heidegger follows with his own observation: "Thus it becomes plain
in what sense the preparatory existential-temporal analytic of Dasein is
resolved to foster the spirit of Count Yorck in the service of Dilthey's
work" (*BAT* 455). *Being and Time* is an attempt to prove the priority of
praxis to modern theory, and to demonstrate that true *praxis* implies the
need for an *ethos*. But it also tries to show that both are dependent on
genuine, awestruck thinking about a source that is itself historical. It is
this last goal that *Being and Time* inadequately accomplished.

15

The "Middle" Heidegger: Heidegger's Confrontation with Nietzsche and the Turn to *Seinsgeschichte*

It has been customary to conclude that, somewhere between 1934 and 1945, Heidegger had a substantial change of heart and a "turn" or "reversal" in his thought occurred. The years during the war, after Heidegger's "retreat from Syracuse," certainly signaled a rethinking. In the posthumously published piece, "Nur Noch Ein Gott Kann Uns Retten," Heidegger tells us his lectures were carefully watched by Nazi informants and that he had to take care in the way he spoke. This care can be seen in his famous lectures on Nietzsche. Heidegger also lived to see the epigonal dilutions of his work and, in the *Letter on Humanism,* reflected upon the change of *language* that was necessary to avoid the misinterpretation of his early works, especially *Being and Time,* in a subjectivist and voluntarist fashion. But the seeming changes during the "middle" years are primarily changes of presentation and emphasis, not of understanding. We must repeatedly remind ourselves of Heidegger's oft repeated maxim: great thinkers think but *one* thought.

It is now customary to see Heidegger's lectures on Nietzsche during the 1930s and 1940s as a sign of both his "discovery" of Nietzsche— "Nietzsche became *decisive* for Heidegger"—and of a great change in his thought. But Heidegger had discovered Nietzsche long before the Nietzsche lectures. By the second decade of the twentieth century Nietzsche was in the very air one breathed on the Continent, and Heidegger's teacher Rickert had lectured on Nietzsche. *Being and Time* shows explicit reference to, and clear understanding of, Nietzsche's work. It is true that Heidegger turned to Nietzsche in a more thematic way than he had done before, but only in that limited sense did Nietzsche became decisive for him. What is really decisive is the environment in which the Nietzsche lectures were given. Nietzsche's work was being used in a clearly misleading fashion to support the Nazi worldview. Heidegger wanted to defend Nietzsche *as a philosopher,* not as a propagandist or cultural critic. In this regard the parts of Nietzsche's writings that Heidegger leaves out of discussion are as significant as what he includes. In the Nietzsche lectures Heidegger clearly signals his rejection of orthodox National Socialism, as he had done in *An Introduction to Metaphysics*. At times this is done fairly openly, at others in a quiet fashion.

Heidegger's method in the Nietzsche lectures is, to say the least, quirky. He takes the posthumously published notebooks as indicative of Nietzsche's genuine philosophy, dismissing the written works as overheated, hyperbolic foreground. Heidegger takes primarily the notes that have been collected as *The Will to Power* but then goes on to castigate the editors for their thoughtless method of selection and arrangement. He also makes it clear that he is uninterested in Nietzsche's *self*-understanding. Heidegger believes he sees what Nietzsche could not and understands Nietzsche better than Nietzsche understood himself. Hence he abstracts from most of the famous Nietzschean rhetoric, which is substantial, as well as from the concrete influence Nietzsche had on other authors.

Heidegger knows that Nietzsche is primarily a philosopher and not an ideologue, propagandist, or critic of bourgeois culture, religion, and morality. Heidegger knows in advance what a philosopher is; all Western philosophy thinks the Being of beings. Heidegger asserts that like all prior Western metaphysical thought, Nietzsche's thought also primarily thinks the Being of beings—in his case as totally recurrent Will to Power. Hence, Heidegger concludes, the Will to Power and Eternal Recurrence are the central concepts in Nietzsche's attempt at a *systematic* philosophy. He further asserts that along with the revaluation of values they form a unity that is indicative of Nietzsche's philosophy. Heidegger asserts that Nietzsche's philosophy is the final and necessary culmination of metaphysical thinking and hence shows our age in the clearest light. When one confronts Nietzsche's philosophy in light of the entire tradition of the West, it becomes clear that that tradition must be brought up for a decision. With Nietzsche we arrive at the end of philosophy—understood as the end of metaphysics. In Nietzsche, metaphysics openly reaches a crisis in nihilism. When one properly understands and appropriates that fact it becomes clear that the history of the West is the history of nihilism, the waning of the light of Being. The West is quite legitimately called the *Abendland*.

Heidegger begins with what at the time was the unconventional comparison of Nietzsche and Descartes. For Heidegger, Descartes set modern man on the path toward the conscious, prior projection and shaping of the perspectives in which beings show themselves. Descartes is indicative of the modern desire to bracket empirical intuition and the "natural" relation to the world. According to Heidegger, Descartes sees in subjectivist metaphysics the predominance of man among all beings and hence the predominance of a being over Being. This is for Heidegger one of the most extreme forms of the Western forgetfulness of Being. Fixing entities in *our* ground comes to dominate attention rather than the clearing process of Being *itself*. According to Heidegger, Nietzsche is the final and most radical spokesperson for this one-sided elevation of human subjectivity. For Nietzsche, man must shape every perspective in advance; he must will it. Nietzsche will not let Being be. He regards human creativity as divine and is completely blind to Being in its *self*-presencing. By bringing modern subjectivism to its completion he brings to a close Western metaphysics.

According to Heidegger, by defining Being as Will Nietzsche remains entangled in the metaphysics of subjectivity. Nietzsche correctly saw that this culminates in nihilism, "consummate meaninglessness," the total devaluation of all values. Nietzsche set as his task a reversal of this phenomena, and hence a *re*valuation of all values. But this remains a self-deluded attempt that cannot disentangle itself from subjectivist metaphysics. Nietzsche remains a subjectivist Cartesian metaphysician, incapable of thinking of Being as *self*-presencing happening or event. According to Heidegger—contrary to what I have argued above—as an eternally recurrent Will to Power, Being is still understood metaphysically as constant presence and temporality is thought using a derivative, inauthentic conception of time.[1] Further, while Nietzsche tries to return man to a reliance on the sensuous realm of appearance, Heidegger sees Nietzsche's sensualism as merely an inversion of Platonism, hence still under its spell. Nietzsche merely wills the sensuous as illusion and the overman as ground and maintainer of the illusion. But as the master and lord of the earth, the overman merely brings to its highest consummation the metaphysical longing for the total mastery of beings. The overman is left to impose his subjective values on the beings he masters. Nietzsche thereby leaves contemporary man lost in the midst of beings abandoned by Being.

Heidegger presents nihilism as the history of the rise to hegemony of human evaluation and, consequently, of the abandonment of beings by the only genuine source of value. Hence at the end of metaphysics

---

1. I have argued that the Will-to-Power represents an attempt to depict Being as a mysterious source that can never—precisely because of its Dionysian unfathomableness —be completely present to thought, and hence cannot be mastered. It is my contention that throughout his work Heidegger is trying to elaborate upon and articulate the same ontological intuition.

nothing remains that is intrinsically valuable and nothing remains other than man's Will. Being, understood as the highest being qua ground, ceases to ground: God is dead. According to Heidegger, man had to be driven to this point, to the experience of God's death, before a new future would be possible. Only by experiencing the death of God and total nihilism could the West have any hope of striking off on a novel path. According to Heidegger, Nietzsche is the author for our age because he brings nihilism to speech in its most radical manifestation and forces a decision.

In his treatment of Nietzsche, Heidegger does considerable damage to the Nietzsche of the published works, the one who had a *public* effect. It would be pointless to show how many things Heidegger disregards and distorts. Paradoxically, Heidegger is unwilling to deal with the rhetorical character of Nietzsche's statements in the published works. He pays little attention to the fact that Nietzsche's point in willing the Eternal Recurrence is to overcome the hegemony of Will. Nietzsche becomes a self-deluded Cartesian entangled in metaphysics, uniquely formulated by Heidegger as a doctrine of Being as total presence. Hence Heidegger's Nietzsche remains in the grasp of nihilism.

By abstracting from the published works, Heidegger is able to free Nietzsche from the Nazi propagandists and win back for him a place within philosophy. He quite rightly points out the centrality in Nietzsche's thought of the doctrine of Eternal Recurrence, which until then had been either overlooked or summarily dismissed as a superficial embarrassment. Heidegger emphasizes the altogether Nietzschean notion that the West arrives at a point of closure, tantamount to nihilism, that calls for a decision about the entire Western tradition. But he goes on to isolate in the thought of Nietzsche all of the things he (Heidegger) wished to downplay in his own early work which could be misread or misused. By laying charges of voluntarism, subjectivism, metaphysics, and nihilism at the door of Nietzsche he could distance himself from those things. In the last analysis, Heidegger primarily attacks the Nietzschean rhetoric aimed at fostering a *transition* to the future and is largely silent about the contours of the future that Nietzsche articulated more quietly.

That said—and much more could be said—I believe the "middle" Heidegger either misses or, much more likely, refrains from discussing the ideas he and Nietzsche shared. As should be clear from my argument to this point, Nietzsche and Heidegger share far more than Heidegger understood or was willing to acknowledge. Each saw a moment of decision coming. Each saw the need for a reconstituted thinking in the future. Each plotted a return to the immediacy of pretheoretical lived

experience and a recovery of the autonomy of *praxis*. Each saw the need
to overcome the Will, transcend subjectivism, open a path to "community," and quit the Spirit of Revenge. The things upon which Nietzsche
and Heidegger agree are the ones that are central to the possibility of *post*
modernity.

In *Nietzsche,* Heidegger also announces his new attempt to discuss
the historicality of Being, this time as part of a discussion of the history
of nihilism. This history he views, not as a random, accidental occurrence or even as an occurrence caused by man's turning away from
openness to the source, but as part of the history of Being itself
(Seinsgeschichte).[2] Nihilism is now explicitly presented as no doing of
man; hence, man alone could not reverse it. Nietzsche's desire to will
an overcoming of nihilism and a revaluation of values mistakenly took
man himself as the source of nihilism. Heidegger now stresses that nihilism is the outcome of the "default" or withdrawal of Being itself at
the origin of the West. The history of Western philosophy must be read
as the history of the default of Being. Nietzsche was blind to this fact
and hence still part of the history of default. From his earliest works on,
Heidegger had indicated his understanding of nihilism in such locutions as the "darkening of the earth," the "oblivion of Being," and
"destitute times." In the early works nihilism was caused, at least to
some degree, by man's turning away from openness to Being. In the
later works Heidegger stresses that it is Being that turns away from
man—we simply cannot know why. But even in the later works, man
must adopt a new posture of openness if Being is to return. To my
mind, it is primarily the *emphasis* that has changed.

From the very beginning, metaphysics leaves Being unthought. It
conceives of Being not as it is in itself, but as an *a priori* cause. In so
doing, it inevitably comes to think Being as a being, the supreme being
as first cause, behind which there is utter emptiness. For metaphysics,
No-thingness is the worst evil of all. Christianity is but one manifestation of metaphysical onto-theo-logos. Christianity shares, therefore,
with all metaphysics, in the oblivion of Being that is the foundation of
nihilism.[3] For metaphysics, the highest being, even as transcendent, is
present; it has come into the light, into unconcealment, once and for
all. Hence metaphysics cannot think Being itself, *the event of presencing
that simultaneously holds back,* because it cannot deal with absence. Hence

2. Heidegger, "Nihilism as Determined By the History of Being," *Nietzsche,* 4:209.
Henceforth designated in the text as *N,* followed by the volume and page number.
3. Heidegger's version of Nietzsche's observation that Christianity is but Platonism
for the masses instead holds that Christianity is metaphysics for the masses.

what is unthought in metaphysics—presencing out of concealment—
withdraws and is never attended to. By reifying and personifying Being as the highest being, metaphysics passes by and never allows Being
to presence as it allegedly is in itself. Instead it focuses more and more
on the cultivation of beings. The eventual outcome is that Being withdraws from beings, which then lose their ability to be in the open and
are cast off to a groundless, autonomous existence of their own.
Heidegger calls this the nothingness of beings. Of course something,
even if inauthentic or destitute, remains present; this Heidegger terms
the presence of absence. Present things announce their lack of Being
and thereby announce the withdrawing ground.

Until now, Being has given itself only in the mode of staying away.
Only now and *for the first time* does thinking observe the default. The
darkness of completed nihilism was needed for it to grasp the "trace" of
the withdrawal, opening a path to "It" that has never before existed.
Now that this novel understanding has come into the open, It achieves
a new and unique kind of presence. Of course, It can never reveal itself
completely, for something like self-refusal or self-withdrawal is necessary for It's preservation. Yet It apparently can presence in a way that is
not dominated by default. What that would mean in concrete terms is
in principle impossible to think in advance of an authentic future presencing by It itself. But considering the fact that only now do we grasp
the withdrawal that happened long ago, it is *possible* that It is ready to
presence in some new way.[4]

Since the beginning of Western metaphysics—since man made that
leap that brought forth philosophic man—language has been the language of metaphysics, the language of withdrawal and oblivion. But
there was language—and present beings—before language became
dominated by metaphysics. In some sense, we seem forced to conclude
that Being had a premetaphysical destiny and not only a metaphysical
one. Likewise, there is the possibility of Heidegger's longed-for postmetaphysical or postphilosophical revelation. The pre- and the post-
have at least one thing in common—neither would be metaphysical.
But what can we conclude about the premetaphysical epoch? If with
the advent of metaphysics It presenced in the mode of absence, can we
conclude that It presenced before that in a more positive form? If so, did
beings during the premetaphysical period have more Being? In his relation to those beings, was premetaphysical man closer to Being, and
was this revealed to him through his prephilosophic language? The an-

---

4. Heidegger's novel "recovery" of the sense of Being embedded in early Greek
thinking is presumably part of that sign; it may even be the new presencing itself.

swer seems to be yes and no. In the premetaphysical epoch man may
have achieved a greater oneness with things-in-themselves, albeit not
directly to Being, since that is accomplished in thought and presupposes the advent of thinking. That was premetaphysical man's short-
coming. The metaphysical age, while nihilistic, paves the way for a
possibility not previously available, a new form of openness to things
and simultaneously to Being itself. On a new plane, future man could
accomplish a redemption such as has never before been available. As
such, we are in a position to receive the advent of a new dispensation, a
new "event of appropriation" *(Ereignis).* But this possibility of being
saved is only available after nihilism has been driven to its extreme and
out into the open, and only after "authentic" nihilism has replaced "inauthentic" nihilism.

According to Heidegger, Nietzsche's nihilism is still inauthentic nihilism. Only the authentic nihilism that grasps the essence of nihilism
as the withdrawal of Being holds out hope (*N* 4:219–21). The "saving
grace" requires the heightening of nihilism in its inauthentic public or
ontic manifestation. But even inauthentic nihilism is determined by
Being itself. Late-modern nihilism rests on more than the negation of
one being—the death of God or any other being, man included. Nihilism has brought it to pass that there is no true presence and no openness
to the source. The eventual outcome of It's withdrawal that affects man
most concretely is that in the process beings get covered and occluded,
no longer showing themselves or appearing as they are in themselves
(the "darkening of beings"). In the language of *Being and Time,* semblance replaces true appearance. No amount of pure willing will be of
service in overcoming this fact. There is nothing man can accomplish
on the basis of his own planning and calculating activity, nor on the
level of *praxis.* Heidegger now tells us we require a "step back" from all
planning and calculating, all *praxis* and *technē,* rather than any hastily
planned overcoming of nihilism. We must not try to interfere in the
course of destitute contemporary beings. To do so would be to miss the
point (*N* 4:240–41). Genuine *praxis* now awaits a future revelation of It.
Something like anticipatory resoluteness can no longer be of help. In
the interim we must allow nihilism to develop (*N* 4:243–46). Heidegger came to see National Socialism as part of that development.

Late-modern humanity is lost among Beingless beings, hence no
genuine dwelling is possible. Instead of being rooted in beings, or open
to Being, man seeks "primal truth" and certainty in himself. Man becomes the being which posits itself and all other things (*N* 4:235). Contemporary humanity plans and calculates everything in conscious
production in the hopes of feeling at home amidst beings from which

Being has withdrawn. As a result, we experience ever intensified forms of homelessness. As man wanders endlessly among man-made beings—and among natural beings that have their Being only in the way they fit into human projects—his alienation increases. Everywhere there are cries for new "ideas" and "values," a sign of the "abandonment of Being" and the resultant lack of any historical destiny.[5] We even try to plan and calculate the past; we study History to impose upon it a causal picture ("metanarrative") so that we might better secure our place among the beings of the present. Historicism replaces true historical dwelling. The world becomes an unworld. Heidegger explicitly refers to *Being and Time* when he asserts that the primary truth of Being is world (*OM* 104). As Being withdraws, the world withdraws and Being itself keeps completely to itself, not showing itself to most men even as default. In the process, man's essence is endangered, and since Being's advent requires man as its abode, this is a prospect of supreme significance for Heidegger. In its most intense manifestation, the withdrawal of Being works itself out as a blind, runaway commitment to autonomous technology which threatens both man's ontic and ontological existence (*OM* 99).

In the distress of the age of his most intense abandonment by Being, man looks for security and assured stability. His search eventuates in a constant using-up of things, which creates an "erring vacuum." Man himself becomes the most important raw material, and the most assured and decisive suppliers, those most adept at planning and calculation, are regarded as "leaders." Man is reduced to the *subhuman,* an instinctive animal, because the *superhuman,* the rational calculators, can best predict the supply of man as unrestrained raw material when "instinct" is unleashed (*OM* 106). Even the "leader natures" must have "assured instincts"; they too must be put in the service of consumption for its own sake. They are rewarded by having the quantitatively and qualitatively greatest consumption. Every event that does not fit the ideal of assured calculability, no matter how ordinary or routine, becomes a "crisis." Man rattles from one "crisis" to another and falls into the hands of ever more intense calculability. This culminates in ever greater and more aimless, ahistorical drift. Distinctions between nations and countries cease to be essential determining factors. When the uniformity of the "instinctive" becomes the precondition for predictability, nations become a nuisance. For the same reason, there is also a *necessity* of a complete lack of "order of rank" (*OM* 108). But this uni-

---

5. Heidegger, "Overcoming Metaphysics," in *The End of Philosophy,* 103. Henceforth designated in the text as *OM,* followed by a page number.

formity is in turn the ground of war and conflict. Just as the distinction between national and international collapses—bringing a global "leadership" of assured suppliers beyond national differences—the distinction between war and peace collapses. Peace is filled with conflicts and crises; war is just an interruption of fully secured predictability. Everywhere Being, destiny, and genuine difference stay away.

According to Heidegger, no consciously willed action can counteract this inevitable nihilistic outcome. It must be driven to its most extreme possibility; the later Heidegger no longer has any hope of circumventing this. We must get "in step with" the nihilism of completed metaphysics. All present action is determined by the mode of revealing that reduces everything to an object to be calculated in the service of total predictability. Hence *praxis* as a form of truth, which retains centrality in the early works, recedes. No *praxis* will succeed until there has been a new appropriative event of Being, and that event has been poetically brought to speech, and again become the ground of a shared world.

16

Technology as the Culmination of Metaphysics

Metaphysics and technology are customarily seen as antagonistic. According to Heidegger, completed Western metaphysics necessarily culminates in the total hegemony of modern technology as manifested in the aimless, unlimited Will to Will.[1] This hegemony will hold sway for a very long time; any concerted attempt to overcome it would be like struggling in quicksand. But it can be appropriated anew if one is able to grasp—i.e., to make present—its *essence* in a way not seen before. Heidegger tries to supply that novel understanding.

Heidegger asserts that, contrary to the customary presumption, the understanding underlying the modern age is not more correct than, for example, that of the Greeks, nor is modern science more "precise" than Greek science; they are fundamentally, *essentially,* different. Modern science projects in advance, mathematically, what must be taken as Nature or reality. Nature is projected as extended matter in motion; Being is defined as spatiotemporal magnitudes in motion. All research then is bound by the mathematically projected plan of Nature.[2] The pro-

---

1. For an extended treatment of the issue of technology, see my "Heidegger, Technology and Post-modernity."

2. Heidegger, "The Age of the World Picture," in *The Question concerning Technology and Other Essays,* 119, 118. Henceforth designated in the text as *QT,* followed by a page number. The modern technological understanding and its "science" are characterized by "research." According to Heidegger, there are three fundamental features of modern scientific research: (1) the projection in advance of a "plan" or "frame"; (2) a methodology which establishes and verifies rules and laws; and (3) institutional organization of experimentation as an ongoing activity (*QT* 120–24). But methodology and the possibility of institutionalized experimentation all rest on the first characteristic, the prior projecting of a plan.

In this projecting there is always the tendency to the mere averageness of busywork because scores of researchers, unaware of the status of the larger frame, or even of the smaller "paradigm" that supports their work, labor collecting small bits of data (*QT* 138). As a result, Heidegger asserts, the "scholar," who is fundamentally different in his

jecting of the plan and the institutionalization of research are possible only because of a prior phenomenon: modern man has become the being who has a "World View" (*QT* 128–34). To say that modern man has a worldview is to say that the world is conceived and grasped as a picture. Such pictures are not the imitation or representation in thought of a world that stands *on its own*. There is no world that stands on its own. Man becomes certain of the world only when it is the representation of his own plan. In the process, man becomes the underlying stratum, the *hypokeimenon* or *subjectum*—that which "lies before" (qua prior). Modern technological thinking is based on the transformation of reality into something present-at-hand as an object over against *(Gegenstand)* a projecting subject as *hypokeimenon*. Under these circumstances, all that is left to debate is whether man is a subject as an "I" or as a "we" and, if the latter, whether the "we" represents a state, nation, common humanity, or something else. Taking man as *subjectum* does not necessarily imply individualism; it can also imply *consciously constructed* "nationalism"—a phenomenon that Heidegger, like Nietzsche, deplores.

There could never have been an ancient or medieval worldview (except retrospectively). The medieval world was conceived as *ens creatum*—created by a personal god; for the Greeks, the world was that which arises and opens *itself (physis)*. In each case, man was the one who *apprehended* that which is independently of human projection. Nonetheless, according to Heidegger, the emergence of the "Age of the World View" can be traced to Plato. Plato transformed the pre-Socratic notion of Being as *physis* and *alētheia* into Being conceived as *eidos* and *idea*. But for Plato man was still the apprehending being who stood in the presence of that which brings *itself* to appearance. Initially, the realm of the ideas remained something at which we merely gazed; the ideas were not seen as constituted by man. But in transforming Being into an idea, Plato paved the way for the modern projecting of Being as *man's* idea. That in turn made possible the transformation of Being into the "object" of a "subject," a prerequisite for modern technology, which transforms the realm of objectivity into "standing reserve," that which is not an object, does not appear, and is less and less present.

---

habits and character than the researcher, is replaced by the individual who has no gentlemanly traits, no understanding of leisure, no grasp of rank and hierarchy: The modern researcher goes hand in hand with democratic homogenization. For Heidegger, mass democracy and the hegemony of research are parallel phenomena (*QT* 125). They both occupy the ground of completed nihilism. On this, Heidegger and Nietzsche agree.

Plato set in motion the long process by which man lost presence altogether. Eventually, in the technological conception of reality, everything that surrounds us simply dissolves, and humanity is expelled
from the here and now. Man comes to be a being who has no place,
stands nowhere, and is dominated by the abstract and the absent. For
Heidegger, the total withdrawal of presence is the same as the withdrawal of Being. The complete withdrawal of Being in the modern age
is what Heidegger means by nihilism.

In the late-modern age, metaphysics reaches its culmination in the
form of a confrontation of worldviews as the ground of rivalry for
world domination (*QT* 134). In the service of the competition of
worldviews, man brings into play his unlimited powers of calculating,
planning, and molding things. Eventually one gets unlimited technology in the service of the competition between what Heidegger sees as
the most extreme worldviews. The rootlessness and homelessness that
ensues keeps modern humanity careening from one crisis and world
war to another. But with the full flowering of the age of the worldviews it is possible for the *essence* of technology to finally emerge.

The traditional understandings of technology, which see it either as
a neutral means to an end (instrumental) or as one form of *human* activity among many (anthropological), are finally seen as inadequate.
Heidegger believes they fail to distinguish the ontic manifestation of
technology from its *essence*. In the instrumental and anthropological
approaches, everything depends on our manipulating technology in a
"humane" fashion, but, Heidegger says, we cannot consciously control the *essence* of technology as if it were some neutral tool. We are
mastered by and totally under the spiritual control of the *essence* of technology, for the *essence* of technology determines the way we perceive
ourselves and all beings; hence we always come along too late in our
attempts to control it.

Heidegger asserts that modern technology is a form of *poiēsis*. Poiēsis, like *physis,* is a form of "bringing forth." Modern technology is
not a mere means; it is not to be understood as a mere instrumentality.
It is a mode of revealing, hence, *a* mode of truth. The essence of technology is to be found in a particular kind of bringing forth.

As a form of revealing or bringing forth, technology is a form of
causality in the sense of the Greek *aition,* to be responsible for, to occasion. Heidegger argues that the traditional four causes—formal, final,
efficient, material—are ways of being responsible for something. In
the modern age, efficient causality increasingly define causality, and
the consciously willed actions of autonomous subjects defines efficient

causality. But Heidegger asserts that this reflects a misunderstanding of the true nature of causality and bringing forth. Heidegger uses the example of the bringing forth into appearance of a silver chalice intended for use in a religious ceremony. He claims that it is wrong to conceive of the silversmith's efforts, especially if understood as the self-willed action of a primary or autonomous subject, as the efficient cause. The smith merely binds together the other three causes—material (silver), final (the ceremony), and formal (the need to hold wine). These other causes, he argues, are fundamentally responsible for bringing the chalice to appearance. The efficient cause—the smith—is determined by the matter and the historical destiny that calls forth the formal and final causes. Modern technology can proceed as if efficient causality were primary and autonomous only because man has ceased to be a historical being. He wanders aimlessly, alienated from earth and world, i.e., material and final/formal causality. As technology becomes more and more successful the specific historical destiny that occasioned it recedes from view; it both loses sight of its own roots and destiny and wards off any further historical destinies (bringing about, that is, the end of history) (*QT* 6–9).

Modern *techné*, as a form of *poiésis*, reveals that which does not bring *itself* forth. It is a "challenging forth" that "puts to nature the unreasonable demand that it supply energy that can be extracted and stored." According to Heidegger, there is a "monstrousness that reigns here" (*QT* 14, 16).[3] This is initially possible only because all of Nature has been objectified, which in turn is possible only because we live in the age of the worldviews. But modern technology eventually goes far beyond this. In modern technology everything is ordered to "stand by," to be immediately at hand for further ordering. Everything is revealed, according to Heidegger, in the mode of "standing-reserve"; nothing stands on its own any longer (*QT* 17). Modern technology, viewed as a revealing that is a challenging forth, does not simply combine natural givens in novel ways. It sets upon Nature, unlocks it, exposes it, and challenges it to do man's bidding. Matter is transformed from its natural state and kept at the ready in its new state until it is needed by modern industry.

When all of reality is transformed into standing reserve *(Bestand)*, there is nothing left that confronts man as *self*-presencing. What remains as the fundamental reality is not truly present at all. Reality con-

---

3. How this challenging differs from the "wresting of truth" performed by art, poetry, and statesmanship is never entirely clear.

ceived as standing reserve—as malleable, transformable, and capable
of being stored in transformed states for eventual use—is revealed to
man as something entirely different than reality as object *(Gegenstand),*
that which stands over and against a subject. A situation arises in which
nothing stands in any sense, and reality dissolves into such abstractions
as "capital" or "energy." Only by initially treating reality as the object
of a projecting subject can modern technology transform the world
into standing reserve. The irony is that in the process objectivity dissolves completely. Absence takes precedence over presence in our daily
lives.[4] Being withdraws; nihilism ensues.

Modern objectification inevitably transforms itself into the loss of
physis. When this happens, the subject, having lost its objects, no
longer has any place to stand. In the language of *Being and Time,* modern man is "everywhere and nowhere" *(BAT* 221). The lack of a
"there" yields what the early Heidegger called inauthenticity, characterized in part by "ambiguity" (as to the where of our existence), "idle
talk" (love of the superficial play of surfaces), and an aimless, superficial "curiosity" *(BAT* 211–24). In the more poetic account of Heidegger's later work, modern man becomes homeless; he loses all
rootedness in the earth or native surroundings. Everything disappears
in the objectlessness of standing reserve. Needless to say, Heidegger
does not see a return to objectification, which necessarily transforms
itself into the technological revelation in which the concrete world dissolves, as an alternative.

Whether we are talking about modern physics or price theory, the
technological approach to reality sets about seeing how Nature responds when conceptualized and challenged theoretically. If the response is "positive," that specific form of challenging is projected as
reality. If not, another attempt is made. But as life becomes more
abstract and as the world becomes more absent it is difficult to know
how to evaluate the competing conceptualizations: what constitutes a
"positive" response? Hence the process of challenging becomes self-
generating, without any external referent, without rhyme or reason.
Eventually technical and organizational sophistication become ends in
themselves and man too becomes standing reserve, organized rationally and bureaucratically, for in the late-modern age man is incapable
of differentiating himself from the rest of reality. There remains no
way to relate to the essence of the human as something distinctive.
Hence man, like majestic redwood trees revealed as merely so many

4. For a concrete and striking presentation of this phenomenon see Steiner, *Real
Presences,* esp. chap. 3, "Presences," 135–232.

board feet of lumber, is challenged forth, manipulated as an abstract integer in calculations of productivity, unemployment statistics, demographic shifts, and so on.

Despite standing reserve's basis in subjective willfulness, man eventually loses control over this fated mode of truth; thrown into this realm from the beginning, he takes up a relationship to it only subsequently. He is himself ordered by this mode of revealing, but it is no longer part of his handiwork. This is late-modern man's destiny, a fate from which he can never abstract himself through his own endeavors. He attains his "freedom" only by appropriating his destiny correctly, i.e., by realizing the *essence* of that which determines him and holds him in thrall.[5] Heidegger asserts that only when we come to grasp the essence of technology, and thereby gain freedom *within* it—not simply willing the overcoming or reining in of a merely instrumental technology—will a new dispensation or revelation of Being become possible. Whatever "saving grace" is possible must follow from an understanding that we tighten our chains in trying willfully to quit the modern technological view of reality. When we recognize this, we have come into a new relation to our world. That relation may be yet another sign of the approaching return of It from default, but until there is a new happening of truth it is impossible to know.

Our destiny is fulfilled in that the essence of technology as enframing and standing reserve has now been revealed to us. Never again can we experience technology in the naive way that we once did, or share the modern faith that technology is based on a science that gives a simple explanation of reality. This collapse of the reigning faith, although the prelude to a solution, leaves man exposed, stripped of what has been the driving force behind modern thought, the faith that science and technology could emancipate us from natural limits, making possible universal, prosperous freedom and equality. Without this faith, man stands naked and alone, lord of the earth, but himself no more than standing reserve ready to be ordered (*QT* 26–27). A perilous time approaches. In the age of the hegemony of the essence of technology, man encounters nothing in existence but himself, and he does not encounter himself in his essential nature; hence he "fails in every way to hear in what respect he ex-sists" (i.e., qua Da-sein) (*QT* 27). Heidegger asserts that in comparison to this threat to man's essence the threat of lethal machines and techniques is minuscule.

5. Heidegger, *QT* 25. This bears some resemblance to the notion of freedom that holds sway in German Romanticism. From its inception in Rousseau to Hegel, freedom requires aligning oneself correctly with something more comprehensive than one's own subjective desires.

As Heidegger poses the matter, when we finally realize that "en-framing" is the "destining" (deferred ramification) of a previous mode of revealing (the Platonic, metaphysical), the "saving power" draws near and sets in motion the *possibility* of a new, future mode of revealing (*QT* 30). We open, in short, the possibility of a new, postmodern—which here means postmetaphysical—recovery of the Other as *self*-presencing. Technology is immune to simple willful control but not to another form of revealing. Unfortunately, by this logic, we cannot will that new mode of revealing; all we can do is prepare for it. Put another way, Heidegger's philosophy can clear the ground, but someone else must do the planting. Art and poetry are what the later Heidegger focuses on as the most fecund possibilities in this regard. Hence he approvingly quotes the poet Hölderlin: *"Poetically dwells man upon this earth"* (*QT* 34). The metaphysical thought of Plato, by winning a "victory" for philosophy over poetry, started the trek toward the dominance of "standing reserve." Heidegger would reenthrone the poets and artists. If one properly understands the modern predicament, Heidegger believes, it becomes clear that a new understanding or revelation will have to come from genuine, inspired, autochthonous *poiēsis,* not conscious, rational, representational thought. Hence the later Heidegger turns to discussions of the ontological foundations of genuine poetry, and more generally, art.[6]

According to Heidegger, late moderns cannot consciously transcend their age; that would imply the action of subjects merely projecting different pictures of the world. Neither can we simply go back to the premodern understanding. Both the Greek and medieval understandings differed from the modern but contained within them the seeds from which the modern understanding grew. Modern technology is the ultimate outcome. By grasping the essence of technology,

6. According to Heidegger, poetry is not something that merely occupies the realm of the production of the beautiful—the arena of aesthetics—but is a distinctive mode of revealing reality that is potentially more authentic than that of modern technology. Authentic poetry might open us to a new relation to nature and ourselves. Heidegger attempts to reverse the reigning hierarchy between poetry and the "hard" disciplines. Poetry as a mode of truth, he argues, is superior to technological revealing in that it does not reduce all causality to the efficient causality of a willful subject; thus it allegedly allows the Other to *self*-presence. The technological mode of revealing—in which reality is revealed as standing reserve, as something absent and abstract—drives out the possibility of alternate manifestations of truth, including art, statesmanship, and religion (*QT* 27–28). We become locked within the monotonous, agitated, ever-changing challenging of one monolithic mode of revealing. With no new revelation possible we arrive at the end of unique historical possibilities; man's essence as openness to Being in all its possible manifestations is destroyed. Life becomes not only abstract, homeless, and worldless, but also uniform, monotonous, unchangeable, and alienated from Being.

we enter into a new, authentic relation to It, in the same way that we enter into a new relation to the essence of nihilism. We live in the fated time when these essences are available to us for the first time. Only by grasping those essences do we become free of the inauthentic dominance of technology and nihilism. No freedom comes from railing against modern technology and late-modern nihilism, or from believing we can control them through our autonomous Will. Hence we need not curse technology as the work of the devil, rebel helplessly against it, or push blindly on with it: "Quite to the contrary, when we once open ourselves expressly to the *essence* of technology, we find ourselves unexpectedly taken into a freeing claim" (QT 25, 26). Heidegger opposes the Nietzschean *rhetoric of transition* and tries to make a radical break with the hegemony of the Will. But it leaves him in the grips of an immense hopefulness.

17

The "Late" Heidegger: Mid-Course Corrections

Determining precisely when Heidegger's "middle" or "transitional" period ends is not important to the present undertaking. Indeed I have bracketed the designations "early," "middle," and "late" whenever they enter the discussion to indicate my understanding that the continuity in Heidegger's thought is far more significant then any alleged reversal. Following convention I have placed the end of Heidegger's early period roughly at the point at which he resigns his position as rector, in 1934, although I consider his *Introduction to Metaphysics* an early work. There is no comparable consensus as to the end of the middle period. It occurs sometime after the lectures on Nietzsche and the move to seeing the centrality of technology. I have assigned most of the discussions of technology to the middle period as a logical extension of the Nietzsche lectures, which almost every Heidegger scholar takes as indicative of a transition in Heidegger's thought. Those lectures culminate in the conclusion that with Nietzsche metaphysics reaches its highest manifestation, in the Will to Will; from there Heidegger moves straight to the conclusion that technology is the highest manifestation of completed metaphysics qua Will to Will.

For the sake of having a straightforward date, one could pick the first lectures Heidegger was allowed to give when he resumed his formal teaching duties after the war—*What Is Called Thinking?*—as the beginning of his late period. But the central themes of the late Heidegger—a new postmetaphysical thinking, language, and the centrality of poetry and art—are already clearly to be seen in the *Letter on Humanism* of 1947, and the famous lecture "The Question concerning Technology" was not given until 1954. Hence, the analytical distinctions I have presented between "early," "middle," and "late" do not easily correspond to any simple temporal sequence. Some minimal consolation can be taken from the fact that no one else has been able to deal with these murky irrelevancies any more clearly. There is, in any case, something artificial about attempts to periodize the thought of great thinkers. Such temporal designations have a certain utility, but, to use a Heideggerian coinage, none gets to the matter itself. In general, we should be suspicious of such maneuvers, which usually indicate a failure on the reader's part to grasp the matter being thought by the thinker in question.

That said, I will begin my discussion of the "late" Heidegger with the *Letter on Humanism*. In what might superficially seem to be a shift from *Being and Time*, Heidegger asserts in the *Letter on Humanism* that "all effecting, in the end, rests upon Being."[1] Instead of stressing Dasein as historical, Heidegger now stresses Being as historical. Man now seems to be the passive being who by "letting be" allows Being to presence through him and eventuate in speech, which now seems to happen primarily through the thought of the great thinkers. Thought "lets itself be called into service *by* Being in order to speak the truth *of* Being" (*LH* 193; emphasis mine). To achieve "thought" in Heidegger's new sense, thinking must be freed from the "technical," metaphysical interpretation, under which it is seen always from the viewpoint of doing and making. Genuine thinking is prior to all doing and making—and to all *theoria,* which Heidegger claims has, up until now, attempted to save thought in the face of doing and making, thought qua *theoria* being what is left after we abstract from doing and making. Heidegger asserts that in this way thought abandons its true element—the thinking *of* Being (*LH* 194–95). Man is no longer the "violent one" who must "wrest" Being from concealment; now Being clearly takes the initiative. To give manifestation to the thought of Being, language must be freed from being a tool of our mere willing and cultivating, an instrument in the domination of beings. Only then can Being itself speak, rather than man. Only of the speech emanating from Being itself can it be said that "Language is the house of Being." Man must project out into the mysterious and "nameless," which is accomplished in the acquiescent posture of "letting be." Seen in this light, thought is *identical* to the reticent, silent, solitary projection into the No-thing in anticipation, except that somehow such projection now is capable of getting beyond silence to speech.

Heidegger asserts that only after such a presencing of Being in

---

1. The *Letter on Humanism* is an important document in that it is explicitly intended to present a gloss on *Being and Time* and advance the project begun there. It links the thought and jargon of the early and late Heidegger in a way that shows that he continued to pursue the same goal throughout his life. Heidegger, *Letter on Humanism*, 193. Henceforth designated in the text as *LH,* followed by a page number.

speech can man rest in his essence and be human. Thus Heidegger claims that his teaching is a "humanism," but only in its calling man toward his essence, which is to be found in openness to that which is not man. According to Heidegger, all past humanism has impeded understanding of the relation between man and Being, because all past humanism eventuates, in one way or another, in metaphysics and thinks that the essence of man arises from *animalitas*, e.g., as the *animal rationale*. But man's essential *humanitas* lies in his ecstatic being, his ability to exist outside himself, projected out toward the overpowering, nameless No-thing.[2] Hence man's essence is "ex-sistence." In ex-sistence, man stands outside himself, out toward Being. Heidegger's new metaphor for this occurrence is "standing in the clearing *of* Being." Past metaphysical thinking closes man off from this possibility.

Man's essence is to be a *Da*, a "There," an openness in a unique sense. One becomes a There by being in the clearing *of* Being. As a Da, so understood, *Da*-sein "stands outside itself [as an ontic Being] within the truth of Being." In this sense, the essence of Da-sein is existence—with ex-sistence taking on an entirely different connotation than that contained in the traditional concept of *existentia*. Heidegger now says that it is in this new technical sense that the statement in *Being and Time* that the essence of Dasein (Da-sein) is existence *(ek-sistenz)* must be understood (*LH* 200). If we survey *Being and Time,* only in anticipation can we say that Da-sein achieves ex-sistence, not in that resoluteness that takes over the factical situation and projects future ontic possibilities.

Heidegger now asserts that in ec-static Being-there, Da-sein qua existence achieves openness to Being, and thereby makes possible a world. World has an ontological foundation; it is not a subjectively willed "horizon" as with Nietzsche. Da-sein exists in the ecstatic relation to the repeated clearing *of* Being by which worlds come to pass. Heidegger observes that Sartre's version of existentialism, and popular existentialism in general, misses his main point entirely. In saying that existence precedes essence, Sartre means that existence conceived ontically precedes essence. For Sartre this means that ontic man must make a concrete something of himself through his *own* subjectively willed acts, prior to coming to have an essence; we are what we do. Heidegger states explicitly that this is not what he meant in *Being and*

---

2. Heidegger reasserts his familiar ontological premise, that in Being there is also nihilation *(das Nichten)*. Nihilation is essential to Being itself; Nothing is part of Being: "The nihilating . . . in Being is the essence of what [Heidegger calls] the Nothing. Because it thinks Being, Thought thinks the Nothing" (*LH* 220, 221).

Time. He asserts that in effect Sartre has missed the distinction between ontological and ontic and, one must add, between anticipation and resoluteness. Sartre's existentialism is an account that explains man entirely on the basis of resoluteness. In effect, Sartre believes, as Heidegger never did, that resoluteness can be autonomous.

Heidegger asserts that Da-sein "endures" openness to Being so that "civilization and culture may be vindicated" (*LH* 202–3). In doing so, Da-sein gives up self-consciousness, quits all subjectivity, and allows something more comprehensive to work through it. As such a Da, Dasein stands outside not only itself, but outside its time and place, yet it comes to be the ground for language and world. "Man is the guardian of Being." But "whether and how it appears, whether and how God and the gods, history and nature, enter, presenting and absenting themselves in the clearing of Being, is not determined by man. The advent of *beings* rests in the destiny of *Being*" (*LH* 203; emphasis mine). Heidegger claims he is still trying to say and accomplish the same thing as in *Being and Time,* even if he did it there "rather clumsily." His early work was co-opted to support subjectivism and voluntarism, despite his efforts to avoid precisely that. Heidegger explicitly claims that *Being and Time* aimed at a "thought that abandons subjectivity" (*LH* 202). Consequently, Heidegger changes his language in an attempt to avoid being inappropriately co-opted. He is explicit in stating that his reversal in *language* is not a reversal of *intention:*

> [The "Time and Being" section was not published in *Being and Time*] because the thinking failed to find *language* adequate to this reversal. . . . This reversal is not a change from the standpoint of *[Being and Time],* but in it the intended thought for the first time attains the place of the dimension from which "Being and Time" is experienced; and, indeed, experienced from the basic experience of Being. (*LH* 202; emphasis mine)

Heidegger's "reversal" is, in short, primarily a rhetorical change. What is presented circumspectly in *Being and Time*—the discussion of thinking qua anticipation—now takes priority, while what was stressed in *Being and Time* and *An Introduction to Metaphysics*—resoluteness, struggle, *polemos,* "wresting"—now remains only on the periphery.

In *Letter on Humanism* Heidegger now asserts that only as Da-sein, in ex-sistence, is one authentic (*LH* 204). Any other sense in which one can be authentic—e.g., in relation to other beings, including other Daseins—is derivative. As I have stressed, the same point is made explicitly in *Being and Time*. Heidegger no longer emphasizes the ecstatic intermingling of the three ecstases of temporality, because he wishes to make clear that it is not man that accounts for Being's presencing; on the contrary, "It gives," "there is" *(es gibt)* Being (*LH* 204–5). "It" gives *itself* in a mysterious fashion, not logically but in a variety of unique, discontinuous ways. Hence "the thought that thinks the truth of Being thinks historically" (*LH* 206). There is always a fate or destiny which thought cannot master but only record and bring to speech, thereby giving Being a presence. This record cannot be reduced to a system because "It" is more mysterious in its grantings than even the revelations and miracles of the god of the Old Testament.

Heidegger now asserts that the history of Being (how It brings itself to presence) finds expression primarily in the words of the "*essential Thinkers.*"[3] The history of Being is primarily the history of thought. Without the ontological openness of the essential thinkers, man becomes homeless. Statesmanlike *praxis* recedes (*LH* 207). Nonetheless, within a unique, future world granted through grace, one presumes it is still necessary for man to resolutely hold together past, present, and future and be authentically temporal until another dispensation of Being arrives. Heidegger had become less sanguine than he was at the time *Being and Time* was published that an act of *praxis,* as one possible manifestation of truth, could reverse the technological domination of things. Technology's monolithic mode of revealing blocks that possibility—at least for now. Here Heidegger begins to diverge from Nietzsche, who still saw the need for a political propaedeutic. In the later Heidegger's eyes, the solution to the problem posed by modern nihilism would have to come from a new revelation of the meaning of Being itself by an essential thinker such as himself. Then that idea would have to sink down poetically to the commonality of mankind so that beings could be revealed anew.

Heidegger still fears he will be misconstrued. Hence he explicitly states that his attack on metaphysics—and its final manifestation in modern technics and logic—is not meant to lead to subjectivism and irrationalism; his attack on past humanism is not a glorification of the inhuman; his attack upon talk about humanly imposed "values" (that is, subjectivism) is not a dismissal of the highest goods; his claim that man is a Being-in-the-world does not justify positivism, for world is the openness *of* Being; his emphasis that our destiny is ruled by "God is dead" is not a submission to atheism, for his thought of Being is neither

---

3. As an example, a thought overpowers a thinker like Heidegger. It comes from he knows not where. He brings it to speech. It has ramifications he cannot predict. But by bringing something novel to speech, and by forcing others to look at the world differently—e.g., to reconsider the nature of modern nihilism or technology—he occasions change.

atheistic nor theistic; and his attempted deconstruction of the tradition, which aims to recover a relation to Being, is not nihilism. Heidegger claims that none of these are implied in *limiting the scope of thought.* Thought must not exceed its limits, which are determined by its need to be related to Being—the only true matter of thought—to the exclusion of meditating on things. Again, unlike Socrates' "second sailing" there must be no approach to Being through the interrogation either of beings or speeches about beings. That allegedly leads to metaphysics. One must approach openness to and oneness with Being (Identity) without the mediation of beings. But that leads into silence. Therein lies the problem that Heidegger never surmounts.

Heidegger closes the *Letter on Humanism* by reflecting on how the silent, reticent thinking he has presented is related to ethics. He asserts that ethics always involves the prior need for an *ethos,* which he defines as "abode, place of dwelling, . . . the open sphere in which man dwells" (*LH* 218). Heidegger again admits that an *ethos* is implied in every ontology, and vice versa (*LH* 219). In a future world that has overcome "the oblivion of Being," a distinct discipline of ethics would not be required; it would already be included in a "way of life." Heidegger is explicit in stating that the fundamental ontology of *Being and Time* already presupposed an *ethos,* which does not differ from the one presented in his later works. But he says that *Being and Time,* as a first step, had to remain within the recognizable and understandable terminology of existing philosophy. "In the meantime, I [Heidegger] have come to be convinced that even these terms must immediately and inevitably lead astray." This is indicative of the primordial problem of moving from silent insight to speech. Heidegger asserts that, nonetheless, *Being and Time* attempted to think the essential thing that must be thought, and hence brought ontology and ethics together in the only serious way it could be done (219–20).[4]

Living in an age of the rapid dissemination of ideas, Heidegger saw his ideas suffer a vulgarization he had apparently not completely anticipated. He had seen his early works interpreted as a simple call to the willfulness of an autonomous subjectivity, which was precisely what he had attempted to overcome even in *Being and Time.* There is no indication that Heidegger had consciously plotted epigonal dilutions as had Nietzsche, who foresaw that his works would be vulgarized and used for ends he found anathema and adapted his mode of writing accord-

---

4. Once again it is worth noting that Heidegger's deconstruction of the tradition is not in the service of endless deconstruction, but is the prelude to reconstruction, to finding a genuine *ethos,* which is the only way to ground "unique historical action" or *praxis.*

ingly. Heidegger adjusted after the fact by trying to develop a form of speech that would not be so easily co-opted—contemporary post-modernism is an indication that he was not altogether successful—but his understanding of the good for man did not change even though his vision was never one of more than broad outlines. He had always intended an assault on subjectivism, technological civilization, mass society, liberal individualism, communist collectivization, and the general totalization of existence. That intention never changed, though his perception of how to pursue it did. Heidegger always intended to recover the possibility of a genuine historical existence, and that always meant with and for a distinct community. And Heidegger always intended to overcome the old tradition of philosophy, and to provide a different vision for a future thinking.

18

The Transition to Postmetaphysical Thinking

In the "late" work *What Is Called Thinking?* Heidegger returns to a confrontation with Nietzsche. What he focuses on now is Nietzsche's attempt to foster a transition, an issue he had more or less ignored in his earlier attempts to secure Nietzsche's thought *as philosophy*. According to the later Heidegger, only a dialogue that is *preparing a transition,* as was Nietzsche's work, can meet Nietzsche's thought. Heidegger asserts that his work, if it is successful, will like Nietzsche's take its place on the side *the transition leaves behind to move to the other.*[1] We must hope that we will eventually find ourselves on the other side of completed metaphysics and nihilism, but we are still not thinking in a postmetaphysical fashion. Heidegger includes himself in this assertion. Hence, yet another transition is required in his thought. Heidegger intimates that various forms of transitional thinking—part *Verwindung* and part *Andenken*—could serve as a prelude to a future, nonmetaphysical thought.[2] Heidegger now prepares for the long wait and the lonely vigil, and a thinking consistent with it. That transitional thinking will be neither metaphysical in the old sense, nor postmetaphysical in his longed-for sense; rather it will exist between eternities.

According to the late Heidegger, the world wars settled nothing about man's fate on earth. The world government which he now assumes is inevitable will be forced into moral, social, and political categories that are too small. European moral and political ideas can no longer cope with what is looming. Quoting Nietzsche, Heidegger approvingly concurs that "our institutions are good for nothing any more. . . . We have mislaid all the instincts from which institutions

---

1. Heidegger, *What Is Called Thinking?* 50, 51. Henceforth designated in the text as *WCT,* followed by a page number.
2. For an elaboration of this issue see Vattimo, "Nihilism and the Post-Modern Philosophy," in *The End of Modernity,* 164–81. See also my "Ancients, Moderns and Postmoderns."

grow." What is needed is *"the will to tradition, to authority, to responsibility for centuries to come"* (*WCT* 67; emphasis mine).[3] But for Heidegger, the resolute "solidarity of chains of generations forward and backward *ad infinitum*" must rest on something other than *willing* the Eternal Recurrence. Heidegger agrees with Nietzsche that the last man is incapable of wielding to high purpose the powers he is soon to possess. A shaking and collapse of foundations will be the ultimate outcome: "But we must not equate such a shaking of the foundations with revolution and collapse. The shaking of that which exists may be the way by which an equilibrium arises, a position of rest such as has never been—because that rest, that peace, is already present at the heart of the shock" (*WCT* 65).

As in *The Letter on Humanism,* thinking remains that which is most essential to man's essence only as long as it remains attached to "It" that must be thought. Heidegger's new locution is that It is what is most "thought-provoking." Conjoined with this, he now observes that "most thought-provoking [of all] is that we are still not thinking," that we have never in our historical journey thought It that must be thought. And this is because that which must be thought turned away long ago, and keeps turning away constantly. For now we must contemplate this withdrawal. If man is ever to accomplish true thinking, he must "leap" away from the thinking that has held sway until now. If he does so, man can potentially be touched by the mysterious It that withdraws, and It can come to be more present for us than what is actual as present-at-hand (*WCT* 5–10). Oddly, Heidegger now also asserts that Socrates is the *purest* manifestation yet of going with "the draft" of that which withdraws which is the essence of thinking. Socrates' life represents a reaching out after that which one senses as somehow present, which is nonetheless not quite graspable and always retreating (*WCT* 17).[4]

But Heidegger asserts that the purest thinking is not to be confused with the greatest. The term "greatest" is reserved by Heidegger for Nietzsche, who brings an epoch to its culmination by drawing out its most radical possibilities. The ultimate outcome of the previous epoch, begun by Plato, is brought to speech by Nietzsche in the phrase "the wasteland grows." While Heidegger cautions that he is not co-opting

---

3. Quotations are from Nietzsche, *Twilight of the Idols,* the section "Critique of Modernity." Cited in Heidegger, *What Is Called Thinking?*
4. For Heidegger, it is Plato who sullies this noble Socratic instinct. This reverses Nietzsche's understanding of the relation between Socrates and Plato. For Nietzsche, Plato was the noble phenomenon who tried to mitigate Socrates' ignoble impulses.

Nietzsche's phrase in the sense of melancholy, pessimism, and despair fashionable in his age (nor in an optimistic sense, for that matter), he does assert that Nietzsche's words about the wasteland are true (*WCT* 30–31). Heidegger says that for Nietzsche, the phrase means that devastation is growing wider.

> *Devastation* is more than *destruction*. Devastation is more unearthly than destruction. Destruction only sweeps aside all that has grown up or been built up so far; but devastation blocks all future growth and prevents all building. Devastation is more unearthly than mere destruction. Mere destruction sweeps aside all things *including even nothingness,* while devastation on the contrary establishes and spreads everything that blocks and prevents. . . . The devastation of the earth can easily go hand in hand with a guaranteed supreme living standard for man, and just as easily with the organized establishment of a uniform state of happiness for all men. (*WCT* 29–30; emphasis mine)

Perhaps the most significant point in this distinction is the assertion that a healthy destruction can sweep aside *even the Nothingness*— presumably the inauthentic Nothingness of our inauthentic relation to nihilism and not the essential relation to the No-thing. *Present* thinking must aim at a healthy "destruction" if a new postmetaphysical thought is to emerge.[5] For now we must contemplate the nihilism that surrounds us just as we must reflect on the withdrawal of Being. In our destitute time nothing else is left to us. But eventually we must hope to leave the devastation of the present behind—and presumably the transitional thinking that goes with it.

Again approvingly quoting Nietzsche, Heidegger asserts that we must first find his (Nietzsche's) thought and then must lose it: " 'To lose' here means *to make ourselves truly free of that which Nietzsche's thinking has thought*" (*WCT* 52; emphasis mine). Despite the necessity of a transition and the need to lose what Nietzsche has thought, Heidegger asserts that Nietzsche knew "that through him something was put into words that can never be lost again. Something that cannot be lost again *to thinking,* something to which thinking must forever come back again the more thoughtful it becomes" (*WCT* 53; emphasis mine). Even future postmetaphysical Thinking will retain an element of recol-

---

5. Part of that destruction is the destruction of thinking as it has reigned in the West up to this time, the metaphysical thinking that only thinks Being as constantly present *(Anwesen)* and not as coming to presence *(Anwesenheit)*. But it would be naive to think this was the only destruction Heidegger had in mind.

lection *(Andenken).* But how can it be true both that what Nietzsche said must be left behind, and that something he said can never be lost? The answer is found in the simple observation that, for Heidegger, not everyone does or will think.

Heidegger asserts that Nietzsche's thought has still not been found; hence the devastation has not yet reached its ultimate peak. Heidegger now makes clear that he realizes that Nietzsche primarily limited himself to carrying to completion the devastation that was already fated, on the assumption that until that is accomplished, no rebirth is possible. Heidegger's "late" confrontation with Nietzsche shows a greater appreciation for Nietzsche's rhetoric and his expectation of the need for a transition than he showed in the Nietzsche lectures of the war years. Heidegger now has greater freedom to speak. But he has also now concluded that a period of extended transition remains the order of the day. Nietzsche saw correctly that "in the history of Western man something is coming to an end." And yet, Heidegger now asserts, the modern age is in no way at an end; it is just entering its long, drawn-out culmination. The transition will continue for a long time *(WCT* 55–56).

In part 2 of *What Is Called Thinking?* Heidegger turns to an elaboration of the recollective component of the transitional thinking, which could be different from the representational/metaphysical thinking he has characterized as culminating in the thought of Nietzsche. He prefaces this elaboration with a repetition of his ambiguous observation that future, postmetaphysical thought has as its object the "That" which calls on us to think, rather than a thinking that revengefully sets up things in and by a subject. Such thinking occurs only when we are open to and claimed by "That which calls," by that which *needs* us to think. We think to the extent that we listen to the *silent* call, which "calls even if it makes no sound" *(WCT* 124). In a way that has been prepared in previous works—and that reminds us of Nietzsche's discussion of the Free Spirits of the future—Heidegger asserts that such thought always occurs in a high and unsentimental solitude. For this reason, he says,

> No thinker ever has entered into another thinker's solitude. Yet it is only from its solitude that all thinking, in a hidden mode, speaks to the thinking that comes after or that went before. The things which we conceive and assert to be the results of thinking [i.e., writings, interpretations], are the misunderstandings to which thinking ineluctably falls victim. *(WCT* 169)

Postmetaphysical thinking will be silent and eventuate in no *logoi.* To translate this *alogon* experience into speech raises problems to which I have already pointed. But, that thinking limits itself to responding to an "unspoken call" is as it should be, for "it is not fitting anyhow to let the way [that is cleared] be seen in public" (*WCT* 170). Writing primarily occupies those who do *not* think, or who have at the very least ceased thinking for a time. Heidegger asserts that a future, nonmetaphysical thinking would be a "way of life" and a path, not a concrete outcome— a modest way of life, a movement that does not cease, an anxious wandering and wondering that cannot come to rest. This new thinking could never become a saying without quitting its element and ceasing to be. Nevertheless, even though it would produce nothing, Heidegger asserts that such thinking necessarily "precedes" all saying (*WCT* 198).

Only thinking so understood is in accord with man's essential nature. Since we have never yet thought, we have never yet reached our essence. In Nietzsche's terms, we are the still undetermined beings. So understood, science does not think, nor does worldly man in his relation to things. Yet Heidegger claims that postmetaphysical thinking, while different from poetry, would nonetheless be *closer* to poetry than to science (*WCT* 131–34). Poetry is the saying that thinking requires if it is to eventuate in authentic *logoi*. Such thinking is something we can prepare for, but it is not something for which we are primarily responsible: it is a kind of "thanking," a form of "memory" that thinks "back" to what must repeatedly be rethought. We must give thanks for this gift of thought before it will be possible, even though it is granted to very few. Until we accomplish such thinking in the future, various forms of preliminary, *transitional* thinking are needed.

While it is true that we are still not thinking, there was, Heidegger asserts, a time in the past when we came close. In our beginnings, we have an intimation toward which we must think back. As a transitional undertaking, "we are asking for the unspoken call that points to the beginnings of Western thinking" (*WCT* 178). Had we not this past intimation, it is not clear that we could make the "leap" that might open a path to a novel future. As part of his discussion of this preliminary recollective thinking, Heidegger turns to a reflection upon a saying of Parmenides to show how Parmenides responded to "the call." The operative Parmenidean phrase is: "One should both say and think that Being is." When Heidegger is finished deploying his customary etymological devices, the phrase is presented anew as "It is useful to let-lie-before-us and so the taking-to-heart also: beings in being" (*WCT* 171, 223).

For Heidegger, the key terms in this phrase are *noein* and *legein,* usually translated respectively as "thinking," on the one hand, and "saying" or "stating," on the other. Heidegger reinterprets *legein* as "laying

out," or "letting lie before one in presence." By Heidegger's understanding, *noein* implies "to apprehend," to perceive that which lies before, "to receive," although not in the passive, merely receptive
correspondence of a mirror. We apprehend or perceive in this sense
only in taking something up and doing something with it. In other
words, only that which is useful can lie before us—the resonances from
Being and Time should be clear: the useless cannot appear. But unlike
modern technology, in authentically using something the thing remains what it is; it is not transformed into standing reserve (*WCT* 187).
For Heidegger, Parmenides' saying responds to the silent call that lies at
the heart of all Western thinking.

Heidegger also asserts that the initial silent call to which we must
think back includes the necessity of thinking the *duality of beings and Be-*
ing, that is, ontological difference in Heidegger's sense. The original
determination of the basic ontological duality set forth the historic fate
of metaphysics and of the metaphysical manner of presenting beings.
But this initial duality could, according to Heidegger, have manifested
itself in ways other than it has in the metaphysical tradition; different
deflections were possible. Heidegger argues that the original call, now
that it has been remembered, can perhaps be determined in a different
way. Nonetheless, this thinking back is primarily a transitional, propaedeutic kind of thought. It is not an end in itself, but it provides a
better point of departure for a move toward a future, nonmetaphysical
mode of thought than does the thinking of completed metaphysics. We
must find a way to get a purchase on our age without falling into metaphysical willfulness. A second beginning from the same roots might
thereby ensue, or that might lead to another, entirely different, silent
call. Heidegger works both sides of this street because he is not sure if
getting beyond the second beginning is possible or if an entirely new
beginning will be forthcoming. But since the period of transition will
be long, there is time to explore options.

Heidegger also addresses what he considers the other great initial vision or silent call of Western thought: the perception that Being and
thinking are the same. He attempts to clarify this by reflecting on Parmenides' saying "For it is the same thing to think and to be." Heidegger
transforms the traditional translation into "for the same: taking-to-
heart is so also presence of what is present" (*WCT* 240–41). For
Heidegger, because "perceiving" and "taking to heart" are only possible where something already has been brought to "lie before" or has
come to presence, *legein* and *noein* occur simultaneously. They are the
same not because human thinking constitutes the Being of objects, nor
because Being itself is thought thinking itself, but because if one does

not take *cognizance* of presence there is no presence. Without thinking, there is no Being, for there is no presence without apprehending. Being and thinking are the same, and all Western thinking moves necessarily in this sphere (*WCT* 240).

Heidegger is not sure this sphere can be transcended. He now admits that this may mean we must always think first from beings as an ensemble toward that which makes them possible, because it is always the ensemble of beings that are immediately present. But according to Heidegger, therein lies the danger that we will never get beyond our preoccupation with things in our pursuit of that which makes them present. It may not be possible to think Being *without* regard to beings. Only by doing so could one think directly about the abundance of transformations of Being and the sequence of the epochs of Being.[6] But if the beginning always holds a variety of possibilities, even if a radically new beginning never comes, we are not entirely without options.

In yet another transitional experiment, Heidegger asserts that by now asking, "What is the event of Appropriation *[Ereignis]*?"—what, that is to say, grants the presence of present beings—we might make a new beginning (*OTB* 13–16, 19–20). Such a question is consistent with the original call, while potentially pointing beyond it to something totally postmetaphysical. Heidegger asserts that *Ereignis* would have to be thought of as a giving that is simultaneously a sending and extending of primordial spatiality and temporality (in the sense presented in *Being and Time*) which opens and appropriates beings, especially man. This is one way a preliminary thinking could think It without thinking It in relation to *specific* beings. Following this intimation, Heidegger asserts that presence should be seen as destiny's (the mysterious Its) gift, the gift granted by also giving primordial temporality: "Being proves to be destiny's gift of presence, the gift granted by the giving of time. The gift of presence is the property of Appropriating" (*OTB* 22). Thinking in this fashion *might* point toward a new, as yet unforeseen, silent call. Hence for the time being, we might think the question of *alētheia* not as truth, as it was posed in *Being and Time*,

6. Heidegger, *On Time and Being*, 2, 6, 9–11. Henceforth designated in the text as *OTB*, followed by a page number. If it is true that we have never yet been thinking, only through a future silent call could we find a way to think Being totally without relation to beings. We of the present must still think within the confines of ontological difference even when we think the epochality of Being. In principle, that must still be metaphysical thinking in Heidegger's terms. Hence the late Heidegger no more transcends metaphysics than does the early Heidegger; totally postmetaphysical thinking remains only a hope. Thus the thinness of Heidegger's articulation of what postmetaphysical thought would be like is to be expected.

but as "opening." Instead of "Being and Time," we could now think "opening and presence."

Heidegger's various discussions of transitional possibilities are far from concrete. But his intimations of a future, postmetaphysical thinking are, to say the least, even more ambiguous and frustrating. They hardly get beyond depicting the new thinking in purely negative terms. But we must recognize the necessity to which Heidegger believes he is responding. To project the concrete features of a future thinking in detail would be to fall into the totally modern trap of projecting a frame unto the future, and that is precisely what must be transcended. Nonetheless, if only because it put prior thought in a novel light, Heidegger's thought cannot help but have deferred ramifications. What those ramifications will be cannot be predicted with any precision. But, having admitted this, it is not unfair to say that the deferred ramifications of Heidegger's novel understandings are likely to include novel possibilities, even if his teaching merely destroys the plausibility of many (usually suppressed) late-modern premises.

For now we remain at the end of modernity. At one point Heidegger observes that "the ending [may last] longer than the previous history of metaphysics."[7] Since we are just entering the period of the end of metaphysics, that would mean that more than twenty-five hundred years of *preliminary* thinking may be required before we transcend our present impasse and move on to whatever genuinely new thinking might be granted to us through an act of grace. Even if it is a shorter period, Heidegger has, in his own way, concluded that "the last man lives longest." When the late Heidegger talks about "overcoming metaphysics" or "overcoming technology," he has in mind an overcoming qua long-term, preliminary "learning to live with," "becoming accommodated to," or "approaching in a new fashion," rather than any hasty obliteration of something completely defeated and left behind. We are destined to remain in that transition for an extended period. This is the only "overcoming" or "destruction" that is appropriate to the *transition* from the domination of completed metaphysics to a totally novel future thinking.

For now, all we can do is to (1) think back to the beginnings—to the original silent call of the West—to explore whether other paths away from the beginning are possible; (2) think through our nihilism, exacerbating the reigning devastation in hopes it will lead to a cleansing destruction; (3) think how the mere presence of the ensemble of things and their coming to stand is related to the various epochal dispensations

7. Heidegger, "Overcoming Metaphysics," in *The End of Philosophy*, 85.

of "opening"; and (4) wait openly and expectantly for a new event of appropriation. Ultimately all of these experiments are *transitional* and preliminary. Whether a thoroughly postmetaphysical version of thought will ever replace Heidegger's transitional experiments, only time will tell. And since, in Heidegger's view, all genuine, unique historical *praxis* rests on a novel openness to the mystery accomplished by thinking, it too awaits a future possibility which remains but a hope.

19

From *Eigentlichkeit* to *Gelassenheit:* Poetry and Phenomenological Openness to the World

In the early works, rooted dwelling with others seemed to rest primarily on the resoluteness discussed in *Being and Time*. Somehow that was linked with the foundational experience of the No-thing. The nature of that linkage remained unclear, resting on the ambiguous bridge phenomenon "anticipatory resoluteness." The problem for Heidegger is always how to speak about the issue of ontological difference, i.e., the difference yet relatedness of beings and Being. In the later works, this problem takes the form of relating "openness to the mystery" and "releasement to *things.*" This duality, which is at the center of Heidegger's thought from beginning to end, is presented with particular clarity by Thomas Langan:

> Two tendencies in the interpretation of Heidegger's philosophy have been calling to one another from mountains which are farthest apart. . . . Two responsible interpretations have come about because of an ambiguity in Heidegger's thought which has been reigning there from his analysis in *Being and Time* of the hermeneutic circle of interpretation to his call in "Time and Being" to think Being directly, without the mediation of the beings *(Seienden)*—in other words, to go beyond metaphysics definitively. How can Heidegger ask us to do that when he has said in *Holzwege,* "Being never comes to be without the beings"?[1]

These two sides of Heidegger's thought converge once again in the quintessential late discussion in *Gelassenheit.*[2] Heidegger begins his discussion in *Gelassenheit* by praising his homeland. It is the possibility of

---

1. Langan, quoted in "Panel Discussion," in *On Heidegger and Language,* ed. and trans. Joseph J. Kockelmans (Evanston: Northwestern University Press, 1972), 270.
2. The English translation of this text is *Discourse On Thinking.* Heidegger, *Discourse on Thinking.* Henceforth designated in the text as *DT,* followed by a page number.

having a homeland that has been lost and must be recovered. The thinking now said to be consistent with having such a homeland is called "meditative thinking." Like postmetaphysical thinking—in either its transitional or future manifestation—it is opposed to scientific, calculative thinking. But such thinking is categorically different from the thinking that strives for openness to It, engages in *Verwindung* or *Andenken,* waits for a novel event of appropriation, and so on. And it clearly does *not* eventuate in the solitude of Da-sein or that of the "essential," solitary thinkers. While calculative thinking reckons up the possibilities inherent in the conditions that are given, Heidegger asserts that meditative thinking contemplates the meaning that reigns in ever*ything* that is, everything that is present (*DT* 46). "Meditative thought" thinks *beings,* not Being or "It." We must come to meditate on what is closest and most *concerns* us, i.e., the beings among which we live out our lives. Compared with openness to It, this thinking is undoubtedly a kind of "falling." Yet for the later Heidegger, proper openness to beings no longer has anything resembling a pejorative connotation. Heidegger asserts that this meditative thinking is a kind of thinking that *everyone* can follow in his own way (*DT* 47).

The praise of a homeland goes hand in hand with meditative thinking, just as resoluteness had required correctly appropriating the destiny of one's own people. For modern man to move beyond living in a world that is an unworld requires "a life-giving homeland" between heaven and earth (*DT* 47–48). Heidegger asserts that everything lasting must have its roots in a native soil. Only in a genuine homeland can one avoid having everything falling "into the clutches of planning and calculation, of organization and automation" (*DT* 49). Previously we were told that what is threatened in our age is the essence of man, which is found as "openness" and as a "site." Now we are told that the essence of man requires an autochthony that is threatened by our technological unworld (*DT* 52–53).

For Heidegger, our transformed modern relationship to Nature threatens our essential being as much as the oblivion of Being. Nothing stands or is really present for us in our abstract world: "All that with which modern techniques of communication stimulate, assail, and drive man—all that is already much closer to man today than his fields around his farmstead, closer than the sky over the earth, closer than the change from night to day, closer than the conventions and customs of his village, than the tradition of his native world" (*DT* 48). As a result, man no longer dwells calmly between heaven and earth. "Meditative thinking," releasement to and oneness with beings, is the new resoluteness. Reawakening this meditative, nonself-conscious, outer directed "thought" is necessary to saving man's essential nature. We cannot know how long it will be before—or if—we can accomplish the transition to this new rooted thinking. Until we do, the greatest peril will be upon us, not because of the possibility of atomic war, but rather "precisely when the danger of a third world war has been removed" (*DT* 56). The greatest danger is that we will find an anesthetized way to accommodate ourselves to alienation and rootlessness, such that we will never leap away from the modern relation to reality into a meditative lingering alongside genuinely opened *things*.

What does "releasement toward things" mean in more concrete terms? It is a thinking that thinks about what *already* has presence. It contemplates temples, fields, animals, and armies, constitutions and sacred texts. It takes them seriously and unironically. It does not think about the ground of their possibility. This nonwillful meditative thinking is not yet available to us but could be at any moment. It is not as distant a possibility as genuine postmetaphysical thought. In an extremely Nietzschean turn of phrase, Heidegger observes that in our age we still have to *will* nonwilling (*DT* 59–60). Only in this way can we "release" ourselves to a future relation to reality that is not a form of willing. A "stepping back" takes the place of anticipatory resoluteness. Yet even in "willing" the overcoming of willing, we do not awaken releasement on our own. It remains a gift from afar—i.e., the deferred ramification of the thought of an essential thinker. Hence we must simultaneously remain "open to the mystery," waiting for a new dispensation of Being, a new event of appropriation.

Heidegger stresses that meditative thinking is not a simple passivity that allows everything to "slide and drift along" (*DT* 61). It is not a letting go of self-will in favor of divine will; nor is it a form of transcendental horizontal re-presenting. With regard to the last, Heidegger observes that we do not know what the horizon (world) really is. It is the "enchanted region," it comes and goes; it loses and regains its enchantment mysteriously. Present *things,* as they appear for all, must be given dignity again (*DT* 79). This means that we of the present must be released to objects that are in most instances products of modern technology. But we will relate to them differently than as standing reserve. This eventuates in a waiting, but not the idle "awaiting" of inauthenticity. Heidegger asserts that when man is under the spell of "releasement toward things" in his world, he has been seized by resolve: "Something like power of action and resolve also reign in releasement." Heidegger observes that in retrospect, resolve in *Being and Time* could be understood as "the opening of [Dasein] *particularly* undertaken by him *for* openness" (*DT* 80–81). Resolve is now depicted as a steadfast openness to *self-presenting otherness,* to what surrounds one as an untranscendable dispensation of fate and destiny, to the realm of appearance as a manifestation of truth. The immediate world that appears should not be taken as an accident to be negated by human will; it always has a supreme necessity from whose draft one can be freed only at the greatest peril to one's true essence. As such, resolve and releasement are identical; they make possible all "in-dwelling." We must relinquish the Nietzschean willing of horizons and meditate on the curious and amazing things that litter our landscape.

Furthermore, "in-dwelling in releasement . . . would be noble-mindedness itself" (*DT* 81, 82). The steadfast acceptance of what is given, the resolute development of what is implied and required within a given world, is the noble, as Heidegger understands it. We must will to release ourselves to a future that is dominated by such "noble-mindedness." The noble being is justified as higher than any autonomously willful being. And as was true for Nietzsche, for Heidegger the noble is what has "origins" (*DT* 82–85). Noble "releasement toward things" is the basis of the new rootedness, the new autochthony. Something like the following equation ensues: noble-mindedness = resoluteness = releasement = in-dwelling = rootedness = living correctly in a traditional world within a technological setting, surrounded by the products of technological willfulness reappropriated in a new way. Properly approached, the technological world, the great enemy and destroyer of past traditions and traditional horizons, can be incorporated into new traditions.

> Releasement toward *things* and openness to the mystery belong together. They grant us the possibility of dwelling in the world in a totally different way. They promise us *a new ground and foundation upon which we can stand and endure* in the world of technology without being imperiled by it.
>
> Releasement toward things and openness to the mystery give us a vision of *a new autochthony which someday even might be fit to recapture the old and now rapidly disappearing autochthony in a changed form.* (*DT* 55; emphasis mine)

A new, noble dwelling is as much a part of what Heidegger is "on the way" to as the new postmetaphysical thinking. In the essay "Building Dwelling Thinking," which reworks a theme opened in *Being and Time,* Heidegger also asserts that man's essence is to dwell.[3] It is pri-

3. Heidegger, "Building Dwelling Thinking," in *Poetry, Language, Thought.* The

marily the artist who makes possible this "sojourn in the nearness of *beings*." Heidegger poetically designates the primal place of our dwelling "the Fourfold"—on the earth, under the sky, before the divinities, and with other mortals. Man can dwell only by keeping the Fourfold *in* things (*PLT* 150–51). Authentically revealed beings include within them the divine, earth, and sky. Such things, which allow a site for the Fourfold, are primarily "buildings," which make possible "locations" that in turn open up a space for other things. Genuine building opens a unique space into which the Fourfold is admitted.

A world locked within primordial spatiality is dominated by a qualitative multitude of locations rather than the uniformity of quantitative space (*PLT* 154–55). Contemporary space no longer contains distinct places or locations, and it does not invite in the divine. Where the sky becomes uniform space, where the earth becomes matter, where the divine withdraws and mortal man longs to be immortal there is no building or dwelling, there are no locations, and hence there is no openness for things. In contrast, the enchanted locations that are opened by true building bring limit and measure (*PLT* 157, 158). This is what makes possible a true homeland.

Dwelling is not something that is possible simply by "Nature." Man must build to be able to dwell. He must open the space that allows for the presencing of the Fourfold; he must open the earth and heavens—a spiritual world is required. Otherwise, the divine does not presence, and man's mortality and finitude are not even available to him: "only if we are capable of dwelling, only then can we build. . . . The real dwelling plight lies in this, that mortals ever search anew for the nature of dwelling, that they *must ever learn to dwell*" (*PLT* 160, 161). And this means they must ever build anew, because even genuine buildings become mere objects; they cease to be the site of the Fourfold. At that point man's dwelling must be refounded. Every work of art is unique. It can never be torn out of its native sphere without becoming a mere object. Works of art have their truth for a time—and a place—and then their time passes. "World-withdrawal and world-decay can never be undone" (*PLT* 41). There is no going back and recovering the world made possible by previous works. Hence when its world collapses, the work of art becomes a mere unenchanted, present-at-hand object.

The modern project, which thought it could make man at home in his world once and for all, was mistaken from the beginning, and by bringing him to live among a forest of mere objects of his own will—

published essay is taken from a lecture given in 1951. *Poetry, Language, Thought* henceforth designated in the text as *PLT*, followed by a page number.

and eventually the abstract objectlessness of standing reserve—made him homeless instead. Dwelling requires a proper relation to *things;* man must become surrounded and in their vicinity in a proper way, a way that incorporates the sacred, accepts mortality, and takes earth and heaven into account in a prescientific, pretheoretical, "phenomenological" fashion (taken in a sense to which I will return in part 4). In short, according to Heidegger, there can never be a secular world; any genuine world bears the stamp of the sacred. And there can never be a genuine world that is not in some way rooted in the indigenous—which includes not only an indigenous landscape, but also an indigenous language.

It is the poets who are most related to and capable of opening up things in the correct phenomenological fashion. It is the poets who "build" in the highest sense: "Poetry first causes dwelling to be dwelling. Poetry is what really lets us dwell" (*PLT* 213, 215). Genuine poetry is not the result of self-conscious creative will, and unlike genuine, essential thinking, it cannot stand outside the particular and indigenous: "Poetry does not fly above and surmount the Earth in order to escape it and hover over it. Poetry is what first brings man onto the Earth, making him belong to it, and thus brings him into dwelling" (*PLT* 218). This is how the poet differs from the thinker. Of course, poets should always, in some mysterious fashion, be tutored by a thinker who has experienced the silent call. The thinker who has achieved openness to the mystery is the true foundational phenomenon, but he can have no immediate echo in the world. The poet is the "teller of language." Only the poet brings silence to speech. Without this saying, there is no *logos,* and hence no limit or measure—no *nomos* or *peras.* The experience of No-thingness is limitless. The thinker needs the poet.

Heidegger asserts that enveloped in a world that uncovers the Fourfold in things, we are safe in the nearness of Being. In genuine dwelling, we are shaped by our world; we are the "mirror" of the world: "Thinking in this way, we are called by the thing as the thing. In the strict sense of the German word *bedingt,* we are the be-thinged, the conditioned ones. We have left behind us the presumption of all unconditionedness" (*PLT* 181). When truly dwelling, man is constituted in relation to the indigenous, poetically revealed things that surround him. Man is part of the whole. This is the correct state for man, the way in which the world should be primally, pretheoretically, poetically revealed. This "be-thingedness" cannot be confused with thinking the No-thing. But it is in a world where this be-thingedness exists that Heidegger believes genuine thinking is most possible.

But a vicious circle raises its head in this account. The poets who bring into existence a speech that opens space for building grow only out of a genuine world; they exist primarily within a world where men are *already* correctly related to things. But the charmed circle of *praxis* has failed contemporary man. An immediate phenomenological relation to reality is unavailable. The "natural" relation to things must be recovered. The poets of the future will reach into the earth for their ground. But poets for our "destitute time," *for now,* must reach into the abyss.[4] Our age requires a unique brand of poets, more philosophical than those who will follow. We need interim poets, just as we need a preliminary thinking. For Heidegger, Rilke is such a poet, even though he still thinks metaphysically. In Rilke's speech, the abyss is endured and phenomenological rootedness is prefigured.

According to Heidegger's Rilke, the higher our self-consciousness, the more we are excluded from the world. To live immediately or "naturally" among things is to be drawn by the "whole draft" (*PLT* 108). Humanity must repeatedly bring itself into this draft, a feat more "benumbed" things accomplish without effort. If individuals engage in conscious, willful, productive activity, they merely cast themselves out into "unshieldedness" (*PLT* 114–15). According to Rilke, purposeful self-assertion, i.e., the attempt to "render the human condition, man's being, tolerable for everybody and happy in all respects," threatens man's essence. As a result, protection is withheld from man. For example, it is important for man to take a stance toward death, to accept mortality. Some must die so others may be born. One must not rail against this necessity. A willful refusal to accept such limits is a "parting *against*" the "pure draft" (*PLT* 116). But "to be secure is to repose safely within the drawing of the whole draft" (*PLT* 120). Since we moderns are allegedly "be-thinged" beings, caught in a "mirror play" with what surrounds us, we cannot avoid becoming objectified; he who knows nothing but objectifications presented through representations "knows nothing immediately perceptual. What can be immediately seen when we look at things, the image they offer to immediate sensible intuition, falls away" (*PLT* 126–27). Reliance on "immediate sensible intuition" is the realm of safety. One must be able to lean on the realm of appearance and accept it as reliable. This is but another way of saying that man must be reintegrated into Nature, understood as recovering an immediate phenomenological relation to what appears.

---

4. This does not seem to differ that radically from saying that during an interim period we need "anticipatory resoluteness."

To be human, we must again become "attuned" to the world, to the things in our world, to the earth. Picking up a theme from *Being and Time,* Heidegger asserts that feeling and mood are the earth within us invisible, and are more reasonable, more open to Being, than all *ratio*.[5] In the words of Rilke, "Earth, your will, is it not this: to rise up / in us invisible?" (*PLT* 138, 140, 141). The poets are the best hope for this recovery. Only through the poets can we come to experience things as they present *themselves*. For example, poetically we never experience reality as a confusing manifold in danger of flying apart; we always experience something whole, like a rainstorm. To abstract from the wholes that we experience and see a phenomenon as an ensemble of characteristics is to fail to grasp it immediately as it presents *itself*.

Since the earth—which implies the Fourfold in general[6]—has to be opened by a work of art to be earth, it always remains intimately related to a world. Earth cannot be taken as primary Nature, for until earth is opened and displayed by world, it cannot emerge on its own as *a native ground*. But every genuine world has this limitation: it cannot fly away from earth. Heidegger asserts that every true world must be set upon the earth, understood as the dark, mysterious, concealed, primal ground. Otherwise, one has an unworld. Every true world belongs to a certain place, a certain group, sharing a distinctive language, past, religion, climate, terrain, *ethos,* and so on. So understood, "upon the earth and in it, historical man grounds his dwelling in the world" (*PLT* 46).[7]

For Heidegger, earth must always be approached as the concealed and mysterious that shatters every attempt to penetrate it. To present earth as an ensemble of atoms, or subatomic particles, is no longer to see it whole, as earth, just as to see a thunderstorm as the relation between high and low pressures or light as an electromagnetic wave phenomenon is to cease to see it as the phenomenon that is immediately

5. Heidegger, "The Origin of the Work of Art," *PLT* 25. This represents a lecture given in 1935, revised for publication in 1950, and revised again in 1960. Therefore it spans Heidegger's various periods.

6. Heidegger asserts that whenever we speak of one of the Fourfold, the other three are always implied. Heidegger, "The Thing," *PLT* 178.

7. All human dwelling requires the reciprocal relation between world ("self-disclosing openness of the broad paths of the simple and essential decisions in the destiny of an historical people") and earth ("spontaneous forthcoming of that which is continually self-secluding and . . . concealing"). "The earth cannot dispense with the Open of the world if it itself is to appear as earth in the liberated surge of its self-seclusion. The world, again, cannot soar out of the earth's sight if, as the governing breadth and path of all essential destiny, it is to ground itself on a *resolute* foundation" (*PLT* 48, 49; emphasis mine).

available. When taken in the way it is immediately experienced, earth is allegedly grasped as the self-concealing mother of all. This manifestation is primary; it has a status of its own, best revealed by poets, not scientists. Nothing about modern science changes the primordial relationship we have to whole things in pretheoretical experience. As with the idea earth, the idea sky presents its own immediate phenomena, regardless of whether its scientific elaboration be that of Ptolemy, Copernicus, or Einstein; primordially, the sun rises and falls, the seasons follow one another, the planets wander, and so on. It is this with which we must renew a oneness.

In asserting that any genuine world must remain in contact with the earth, Heidegger is not speaking in favor of a return to a rural or agrarian civilization. Nor is he condemning the "idiocy of urban life." Rootedness in the earth means rootedness in a distinctive place poetically opened up for a specific group in a way which *affirms life* in all its unfathomableness. Presumably, one can be grounded in the earth within an urban, technological environment as well as in the Black Forest (although perhaps not as easily). Likewise, in properly opening the earth, the genuine artist never *uses it up* any more than the painter uses up or transforms his colors into standing reserve. When Heidegger asserts that no world is acceptable which destroys the earth and its self-concealing, self-subsisting rhythms, he is trying to bring about a recovery of a certain relationship between man and what surrounds him, one that is not antagonistic, and does not lead to an objectifying negation of self-presenting difference. He wishes to integrate man into a redivinized, self-presencing Other, to reconstitute immediacy. The hegemony of earth can be reestablished in a variety of ways other than in a longing for the pristine and bucolic as long as earth is not revealed as mere object, as standing reserve, or as capable of being totally unconcealed. Beyond these general observations, the specifics of the alternative presented by the concept earth remain allusive and thereby illusive, a matter for a poet to determine.

Any dialectical attempt to overcome the tension between world and earth will destroy the possibility of human dwelling.[8] For Heidegger, existence requires this primordial opposition, just as, by its very nature, truth requires untruth, freedom restraint, cultivation ignorance, and so on (*PLT* 54). Within broad-bosomed earth as it reveals itself phenomenologically, opposition always reigns. Any world that tries to destroy opposition (difference) destroys dwelling. This "is the opposi-

---

8. This argument is similar to Nietzsche's point that we must not attempt to overcome the tension between Dionysian and Apollonian.

POETRY AND PHENOMENOLOGICAL OPENNESS

tion of the primal conflict" (*PLT* 55), which no dialectic can safely replace.[9] Setting this conflict in place is the task of the true artist (*PLT* 59–61).[10] And "artist" must be understood broadly—"Another way [besides the work of art] in which truth occurs is *the act that founds a political state*" (*PLT* 62; emphasis mine).

Among all the modes of revealing, Heidegger asserts that the linguistic work has priority.[11] It is always language that brings some*thing* into the open for the first time (*PLT* 73).[12] This is why the post-metaphysical thinker will need poets as epigones as much as Nietz-

9. Modern capitalism, which prides itself on institutionalized conflict, apparently does not represent a "primal" conflict, for it is in the service of the mastery of Nature and a once-and-for-all secured existence and leads inexorably to a technological destruction of allegedly primal conflict.

10. We are inevitably brought to pose the question of why we should choose this poetically induced conflict over modern technological making. Ultimately, the only answer is that Heidegger has reached an empirical conclusion, based on some theoretically unexplained practical wisdom that allows him to know what is most conducive to human well-being, that is, the preservation of man's essence. It is more than a little disquieting, therefore, to reflect upon how defective Heidegger's actual practical judgment was. But theoretical genius and practical wisdom are frequently not found together. On this level Aristotle's radical separation of *sophia* and *phronesis* seems compelling. The saving grace is that theoretical insight may be deflected in a variety of ways.

Aristotle's radical separation of theoretical and practical wisdom has a parallel in Heidegger's projected chasm between being-toward-Being in an unmediated fashion and being-toward poetically opened beings. I would argue that this radical split, which Aristotle initiated, is one of the causes of the nihilism that Nietzsche traces to Socrates and Heidegger to Plato. Aristotle's radical deflection of Plato's thought is the ground of many of the problems Nietzsche and Heidegger diagnose. But a similar chasm between thought and *praxis* is still manifested in their thought. To that extent they both remain determined by Aristotle's deflection of Plato. Since Aristotle's was not the only deflection available, a "second beginning" may be possible starting from Plato's work rather than that of the pre-Socratics.

11. Heidegger asserts that language is always a saying for a world historical people, i.e., a people with a genuine world, a shared enchanted, charmed circle. Hence statesmen seem necessarily to follow poets. Homer, for example, must shape the Greeks as a people before a Solon or Lycurgus can perform their acts of statesmanship.

Further, true art is always art for a people, not for man per se. For Heidegger, to say that there can be world art means only that all art simultaneously presupposes and helps constitute a world. With each establishing of truth, something unique occurs; hence, even technological objects could in the future be uncovered in a novel fashion (*PLT* 62). In other words, their Being could become different, as different as when what was once seen as a sacred cow comes to be seen as only so much potential ground beef.

12. For Heidegger language is always the language of a pregiven community, never the consciously projected "language-game" of a self-constituting group. The idea of choosing among language games is a delusion; there is always a primordial shared language—or at least the remnants of one—that predates such efforts and shapes our choices.

sche's future Free Spirits needed them. Poets are the ones who make a *logos* and *nomos* possible and who can ground the unique historical action of a people in immediate experience. That cannot be done by the thinker projected out into the No-thing waiting for the silent call, trying to think Being *directly* without the mediation of beings.

20

Variations on a Theme: Postmodern Elements in Heidegger's Teaching

The later Heidegger returns to the themes that he pursued in his early works. The project of *Being and Time* is reappropriated under the aegis of a new rhetoric. But whether we talk about the new thinking or about anticipation, releasement toward things or resoluteness, dwelling, rootedness, and autochthony or authentic being-in-the-world and being-with those of one's own generation, we are *on the way* to the same vision. Heidegger's problem always remained the same—how to bridge the gap between the silent, solitary openness to the primal source and the action within the world that presupposes a shared *nomos, ethos,* and *logos.* He pursued a new thinking *and* a new basis for *praxis,* a new relationship to both Being and beings, but he never adequately succeeded in integrating the two.

For Heidegger, authenticity, as well as rootedness and dwelling, is genuinely possible only in a future in which one is reattuned to a world accepted as *self*-presencing. But that is what eludes us at present. The gap between the silent thinking that eventuates from openness to the *Abgrund* and closure within a world, which requires a distinct *logos* and *ethos,* is never completely closed. Still, in Heidegger's mind, genuine rootedness requires a prior theoretical propaedeutic; it rests on a *transition* made possible by the Heideggerian deconstruction and *the reconstruction which it awaits.* Heidegger has no intention that we remain deconstructionists forever. He is clear, however, that *he* cannot consciously provide the reconstruction but must instead prepare for the existence of others. This is a notion Heidegger shares with Nietzsche. Poets, statesmen, and others take on the same autonomy from theory for Heidegger as they do in the thought of Nietzsche. Thinking must withdraw from the modern stance of projecting the future—what Nietzsche categorized as the Spirit of Revenge. What is required is to quit the manipulative, revengeful stance of the modern theorist. Then one might hear the silent call of Being. But since Heidegger cannot explain how the silent call gets *correctly* translated into a *logos,* he cannot explain what the future *nomos* will look like except in negative or purely formal forms. Nonetheless, his project, like Nietzsche's, rests on the necessity of fostering the recovery of an autonomous *praxis* and a new future thinking disencumbered of the modern task of projecting concrete futures and manipulating *praxis.*

I suggested above that the *post*modern elements in Nietzsche's thought could be found in his attempt to sever *praxis* from theoretical determination while simultaneously offering a new vision of thinking freed from the Spirit of Revenge. These postmodern elements can be found in Heidegger's thought as well. But Heidegger gives a deeper ontological exploration of the presuppositions of that shared understanding.[1] He strips away the modern rhetorical elements of Nietzsche's thought and tries to ontologically ground the longed-for future. In the process, Heidegger tries to give the return to immediacy both he and Nietzsche see as essential an ontological depth that is missing in Nietzsche's thought. Like Nietzsche, Heidegger tries to return man to the surface, to recover immediacy, a phenomenology of the experience of otherness taken as self-presenting—this is Heidegger's version of the reintegration of man and nature, which Nietzsche thought was possible only on the basis of illusions or consciously willed myths. Heidegger tries to show that *mythos* is not a form of self-consciously willed illusion, but a mode of the revealing of truth. As such, *mythos* has truth about it, and the things it reveals also stand in the truth. Consequently for Heidegger, the things that appear for all in shared sensory intuition and shared opinions are not illusions, but self-standing in truth. Likewise, for Heidegger, appearance is a manifestation in truth. For Nietzsche, all future *praxis* rests on consciously projected myths; for Heidegger, genuine *praxis* is also a manifestation of truth.

In his attempt to free Nietzsche's project from metaphysical ele-

1. The middle and late Heidegger confronts Nietzsche thematically. There is an explicit attempt to distance himself from the Nietzsche who gave preeminence to the Will to Will and what Heidegger presents as the mere reversal of rather than escape from metaphysical dichotomies. I have argued that the primacy of willing, along with other metaphysical elements, was part of Nietzsche's understanding of how to foster a *transition* and not part of his hoped-for future. Heidegger's criticism of Nietzsche, then, ultimately reduces to the same criticism he eventually made of his own early rhetoric—that it is infelicitous to make the Will even appear central to a teaching that is attempting to overcome the hegemony of the Will. Put another way, Heidegger is more sensitive than Nietzsche to the problems involved in using modern means to a *post*modern end. In the last analysis, Heidegger's critique of the rhetoric Nietzsche used in the service of fostering a transition should not divert us from recognizing that Heidegger pursued many of the same *ends* as Nietzsche.

ments and provide an ontological foundation, Heidegger transforms Nietzsche's discussion of "horizons" or "perspectives" into his discussion of world, and then tries to show that it is the No-thing that worlds in the world. Like Nietzsche, Heidegger sees the world of his time as an unworld that threatens man's essence. Like Nietzsche, he sees man's essence requiring rootedness in a shared *ethos*. While Nietzsche pursued the ontic, more concrete ramifications of this fact, Heidegger explored its ontological presuppositions. But Heidegger makes explicit throughout his works that there is a reciprocal relationship between one's conception of Being and a specific *ethos,* and he concludes that a certain view of Being, which he attempts to articulate, is required for the existence of a genuine world. He also tries to articulate a view of Being consistent with a new kind of thinking that would not become calculative and manipulative (or "legislative"). Whether Heidegger actually believes his ontological account or is simply deeper and more clever rhetorically than Nietzsche is a matter for speculation. I am inclined to believe that his ontological longings are genuine and that he articulates well the experience of absence that is inarticulately widespread in the abstract world of late modernity.

Heidegger puts substantially greater emphasis than does Nietzsche on the idea that at the heart of all truly individual thought lies what can only be explained as a silent, mystical, religious longing for oneness, or identity, with the source. Heidegger agrees with Nietzsche that the true thinker exists outside the *ethos* of a community, and is primarily a solitary. Any direct intercourse with a community sullies the silent reveries of the true thinker. However, as cospokespersons for the religious, Heidegger's thinkers and the poets need not be at odds. Thereby they need be intrinsically at odds with the requirements of a distinct people, which always requires a relation to the divine. What Nietzsche put forward as a possible public persona for the philosophers of the future—priests of an atheistic religion—Heidegger appears to have actually pursued. Unlike Nietzsche, Heidegger leads us to believe that there truly is a Dionysian core toward which one must be open. Here I am admittedly engaging in speculation, but when Heidegger stands in his solitude peering into the dark, mysterious core of reality, he seems— unlike Nietzsche, who openly says that the Dionysian must be willed— actually to be waiting for a silent call to course through his or some future thinker's being. Heidegger has definitely put into speech a vision that no one else previously had. Whence did that vision emanate?

Like Nietzsche's Free Spirits of the future, Heidegger's future, postmetaphysical thinker ceases to stand as the self-willed, self-legislating

ground of *praxis*. In this Nietzsche and Heidegger stand at the pole opposite that occupied by modern philosophy, which set out to dictate
theoretically to both nonhuman Nature and the human political and
ethical world. What can appear to be substantive disagreements over
the meaning of nihilism, the status of the Will, the nature of metaphysics, and so on are, by comparison, a contest over means to an
agreed-upon end: a future rooted in an enchanted circle where *praxis* is
self-generating, and a new thinking which is freed from the Spirit of
Revenge so that it may be open to and affirm life in all its mystery and
self-generating difference. But Heidegger goes far beyond Nietzsche in
attempting to ontologically ground his project in something that is not
willed by man. Heidegger spent a lifetime trying to put into words that
central ontological sense, an effort he understood to be both necessary
and ultimately unlikely to succeed, because the great thinker of vision
is rarely the great poet as well. As a philosophical poet, Heidegger is
certainly no Plato.

While Heidegger certainly gives ontological depth to the Nietzschean project—and the potential *post*modern elements it entails—the
central novel aspects of Heidegger's thought for my purposes are to be
found in his attempt to recover the notion of something self-
presencing, his notion of ecstatic temporality, his discussion of the primacy of the pretheoretical, and the idea of multiple possible deflections
that can be extrapolated from his notion of a "second beginning." Perhaps most importantly, postmodernity requires a recovery of a public
world that "appears for all" as self-presencing rather than as the prior
projection of a self-conscious, self-legislating "subject." Likewise, it
requires a new relation to Nature, which in turn rests on a recovery of
physis, understood as that which is self-presencing. Those possibilities
lie at the heart of Heidegger's thinking.

In the face of the hegemony of scientific and technological revelation
of reality, Heidegger tries to give dignity to fundamental thinking, poetry, statesmanship, and authentic doing and making. He is intent
upon giving man back the possibility of genuine, unique, historical
action—i.e., the political.[2] Deflected in what I believe is a consistent
postmodern direction, the ultimate concrete outcome is what in part 4 I
will call the return to the political, understood as a realm of *praxis* freed
from the theoretical Spirit of Revenge. In Heidegger's thought, that
possibility always presupposes the recovery of certain primordial expe-

---

2. For Heidegger, the political arena *is* the historical place where genuine and unique
history can be made, not the endless repetition of the same, nor the replacement of political action by technical decision making.

riences, possibilities obliterated by the monolithic revelation of reality of techno-modernity. For Heidegger, what I will call the political requires "community," not the modern bureaucratic state, and a shared *ethos,* not a universalizing legalism.

Even more resolutely than Nietzsche, Heidegger tried to reflect on the actual presuppositions of genuine community—realizing that communities cannot be willed. Like Nietzsche, Heidegger saw shared principles and ideas, not biology or race, as what forges communities. Contrary to the modern understanding, it is not questions of penury, scarcity, unequal distribution, fear, and mortality that occasion the political. Hence the abolition of those limitations would not bring with it the abolition of the political except by threatening man's essence. The political cannot be reduced to the economic—or to the subpolitical in all its "instinctive" forms—and thus transformed into a problem with a technical solution. Further, for Heidegger, the recovery of the political is linked to the recovery not only of peoples, but also of the holy. Historical existence requires the holy. As Heidegger argues in his studies of Hölderlin, any "second beginning" must let the truth be seen as the holy, beyond the death of God. The Fourfold can only hold together if the holy is kept in things. Every high civilization to date has been a religious civilization. Primordial poetry, which is always the language of a historical people, must speak the holy. The political and the religious cannot be sundered.

Heidegger's argument for the primacy of the pretheoretical revelation of reality likewise opens a variety of possibilities. It shows modern science and technology in a far different light than that contained in the early modern understanding. As late-modern science ceases its ontological pretensions, or even the search for a "unified theory," and becomes increasingly abstract and dependent upon hypotheses that in principle can not be verified empirically, what makes one theory better than another comes to rest increasingly on aesthetic phenomena. That raises the question of the basis of such aesthetic judgments. Heidegger would force one to conclude that those judgments will always be ontologically, morally, and politically loaded. While late-modern science—especially physical science—increasingly eschews ontological pretensions and the search for ontological foundations, it still surreptitiously retains ontological presuppositions. Its theoretical status —it remains worth pursuing for utilitarian reasons—is diminished in light of that fact, as are its pretensions to be able to arbitrate the most important questions. And the status of modern scientists as cultural heroes can remain plausible only on purely utilitarian grounds.

Heidegger's analysis of the priority of the pretheoretical also points toward a valuable qualitative understanding of primordial spatiality and temporality, which leads to his discussion of the ecstatic nature of existence. This represents a significant emendation of Nietzsche's longing for an ahistorical "innocence and forgetting," in which there is the danger of falling prey to all manner of ignorant and venal manipulation. Heidegger's understanding can explain man's existence as historical—and hence open to novelty and the transcendence of any possible end of history—without succumbing to any thoroughgoing historicism or fostering ahistorical illiteracy.[3] But it must be disassociated from Heidegger's apocalyptic vision, which made it easy for him to fall prey to the preposterous pretensions of National Socialism. National Socialism and the essential things for which Heidegger longed need not have anything in common. Further, apocalyptic visions can hardly avoid being sullied by the Spirit of Revenge against the present as it is constituted. Still, Heidegger's thought opens many paths which provide a variety of possible deflections. These postmodern elements, along with the need to sever the modern amalgamation of theory and practice and transcend the Spirit of Revenge, are the ones I will try to deflect onto a resolutely postmodern path in part 4.

We must still attend to the main difficulty of Heidegger's presentation. What is the primary agent for the *transition* to a more healthy future, man or Being? There is a tension here that Heidegger did not—and in principle, could not—remove. If man is caught in the grips of an overpowering fate, Heidegger can do no more than restate the problem of nihilism. Man must be capable of doing something, even if it is only adopting the stance of openly waiting for the advent of a new event of presencing. But if man becomes a self-grounding agent, the problem Heidegger is trying to transcend reemerges. In the early works, Heidegger put the accent on man's need to take responsibility for his existence, in the later works on the saving grace of Being itself; but neither emphasis offers all that is required if one wishes simultaneously to evaluate the contemporary world in a way that has an ontological foundation and to be of use in transcending elements of it. Heidegger's various attempted solutions lead into an unnecessary opacity. The Heideggerian gulf between action and silent hearing need not open; as suggested above, that dichotomy is a residue of a premodern premise that descends from Aristotle's infelicitous deflection of Platonic/ Socratic thought.

Finally, Heidegger argued that all Western thought, including his

---

3. If we are always at least partially determined by our "having-been," an element of *Andenken* is always required.

own, thinks within the confines of the Being/beings dichotomy. He wished to reopen contemporary *beings* in an authentic way and to think Being directly. I will argue that the cost of his eschewing dialectical mediation in the approach to Being is that it is never clear that beings, and the practical world in general, are not cut off from the ground, whether understood as *Abgrund* or otherwise. Likewise, it is never clear how the highest and most primal philosophic experience comes to speech. As a result, we are left with a thinking that cannot explain the difference between decent activities shared with others and barbaric viciousness, nor the difference between a thinking that is rigorous and a vacuous hopeful waiting that cannot help but be enervating. Despite all the novel possibilities and deflections Heidegger opens, his thought therefore contains fatal flaws that point toward the need for further reflection.

PART FOUR

Deflections toward a Postmodern Future

Late modernity is the place where, perhaps, a different possibility
of existence for man emerges. When seen in this light,
the prophetic overtones of philosophies like those of Nietzsche
and Heidegger appear less apocalyptic and more in line
with our own experience. . . . The ideas of Nietzsche and Heidegger,
more than any others, offer us the chance to pass from a
purely critical and negative description of the postmodern condition,
typical of early twentieth-century *Kulturkritik*
and its more recent offshoots, to an approach that
treats it as a positive possibility and opportunity.

Gianni Vattimo, *The End of Modernity*, 11.

21

Unending Modernity or Postmodernity?
Severing Theory and Praxis

Nietzsche and Heidegger are the primary philosophical progenitors of contemporary postmodernism. But I want to argue that they also open a door to the *genuinely postmodern* as a positive possibility. Nietzsche and Heidegger are *the* authors for our time. We can ignore their thought but will not thereby transcend them—quite the opposite. The thought of Nietzsche and Heidegger will have deferred ramifications, and we cannot be assured of deflecting the less than sanguine possibilities their ideas point to on the basis of any easygoing eclecticism. Without a deflection that moves within the essence of the thought of Nietzsche and Heidegger, we cannot be assured of avoiding outcomes that are unsettling from the perspective of individual dignity and constitutional government.

As I have already argued, I do not want my treatment of the postmodern confused with contemporary postmodernism. Contemporary postmodernism is only one conceivable deflection of the thought of Nietzsche and Heidegger—and not the most essential deflection given that it deflects Nietzsche's and Heidegger's thought back onto a fundamentally modern path. Postmodernism abstracts elements of the thought of Nietzsche and Heidegger and uses them as weapons to defeat the essential core of Nietzsche's and Heidegger's thought. That more essential core is what opens a door to the genuinely postmodern.

My understanding builds on the premise that there are certain authors who, for a variety of reasons, dominate their age. All other thinkers operate under the umbrella of thought those authors construct. Nietzsche and Heidegger are such Titans for our age. If one could presume to equal their stature, then one might presume to think one's way out from under the umbrella and begin simply from "the things themselves." The evidence convinces me that only a rare few accomplish that.[1] Part of what my idea of deflections implies is that we are always forced to begin from the resources that are available to us and cannot pick and choose at will. The reigning climate of thought is one of the givens that conditions our efforts. To speak with others one must at least *begin* with a shared set of idioms. This is not caving in to historicism; it is simply an empirical fact. The world of ideas, like the moral and political world, is always a shared world. The belief that we can construct an Archimedean point outside of that world *as a point of departure* is a chimera.

Another premise of this study is that far more deflections are possible the closer in time we are to the source; hence, we have available more possibilities with regard to the thought of Nietzsche and Heidegger than we would if we were to attempt a return to Hegel, Locke, Aristotle, Aquinas, or Plato. If philosophical wishes were horses I might wish to ride someone other than Nietzsche and Heidegger. But my preference for Plato or Aristotle, Augustine or Aquinas, Locke, Kant, Hegel, or Marx is irrelevant. One cannot pick and choose in that fashion. History moves in only one direction. We cannot in any simple sense go back. For example, although I would argue that significant preontological and premetaphysical deflections of Plato's thought were never opened, a point arrives at which the opening of those paths becomes at best unlikely.[2] While I would similarly agree that a variety of possible deflections existed within modern thought—Rousseau's crucial deflection was not inevitable—as I have suggested above, a moment of irreversibility has arrived, primarily due to the success of modern thought. Hence no attempt to go back and deflect earlier modernity is likely to redirect the momentum of late modernity.

In exploring the possibilities latent in the thought of Nietzsche and Heidegger, I have tried to avoid either uncritically accepting or summarily dismissing everything in their thought.[3] I have tried to reontologize the thought of Heidegger in the face of contemporary postmodernism,[4] just as I have tried to avoid the misleading attempts

1. It certainly will not be accomplished by those who take their bearings by attempting a primarily negative stance with regard to the thought of Nietzsche and Heidegger.
2. See my "Paths to and from Plato" and "Dialogue and Dialectic in Plato's *Phaedo*." I intend to return to this issue in a forthcoming sequel to this volume, *Paths to and from Plato*.
3. As examples of those who would reject almost everything, consider Ferry and Renaut, *Heidegger and Modernity,* and Pangle, *The Ennobling of Democracy.*
4. Derrida provides the classic example of this maneuver that tries to arrive at a deontologized Heideggerian thought. He approvingly presents Nietzsche as freer from

to divorce what might seem to be the radical "individualist" teachings of Nietzsche and Heidegger from the clearly "communitarian" elements in their thought.[5] As a result, I have tried to reverse those deflections which strip the thought of Nietzsche and Heidegger of political and ethical content. And I have tried to point beyond those views that see the death of God as a great emancipatory boon rather than the most significant problem humanity has ever faced.[6]

---

metaphysics—in Heidegger's sense—than is Heidegger himself. According to Derrida, for Nietzsche there is no source, whereas Heidegger will not let go of the search for a source. This gets Derrida into a contest of nonmetaphysical one-upmanship with Heidegger. This is one of the trademarks of postmodern*ism*—the retreat from any source or foundation. For Derrida it is far better that we believe there are only traces of an absent source, arrows pointing in the direction of a source we somehow "know" is not there, so that the traces will not entice us into believing they point to something when they do not. Derrida is correct that Heidegger ("early" or "late") was no antifoundationalist. But his attempt to deontologize his discourse is just the latest and most intense manifestation of modernity's antinature animus. Hanging on to that modern premise makes movement toward any genuine postmodernity impossible, because modernity's antinature animus is at the heart of its Spirit of Revenge and its refusal to affirm life. See Derrida, *Spurs: Nietzsche's Styles,* and my "Cacophony or Silence."

5. See Kateb's prescient remarks in "Thinking About Human Extinction II: Nietzsche and Heidegger," *The Inner Ocean,* 127–51. My premise is that Nietzsche and Heidegger posited a form of individualism only for great thinkers. Kateb, who notes their "antidemocratic individualist doctrines" (p. 129), sees this clearly: "Nietzsche feared that most people needed what new philosophers, in their strength, could do without and, in their honesty, had to do without. The spreading beliefs that God is dead and that life is morally unjustifiable, indeed condemnable, produce despair, which then may turn life denying and life destroying. . . . Only a few individuals, a few philosophical spirits, radically unlike and cut off from most people in society, can make themselves immune to the blindness of doctrine and the ravages of its absence" (p. 133). I am also in complete agreement with Kateb's observation that "Heidegger enriches and revises these suggestions but seems to retain Nietzsche's spiritual elitism" (p. 133). I would like to think, however, that one can deflect the thought of Nietzsche and Heidegger in a way that avoids "a political theory or a vision of the good society from their work [that] ends up fascistlike, or reactionary, or communitarian-conservative, and self-deluded to boot" (p. 135).

I believe Kateb is correct to take as the central longing of Nietzsche and Heidegger the attempt to criticize the desire to "convert all nature, and man himself, into something manmade." I agree completely that their "saving implications" are to be found in a "preserving attachment to existence" (pp. 135, 134), which affirms existence by opening man toward the "radiant look of things" (p. 143). But in my terms, when one is freed from the Spirit of Revenge against life, one opens oneself to a genuine individualism. I would go beyond Kateb and argue that the emancipation of genuine individualism within an *ethos* of rights is precisely what fosters "community" and that there is nothing fascist about it.

6. Vattimo is one of the few postmodernists who makes the explicit point—with

If we look at postmodernism as the final stage of modernity, we reach the conclusion that we have entered a period of seemingly permanent critique and deconstruction.[7] Put another way, we are faced with the prospect of permanent fragmentation. An unending modernity seems likely to leave us with a cacophony of voices, adrift yet monotonously unchanging, armed with immense technical sophistication but without a long-range perspective or the possibility of perseverance. We are confronted with the paradox that as we get more and more intensified manifestations of "rational" planning and manipulation we seem to get less and less concerted action, and less and less collective, cross-generational staying power. We seem consigned to endless historical zigzagging. Faced with the prospect of cacophonous, manipulated drift as the most likely outcome of unending modernity, it is no idle speculation to reflect upon what a genuine *post*modern alternative might look like, considering how one might deflect its potential vices in the direction of virtues while saving as many of the virtues of modernity as possible. It is particularly important to save a commitment to individual dignity and the limitations of authority made possible by constitutional government. In this regard, Heidegger's explicit conclusion that liberal constitutional institutions will not be equipped to confront the coming world—Nietzsche reached the same conclusion—is disquieting.[8] My argument will be that a constitutional postmodern alternative is conceivable.

It is difficult to predict whether the disintegration evident in late modernity will yield something novel, or whether the simultaneous intensification of modern principles will bring unending modernity. Theoretical modernity may have so established the instinct to critique that authors like Robert Pippin are correct in stating that it is impossible

which I am in full agreement—that postmodernism must be understood in conjunction with late-modern nihilism as a *transitional* phenomenon. See Vattimo, *End of Modernity*, 113–29, 164–81.

7. Pippin's presentation is the clearest I have seen in this regard. He concludes that modernity is a terminus, and ongoing, late-modern (a.k.a. post-Kantian) critique an inevitability; see Pippin, *Modernism as a Philosophical Problem*, esp. 148–67. Pippin seems to me, however, to underestimate the originary potential of *praxis*. Pippin comes close to reducing reality to a movement of thought qua critique. *Praxis* seems to have no potential, self-standing autonomy for him. Rorty, on the other hand, seems to me—in his belief that we can discard modern theoretical premises, yet prop up liberal politics with a variety of "new vocabularies" or narratives—to overestimate the autonomy of *praxis*.

8. See Heidegger, "Nur Noch Ein Gott Kann Uns Retten." Heidegger is not alone in seeing a need to look toward authoritarian solutions for problems created by modernity in general and technology in particular. See for example William Ophuls, *Ecology and the Politics of Scarcity*.

to transcend it.[9] And concrete techno-modernity may have gained so much momentum that it could roll on autonomously for an indefinite time. It is entirely possible that postmodernism will succeed in deflecting the thought of Nietzsche and Heidegger back onto the modern path each tried vigorously to transcend. Perhaps late modernity can continue to build its house in theoretical midair indefinitely; some antifoundationalists think so. Perhaps there is no problem in reveling in the antifoundationalism Nietzsche and Heidegger equated with nihilism. I think the more likely outcome is that the limited consensus that still exists will ultimately fail; cross-generational perseverance will become impossible; and the all too prevalent inarticulate, unfocused despair and anger of the present will only grow and have manifestations far beyond what we have seen to date.

Will there be something beyond modernity, or is modernity an end, a culmination? Has History ended in endless critique and deconstruction? I cannot definitively answer those questions and have set myself a more modest one: What could the term *post*modern mean if we took the *post-* seriously? Although I will articulate such an alternative, there is no assurance it can be given any concrete manifestation. I admit in advance that I will not be able to give concrete institutional manifestations of postmodernity. I do not consider that a liability. I have not set out from a concrete end only to work backwards to a justification. I have tried to take an argument, develop its logic, and follow it where it leads. The alternative is the modern maneuver of projecting theoretical pictures upon the future and repeatedly trying to actualize them. Therein we reproduce again and again the modern priority of the future as well as the modern Spirit of Revenge against the present. At the same time the past remains closed to us. We produce the situation Tocqueville noticed when he observed that "as the past has ceased to throw its light upon the future, the mind of man wanders in obscurity."[10]

Something truly postmodern would have to come into being on its own, from "within." It would have to grow out of life itself—affirming life in all its diversity and difference, past, present, and future—and out of a respect for the originary potential of *praxis*. Put another way, we will have to live, more than think, our way out of modernity—albeit, it is hoped, in a reflective fashion. Hence in advance, all that can be done is to give thought to the conditions for that possibility.

9. Pippin, *Modernism as a Philosophical Problem,* 148–67.
10. Tocqueville, *Democracy in America,* 2:349.

In late modernity, as I attempted to show in part 1, the universal gains almost complete hegemony, and the particular is almost totally delegitimized. This is the inevitable outcome of the culmination of modernity in the idea of metaphysical freedom. We have the paradox that modern theory continues to take its stand on willing the abstract universal at a time when the energy, as well as legitimacy, of the great proselytizing, modern, universalist empires—e.g., Marxist communism —seems to be spent. Into this confusing mix must be added the ethnic balkanization we are witnessing. But that manifestation of the particular will not prosper if it aims only at the recovery of traditions born of a previous time and place, which will inevitably become more sterile with each passing generation. As Heidegger argues, the longing for one's own clearly is a primordial longing if allowed room to operate. But it must discover its own place and space within its contemporary world. Only a new thinking which consciously quits the Spirit of Revenge will allow that to happen.

Since the idea of metaphysical freedom is where late modernity must make its last stand, to transcend modernity and arrive at something genuinely postmodern, we would have to transcend the attitude that turns the world into our projection.[11] We would have to quit the

11. This realization is manifested in the work of two of the more clear-sighted and unrepentant late moderns, Luc Ferry and Alain Renaut. They argue that in any critique of modernity there is a great danger, for modernity is the only basis for decent political and moral life. Criticizing modernity is equivalent to destroying decent political and moral life. And modernity can only be defended on the premise that man's essence lies in being a nothing. See Ferry and Renaut, *Heidegger and Modernity*, and Ferry, *Political Philosophy*.

Only our essence as nothings, (which conditions our fundamental equality as abstract universals) allows us to distance ourselves from being sullied by particularity, which allegedly leads inevitably to reliance on such hateful particularities as race and gender. Our essence as abstract universals allegedly points toward the need for "communication" with others. It is asserted that this communication of abstract universals is the prerequisite for "community," though how that works concretely is not well articulated. This conception of humanism, which begins from abstract universality, allegedly culminates in the inevitability of democracy and human rights. It represents Ferry's and Renaut's version of "critical theory," which they assert originates in Rousseau and passes through Adorno and Sartre to them. In short, Ferry and Renaut agree with Heidegger's understanding that humanism rests on the modern premise that man has no nature or essence but is an open possibility determined by no pregiven code descended from Nature, God, or History: i.e., man's essential humanity is to be found in his "metaphysical freedom." They further argue that the fact of human nothingness leads to the necessity of a minimalist conception of subjectivity and the inevitability of "willing the universal." For them, it is absolutely imperative that Reason be transformed into Will.

I cannot here give this argument the detailed response it deserves; I have, however,

attitude that it is incumbent upon us to project ourselves and the world in continually repeated, self-legislating acts of legerdemain. That requires a change of philosophic perspective—i.e., in the understanding of the task of the thinker—precisely the sort of change in understanding that stood at the origin of modernity: only a counterchange will get us beyond modernity if that is still possible.

Both Nietzsche and Heidegger attempt to foster a *transition* to a future in which man could be open to something which was not seen as a mere projection of himself. Unfortunately, in modern fashion, Nietzsche still placed his hope of recovering the Other in consciousness, i.e., in a deliberately manipulated consciousness that is shielded from the whole truth. Just as is true for Hegel, who views Nature as but one moment in the history of consciousness, for Nietzsche Nature is a phenomenon to be recovered in consciousness. Nature remains a fable.

The hegemony of the Will in Nietzsche's thought, and his longing

---

dealt with it more fully in my "Ancients, Moderns and Postmoderns." My present point is that Ferry and Renaut are correct; the abstract universal—i.e., metaphysical freedom—is where late modernity must make its stand, just as Pippin is correct in saying that unending modernity would lead to unending critique. For both of these reasons modernity is an untenable place to stand.

As Ferry and Renaut are themselves perfectly aware, there is the great difficulty of finding limits. What limits are there to the constant self-creation, manipulation, and domination of a being who is a nothing? This question is especially poignant in light of rapidly advancing biomedical technology. We seem unable to get clarity on the issue of abortion, which philosophically is almost trivial compared to the questions posed by, say, genetic engineering. What limits are there to the use of such technologies if man has no essence that should be guarded and from which he becomes alienated only at his peril? Second, if it is true that late modernity must make its stand within the idea of metaphysical freedom, which is part of modernity's antinature animus, it will be impossible to develop an environmental ethic. How can we be antinature ethically and politically and hope to be pronature environmentally? Third, in light of the failure of Marxist communism, who remains willing to argue the beneficence of the complete hegemony of the universal? In light of the ethnic balkanization under way in Europe, who is still so bold as to argue its inevitability, especially without the comforting support of History? Heidegger's argument for the importance to human beings of the desire for the preservation of "ownness" and exclusivity seems to have at least as much force in our late-modern world as the longing for the abstract universal. Yet to turn the matter around, who cannot see the potential malevolence of autonomous ethnic balkanization? Who could will the simple hegemony of the particular? Is this what the choice between the universal and particular offers in our time? If this is how the matter presents itself, *it is impossible to take sides:* Do we choose the revengeful tyranny of the unmitigated attempt at the installation of the universal or the chaos of a simple immersion in the particular? Fortunately, I think we are forced to pose the issue in this either/or fashion only from a modern perspective.

to put an end to what he depicts as the hegemony of chance and accident in all past history, is thoroughly modern. The modern longing for human control goes so far in Nietzsche that he even presumes to will the past. And yet the Nietzschean hypertrophy of the Will eventuates in a willing that tries to overcome the Will, a willing that would translate man back into a reintegration with Nature, a oneness with something that is Other than man. That understanding is the necessary extension of Nietzsche's critique of prior thought—especially modern thought—as a form of the Spirit of Revenge. But for Nietzsche transcending the Spirit of Revenge is accomplished only on the level of myth or illusion, presupposing a prior ahistorical innocence and forgetting. Hence there must remain on the fringes the modern manipulators, i.e., overmen qua Free Spirits, who can arrange, no doubt indirectly, to keep the sovereign illusions in place.

For Heidegger, a comparable openness of man to something Other is intended. That Other is alternately Being or things, the mysterious source or one's *Volk,* It or the Earth. But the possibility of openness to something *self*-presencing is not, for Heidegger, based on illusion or consciously willed myth. Heidegger goes much further on the path that Nietzsche opened by presenting Being as self-presencing, and the "look" of things as part of Being itself. Especially in his later works, Heidegger develops what I have called a phenomenology of "natural" experience. For Heidegger, Being qua *physis* is not our projection, although we must open ourselves to it in a correct fashion if it is to have presence. For Heidegger there must be a new orientation toward *physis,* one of awe, joy, and acceptance—*thaumazein* represents the correct posture in relation to Nature. When Heidegger's notion of Being as self-presencing is added to Nietzsche's critique of the Spirit of Revenge, we have an entree to the discussion of postmodernity.

Both Nietzsche and Heidegger try to recover a form of the "natural consciousness" or "immediate consciousness" grounded in lived experience and that which appears for all. This points toward the priority of the social, especially as articulated in Heidegger's discussions of ecstatic spatiality and temporality. From the time of *Being and Time* Heidegger explicitly tried to show the priority of the practical, pretheoretical, social disclosure of the world. In Heidegger's thought, pretheoretical reality presents *itself* in fundamental phenomenological wholes. To doubt those experiences that present themselves—taking them apart in Cartesian fashion, rebuilding them from humanly posited building blocks—simply alienates us from the world as it presents itself. In the process the world withdraws: There is no There there. Heidegger tries to go beyond Nietzsche to give an ontological foundation to this phenomenology of natural experience: Appearance *is* part of truth. Again, by merely inverting the *textbook* Platonic understanding of the relation between appearance and reality, Nietzsche was left believing that appearance was an illusion.

Heidegger argues that man's being-with-others is always prior to any autonomous individuality or theoretical detachment and always shapes it. Even the Nietzsche who is seen as a proponent of a radical individualism—though only for the Free Spirits—takes the side of the importance of "community." But Nietzsche accepts the *pre*modern notion that the element in which society exists is dogma or myth, a *mythos* that hangs in midair, balanced on the projects of the respective philosophers. *Mythos* is in principle *untruth*. Heidegger goes much further. He tries to show that *mythos* is one form of truth. Heidegger attempts to expand the concept truth beyond a locus in statements or logic and thereby also opens postmodern possibilities.

Despite their differences—and where they differ, I believe Heidegger moves further in the direction of the genuinely postmodern than Nietzsche—both agree that a novel future requires a new understanding of the status and nature of thinking. For both, future thinking must—to a greater or lesser extent—refrain from the modern revengeful projecting of frames upon *praxis*. This in turn requires a rethinking of the nature and ground of *praxis* once it gains autonomy from self-grounding, self-legislating theory. Neither was trying to foster an an-archic *praxis, except in the sense of freeing praxis* from the stranglehold of *modern* theory. Their efforts are antifoundationalist only for those who conclude in advance—in thoroughly modern fashion—that there is nothing which presents *itself,* or that "we" will allow to be legitimate (i.e., refrain from deconstructing) if it does present itself.

Further, freeing *praxis* from the Spirit of Revenge leads to irrationality *only* for those who think modern theoretical reason is the only manifestation of Reason. Postmodernity points toward the need to find a mode of Reason that is not primarily hypothetical, but instead takes its bearings from a phenomenology of immediate experience. The modern longing to expel Chance required the manipulation and domination of *praxis* by theoretical Reason as well as the domination of Nature by modern theoretical science and technology. Modern theoretical Reason refuses to allow *praxis* to have any autonomy. A world in which *praxis* is severed from modern theory opens the possibility of reestablishing the sovereign dignity of something like practical wisdom or prudence *(phronesis)* in the face of the modern hegemony of projecting, theoretical Reason qua Will.[12]

There is no necessity that the postmodern eschew Reason and endorse the "irrational" in any of its either/or modern manifestations—

12. Here I join company with a number of thinkers—including Hans Georg Gadamer, Hannah Arendt, and Ronald Beiner—who see the need to focus on the centrality of practical wisdom, by which I mean something more like *phronesis* than *Verstehen*. See especially Beiner, *Political Judgment;* Arendt, *The Human Condition* and *Between Past and Future;* and Gadamer, *Philosophical Hermeneutics* and *Reason in the Age of Science.* I agree with Beiner's observation that "if all human beings share a faculty of judgment that is sufficient for forming reasoned opinions about the political world, the monopoly of the expert and technocrat no longer possesses legitimacy. Political reason, from being a technical science, is restored to a practical science" (Beiner, *Political Judgment,* 2–3). I also agree that this points to the need to "open up a space of deliberation that is being closed ever more tightly in technocratic societies" (*Political Judgment,* 3). I doubt that Kant, the great proponent of metaphysical freedom, and Habermas, for the same reasons, will be of use in this undertaking. I do, however, endorse Beiner's turn toward Gadamer and Arendt. Beiner correctly sees that both Arendt and Gadamer "derive their essential inspiration from Heidegger" (*Political Judgment,* 23).

Below I will develop *a* version of what, if I understand her correctly, Arendt was attempting to accomplish in her discussions in *The Human Condition* of the need for a shared *public space* and a shared *realm of appearance.* I agree that political reality is an activity of collective self-disclosure. Further, living well presupposes speech and action, and that presupposes a public arena. This need not overwhelm individuality—quite the contrary. True individuality cannot act itself out in solitude. The implications of this understanding are not fascist, an all too easy and lame assertion we hear all too often. What is implied is a move closer to a reality Aristotle called ruling and being ruled in turn, where persuasion is at a premium.

Gadamer tries to articulate the fundamental principles of the shared "understanding" that could make this possible. What he stresses is that understanding requires mutuality, is prior to any possible science or art, and exists—here he simply follows Heidegger— prior to any doing or making. Further, understanding is always conditioned by a shared *ethos* or tradition. For Gadamer it is inappropriate to characterize that *ethos* pejoratively as a "prejudice," which would be possible only from the point of view of some detached Cartesian, autonomous subject.

I agree with Gadamer to this extent: one cannot *begin* by bracketing one's shared *ethos.* That is a prior given—i.e., the "hermeneutical situation." I will, however, part company with Gadamer and agree with Vattimo and Heidegger that we are presently in a situation where traditions and *ethoi* have substantially collapsed because we do not—in Arendt's terms—have a shared public space. Vattimo is correct in saying that everything in our time points toward fragmentation, and that modern mass communication technologies exacerbate that tendency. We are confronted with an arena of multiple, parallel, conflicting perspectives, not a shared *ethos.* See Vattimo, *The Transparent Society,* chapter 1.

Nevertheless, I fundamentally agree with Gadamer that the past is always transmitted into the present and that understanding rests on an act of transmission so understood. But for that transmission to happen we have to remain open to the past, and open to the possibility of a novel future for which we are willing to take responsibility. We have increasingly lost the relation to the past, and our modern relation to the future is

e.g., as blind tradition, emotion, or instinct.[13] What is needed is a different conception of Reason. Nietzsche and Heidegger, in trying to sever *praxis* from modern theory, move *in the direction* of freeing practical action so that it can have principles of its own that are not dependent on or derived from the theoretical. Both try to give to practical action an autonomy and independent dignity that it had lost in the face of Christian and modern dogmatism, and to recover the flexibility *praxis* requires. But while I accept that a postmodern severing of *praxis* from modernity's Spirit of Revenge is necessary, I will argue that the complete severance of *praxis* and thinking poses serious problems.

Modern thought consciously reined in the flexibility of *praxis,* eventually replacing the need to respond to the unique and unpredictable with the bureaucratic control of a mass society. Predictability in such a society is based substantially on a uniformity supported by modern science and technology and abstract, universalistic ethical theory, the reduction, that is, of the play of self-presencing difference. Nietzsche and Heidegger—in different ways—open an alternative path toward a respect for the play of differences. Contrary to the modern longing to pacify existence and bring on the reign of the predictable, Nietzsche and Heidegger try to reenthrone the unique, the unpredictable, and the changeable—i.e., difference. *Post*modernity would have to *start* from a severing of modern theory and *praxis,* together with a respect for spontaneous outcomes. It should be added that one can respect spontaneity and spontaneous outcomes in a postmodern fashion without submitting uncritically and optimistically to various "invisible hands."

Nietzsche—who saw the foundations of nobility in Machiavellian terms, as harsh, predatory, and brutal—attempted the emancipation of a predatory "noble," from whose "instinctive" Will could come a *nomos* that might become the ground for a new set of traditions—softened and embellished eventually by the poets and artists. Only within a closed cultural whole so constituted could *praxis* regain autonomy. In short, Nietzsche wished to recover by act of Will what premodern authors could presuppose. While Nietzsche's noble individual bears some vague resemblance to Aristotle's "great-souled man," in the last analysis he is closer to Hegel's characterization of the "master."

---

determined by the Spirit of Revenge, which will not allow the future to present itself. The proper relation is what Gadamer refers to as a "fusion of horizons," which is close to Heidegger's understanding of the ecstatic fusion of past, present, and future.

13. The postmodern would have to transcend the entire ensemble of false, modern either/or dichotomies: Reason/tradition, Reason/instinct, Reason/emotion, individualism/community, identity/difference, universal/particular, and so on. I will return to this issue in chapter 24.

Most telling is that for Nietzsche, nobility is a phenomenon of consciousness that exists in relation to the consciousness of another who is ignoble. For Nietzsche, all difference is a function of differential consciousnesses. Consequently, Nietzsche's nobles are definitely the modern children of Hegel—and thereby of Descartes. For Nietzsche, there is no intrinsic ontological hierarchy; distinctions like noble and ignoble must be willed for the sake of life. For Nietzsche, this, like all other forms of difference, must rest on the evanescent play of willed surfaces for which there is no deeper source. To the extent that it remains a conscious projection, Nietzsche's effort is thoroughly modern. And his work raises the troubling question of whether it is possible to get to the autonomy that allows *praxis* to proceed with a good conscience without brutality and an intervening chaos.

Heidegger likewise wished to recover an indigenous world with a shared *ethos*. Unlike Nietzsche, he abstracts from any concrete discussion of virtues or regimes. His discussions culminate in formal categories like "resoluteness" or "releasement." This is both frustrating and understandable. Heidegger understood that to will concrete futures was to remain modern, all too modern. Our shared world must be allowed to constitute *itself* from *within;* horizons cannot be willed. But in Heidegger's account, authentic *praxis* requires for its existence the prior existence of a rooted community, which for contemporary man remains only a future possibility. Hence like Nietzsche, Heidegger was willing to contemplate an apocalyptic transition to that future, rooted world. What such a world would look like could not be determined in advance, only by those already locked within it. In that way Heidegger follows the logic of the *post*modern. To consciously project a concrete future is to remain within the Spirit of Revenge; and the future never comes. But he delivers us over to the thorough hegemony of chance. When thinking abdicates public responsibility, no other outcome is possible.

In neither Nietzsche's nor Heidegger's case did the autonomy of *praxis* point to the abolition of thinking as an end in itself. My argument is that for both Nietzsche and Heidegger, the future autonomy of *praxis* is linked to an epicureanization of thinking.[14] In each case, the

14. In this regard, Rorty represents an interesting hybrid of modern and postmodern elements. On one level he comes close to epicureanizing thought; on another level the Rortyean philosopher still offers up theoretical visions to impose on reality. For Rorty, philosophy must now adopt a new stance. It can no longer be foundational. This is the lesson he learned from Wittgenstein, Dewey, and Heidegger. No longer can philosophy be the discipline that grounds other disciplines. We must recognize the incommensurability of various kinds of discourse—understood as Wittgensteinian language games. Hence Rorty concludes that philosophy's task must now be edifying rather than

thinker withdraws to the solitary contemplation of the "first things"
—the *Abgrund,* one's own self, the relation between the two, the mystery that there is anything at all. Both Nietzsche and Heidegger attempt
to reconstitute the possibility of thinking in the face of its post-
Hegelian demise, not in modern fashion as a public weapon, but as a

---

systematic. Once we realize this, we can make the move from epistemology to hermeneutics, where philosophy can operate using narrative or metaphor, which is indistinguishable from Nietzschean myth making. See Rorty, *Philosophy and the Mirror of
Nature,* esp. 3–13, 315–94.

Rorty admits that he is still intent, in modern fashion, on imposing a "liberal utopia." And he admits it is "his utopia" which rests not on inquiry but on imagination
(Rorty, *Contingency, Irony and Solidarity,* xvi). His "liberal solidarity" is not discovered
by reflection but created—and that means created by imaginative thinkers, apparently
when they are not creating themselves. Rorty reverts to the perfectly modern desire to
impose a theoretical picture on his community. Nothing is changed by saying it is
merely a narrative rather than theoretically grounded. One way or another it is a picture
imposed by the theorist. Lyotard is correct in stating that Rorty is still presenting metanarratives.

The thinker qua Rortyan hermeneuticist is also presented as the "polypragmatic di-
lettante" who "sees the relations between various discourses as those of strands of a possible conversation . . . which unites speakers but where the hope of agreement is never
lost so long as the conversation lasts" (Rorty, *Philosophy and the Mirror of Nature,* 318).
Philosophers must now become multiconversant, rather than assuming to be in possession of *the* common ground. Philosophy should take as its model getting acquainted
with a person more than following a demonstration. Hence the culture that we will
mythically try to create is one of conversation rather than one that believes it is erected
on solid foundations. Rorty's myths assume we should get rid of the belief in foundations, but keep the Enlightenment moral and political *faith* as our best hope. The fact
that the two views were once conjoined does not mean they have to be. Rorty does not
explain *his* faith in the Enlightenment moral and political project. He simply asserts the
priority of democratic practice, at least his own intellectually cramped version of democratic practice.

Having said these things, Rorty turns around and observes that, contrary to
Lyotard, future philosophers should cease to see their role in modern fashion as an
avant-garde because he is after a "de-theoreticized sense of community." Rorty wants it
both ways. See Rorty, *Essays on Heidegger and Others,* 174. In his later essays, Rorty ex-
tols a form of private, self-created, autonomous searching for "human perfection" as the
end of philosophy. Kierkegaard, Nietzsche, and Heidegger are examples of such
thinkers from Rorty's point of view. Marx, Mill, Dewey, and Habermas he describes as
more concerned with being fellow citizens than exemplars of perfected individuality.
They aim at fostering solidarity. Rorty advises us to synthesize the epicurean longing
for private self-creation and solidarity. This can only be accomplished by a "liberal
ironist"—i.e., a liberal who thinks cruelty is the worst thing we do synthesized with an
ironist who faces up to the contingency of all central beliefs (Rorty, *Contingency, Irony
and Solidarity,* xv). But it is hard to believe that the irony of this model of philosophy will
not spill over into the political community. Rorty admits that nonintellectuals believe
there is a ground or foundation.

I am in some agreement with Rorty's early picture of thinkers as codiscussants, but

primarily private, solitary affair. Precisely what occurs in such thinking is presented only metaphorically. Such future thinking would have a public effect only in the most indirect way. I believe this point is fairly clear in both Nietzsche's discussion of the Free Spirits of the future and Heidegger's depiction of thought as silent hearing. Just as the Free Spirits abandon the public forum, leaving it to the nobles and poets, Heidegger's philosophers abdicate in favor of the poets and artists. Indeed in Heidegger's case, one replaces the extreme wakefulness and "seeing" of ancient *theoria* with an *alogon* silent "hearing." Thinking requires remaining in a posture of "openness to the mystery," an openness to and longing for a kind of revelation; it must come to see itself as a form of thanking, a kind of piety.[15] Philosophy and *theo-mythos* seem to merge in a way they do not for Nietzsche, for whom future philosophy seems to remain equivalent to a deep, penetrating, psychological

---

for me it is primarily a practical discussion that is needed, not the imposition of a theoretical frame. It is unclear how that imposition counts as "conversation." When one looks at the kinds of things of which Rorty concretely approves, it is clear he has limited knowledge of where his fellow citizens are to be found in *their* discussion. At best it seems that what he is capable of adding to the discussion is a perfectly modern left egalitarianism—hardly an impressive act of imagination. If Rorty really believed in contingency, he would let the future present *itself*. One would prefer Rorty's picture of an epicureanized thinking that dabbles in private self-creation to his meddlesome vision of ironist utopian projections.

Finally, as part of his new mode of discourse Rorty claims he offers "redescription" as a form of "changing the subject" (*Contingency, Irony and Solidarity*, 44–45). The liberal ironist should not waste time trying to persuade those who disagree or are suspicious of his myth making; he should simply start talking about something else as if everyone already agrees with the new discourse. This glib proposal could justly be met by saying that the rest of us should simply do the same. But that would eventuate not in the conversation which Rorty claims to desire, but in cacophonous voices speaking at once—or the simple attempt to impose one's vocabulary by force, a situation philosophy in the foundationalist sense was invented to avert. More to the point, Rorty has poorly grasped the world that is coming if he assumes that his voice will be heard. One may always try to change the subject and change vocabularies, but why should anyone listen? If they do, why should they listen sympathetically rather than laughing, yawning, or barbarically silencing the speaker?

It seems to me that Rorty assumes far too much. He assumes the inertia of contemporary liberal institutions. And he assumes a plurality and "otherness" which is precisely what is endangered. Vattimo is correct; in an age of the increasing Europeanization of the planet, alterity and otherness will become more and more difficult to find (Vattimo, *End of Modernity*, 159). I deal with Rorty at greater length in my forthcoming "American Postmodernism: The Case of Richard Rorty."

15. Given the centrality of the issue of God and the gods, the divine, the Fourfold, and so on—especially in Heidegger's thought but also in Nietzsche's—the almost complete silence of postmodernism on this issue is, at the very least, telling. That silence ceases to be curious when we reposition postmodernism as modern, all too modern.

autoanalysis, which in modern fashion is still seen as a penetration of the primary ground of existence. Regardless of the concrete contours of future thinking, for both Nietzsche and Heidegger thinking retreats to pursue its object in solitude; this is how it frees itself from the Spirit of Revenge and the need to come forth in a vulgarized public form. The question is whether thinking can free itself from the Spirit of Revenge only by epicureanizing itself. I will argue that there is a way to give flexibility back to *praxis* other than radically severing it from thinking.

Beyond the transitional period that each author anticipates comes a radical separation of a newly reconstituted thinking and a newly autonomous *praxis*. The autonomous "community" of the future is left to generate a *nomos* from within using nontheoretical resources. I would agree that the severing of *praxis* and *modern* theory, together with a new appreciation for pretheoretical, "natural" awareness, are prerequisites for the postmodern. But in what follows I will argue that this need not lead to willing "Nature" as an illusion or myth, nor to blind reliance on "nobles," poets, or artists as the spokespersons for Being. And more importantly, it should not lead to the epicureanization of thinking.

22

The Problem of "Nature": Beyond the Sublimation of the Political

Modern man, Hegel observed, can no longer begin from "immediate" or "natural" experience in his attempt to achieve understanding. Modern reality is mediated by constellations of concepts and ideas. For Hegel, this conceptual mediation is a sign of human advance and perfection; it differentiates human from mere animal existence and explains the superiority of the moderns to the ancients.

> The manner of study in ancient times differed from that of the modern age in that the former was the proper and complete formation of the *natural consciousness*. Putting itself to the test at every point of its existence, and philosophizing about everything it came across, it made itself into a universality that was active through and through. In modern times, however, the individual finds the abstract form ready-made; the effort to grasp and appropriate it is more the direct driving-forth of what is within and the truncated generation of the universal than it is the emergence of the latter *from the concrete variety of existence*. (*PS* 19; emphasis mine)

Our modern conception of the whole is determined by a distinctive mathematical science, just as our senses are in touch with a landscape shaped fundamentally by modern technology. Our political life is moved by systems of ideas (ideologies, worldviews) at least as much as by natural desires and longings, and our morality is not based primarily on habits formed by a distinctive shared *ethos* or set of religious beliefs, but on the imperative that we must live in accordance with various abstract theoretical prescriptions, whether they be categorical imperatives, difference principles, or any number of other theoretical visions posited for the sake of reshaping the world. Even our relation to ourselves is shaped by psychological explanations based on posited phenomena unavailable to us in day-to-day experience.

After Hegel this unique modern situation came to be associated with the breaking to the surface of nihilism. It was seen as life in a rootless, nomadic "unworld," cut off from necessary experiences that must be recovered if we are to recover our essential selfhood. Despite significant differences, this basic understanding, that modern theoretical attempts to transform our "natural" or "immediate" relation to reality have caused alienation and nihilism, informs the thought of both Nietzsche and Heidegger. Both point us toward a recovery of a pre-scientific, pretheoretical understanding of the world which is to be found in our "immediate," "primary," "natural," "primordial," "ordinary," "everyday" experience. The possibility of freeing *praxis* from the Spirit of Revenge requires grounding it in primary, lived experiences. We can call these the experiences of the *Lebenswelt*.[1]

I want to discuss this possibility under the rubric "the problem of Nature." First, modern human beings are no longer confronted by primary Nature. That which is immediately available to all in ordinary, sensuous appearance bears the significant stamp of man's *technē*. No "phenomenology of immediacy" is possible, if by that one means being in touch with something primally natural. A "natural" relation to things must be conceived differently.[2] Further, the problem of Nature overlaps with an issue central to contemporary postmodernism, the question regarding difference. I will argue that this issue is central for any genuine the*post*modernity as well. I have argued that at the heart of modern thought is an antinature animus. The postmodern requires transcending this animus—not by *willing* the natural as a myth, as with Nietzsche, any more than by affirming that *no* part of difference is a social construct—but by legitimizing self-presenting difference, respecting it and the interactions that flow from it. The refusal to say yes to difference manifests itself in the theoretical Spirit of Revenge, and in time in the intensification of the Spirit of Gravity.

Contemporary postmodernism argues that all difference is rela-

---

1. It is not my intention to import any of the implications of altogether modern, Husserlian transcendental phenomenology along with this term. I use it as indicative of pretheoretical lived experience in all its diversity.
2. The "problem of Nature" in our time is not only that we are no longer immediately confronted by primary Nature, but that, even if we could easily isolate that which is simply natural, we are armed with techniques that allow us to manipulate, transform, and, in extreme cases, eradicate it. I have in mind here not only the capacity to transform matter and create nonnaturally occurring elements, but genetic engineering. This is an unprecedented reality that determines the late-modern world. We are confronted not only with the question "What is Nature?" but also with a more radical question, "Why should we keep it?"

tional, based on the play of evanescent surfaces, where, with Derrida for example, the surfaces are seen as signs that point to no ultimate signified or source. Yet this, like all prior manifestations of the modern, revengeful antinature animus, represents a thoroughly theoretical imposition upon the phenomena. Postmodernists have written "natural" difference out of existence only to extol difference as a free-floating, ever-changing, contingent surface. This deification of the surface is perfectly Nietzschean. It refuses to accept *physis* as self-presenting and not based on our projection.

It must be admitted that *physis* presents itself in a variety of ways and there is very little primary Nature left to us as a benchmark to which we can return[3]—no "primitive" state, no Arcadia, no "wilderness" of the soul or the forest.[4] Something genuinely postmodern—unlike contemporary postmodernism, which falls into the perfectly modern antinature animus, siding with the hegemony of *nomos* as opposed to *physis*— would have to start from the given as self-presencing and abstract from the traditional *nomos/physis* distinction. Rather than debating the precise relation between *nomos* and *physis* in traditional terms—or in a modern either/or fashion—we should limit ourselves to the observation that there *is* difference and it is self-presenting if allowed to be so. The origin of that difference should cease to be our primary, present preoccupation.[5] In common sense terms, Nature and habit always meld in a way that makes attempts to differentiate the parts of the whole difficult, and in the late-modern world focusing on differentiating the two opens a path to a theoretical exercise in the Spirit of Revenge.

What I am suggesting is an attitude something like the following: When we look phenomenologically at human reality, we see self-presenting difference. That should be affirmed, legitimized, and respected. Rather than dream (qua theoretical projection) about what the present given should be transformed into, we should look with affirmative eyes

---

3. Heidegger is correct in asserting that in our time longing for Nature, understood as primary Nature, can lead only to a glorification of instinct and the divine animal in us qua *brutalitas*.

4. Modern science cannot adjudicate the debate over the relation between the natural/genetic/instinctive and the habitual/learned/socially constructed. We must now accept the thoroughly hypothetical, nonautonomous nature of the modern, scientific approach to reality and recognize that it is grounded in *a* pretheoretical, prescientific revelation of reality.

5. We can trace the origin of the traditional *nomos/physis* distinction to a specific time, i.e., the time of the origins of philosophy in ancient Greece. See in this regard, Strauss, *Natural Right and History,* esp. chap. 3, "The Origin of the Idea of Natural Right." The question is, Why should we continue to be determined by this distinction in precisely its original form?

at what presents itself. On the level of what could be termed a phenomenology of the lifeworld, reality—especially human reality—presents
itself as a heterogeneity of different types. That must be affirmed as the
appropriate and untranscendable postmodern point of departure. To
that extent the traditional *nomos/physis* dichotomy recedes—at least in
the beginning. By my understanding, the resulting respect for heterogeneity means the postmodern would be "individualistic." But as I will
argue shortly, this does not preclude its being "communitarian." There
is no need to be locked into such dichotomous choices.

What I have suggested opposes postmodern thought to the search
for a universal definition of man. The interplay of an irreducible, self-
presenting plurality of different types and manifestations of human beings must be respected.[6] I will argue that this respect for self-presenting
difference need not lead to the obliteration of a basis for unity or identity. That can be pursued by a respect for a transformed, affirmative
kind of thinking, freed from the Spirit of Revenge, which is "dialectical" in the sense I will propose. The appropriate metaphor for postmodern thinking is neither the epicureanized solitude of Nietzsche and
Heidegger nor the theoretical projecting of modernity (and, one must
add, of postmodernism, which by and large continues to project egalitarianism, pluralism, democracy, an antinature animus, and so on), but
"weaving"—that is, the weaving together of self-presenting difference. I think this can eventuate in an understanding of the need to attend to both identity and difference, unity and diversity, the universal
and the particular. These need not be viewed as either/or dichotomies;
we are not forced to choose one or the other.

A postmodern alternative would require that that which is immediately available to all *in the present* be respected as it presents itself. That
which shows itself, as it shows itself, need not be viewed as unreliable

6. This sword seems to me to cut against both the "left" and "right" as presently
constituted. For example, respect for gays and lesbians must be accompanied by respect
for the spirited, competitive, naturally gifted, beautiful, and so on. Our legitimizing of
difference should not wallow in a narrow "accept me" mentality that then turns around
and vengefully assaults other forms of difference. It is but one step from the now-
common assertion that "my" difference is "natural" and yours simply learned or conventional to an insistence that mine should be "liberated" and yours "retrained." In the
late-modern world, the traditional *nomos/physis* distinction cannot help but become a
weapon of the Spirit of Revenge and its unavoidable manifestation in the Spirit of Gravity. *Nomos/physis* is one of many dichotomies that must be not so much simply jettisoned as understood as a continuum. Since any line we might draw between *nomos* and
physis will be imprecise, I would argue we are better served by dispensing with such
distinctions as a form of false knowledge and accepting what self-presences as an immediately given *point of departure*.

or as sullied in relation to some higher reality. The realm of appearance is not unproblematic, but neither is it an illusion. It is the arena in which truth happens. One does not have to prove the reliability of pretheoretical awareness. *That should be taken as the given.* One must refrain from repeatedly making it disappear theoretically. Heidegger argues, persuasively I believe, that all theoretical relations to reality are grounded in pretheoretical awareness which they nonetheless eventually threaten. Theory always grows out of *one* form of experience and then tries to objectify it and close off recurrence to other everyday experiences and subsequent manifestations of difference. But in light of the problem of Nature, why should not modern theory be allowed to obliterate pretheoretical, immediate experience, and "colonize the lifeworld"?[7] The answer is that nihilism is the inevitable outcome. Life will devolve into the endless, manipulative battle of world pictures.

7. This phrase points to Habermas's voluminous body of work. In using it I do not by any means intend to signal my agreement with Habermas—quite the contrary. Habermas remains a modern, even though various Heideggerian elements have entered his thought in diluted form through his Frankfurt school roots. Habermas agreed with his mentor Adorno that the Enlightenment project, based on the domination of nature as a means to human emancipation, had turned into a domination of man. But where Adorno and Marcuse looked to art for a critical stance outside of the dialectic of modern, technological rationalization, Habermas continued to look for a "rational" and modern stance.

In his later "theory of communicative action" Habermas differentiates technical/purposive action and symbolic/communicative action. Each aims at rationalization, one at technical rationalization, the other at freedom, equality, and emancipation. Hence there are two rationalization processes working simultaneously. Habermas admits that the technical rationalization process is *colonizing* the latter, which has its operation in the *lifeworld*. But he argues this need not occur if we get rid of the hidden forces that block the kind of communication that is indicative of the lifeworld. Paradoxically, this requires a theoretical picture of ideal noise-free, nondistorted, noncoercive communication and action.

Throughout his corpus Habermas tries to show that Reason has more than one manifestation, but that all of its competing interests require a nondistorted free flow of communication. It is thus allegedly necessary to foster the social conditions that will allow such communication to take place. I agree with Habermas about the centrality of communication in lived experience and the need to foster an arena for its exercise. But Habermas's theory of communication is still an example of a theorist imposing theoretical frames on life rather than allowing actual communication to present itself. Habermas is unwilling to affirm spontaneous outcomes. According to him to do so will lead to irrationality. But it seems to me, and here I side with Gadamer, that practical judgment is perfectly adequate to avoid irrationalism without the need for a *theoretical* construct soaring high above lived experience. Habermas's theory itself seems to me to intrude upon the integrity of the lifeworld and *its* communication. I must again agree with Lyotard that Habermas is trying to impose just one more metanarrative. Habermas's response is that without the modern premise that one needs a theoretical ideal to

I wish to pose the matter in the following fashion: The issue in our time is to take a stance for or against Nature as that which is self-presenting. Strictly speaking, that was never an issue for premodern thought. The "problem" is that even if there is a fundamental natural substratum to existence, a primary Nature, it can now be so easily manipulated and transformed that we may no longer take it as unproblematic. We must now choose *not to transform* that which is other than man's Will and instead allow it to present itself. We must respect the earth, especially as it rises up in us, even though we may realize that some of what will present itself is the deferred ramification of prior human action and thought. We must affirm that as well. Only in that fashion can we transcend the Spirit of Revenge and affirm past and present.

The success of modern theory in transforming the world means that no simple return to primary Nature would be possible even if it were desirable, *which I do not think it is.* A return to immediate experience need not concoct for itself the romantic notion that it has recovered some primordial state that existed in the past. What must be recovered is an appreciation for that which is other than our positing Will, for that which self-presences and appears for all in pretheoretical awareness. A natural relation to reality in our time will open itself to a fundamentally novel, modern world of appearance. Nonetheless, this relation to reality represents a reversal of modern values. It is the *opening* to the postmodern.

Following Heidegger, I will call the self-presencing Other "Nature" *(physis).* I will call openness to a self-presencing Other "immediate experience," realizing fully that from a purely theoretical perspective it is mediated by everything from one's regime and language to past objectivizing theory. That said, both Nietzsche and Heidegger—albeit Heidegger in an ontologically more substantial way—open the possibility of recovering *the ground out of which* Western thinking initially grew. That ground was immediate, lived experience. Nietzsche and Heidegger also reopen the *question* of the proper relation between thinking and *praxis,* and between man and what is other than man. Even more than that, they open again all the seemingly closed questions: Why science? Why Nature? Why Reason? (In other words, can

---

guide action, one is driven into a blind positivism that deserves to be called "neoconservative." For Habermas everything that is not based on or that attempts to transcend a late-modern "emancipatory" projection of reality is neoconservative—i.e., a desire to go *back*—because, in principle, nothing novel, that is, genuinely postmodern, could possibly come in the future. That is a very self-serving either/or dichotomy indeed. I reject that premise, which rests on a hidden end of history thesis. See primarily Habermas, *Knowledge and Human Interests* and *The Theory of Communicative Action.*

there be a rational ethics? Is habit the basis of morals? Is Reason superior to revelation?) Why technology? Why Enlightenment? Why the political? Why cosmopolitanism? Why the overcoming of Chance and contradiction? Why thinking itself? (I.e., Is it good?) This reopened horizon points to *post*modernity as a "second beginning."[8] The second beginning will differ from the first in almost everything except its rootedness in immediate pretheoretical experience.[9]

Nietzsche and Heidegger lead us toward a recovery of *the ground* out of which Western thinking grew, and in which a *praxis* freed from modern theory is conceivable. As far as I can see, only a thinking that affirms immediate experience can free itself from the Spirit of Revenge, and only a thinking so freed will allow *praxis* to be what it is, a manifestation of truth. Again, I will part company with Nietzsche and Heidegger by trying to show that such a thinking can avoid the Spirit of Revenge without epicureanizing itself—being plunged into silence or abandoning its public role to instinct, emotion, poets, artists, and so on. I will discuss why that epicureanizing tendency is an error and why

---

8. At present I can only assert my understanding of how the postmodern relates to the origins of the Western tradition. Postmodern*ism* builds on the premise that the origin of the West in Plato's thought is the origin of nihilism. Therefore, one surely does not want to return to the origins. Heidegger holds a version of this premise but asserts that we must recollectively return to the pre-Socratics, from which point we might launch a second beginning. Nietzsche also shows a preference for the pre-Socratics and tragic Greeks.

My argument, put simply, is that the West is *not* Platonic. Plato was a premetaphysical and preontological thinker, but his thought was immediately deflected onto a metaphysical and ontological path by Aristotle, neo-Platonism, and so on. By the time the Platonic texts again became available in the West we already thought we understood him; hence we viewed him only through the lenses of the Western tradition—primarily those of Aristotelianism and Christianity. It is only now, with the radical questioning of that tradition, that we gain access to Plato, perhaps for the first time. What we learn when we approach his texts afresh is that Plato was the consummate depicter of difference in its complex interactions, of the heterogeneity of different types of human beings as well as the irreducible and unsynthesizable nature of the whole; thereby his thought is free from the Spirit of Revenge. In short, a possibility similar to those opened up by the genuinely postmodern existed but was never developed. Thus we have much to learn from the Platonic dialogues, not only about the phenomenology of immediate experience, but also about the "weaving" of difference. In his *practical* works Aristotle also presents an inestimable phenomenology of everyday experience—precisely as Heidegger asserted. But in his *theoretical* works he sets in motion the eventual overcoming and transcendence of that immediacy by creating a hierarchical relation between theoretical and practical reason which was eventually deflected onto a thoroughly radical path by modern thought. I will return to this issue in my forthcoming *Paths to and from Plato*.

9. Life can have a foundation in immediate experience without appearances that are indicative of primary Nature or past manifestations of *physis*.

thinking must be a "dialectical" enterprise that gives priority to immediate experience and pretheoretical *praxis*. Thought requires the same
starting point as *praxis*. A refusal to accept that fact leads to the Spirit of
Revenge. I have posed the recovery of immediacy as part of "the problem of Nature." I now want to argue that the recovery of immediacy
goes hand in hand with a respect for and acceptance of "the political."
Our pretheoretical relation to reality is inevitably *politically* constituted. The loss of a relation to the pretheoretical manifests itself as an
alienation from the political, which in a significant sense no longer exists.

The claim that the political no longer exists must initially seem
strange. Wherever we look we find unlimited competition for power
and economic advantage, clashing interests, inflamed passions, nations
armed beyond belief to counter and forestall bitter enemies, and on and
on. Yet in the sense that the political, as something autonomous of revengeful theory, is the realm in which organized and collective debate
about ends takes place, it can be said that we have no politics. In our
time, the question about ends has been answered with the conclusion
that a dignified life, free from pain and anguish, that pushes back fear of
death and affords a decent, predictable, comfortable existence is the
primary, legitimate end. We see a facade of commitment to individualism and the need for individual self-definition, but as an empirical matter, the majority of selves define themselves in very limited ways,
oriented more to quantitative differences than to qualitative ones.[10]

Needless to say, the pursuit of that threshold of self-respect and dignity which presupposes the decent avoidance of abject circumstances is
one of the legitimate ends of human action. And I am by no means unaware that an entire spectrum of activities is included in catch-all categories such as "comfort" and "self-preservation." However, even
when fully elaborated these categories are not exhaustive; there remain

10. One of the many false modern dichotomies is that between "communitarians"
and "individualists." Before we can move beyond this either/or category we must reflect on the extent to which a world that pays lip service to individuality primarily produces homogeneity and resentful, theoretical projects aimed at producing an abstract
equality qua identity; on the paradox of thinking that "community" can be theoretically
projected and imposed from the top down rather than being self-constituted prior to
and independent of theoretical construction; and on the extent to which genuine communities seem by far the most fertile venues for the growth of genuine individuals. The
reason for this growth, we may infer, is that true individuality manifests itself in spontaneous interactions with others, not in idiosyncratic, solitary flights of mythical self-
creation. True individuality is intimately implicated in the possibility of a genuine community and prospers best in its midst, and true individuality requires individuals who
follow different *ends*.

other possible human ends. For example, self-preservation was traditionally seen as belonging to the arena of "economics," the private realm of the *oikos* that deals with bodily needs and things related to them. If the political is the arena of the debate over ends, it does not include the economic, because few seriously debate whether self-preservation is good or comfort desirable. Surely they deserve some place in the constellation of ends we pursue. Instead, one primarily considers the most efficient *means* to those ends. Strictly speaking, that is an economic debate, even if debate about means can be a facade for debate about ends, and vice versa. But one can certainly debate whether comfortable self-preservation is the only or highest end, or where it should fall in a hierarchy of ends. Then the debate has become political.

A society, indeed an entire civilization, always takes some stance regarding the place of self-preservation in the hierarchy of possible ends. If, however, a civilization reaches universal agreement as to its ends, the political can be replaced with the pursuit of the most efficient technical means to those ends. How does this differ from the end of history understood as the cessation of legitimate debate as to ends?

No society can constantly reopen the debate regarding legitimate ends; a relative consensus is necessary if community between different individuals is to be possible. But when a civilization with increasingly global, transnational influence forgets that there is such a question and ceases to consciously articulate its answer, it ceases to be political. And when the same answer to the fundamental political questions is surreptitiously held by whatever reigning antagonists there might be competing for global hegemony, one can say there is the potential for a global transcending of the political. As Heidegger argues, this may go hand in hand with massive efforts at human organization and mobilization and the greatest conceivable manipulation and transformation of human and nonhuman Nature. And because agreement as to ends leads to everyone's pursuing the same, limited things, the likelihood of conflict may in fact be increased.

If we accept self-presenting difference, what we see is the disparate characters and capacities of actual human beings. Hence complete agreement as to ends can only be bought at the price of the radical truncation, suppression, and sublimation of human possibilities or the technological transformation of human nature, all of which are manifestations of the Spirit of Revenge and thoroughly at odds with a serious affirmation of difference. If, for the sake of argument alone, we take Plato as an example, it is "spiritedness" *(thumos)*—substantially transformed versions of which appear as "nobility" and "resoluteness"

—that is a principal ground of the political, *epithumia* being the ground of the *oikos* and true thought belonging to the political community only when it is politically mediated or diluted. For convenience, let us take spiritedness in the broad sense of indicating all of those more intense, spiritual manifestations of difference that modernity consciously set out to sublimate. Let us broaden the account even further and also say that spiritedness manifests itself in the defense of one's own— family, nation, property, self-identity. This defense of one's own is both grounded in and becomes a ground of genuine difference.

One can only attain true awareness of who one is through interaction with others; it is never immediately self-evident. To do so one must give up the belief that one is all things and so malleable as to be or do anything. Likewise, one cannot see as one's own something one shares with billions, or something abstract and without concrete manifestation or an appearance of its own. In the broadest sense, the defense of one's own is intimately related to the ground of the political. In equally broad terms, the objects of the purely political—about which fundamental disagreement is conceivable—can be brought under the general headings of war, sex, and the gods. Under the rubric "war" I include all things that conduce to the preservation of a specific community and its shared principles, together with the protection of its members, their property, and their prerogatives from *external* threats. Under "sex" I include the generational reproduction of the members of a community, their education, the transference of beliefs, and the defense of the shared principles needed for unity from *internal* subversion. Under "gods" I include the collective view of the whence and whither, the origins, the afterlife, and the existence or nonexistence of a nonhuman support of all that presences.

Any society that is truly political would always have significant internal concurrence—*but never complete agreement*—on questions of, for example, who may form a family, how to raise the young, what form and degree of piety is required in a given circumstance, who should lead the army and when, what distribution of goods is just, and so on. But internal concurrence would always be far greater than concurrence with other communities—otherwise all difference would be reduced to identity. The debate within a community over creation and maintenance of consensus on the primary questions is the ground for the discovery of self-identity, i.e., difference. The pursuit of self-identity can also be seen as the pursuit of self-development, self-understanding, and honor—i.e., that which is one's own in the most intimate sense. Such debate is implicated in the legitimate differentiation of oneself from others, as well as of one's community from other communities.

The true pursuit of self-understanding—i.e., genuine difference—can never be merely a matter of self-preservation or a contest over the best means to self-preservation, for example, how best to distribute goods. Needless to say, there may be tensions between self-identity and group identity, but the two are always related and cannot simply be detached.

The political has ceased to exist when all the issues of war, sex, and the gods are believed to be reducible to issues of self-preservation and the pursuit of an excess of the things that conduce to self-preservation for as many as possible. If—and only if—that occurs, debate over techniques of administration can take precedence over political debate. One would then be in no position to smugly dismiss the possibility of the end of history or, as Heidegger puts the matter, the end of genuine, unique, historical existence.

If, however, the fundamental issues of sex, war, and the gods cannot be foreclosed—and the Nietzschean and Heideggerian critiques of the modern, universalistic conception of Reason have made that increasingly difficult—History cannot end. To put the matter in the clearest light, if one believes the best life is one lived in a secular, global, technological, socially and morally uniform and universalistic civilization, then History has ended and the fundamental questions have been foreclosed. All that remains are questions of distribution.[11] That is surely

11. Connolly's *Identity/Difference: Democratic Negotiations of Political Paradox* deserves note at this point. Connolly also sees the significance of the issue of the Spirit of Revenge. But clearly flying in the face of such Nietzschean discussions as "Flies in the Market Place" and "On the Tarantulas," to say nothing of "On the New Idol," he sees the Spirit of Revenge manifested primarily in the state's acting on behalf of the wealthy. For Connolly the modern state is the engine of resentment which eventuates in the "politics of generalized resentment" (*Identity/Difference*, 211). Connolly sees the modern state as Marx did, as the defender of privilege, in this case the privilege of the "neoconservatives." It is the privileged who show resentment toward the others by not allowing social justice (*Identity/Difference*, 166). The alternative view is Nietzsche's, which sees the state as the defender of the mediocre against genuine individuality and difference. Nietzsche's state enforces equality and guarantees a "wretched contentment."

Connolly calls for the "politics of agonism." What is required is an "alternate hegemonic coalition" to counteract the neoconservatives. This presupposes, and is intended to foster, a more egalitarian distribution of material resources. Connolly seems, in perfectly modern fashion, to see difference as an issue primarily of economic distribution, although his "agonistic politics" at places also bears the stamp of "multiculturalism." Connolly also points beyond the modern state to what he calls the "globalization of contingency." This is part of an argument for transcending the sovereignty of the nation-state in the direction of "nonterritorial democratization." He openly projects the need for nonstate, transglobal activism, calling for creative intervention by self-appointed "non-state actors" to bring about a project of "non-territorial democracy." What one sees here is the perfectly modern cosmopolitan longing in a new permutation. But appended to that modern vision are self-selecting Nietzschean Overmen qua nonstate ac-

the modern longing, if not necessarily the present concrete reality. But if modern philosophy were to succeed in actualizing its bourgeois cosmopolitan goal it would, as Hegel makes clear, lead to its own obsolescence—one would need no further theoretical projections. The overcoming of the political and the end of modern philosophy would then occupy the same historical venue.

What could it mean to say thinking had reached its end? If thinking is an end in itself, something to which one is called that is productive of nothing, the end of thinking would come if it could be transformed into a productive enterprise or limited in function to being the handmaiden of other productive enterprises. If thinking is ultimately a desire for self-knowledge—in the sense of explicitly raising the question of the relationship between oneself, the possibility of one's doings, and the rest of what is—thinking could end only if it was believed that all fundamental answers to all important questions had been given once and for all. The calculative, hypothetical-deductive application of reason is everywhere in evidence. Such theory is always informed in advance by some specific project, which, if traced through its many relationships, could in every case be linked to a question of utility as regards the means to the most comfortable self-preservation of the largest number. If thinking transformed itself into a "professional" undertaking that saw its task as subsidiary to some other, prior and autonomous branch of calculative, theoretical reason—solving its muddles (e.g., analyzing language), clarifying its problems (e.g., explaining how properly to form and verify propositions), and in general coming along behind and ministering to its needs—thinking would have ended. The activity involved could no longer be thinking understood as an end in itself, as a calling which, as Heidegger makes clear, cannot be cast aside by those called regardless of the practical outcome.

Thinking, understood as an end in itself, and the political as I have

---

tivists. Since the inevitability of a cosmopolitan outcome is no longer expected, an avant-garde elite must foster it in the name of the global masses but without their participation or even agreement.

Connolly wraps his argument in the accoutrements of the philosophy of difference that Nietzsche and Heidegger originate, and which postmodernism co-opts. But combined with the altogether modern elements of his discussion, it seems to me one gets a synthesis that cannot hold. And with a self-selecting elite still manipulating the substate agonal democracy and the suprastate transterritorial democratization we remain in the grips of the theoretical Spirit of Revenge. Indeed, Connolly explicitly admits he is pointing toward the competition of theoretically projected worldviews (*Identity/Difference*, 220–21). And all of this is in the service of a more egalitarian distribution of material goods, as if that were the primary issue that needed to be addressed.

defined it, would inevitably be brought to confront each other. At the very least, in reflecting on its own possibility and the nature of the whole, thinking must reflect on the practical conditions within which it can pursue its end, for those conditions form a part of the whole about which one thinks. Thinking would likewise be brought to reflect on the variety of ways we have lived and could live (worlds, regimes), their mysterious coming into being and passing away, and what is therein implied. The community, in articulating answers to the political questions regarding war, sex, and the gods, takes a position on the first things, which are the very issues that inform thinking. On some level, the political always thinks and thinking always exists within a certain world or regime and has concrete ramifications as soon as it speaks, no matter how indirect or deferred those ramifications might be.

Politics and thinking inevitably interpenetrate each other, albeit not necessarily in the way they do in the modern world, where they increasingly merge and both are transformed and threatened with obsolescence. The abolition of one may necessarily imply the abolition of the other, unless, on the one hand, genuine thinking is an irreducible, unavoidable phenomenon which always has its public reverberations and, on the other, the pursuit of individual and collective self-definition is likewise irreducible to any other end and the issues of war, sex, and the gods remain matters of passionate concern. If thinking and the political are irreducible phenomena, they should always reassert themselves if emancipated from the restraining, sublimating, transformative effects of the Spirit of Revenge. Likewise the two will always be drawn together in some complicated tension as long as the public world attempts to justify itself with more than force and thinking avoids an epicurean retreat into silence and solitude.

If both the political and thinking are irreducible phenomena, in the absence of counterpressures they will always reproduce themselves.[12] But even if there are irreducible phenomena, they can be obliterated by a technology that increasingly turns itself on man himself. A science that can so transform Nature that it can suppress natural possibilities or genetically destroy their natural base could overcome both the political and thinking. We would be left to explain why they should be saved. In doing so, we would be led back inevitably to the epochal questioning

12. I proceed on the assumption that they are such irreducible phenomena. On the other hand, it should be noted that even if there is an irreducible substratum to human existence, it does not operate as efficient causality. Even Aristotle admits that nature must be completed by art, which means habits that are dependent on a shared *ethos*. And unless we have arrived at the end of history, *ethoi* will change.

of Nietzsche and Heidegger, if not to their answers: What conduces to man's well-being and to life? What is the nature of Being? What is man's place in it? What limits should be put on the Will and the manipulative Spirit of Revenge? What conditions enhance the possibility of those limits? All of these questions and many more lead us back to what I have designated "the problem of Nature." Ours is the age confronted with the unenviable task of deciding for or against Nature, for or against life, for or against difference. Will we open ourselves to life or allow the Spirit of Revenge to obliterate it? That is *part* of the choice between the modern and the *post*modern. Since primary Nature is not available to us in our transformed world, that choice reduces to a choice for or against immediate lived experience in its self-presenting difference as it plays itself out politically.

The central question is whether modern theory will step back and allow reality to self-presence, i.e., allow an openness to the interaction of different individuals with competing ends and allow their spontaneous interactions to determine outcomes that are not theoretically projected before the fact. One must be prepared and willing to appreciate and accept unpredictable outcomes. Otherwise we fall into the modern trap of relying on great founders, puppet masters, legislators, manipulative elites, revengeful theorists, and so on, who try to create predictable outcomes rather than allowing *praxis* to constitute itself. This is still done even by those postmodernists who, in the service of a perfectly modern bourgeois pluralist egalitarianism, put up a facade of praising contingency, "agonism," an-archy, and so on.[13] Without allowing *praxis* to constitute itself, talk about "community" is also a hollow gesture on the part of a deceptive theorist.

Postmodernity would require that the modern Spirit of Revenge step back and allow *praxis* its own sphere, that of the political. This would initially have to be a step back on the part *of the theorists* who must cease to theoretically project outcomes onto *praxis*. The theorists would have to adopt a new stance, precisely as occurred at the dawn of modernity. The problem is that modern *praxis* itself is so in the thrall of the Spirit of Revenge that only theoretical clarity will make it possible to step down in this direction. For now, thinking must foster and shelter *praxis*. Thinking cannot be allowed the epicurean alternative. The recovery of *praxis* must be fostered in the same way endangered species are now nursed back to a self-sustaining status. This is not a manifestation of the Spirit of Revenge, but it is a historically novel task.

13. Those postmodernists who project what the "contingent" outcome *must* be—egalitarian, pluralistic, pacifist, etc.—still operate under the Spirit of Revenge.

There is another reason why thinking must not quit the vicinity of the political. If it wishes to avoid silence, it has nowhere else to *begin*. There is an epistemic necessity that thinking be dialectical. Finally, given the problem of Nature, thinking must at all costs avoid the easy out of faith in unhistorical "innocence and forgetting," for reasons I will discuss below. Consequently, an ongoing knowledge of and openness to the past is as imperative as an openness to the possibility of a novel future: i.e., we need an openness to an ecstatic temporality, not a Nietzschean, unhistorical manipulation. Finally, freeing *praxis* from theoretical projects points in the direction of an opening to the self-subsistent dignity of practical reason operating within the *ethos* of a genuine community, which points toward expanding dialectical "communication."[14] On this level, thinking should see its task as educative rather than manipulative. The thinker becomes codiscussant qua citizen rather than a modern manipulator, Rortyan "polypragmatic dilletante" juggling incommensurable language games, or Habermasean projector of a theoretical stranglehold on actual discussion. "Enlightenment" could then come to be linked with notions like self-understanding and the formation of character. Freedom could come to be seen as requiring self-control, rather than being based on the pursuit of theoretical exactions such as "autonomy" and "metaphysical freedom."

14. While many contemporary thinkers, from Rorty to Habermas and Gadamer, see the centrality of "communication," none pays attention to the environment in which an *actual,* dialogic, practical discourse is possible. Gadamer comes closest, but in believing that the tradition always remains seamless and that an adequate *ethos* already exists he does not turn his attention to how to *foster* a postmodern *ethos*.

23

Dialectical Thinking: From the Phenomenology of Immediate Experience to Poetry

There are at least four potential beginning points for thinking in our time. First, one can begin by articulating what is embedded in the opinions individuals already hold. In our time that is tantamount to mounting a well-funded expedition to "discover" and dig up what was previously buried in the backyard. Contemporary *praxis* is already so thoroughly informed by modern philosophy that it is no longer in touch with immediate experience. Interrogating present opinions will only lead to digging up diluted versions of, for example, Locke or Kant. This circularity can only be appealing to those who are determined to arrive at a modern outcome.

Second, there is the hypothetical beginning in which one posits the foundations, then proceeds "as if" they were the fundamental reality. One can then reduce thinking to a logico-deductive enterprise. Proceeding in that fashion, one's outcomes will always be without ontological foundation. Man becomes the ground, the ultimate foundation of Being and value. That is the quintessential modern approach. Its value is that one can gain a theoretical purchase that allows the manipulation and transformation of reality. The hypothetico-deductive form of thinking can lead nowhere else than to the transformation of thinking into *technē*, which leads to the abolition of thinking.

Third, one can begin from a direct grasping of the first things or ground. Examples include Hebraic revelation, Aristotelian *nous,* or Heideggerian silent, *alogon* hearing. (One should keep in mind that Hebraic revelation is anything but *alogon* even if the source is self-concealing.) This gives an ontological foundation to thinking but poses a problem for those who do not have the direct experiences. Some kind of mediation is always required for those without that experience— e.g., prophets or Heideggerian poets. That in turn raises the problem of true versus false poets and prophets and how to determine the difference. While that raises significant difficulties, the epiphantic in all its

manifestations should not be dismissed. It too is part of human experience. But epiphantic experiences have to be passed through a mediating filter the moment they are brought to speech, and shared language
imposes limits.

Finally, there is what I will call the "dialectical" approach, which one
is left with if, in the absence of a relatively universal, direct, unmediated relation to the first things, one is intent upon transcending modernity. I will try to differentiate my use of this term from Hegel's. The
dialectical approach begins with the immediate, pretheoretical experience of reality as it reveals itself publicly to all. Such a publicly revealed
reality, when freed from the Spirit of Revenge, would be political as
defined above. Following Heidegger, I would argue that pretheoretical
awareness presents itself in such a way that the subject–object distinction and all manner of other *theoretical* conundrums are never encountered. There is no need to prove the reality of what appears or to
explain how we have access to it; it is taken as self-standing and self-
presencing. The fact–value distinction does not appear; facts presence
and stand out as part of our doing and making—i.e., because they have
a value. Reality presents itself in phenomenological wholes: One does
not confront the problems Hegel depicts in his discussions of "Sense-
certainty" and "Perception." No one worries about whether the ensemble of properties that make up an object will fly apart. The list
could be expanded.

That which reveals itself publicly to all is never entirely self-evident
and unproblematic. The problematic nature of lived experience becomes clear as soon as different individuals try to articulate what they
experience. That undertaking invariably manifests itself in different
statements about what is experienced. But the various statements can
then be juxtaposed, compared, discussed, analyzed *(diairesis)*, synthesized *(synthesis)*, and so on. But where that process leads should not be
prejudged. Dialectical thinking does not confront the Heideggerian
problem of translating silent hearing into speech, it is never *alogon*.
Likewise it never begins from the artificial and theoretically derivative
modern stance that what appears to all is intrinsically unreliable. That
which appears for all can be less than apodictically clear without becoming epistemically unreliable. Dialectical thinking proceeds on the
assumption that there is truth embedded in pretheoretical experience as
it appears to all. The opposite conclusion is theoretically derivative,
and ultimately rests on articles of pure faith, e.g., that a transcendental
ego exists and is in touch with something more substantial than immediate experience.

Immediate experience is always determined by the shared experience of the community into which one is thrown, the language it shares, its customs, natural environment, and so on. But what preeminently shapes a community is the collective pursuit of clarity in relation to war, sex, and the gods. Hence to begin from immediate experience is to begin from the perspective of the citizen living in some specific place, whose perspective is shaped by public or authoritative *speech*— that is, by fundamental laws and legislation, but also by an unspoken *ethos*.[1] But given that there is always a variety of communities, each with a shared *ethos*, immediate or natural experience has more than one manifestation, a fact compounded by the variety of languages and natural environments we occupy. This is a ground of diversity. But the existence of diversity does not preclude the possibility of elements of unity or identity. Different nations and cultures succeed in speaking; otherwise, diplomacy would be impossible. When we travel we have no problem seeing that the novel institutions of another group address many of the issues and problems for which "we" have our own institutions. These are not magical and mystical theoretical occurrences; they happen repeatedly and have since the beginning of time. There is no need to prove that this possibility exists.

The pretheoretical understanding of the citizen is not simply fixed and uniform but rests on the nature of the community in which it exists. The variety of communities is determined by the variety of purposes to which groups can be dedicated and the variety of different individuals always included. But every community has a primary end and is dominated by the individuals "akin" to that end. There are a finite number of ends that human beings actually pursue. "There are no recesses of privacy which are simply impervious to" a community's pretheoretical disclosure of reality.[2] This includes philosophy understood as a detached, theoretical activity. This is why dialectical thinking necessarily begins from *within* the confines of a community (which *Socrates* too harshly designated as a cave). This is not due to an act of noble benevolence; it is an *epistemic* necessity. This differentiates the dialectical approach from epicurean approaches to thinking which try to detach themselves from the political. The dialectical approach to thinking avoids the Spirit of Revenge without radically severing thinking and *praxis*.

A simply detached observer would have at best an unclear grasp of the ends pursued by participating and communicating individuals and the order of those ends as they become clear to active and involved citi-

---

1. Cf. Strauss, *City and Man,* 14, 15; Strauss, Epilogue, 310.
2. Strauss, Epilogue, 318.

zens. What this means is that pretheoretical experience is always confronted by a reality that is hierarchically constituted. The world presents itself in a teleological fashion to the involved citizen.[3] The dialectical approach to thinking begins from pretheoretical perceptions and the language used by citizens as they try to articulate their shared understanding as well as the reasons for their differences.[4] Grounding thinking in immediate experience avoids the danger of theoretical hubris, "madness," "blindness," or "silence."[5] What one sees when engaged in dialectically articulating common experience is that ordinary perceptions and the opinions based on them point to definable, differentiable parts. The whole brings itself to sight unavoidably, as a heterogeneity of such parts.[6] The study of the whole becomes a study of the articulation of these parts. No direct apprehension of the whole shorn of the parts is possible from this beginning. The dialectical thinker does not begin from anything like an Aristotelian *nous* that grasps the *arche* or the whole directly. One ends with no Heideggerian movement toward an articulation of Being that completely eschews beings. Contrary to Heidegger, one can *approach* Being through an articulation of the parts without landing in the lap of revengeful manipulation and domination if one is willing to accept the fundamental political articulation of immediate experience as primary, and to respect differences as they present themselves.

Thinking must eventually go beyond immediate experience and

3. Whether the world presents itself in a teleological fashion to the dialectical thinker may be another matter altogether. The dialectical method relies on no specific cosmology and points toward no specific cosmology. It is metaphysically and cosmologically neutral. (I use the term "metaphysical" here in its customary usage rather than in Heidegger's paradoxical sense.) It is also morally neutral; it neither relies on nor points to a specific morality.

4. In this regard we should consider Socrates' discussion in the *Phaedo* of why he changed from his early attempts to understand the whole directly. When he matured, and became Socratic, he adopted a method based on the indirect or mediated approach to the whole. More specifically, he came to take seriously the data of immediate experience as well as the speeches made about reality by individuals in what I have called the "lifeworld."

5. In the *Republic*, Socrates asserts that direct knowledge of the ultimate ground is like looking at the sun directly, which causes "blindness." The *Republic* makes a clear criticism of the kind of philosophy that is a *mania*—whether divine or otherwise—a longing for direct oneness with the ground. That leads to self-immolation. To that extent, in the *Republic*, the ground is presented as self-concealing.

6. See Strauss, *Natural Right and History*, 123. In contemporary parlance, this means language is inevitably "metaphysical" in Heidegger's unique sense—a fact that Heidegger himself came to see. Dialectical thought begins from this fact rather than theoretically dismissing it in advance.

provide speculative explanations of the articulation of the parts. It then takes on a poetic element. Eventually those speculative/poetic articulations become part of what is present and affect immediate experience and the opinions derived from it. Thus begins the unavoidable process by which we become alienated from immediate experience. As the Heidegger of *Being and Time* argues, theoretical detachment is unavoidable, although it can manifest itself in a variety of different forms. But if it leads to a desire to revengefully transform reality—i.e., a refusal to accept difference—it cuts itself off from its only real ground. As a result, the ground withdraws.

Thinking always points toward poetry. Poetry and thinking are not in fundamental opposition.[7] But if the thinker is determined to use poetic projections (e.g., qua mathematical poetry) to change the fabric of natural experience rather than to explain it, articulate its parts, and "weave" them together, a dialectic of a different kind begins. At that point one approaches Hegel's dialectic, the thinking that transforms the world and is in turn transformed in an accelerating cycle. In the process theory becomes increasingly ontologically groundless; by making its objects entirely a projection of itself, thinking eventually abolishes itself and destroys the political. Assuming human beings cannot live without curiosity about the first things and the speculative, poetic attempts to articulate them, the process of alienation from natural experience is built into the nature of human reality. What can be avoided is the desire to quit those roots once and for all. Thinking needs to allow itself the possibility of continually returning to the immediate experience of reality if there is a possibility of transcending unending modernity (qua postmodernism) or future impasses of a like kind. That means thinking must continually return to the political, at times fostering that return. The return to immediate, pretheoretical awareness is always the return to the "surface," to the way things appear, to their *eidē* or "facade." On that surface one may discover "the notion of the beneficence of Nature or of the primacy of the good."[8]

The comparison of the dialectical approach and that of Aristotle yields another distinctive feature. For Aristotle, the theoretical is coequal with the practical; neither is derivative from the other. As Aristotle makes clear in book 6 of the *Nicomachean Ethics,* practical wisdom

7. I attribute this unfortunate disjunction to Socrates, not Plato. Plato is a master of synthesizing *mythos* and *logos*. Having posed this Socratic either/or choice one is inevitably forced into false choices. For example, Nietzsche is still operating within this either/or when he makes his choice for autonomous poetry against self-legislating modern philosophy.

8. Consider in this regard Strauss, *Thoughts on Machiavelli,* 299.

(phronesis) and theoretical wisdom *(sophia)* each have their own distinctive object. The dialectical method contradicts the Aristotelian assertion that theoretical and practical sciences have their own objects. The primary pretheoretical disclosure of reality determines both. If the dialectical method for approaching the study of the whole through the interrogation of speeches *(logoi)* about the various beings as they appear to all is the fundamental form of thinking, it is *the* method for *all* thinking.[9] Since no radical Cartesian detachment is implied in the dialectical view of thinking, one need not overcome all movement away from immediate experience—i.e., all speculative or poetic activity—to overcome a nihilism born of theoretical hubris. Further, the dialectical thinker—contrary to the modern understanding of the philosopher as puppet master—remains in full sight of all as a codiscussant, at most as *primus inter pares*. Hence dialectical thinking leads to a theoretical moderation. Moderation and mythmaking are two different things. Further, moderation is a theoretical necessity, not just a practical one.

Premodernity was initially intent on carving out a place for thinking and defending it *from the political*. Modernity felt the need to carve out a place for thinking in the *face of theology*. Postmodernity would have to try to find a way to defend the practical experience of reality *from the hegemony of autonomous theory*. The problem has changed and thereby the therapy needs to be changed as well. One can preserve a place for thinking in-the-world—which I believe Nietzsche and Heidegger do not—and defend *praxis* simultaneously, but only on the basis of a self-imposed moderation.

A dialectical, postmodern thinking turned loose on a transformed modern reality would certainly produce different speculative and poetic articulations of shared experience than anything that has heretofore existed. The world that appears for us is not the one that was present for previous human beings; hence our immediate experiences will not be identical to those of individuals of the past. Neither will they be entirely incommensurable if we assume the primacy of questions about war, sex, and the gods and the unavoidability of thinking as a way of life. Further, difference is not infinite in its manifestations. What post-

9. Aristotle, departing from Plato and Socrates, established the independent disciplines and set the Western tradition on the way to the radical theoretical/practical distinction, thereby setting the stage for modernity. As I suggested above, most of what Nietzsche and Heidegger lay at the door of Plato should be traced to Aristotle's radical deflection of Plato's thought. The independent theoretical disciplines are only possible on the basis of a unique form of abstraction from the initial results of *a* reflection on immediate experience. Their foundation emerges from an abstraction from an abstraction.

modern articulations of immediate experience would look like cannot be predicted. One would have to free *praxis* from the Spirit of Revenge and turn loose a new dialectical thinking—and the "communication" therein implied—to find out. That such a thinking would have deferred—and again, unpredictable—future ramifications goes without saying. But anyone who genuinely affirms life should revel in the possibility of novelty and be open to a novel future. The alternative is to accept the end of history.

For thinking to strive as much as possible to quit its community and adopt the epicurean stance would lead to a way of being that was far from self-sufficient, precisely because it would be an existence that was not self-consciously aware of its prerequisites. And the fundamental prerequisite for thinking is not primarily the preservation of the body—which admittedly is important and has ramifications—but language. Even if some direct apprehension of the first things—or the nature of the whole—existed, to prove that that experience was not some vagrant phenomenon born of indigestion, one would have to state it, articulate its parts, discuss it, take it apart, and put it together again. That clearly implies speech. Speech is always the speech of a community. Dialectical thinking, which is unavoidably rooted in the pretheoretical, must also use a tool it borrows from a community and at least initially use that tool as it is used in common parlance.

Because it is a tool indigenous to a community, language bears the limitations of its origin. Languages are living things. All languages carry within them ambiguities, accidents, and contradictions. Thinking must exist within those limitations. This does not mean, however, that it relates to those limitations in the same fashion as those who do not think. Thinking inevitably tries to articulate the tensions and contradictions inherent in speech. It must assume that in doing so it is coming closer to a grasp of reality, for there is no reason to assume, and no way to prove, the opposite. In dialectically confronting the tensions within speech, and between different speeches, thinking necessarily engages in a public act and must hold itself responsible for the ramifications of that act. The minute a thinker speaks, thought falls prey to misunderstandings that are not entirely predictable. This is true even when speaking among one's friends or students, to say nothing of speaking to those less prepared or at a greater distance from the speaker's constellation of thoughts.

No thinker can possibly predict the process of the dissemination of thought. Hence no thinker can entirely predict the ramifications of thought. Plato could no more predict that Aristotle would make the crucial transformation of his thought that he did than he could predict the curious fashion by which Aristotle's work found its way to Rome, while his own (Plato's) was fundamentally lost to the West until the fifteenth century. This is not *Seinsgeschichte* in action; it is contingency and accident. One must accept its inevitability. But one can consciously try to guard against infelicitous misunderstandings, using a variety of devices. One should not, however, rely on consciously projected misunderstanding, as did Nietzsche. One best guards against misunderstanding by remaining close to ordinary speech and shared immediate experience.

Thinking is necessarily rooted in a community for many reasons: It must inevitably begin its undertakings with immediate experience, it must borrow a tool of its community, and it cannot avoid having an influence on its community, and thereby on its language. *Neither thinking nor a community stands alone as an autonomous originating principle; the relationship is mutual and reciprocal.* Thinking, to the extent it avoids being mere political ideology, on the one hand, and free-floating poetic *theo-mythos* (or equally free-floating mathematical *poiesis*), on the other, remains linked to speech and the community to which it belongs. Hence at its peak, thinking must be a form of dialectical political philosophy. The question that remains is whether the contradictions present in speech or between different speeches can be synthesized and transcended. For example, are the historical successions of contradictions and competing opinions eternally contingent, or do they sequence themselves in some fashion? In other words, postmodern thinkers will always remain in a primordial debate with Hegel.

The problem with what I have presented is that late moderns do not have access to an immediate experience that grows out of a full range of experiences unsullied by theoretical projects. We must recover a full sense of the immediate experience of reality that should seemingly be part of every generation's legacy.[10] Dialectical thinking cannot be immediately deployed. Contemporary thinking has a different, more im-

---

10. Consider the following observation:

Now, not indeed philosophy, but the way in which the introduction to philosophy must proceed, necessarily changes with the change of the artificial or accidental obstacles to philosophy. The artificial obstacles may be so strong at a given time that a most elaborate "artificial" introduction has to be completed before the "natural" introduction can begin. . . .

People may become so frightened of the ascent to the light of the sun, and so desirous of making that ascent utterly impossible to any of their descendants, that they dig a deep pit beneath the cave in which they were born, and withdraw into that pit. If one of the descendants desired to ascend to the light of the sun, he would first have to try to reach the level of the natural cave. (Strauss, *Persecution and the Art of Writing*, 155).

mediate task of reflecting on the conditions for the return of *praxis* from the brink of extinction. It is predictable, therefore, that my argument will be criticized as being no more than a circuitous way of projecting my own interpretation in place of others considered less desirable, and of hiding the enterprise under talk about immediate experience and postmodernity.

The only response I can give is that I have tried to articulate what would be implied in a genuinely *post*modern alternative, taking into account the available Nietzschean and Heideggerian resources which I believe are the most powerful in our time. I have concluded that the postmodern would require that thinking cease to present itself as a self-legislating ground. It would have to reverse the transformation of Reason into Will and understand that ultimately it can never simply originate anything by itself; it digests and articulates elements that are given prior to its efforts, at most weaving them together in novel ways. Hence thinking must realize that something must be *self*-presencing. The alternative is to accept that the present is never more than the deferred ramification of an absent source (primary Nature, prior thinking) that can never be recovered, and that we are left to generate everything henceforth out of self-legislating speech. To observe that thinking cannot originate its ultimate ground is no more than to state the architectonic status of the practical in its primary manifestation as political. If that primary ground cannot be recovered, thinking could end in endless projecting and ongoing deconstructive critique. As a result moral and political modernity could be unending. The age of the clash of competing worldviews, and their subsequent deconstruction, would go on indefinitely.

Another problem awaits. Does not my understanding *necessarily* historicize thought, as that of Nietzsche and Heidegger seems to some to do? Not if it can rise dialectically to greater clarity than is contained within pretheoretical, natural experience, even if one never arrives at final wisdom about the first things. That we do not know everything does not mean we cannot know anything. A variety of possibilities exist between relativism and apodictic certainty. A further question: Does not direct noetic grasping, epiphantic vision, or revelation take hegemony over dialectical thinking? Not given that any direct experience of the first things must be brought to speech—brought before the bar of speech—if it is to have any manifestation in the world. Put another way, at most only a rare few experience revelatory insight, and only a few others will have direct contact with those rare individuals. For all others, revelation manifests itself only through the words of others. Clearly there are true and false prophets, those who are genuinely inspired and those who are charlatans. And it is possible that even the genuinely inspired at times sound like, and occasionally are, frenzied madmen. There must be a *logoi* that allows one to judge between true and false prophets.

Dialectical thinking stands *between* natural experience and revelation. The thinking that is described by Socrates as a "preparing to die," which would quit natural experience—alternately termed a form of "divine madness" or an erotically intoxicated *thaumazein*—is a philosophy that longs for revelation and a direct noetic grasp of or oneness with the first things. Paradoxically, Socrates shared this longing with Heidegger. This natural longing is as much a part of life as the need to act; hence awareness of it is as important to a revenge-free thinking as a foundation in *praxis*. But it always threatens an altogether human madness. Thinking must always draw in the reins on itself and remain both related to immediate experience and open to the divine impulse without simply collapsing into either.

Modern philosophy presumed it could avoid this suspension between external, originary phenomena through positing the autonomy of objective modern science from either immediate experience or theology. In this attempt, it failed to see the architectonic status of the practical and reduced the political to a problem that could be eradicated by overcoming scarcity and fear. Modern science could emancipate itself from the divine impulse, and thereby dispense with the need for direct apprehension of the first things, only if it could inductively or mediately work up to the first things (the Baconian option), which it quickly realized it could not. When modern science is finally forced to realize that its mythic belief that its self-legislated projections "mirrored" reality was unfounded, it recognized its indifference to the first things per se. It then had to admit that its end is manipulation, not explanation. Modern science, in accordance with its Cartesian roots, projects the first things for itself in consciousness, and then turns its back on the existence or nonexistence of the first things per se—Kant's "thing-in-itself." This may be perfectly adequate from the perspective of generating theories that are useful in manipulating Nature, but it is altogether useless from the perspective of understanding the whole—which is the ultimate, if unattainable, end of thinking. Thinking will forever reproduce itself as long as wonder and curiosity are repeatable possibilities, and the speculative by-products of that wonder and curiosity will continue to have unpredictable, deferred, practical ramifications.

In suspending dialectical thought between revelation and natural experience, have I not destroyed thinking as an end in itself and established the simpleminded autonomy of the political and revelation? On the contrary, the political is always under the sway of something like what Heidegger calls "semblance." Part of political discussion is conscious obfuscation and misdirection. Thought must win for itself a path through such semblance and keep it open. Further, much of what thinking distills from natural experience is irrelevant, useless, or dangerous to everyday *praxis*. It is properly to be enjoyed and shared with friends, but need not be announced. And the coming of the great revelatory experiences and speculative and poetic efforts is mysterious and rare. One cannot simply wait in hopeful silence in the interim.

Several final thoughts about dialectical thinking as I am presenting it are in order. First, the world of pretheoretical experience is not only a political world but also always one of morality and faith. The political is the inlet to the religious. As Spinoza put the matter, we are always confronted by a theologico-political question. No one can avoid openness to the first things, which for the thinker takes the form *quid sit deus*. Openness to the religious question is unavoidable and is also needed to rein in the hubris of autonomous poetry and theory. One may question a community's beliefs—for they always rest on a certainty that is never available—but one must also realize the need for circumspection when it is understood that nothing apodictic can be substituted. Further, atheism is always based on the arrogant assertion that one has complete knowledge about the whole and hence knows apodictically there is no divine support for life. The dialectical thinker knows we can never have that knowledge; hence we can never prove that faith is wrong. None of this means that we might not, for practical reasons, conclude that there is a value in having a secular set of political institutions—the certainty and arrogance of the faithful is frequently as great as that of the atheistic. But every society must remain open to the religious dimension of experience *and thereby point beyond itself.* That openness can only be closed off by the Spirit of Revenge in its attempt to pacify existence by closing itself off from the mysterious.

Heidegger saw that immediate phenomenological awareness had sacred and profane qualities; it necessarily implicated openness to the divine (e.g., the Fourfold). For Heidegger every great civilization had, and needed to have, a religious basis. But he went too far. For him there is no place left for thinking as I have defined it; that place is taken entirely by *theo-mythos*. In Heidegger, poetry and religion attain hegemony; thinking, which needs *openness* to the religious longing for oneness with the mysterious source, abdicates and goes over to the side of the gods of the autonomous poets. Heidegger himself increasingly longed to grasp the mysterious source directly, without the mediation of beings. This led him into silence, positively requiring abdication to the poets. Likewise, his openness to Being that abstracts from beings left the place of the political occupied by mere, formal, committed resoluteness in the early works, and an equally substanceless, parochial, autochthonous rootedness in the later. Finally, Heidegger tried to overcome the crisis caused by the hubris of modern rationalism through a recovery of the East. He found the most fruitful basis of the East *within* the West in pre-Socratic thought. But with this version of the recovery of the distinctive tension between the principles of the East and the West, Western rationalism is completely lost. Dialectical thinking avoids these problems.

Second, in my understanding, at the dawn of the Western tradition, Socrates posed the issue of the relation between philosophy and poetry in an entirely misleading fashion. Contrary to Socrates, the postmodern thinker and the poet occupy the same ground. The poets are the spokespersons par excellence for the natural experience of existence. They give vivid word pictures—at least for individuals who share the same world—of that which most individuals grasp less vividly. Philosophical poetry also provides the speculative articulations of the whole, toward which the parts of immediate experience always point. In articulating natural experience vividly, the poets ground thinking, and thinking in turn points toward speculative poetry. Further, those who equate the "inspiration" of the poets with the "grasping" of the prophets err.[11] That leads in the direction of Heidegger's *theo-mythos*. Poetry brings to speech the experiences we share within this world; prophets try to bring to speech the call from beyond.

Finally, thinking moves away from immediate political awareness precisely because in dialectically and speculatively reflecting upon it, it abstracts from it. What is to keep thinking from moving further and further away until one has a long tradition of thinking leading to, for example, Descartes's radical detachment and ultimately Nietzsche's open glorification of self-grounding philosophic willfulness? The danger of abstractions from abstractions is always present. If there is to be a form of thinking that does not destroy the pretheoretical horizon it will have to be a humble thinking that knows its origins and limitations. That humility comes from the realization of the impossibility of overcoming all manner of tensions, such as those between religion and thinking, thinking and *praxis,* different individuals and different groups with competing ends, and so on. To affirm life and avoid the

---

11. See for example Pangle's Introduction in Strauss, *Studies in Platonic Political Philosophy.*

Spirit of Revenge, one cannot affirm life selectively. Life must be affirmed in all its diversity, tensions, and seeming contradictions.

Henceforth the pretheoretical lifeworld's existence is precarious. To fly too far beyond that lifeworld is to stand nowhere. Thinking must recover its foundation if it is to continue. That is the task of present thinking. A future postmodern thinking would have to appreciate its rootedness in the particular. This would certainly convince thinking of the paradoxes involved when the political strives to be universal. But at the same time, *praxis* must retain its natural openness to what lies beyond it, and hence must eschew all radical particularity, closure, and parochialism. In the process a newly modest postmodern thinking would come to see that care for the lifeworld has become its most significant task. How can we affirm the right to existence of the snail darter or the spotted owl and fail to affirm the autonomy of *human* life in all its diversity?

24

Letting the Future Present Itself: Constitutional Government and Postmodernity

I have argued that a resolutely *post*modern alternative would require overcoming the Spirit of Revenge. That means theory must cease to dictate to *praxis* and must instead affirm life as it develops and presents *itself.* That requires in turn that thinking transform itself. *Praxis,* freed from theoretical determination, has no ground unless it returns to a ground in immediate experience, which I have argued is articulated politically. If there is no immediate experience that self-presences, we will forever be left grounding *praxis* on willed myths or willed theoretical projects, and the difference between the two will be increasingly difficult to discern. In the process, modernity would become unending.

I have argued that *praxis* can be freed from the Spirit of Revenge of modern theory without being radically severed from thinking; hence we need not be thrown into the lap of myth making, irrationalism, predatory "nobility," atavistic ethnic balkanization, or anything of the kind. But thinking must first assume a new role. I suggested above that thinking must stand to *praxis* as environmental scientists now do to endangered species. Let *praxis* be thinking's bald eagle. As a theoretical matter, this discussion may be all well and good, but *we* live in the modern world. First, how can we presume to get from our present to a postmodern future? Second, if we do get out of the blind alley of late modernity, what might we reasonably expect to gain and lose in the process? I will conclude by addressing those two questions.

Despite what until this point may have come close to overstatement for emphasis, it can be admitted that an experience of genuine *praxis* is not extinct. If it were, we would probably have no way out of modernity. We have intimations of immediate experience upon which to draw. Those intimations must be articulated. First, *contemporary* thinking must turn itself to phenomenological articulations of that experience and legitimize its priority.[1] Second, we have the great benefit of a literary heritage that gives us access to immediate experience, so long as we refrain from gross hermeneutic hubris or that version of innocence and forgetting that revengefully dismisses the entire past as hopelessly sullied. Consequently, *contemporary* thinking also has a hermeneutic function. Third, current economic reality will probably require that matters presently administered by technical professionals be accomplished by far more labor-intensive, autonomous, face-to-face local action. This will give a venue for *praxis,* but we must be willing to affirm the spontaneous outcomes born of the interactions of difference as it operates within those venues without projecting in advance what those outcomes will be. It is from out of the complicated nexus of spontaneous interactions that a unique *ethos* can emerge. Finally, *present* thinking may have to engage in acts of artificial insemination. That does not mean that one invents one's materials, only that one weaves together difference as it presents itself in ways that would, without intervention, require multiple permutations and more time than we have to become self-sustaining.

Thinking is central if we are to get from the present to a unique future. But it is central as much for what it should cease to do as for what it must do. Unfortunately, what this means is that we are confronted with the need for yet another transition. But what I am suggesting simultaneously affirms action in the present, an action freed from the Spirit of Revenge (especially revenge against the past) and from frameworks projected onto the future. One can respect present interactions with the thought that through those interactions the future will in due course *present itself,* and when it does, it will in retrospect be as if nothing had transpired by conscious manipulation. I want to argue that in this regard, Heidegger's discussions of temporality are far more useful than Nietzsche's. In looking toward the future we must first find a way to occupy the present with a good conscience while avoiding that innocence and forgetting that obliterates a healthy relation to the past.[2]

Nietzsche projects the need for a future moment that has accomplished innocence and an unhistorical forgetting. That is his under-

1. Philosophically informed case studies from the social sciences can help serve this function. "Community action" studies come immediately to mind, although I am suspicious of most present studies, which are primarily a facade for the imposition of a modern theoretical frame.

2. Common sense alone should make it clear that the spectacle of past human history cannot possibly be *only* the chronicle of unwisdom, error, vice, malevolence, and repression. That conclusion is only possible on the basis of some notion of inevitable, linear History, to say nothing of being totally sullied by the Spirit of Revenge.

standing of the only remaining way for humanity to occupy the present with a good conscience.[3] In that way the present would, for a time, be isolated from past and future. Heidegger's discussion of ecstatic temporality, where the past and future are coequally present in the present moment is more useful. We must bring our past to presence in that loving, intimate and passionate way that allows it to inform and open us to care and concern for the future. Only in that way can we be accommodated to our present. We must lovingly appropriate the past as a great spectacle of difference in all its permutations and take responsibility for the fact that the future will in some fashion be a deferred ramification of how we live in the present. Then the present can become a moment we can accept without revenge. The appropriate relation to time must integrate past, present, and future, not privilege one moment to the exclusion of the others.

I have refrained from suggesting reliance on the resolute and monumental acts of great thinkers, statesmen, artists, and poets, which remains central for both Nietzsche and Heidegger. First of all, that leaves one in a posture of waiting for the acts of great creative individuals without assurance that the waiting will be rewarded. Second, it puts the cart before the horse. The great, creative acts Nietzsche and Heidegger look to as originary and foundational in fact grow out of an indigenous *ethos*. That indigenous *ethos* must be nurtured first; in due course the creative acts will follow. Cultures, traditions, and *ethoi* grow out of countless spontaneous, day-to-day interactions, which are destroyed by the theoretical projecting of modernity. These are the almost extinct realities that must be nurtured. Doing so will open the present for us in the appropriate way. Finally, reliance on great foundational acts seems to go hand in hand with the apocalyptic visions that open authors like Nietzsche and Heidegger to a willingness to endure barbaric interludes of transition. If we are to be freed from the Spirit of Revenge we must eschew these apocalyptic visions and adopt a more temperate and healthy relationship to our present. The last thing we need is more public abyss teachings and anxious handwringing.

How do we get from here to there? My suggestion is in a way so modest as to occasion hesitancy. But this hesitation at least points toward something more benign than that of the Zarathustra who hesitates to offer his version of the Eternal Recurrence because of the

---

3. In this vein I believe Rorty's praise of irony—and other, similar praise—is a mistake. The ironic person cannot occupy the present with a good conscience. That ironic relation to the present—seen throughout postmodernism—leads to cynicism and various forms of epicurean flight. See chap. 21, n. 14.

suffering it implies. It seems to me that one cannot get from here to there unless and until thinking steps back and transforms *itself,* respectfully accepting the spontaneous interactions of different individuals in the present and affirming their outcomes (all of them, not just the momentary favorites of the right or left). That step back from the Spirit of Revenge on the part of thinking rests on a transformation of thinking's *self*-conception. Modernity itself was born out of precisely such a transformed self-conception—well-intentioned but ultimately revengeful.

If we begin from the present, drawing lovingly on the resources now available—yet open to the full range of possibilities the past presents us, in literature, philosophy, art, and history—we can open ourselves appropriately to the future. Only then will a novel future present *itself.* I admit that this conclusion rests on an act of faith, albeit an informed act. This is a postmodern faith that can be opposed to the modern faith in the autonomous, projecting Will, which seems to me to be ill-founded. Armed with this postmodern faith, the modern perception of being always in transition and "on the way"—which drains all meaning from the present—can slowly be overcome. But that will be possible only after thinking ceases to see itself as a form of self-conscious, self-grounding manipulative Will.[4] Postmodernity, were it to come, would in principle be based on a novel *ethos* (actually a multiplicity of *ethoi*) and would eventuate in novel poetic and speculative articulations of experience. What those would be like cannot be projected or predicted. To get from here to there requires slow, modest steps. Contrary to Nietzsche and Heidegger, we need not fear some apocalyptic event.

---

4. It might be argued that now, of all times in our history, with all the dangers we face, is precisely when humanity needs the greatest efforts in conscious planning and prediction. I would respond that intensified doses of such planning seem only to magnify our confusion and frustration. To put the matter in Heideggerian terms, in the process every destiny is warded off, and all cross-generational perseverance lost. We expect too much and as a result get much less than would be possible with a more modest conception of the capacities of thinking.

I cannot stress strongly enough that thinking came into existence at a specific time. It could cease to exist if the ground for its existence was destroyed. Now that thinking is the only ground for restoring openness to immediate experience, the overcoming of thinking would be a world-historical event, one which in due course would not be remembered. It would arouse the same concern that the loss of ornithologists would occasion among bald eagles. This points back toward what I have designated as "the problem of Nature." Ours is an absolutely unique situation, intrinsic to our time and hence in principle never confronted by prior thought. We in the present must find the way around the problem; no "return" to some past moment will be efficacious. But that presupposes modesty.

I have argued that Nietzsche and Heidegger call modernity into question in such a radical way that they open the horizon to positive reflections about postmodernity. I have argued that they are the authors for our time, and cannot be circumvented; what they have said cannot be wished away. But from a consideration of the thought of Nietzsche and Heidegger, it becomes clear that the pursuit of autonomous *praxis* toward which they point is not intended to lead to a republican or constitutional outcome. Does everything I have presented regarding the re-creation of the political run in the face of the republican principles of the modern West? The answer is a categorical No, for I have also tried to argue that multiple possibilities exist in the work of all epochal thinkers. A variety of deflections are initially possible; the closer in time one is to the thinker the more possibilities are likely to be still viable. There are clearly anticonstitutional tendencies in the thought of Nietzsche and Heidegger. These tendencies should not, as has generally been the case, be ignored or obfuscated, because in due course they could well manifest themselves. But intensified doses of the modern revengeful desire to pacify existence, especially when met by the predictable intransigence of reality, are even more likely to tempt many to authoritarian experiments. We should not be so naive as to believe that the collapse of global communism means that the totalitarian temptation is behind us.

Our world—we moderns from democratic, technological mass societies—forms the habit background that must be our point of departure. For example, rights are intrinsic to our constitutional existence. Those rights have been most frequently defended on modern, individualist, subjectivist principles. Can they exist without those modern principles? For their vitality, rights rely primarily on a public that understands, supports, and *lives* them. Without substantial public support, over extended periods of time—which creates an *ethos* of rights—no court or police force could impose a way of life on a people for long. There must be an *ethos* founded on vivid, enduring, lived experience to maintain institutions. Overreliance on courts, like overreliance on technical professionals, leads to the atrophy of the interactions that feed lived experience and the docility that lurks in theoretically legislated and governmentally imposed outcomes.[5] No one has a right to talk of "community" without a simultaneous respect for the spontaneous interactions out of which a distinctive *ethos* grows.

---

5. Kateb rightly points out the ramifications of this societal docility. See Kateb, *The Inner Ocean*, 222–39.

And no one should believe that rights will remain inviolate on the basis of a theory in the absence of a supportive *ethos*.

When deciding what should or will be allowed in the way of self-assertion, average citizens care not at all whether their rights are "natural" or "deontological." And none of them would think that asserting rights was morally neutral; a serious commitment to rights positively requires that there be different ends to assert, and that requires a revenge-free respect for difference. Rights rest on an environment of expectations reinforced by repeated concrete examples. One does not have to "conquer Chance" or accept the great abstract myth of modernity—"metaphysical freedom"—to have rights. Nor must one be an "antifoundationalist." Needless to say, there is a subtle relation between any *ethos* and laws and ideas. But neither laws nor theories alone could ever substitute for an *ethos* of rights. Our political and moral possibilities must grow out of our daily lived experiences, and they will remain vivid only as long as we continue to live in a certain fashion over an extended period of time. Recognizing the priority of a pretheoretical *ethos* will not undermine constitutional government and rights, but it will force us to approach them in a different way. Rather than argue about the theoretical constructions we wish to impose on reality, we should reflect on the ground of the distinctive shared *ethos* or community that supports constitutional government. This hardly calls for anything radically novel. But if one fears the outcomes of spontaneous interactions—with the dialectical thinker as one of the codiscussants—then one cannot hope for "community." All one will get is administered outcomes that result from prior theoretical projections. We need not fear unrepublican outcomes lurking in a return to "the political." There are far greater dangers in succumbing to the administrative and theoretical hubris of modern elites.

Having said this, I do believe there is an unmistakable and unavoidable aristocratic element lurking within the essence of the genuinely postmodern. The aristocratic element to which I am pointing does not imply theoretical or administrative elites ("meritocracy") or a commercial oligarchy. It points toward an openness to *arete*. Contrary to the treatments of Nietzsche and Heidegger—where an aristocratic element clearly exists—the aristocratic element need not be unmediated by other elements—for example, the democratic and oligarchic. And the aristocratic need not be deflected in the direction of Nietzsche's predatory nobles.

The logic of postmodernity points in the direction of having an aristocratic component because openness to the legitimacy of a full variety of competing ends must certainly respect the pursuit of excellence or virtue—in all its various forms—as a sovereign end. A postmodern aristocratic element would open a path to and a concern for "character." Openness to and a legitimization of differences of character would offer a counterbalance to the modern hegemony of technical skill and economic rationality. We already accept the legitimacy of differential outcomes based on differences of technical merit, so differential respect should not appall us. But meritocratic inequality is a simple extension of the modern legitimizing of technical elites. This should not be confused with an openness to "character." The modern abdication to technical elites points to far greater dangers than a respect for *arete* in an environment of equal opportunity. For example, what is this but Jefferson's "natural aristocracy" in a postmodern perspective (albeit we are obviously not pointing simply toward the virtues of agrarianism)?

Further, an openness to smaller-scale community interaction—which is definitely implied in the postmodern reaction against the hegemony of the modern state—carries with it a dynamic that has been articulated in numerous studies.[6] The more persuasive speaker, the more revered person, the preeminent manifestation of moral character, at times the most attractive individual, always acquires preference in *actual* communication. Giving legitimacy to smaller-scale interactive venues inevitably opens a path to hierarchical relations between discussants based on various differences, one of which is character. That outcome can be simply negated only by thoroughgoing revengeful truncation of the full spectrum of manifestations of self-presenting difference and by a theoretical truncation of actual communication. For example, contrary to Habermas, actual communication is never thoroughly egalitarian, nor is it ever free of "background noise," nor does it arrive at the full self-conscious transparency of the Enlightenment ideal. This observation does not in any way bear on the possibility or desir-

---

6. The literature here is extensive, stretching from Robert Michel's "Iron Law of Oligarchy" to what I consider one of the subtlest and theoretically best grounded recent explorations, Jane Mansbridge's *Beyond Adversary Democracy*. Mansbridge's work seems to me to be on the path to many important insights. Exploration of postmodernity should not eschew the "participatory" literature. However, never far from the surface of that literature is the new left political agenda of the 1960s and 1970s. That agenda almost always rests on the thoroughly modern projection of an egalitarian theoretical frame. Put another way, there is only limited appreciation for letting participatory interactions proceed where they may and produce whatever *ethos* may ensue. There are expectations before the fact, which include reflections on the place of theoretical elites, legislated equality, redistributed resources, and so on. In short, they come complete with manufactured outcomes.

ability of a more equal distributions of material goods, nor upon the
need to limit "oligarchy" or "elite" domination. It bears on those who
revengefully refuse to give eloquence, beauty, character, virtue, and all
manner of things that present *themselves* their inevitable due. Once
again, we already have multiple elites in the commercial, bureaucratic,
and academic worlds. *They* seem intrinsic to modernity. Further, none
of those elites is going away in the foreseeable future, although their
hegemony can be counterbalanced.

As the example of Aristotle shows, an openness to the aristocratic
principle can also go hand in hand with equality of citizenship, ruling
and being ruled in turn, broad-based, active participation, and a bal-
ancing of democratic and oligarchic elements.[7] In short, it is possible to
have a "noble" element that is not predatory, and that is altogether consistent with constitutional government and rights. Cannot constitutional government exist without the Spirit of Revenge and in the
presence of an aristocratic *element?* My answer is Yes. What concrete
manifestations would that take? That is for the future to decide. But,
one way or another, I believe there would be an aristocratic element
within any future that is genuinely postmodern. It needs to be deflected
in a sanguine, constitutional direction.

Are there not, however, economic and technological prerequisites
for the possibility of modern constitutional republics that unavoidably
rest on modern theory? I will pursue this issue through another reflection on Aristotle (which should not be interpreted as an endorsement
of Aristotle). Aristotle never considered the possibility of an egalitarian, mass, democratic society. For him, the rule of the majority was
always the rule of the propertyless and uneducated, which would fairly
quickly lead to chaos and eventually tyranny. In this, Aristotle's
thought is indicative of premodern thinking generally, in that it assumes an economy of scarcity as the natural situation. Through the introduction of modern science, we have embarked on a path that
tortures Nature so that we can overcome the economy of scarcity. This
opens the possibility that the vast majority can have enough property
and leisure to achieve the education and enlightenment previously

---

7. As I have suggested above, while Aristotle's theoretical works open the door to
the eventual sublimation of immediate experience, his practical works—especially
Ethics, Politics, Rhetoric, Poetics—represent unrivaled phenomenological articulations of
immediate experience. But again, contrary to Nietzsche, Heidegger, Derrida, and what
is becoming a veritable chorus, I believe the ultimate roots of modern nihilism can be
traced to Aristotle, not Plato. I turn to Aristotle in this instance only to point out the
possibility of alternatives outside the modern.

thought possible only for a few. Would postmodernity inevitably endanger this possibility?

It could be argued that the modern dream is ultimately a chimera; we are merely deluding ourselves by living off the resources of future generations. In due course a number of things will happen: (1) Nature itself will impose ecological limits. We will run out of resources and places to put expended residues. (2) Overpopulation will create shortages and pollution that will occasion necessary limits. Those limits will have to be imposed in some authoritarian fashion. (3) The economy of endless growth will come to be seen as a sham based on faith in the existence of unlimited resources and the need for an ever-growing population. Will Nature itself then impose postmodernity upon us by causing the economy of scarcity—with all its political and moral implications—to return? I do not think that is inevitable. But if that did occur, I think the prospect would be anything but sanguine for constitutional government. Under those circumstances the authoritarian rule of modern theoretical and technical elites would become very likely.

As I suggested above, in our age the question of scarcity reduces to scarcity of energy, not of actual materials.[8] If modern technology can solve the problem of clean, limitless energy—and I see no reason why it cannot—finite natural resources will pose no limitation on the modern technological project. Sensible recycling is all that will be required. And there is no intrinsic reason why technological sophistication cannot bring increases in productivity such that economic growth can be predicated on increases in productivity rather than population growth.[9] Finally, there is the sanguine news that population seems to tend toward a steady state in economically and technologically modernized societies. Perhaps when modern technology achieves its inevitable global dispersal, the population problem will be resolved without authoritarian regulation. I have neither the space nor the ability to deal with this issue in detail. I wish merely to suggest that Nature itself may not bring an end to modernity. If not, we cannot assume that Nature will impose limits and save us from having to face the primarily moral, political, and philosophical questions concerning whether we will allow our species to be reduced to an undifferentiated mass of technicians

8. See chap. 5, n. 7.

9. I admit a great danger lurks here. Will not increases in productivity require ever intensified organizational manipulation of human beings and their total transformation into manipulated laborers/consumers? Where will there be the leisure for the political interaction that is the basis of community? Might it be possible to work the latter into the workplace? Far more thought will be required here than I, or anyone else, have given these questions to date.

and laborers, or open ourselves to being political and moral beings and let difference flourish.

I see no reason to conclude that postmodernity must be antigrowth or anti–open markets. If postmodernity is political, however, it will have to be open to a variety of ends other than the economic. Such openness will inevitably lead to a hierarchy of ends (differently organized in different places) in which the economic is somewhere other than at the top of the ladder. That does not require a resentful, revolutionary onslaught against commercial republicanism, in which we would risk losing all its obvious benefits; it means only that commerce as a way of life will be put in a less elevated position of respect. The same would be true of technical expertise. In short, our hierarchy of cultural heroes would change. Commerce and technology—central to the modern faith—would be seen as means to other ends higher than merely long life and comfort. That is part of what openness to the political, and genuine openness to difference, implies.

Assuming the universal, global victory of the modern project—and that seems fated—what then? Perhaps it is precisely at the point when the modern technological and commercial project reaches its peak that one can step back and reappropriate an immediate relationship to the external world and others. When modern technology reaches its *telos,* perhaps one can step down, foster the postmodern, and recover the indigenous with its rootedness in one's own—e.g., one's own music, poetry, language, art, and natural location. This could become possible precisely because issues of scarcity would cease to be central issues; the political and the economic could be severed, such that the political is no longer seen as epiphenomenal. Postmodernity could be economically classless and still manifest difference.[10] Precisely because of the success of the modern project it might be possible for us to become more than primarily economic and laboring animals without reestablishing an economy of scarcity.

By way of comparison, Aristotle could preference the political because he accepted scarcity and the subsequent economic inequality. While different than the economic, the political was still wound around the economic for Aristotle. A postmodern thinker could preference the political because the economic could be lowered in dignity without leading inevitably to economic inequality—e.g., the postmodern may imply the relative universality of the middle class. Further, it need not be telling if, on a global basis, we eventually all have refrigerators and

10. Consider in this regard, as food for thought and no more, Hermann Hesse's vision of a postmodern aristocracy that is not an economic class in *The Glass Bead Game.*

telephones, so long as the universal ceases its hegemony over the political. The consummation of modernity *need not* be commensurate with the withering away of the political into a universal homogeneity—although it very well could be. It probably would be commensurate with the withering away of the modern administrative state in its present manifestation.

Reflecting on postmodernity opens the following question: Must difference always inevitably be intertwined with economic class divisions? Modern technology within a mass, democratic/commercial environment threatens the hegemony of uniformity and with it the abolition of the political, because it makes it difficult for ends other than the economic to legitimately assert themselves. But is there any intrinsic reason why one cannot return to the political within the technological world without economic class divisions? The political requires interaction of those with different ends. In a postmodern environment that need not mean competition between different economic classes. However, the abolition of economic classes—and the move to the hegemony of the middle class—seems under *modern* conditions to go hand in hand with the victory of one particular end. Regardless of our political affiliations, we must accept that in the modern world we are already living in the most classless state the world has seen and everything points toward the even greater classless hegemony of the middle class. To propose *praxis* as a necessary means to our humanity, rather than economic competition or *technē,* requires only that one *lower the status* of those activities which provide the *prerequisites* for the overcoming of scarcity and thereby the apolitical, utilitarian egalitarianism pursued by modern thought. It need imply no more. And the inclusion of an aristocratic element need not imply economic inequality as long as we keep the aristocratic and the oligarchic conceptually separate.

For example, a postmodern community might distribute its material resources—wealth, health care, education—equally and still grant greater social status to those with greater knowledge, courage, public-spiritedness, piety—or some other preferred virtue—rather than those who produce wealth or have technical skill. And different communities could well preference different virtues. To free *praxis* and *ethos* from the modern hegemony of the universal points toward a variety of outcomes, all open to difference, which hierarchically order the constellation of ends in unique ways. When difference is released from the Spirit of Revenge, one would expect a multiplicity of outcomes. It is not one outcome that would be distinctively postmodern, but a multiplicity of juxtaposed outcomes. Likewise, it is not one kind of human being that is to be expected as *the* exemplar of excellence, but a diversity of individuals.[11]

In pursuing the hegemony of *praxis* over the increasingly autonomous technical and administrative sophistication of our time, neither Nietzsche nor Heidegger anticipated the withering away of the technological civilization that has already come into existence, nor should we. What each argued was that what was at stake was the debate over the purposes for which future technology and science would be wielded. Both argued that science and technology not only should not be autonomous but in fact never are; they are always guided in advance by some moral sentiment—e.g., in the modern dispensation, egalitarianism, hedonism, pacifism, and utilitarianism. Since science and technology can never think, they can never consciously know their own roots, which remain hidden. Only by an act of moral and political abdication do science and technology become autonomous, but they do not thereby become morally neutral. Both Nietzsche and Heidegger preferred to have those with a practical perception of reality—not the modern technical and commercial elites—take priority in revealing the nature of reality, *particularly modern technological reality.* What is required is a world where *praxis,* not the elimination, truncation, or forgetting of technical or commercial proficiency, is legitimized. Barring an apocalypse no sane person could wish for, we will henceforth never forget the technical skills we have acquired, and we will continue to acquire new ones as yet undreamed of. What is at stake is taking away from scientists and technicians the status of ultimate cultural heroes—based on the erroneous assumption that they reside closer to the truth.

In light of where the argument now stands, one can raise the possibility of a slow transition to postmodernity that would require no apocalyptic break. One thing it would require would be a civic pedagogy of participation which legitimizes and fosters community interaction.[12] Only thinking can foster this possibility, a thinking that must

11. Consider Walzer's discussions in *Spheres of Justice,* where Walzer sees different understandings of justice applicable in different spheres of *a* society. I am suggesting that different societies would institute different understandings of the hierarchy of ends—i.e., they would give priority to ends other than comfortable self-preservation. Walzer's account is a subtle version of imposing the universal on all societies.

12. Again, what is needed here coalesces with impending economic necessity in an age calling for decreased central governmental spending. The modern state could see its task as articulating needs and fostering civic action much as an earlier version of pluralist theory saw the task of government as fostering the creation of "interest groups." This would, of course, be only a propaedeutic. Where it leads once it gains momentum is anybody's guess. Reflections on the importance of, need for, and function of universal public service might also be useful. These reflections need be seen as antibusiness; com-

remain aware of the fundamental problems and their origins. Further, in our time there is a crisis in the tradition of thought that calls for a decision. Heidegger is correct in stating that we must confront that crisis in full clarity, armed with a profound and serious awareness of the philosophical past and our present options and limitations.[13] That must remain part of thinking and hence of the education that sustains the possibility of thinking. "Innocence and forgetting" must be avoided in all its contemporary forms and deployments. Education must bring about a deep and serious interpenetration of a civic pedagogy of participation and nonideological knowledge of the past. Those two prongs of education should take priority over technical education in a postmodern curriculum. It is all well and good to have technical education comparable to that of one's economic competitors, but that alone will never assure the success of a community or the happiness of its members.

This pedagogical suggestion culminates in one among many necessary postmodern synthetic tensions. Knowledge of our past and active involvement in what is distinctively our own have to be fostered simultaneously. We are the kind of beings who can simultaneously love our own and that which transcends our own. In classical antiquity a tension existed between simultaneous attachment to Athens, for example, and to the eternal ideas. In the Christian Middle Ages, the tension between the universal and the particular consisted of simultaneous attachment to what was Caesar's and to the universal kingdom of God. Postmodernity requires openness to a new synthesis of the universal and the particular such that neither side can gain hegemony. Civic pedagogy and knowledge of the past offer *an opening wedge* to a new synthesis.

The late-modern world presents the tension between the universal and the particular as an either/or choice (e.g., cosmopolitanism versus ethnic parochialism). It is far more fruitful to see dichotomies like this

---

merce is, after all, what most of us do, and that will not change. Participatory life will require time for its exercise, hence the ways in which we use our time will have to be reshaped. But this need not be antibusiness, as the community-oriented practices of corporations like McDonald's show. There are a variety of venues for civic participation.

13. Contrary to Vattimo, I do not think that this forces us to accept the "weak thinking" that devotes itself to continually rewriting the texts of the past as the last available trace of Being. Then life really is transformed into a text that continually rewrites itself. I believe that the tradition is more than an endless spider web of speeches that represent our last trace of something solid that long ago withdrew; rather, it opens us to a source that self-presences, to which we must continually reopen ourselves. See Vattimo, *End of Modernity,* 164–81.

as poles of a continuum with an ideal venue lying somewhere near the midpoint. We are not forced to choose between globalization, with its mindless, universalistic cosmopolitanism, and ethnic balkanization based on unities formed in epochs past. We have choices other than becoming citizens of the cosmos or being immersed in a closed horizon with all the stupidities such parochialism implies. We need not, when we see the destructive tendencies of modern homogenizing cosmopolitanism, blindly affirm the parochial and the local.

We must be open to both the universal and the particular, identity and difference, unity and diversity. These are either/or choices only within a modern perspective. But our time is unique; hence which side of the various continuums we now need to accentuate is unique. Postmodernity needs to nurse the particular back to health, albeit not simply to immerse itself in *old* parochialisms.[14] What is needed is an openness to and an affirmation of self-presenting particularity. To avoid the apocalyptic situation implied in the simple, unmediated hegemony of the particular requires a new relation to *both* the universal and the particular. Neither side of the equation should be in a position to destroy the other. Thinking must use the available resources to see how that outcome can be woven together.

Likewise, the radical disjunction between Reason and tradition represents an unnecessary modern either/or. Alarmed by the nihilistic implications of modern rationalism, Nietzsche and Heidegger tried to make tradition autonomous. They are by no means alone in this effort. But this understanding of tradition distorts the necessary relationship between Reason and tradition just as much as does the modern belief that Reason can replace tradition. The two must always exist together. The radical distinction between Reason and tradition is historically determined by the world existing in the aftermath of the French Revolution. One can respect the need for a distinctive *ethos* and thinking simultaneously. It must be recognized that Reason cannot originate or will an *ethos,* just as no thoughtful person would proclaim every vagrant, contingent outcome a gift of Being. That is where dialectical thinking, conceived more along the lines of practical than of theoretical reason, comes into play. However, since the modern world is a world of the constant, aimless revolutionizing of existence, it is difficult to

---

14. I think it is fair to say that at present we have erred too much in the direction of the abstract universal. When a new future might arrive and new traditions emerge cannot be known. But "metaphysical freedom" and the abstract universal ward off all true historical destiny, as does the constant flux of postmodernist critique. We need not fear the emergence of blind and malignant traditions if we leave a place in the world for dialectical thinking such that every *ethos* is open to what is beyond it.

maintain any traditions in late modernity unless one plays fast and loose with the term tradition. In those circumstances, one should err in the direction of openness to the *emergence* of genuine traditions, i.e., openness to the conditions under which traditions emerge. It is theoretical arrogance on the part of postmodernists to believe they have a self-appointed mission to deconstruct every concrete habit background that begins to form. That is just the latest version of the modern theoretical Spirit of Revenge directed against tradition (the past and its "it was").

The scattered manifestations of genuine traditions that we still have must be regrounded or they will become extinct. Thought would have to turn itself to fostering the *conditions* for their growth, not projecting *outcomes*. Those traditional institutions that are worth preserving in our world are precarious growths that will survive only given the retrieval of their natural soil. Nietzsche and Heidegger are correct—we must recover the *ground out of which* true traditions grow if we are to have an *ethos,* and we have substantially lost the necessary instincts under the tutelage of the abstract universal. In our time, the necessary balance between Reason and tradition, the universal and the particular, individualism and community, Reason and emotion, and so on cannot immediately be struck, because in each case we have come too close to one of the poles and must move toward the other to effect a balance.

The landscape of the postmodern world would be one where not only would the differences of different individuals be allowed to interact, but where there would be different outcomes in different places. This need not lead either to internal strife or to external hostility. One can best respect difference when one has an identity that is truly one's own, something stable with which one is comfortable. Far more conflict is necessarily implied in the late-modern world, where the evanescence of life makes self-identity difficult and hence self-assurance—individual and national—unlikely. We must take account of the fact that the late-modern world has shown us more frequent, complete, and vicious forms of conflict than our species has ever known. This is easily traceable to a growing sense that we have nothing which is our "ownmost," and hence no self-identity. Opening ourselves to difference qua legitimate self-identity offers the prospect of less conflict, not more. We cannot truly respect the difference of others until we are assured of who we are.

And it is no accident that the late-modern world is increasingly intolerant. The Spirit of Revenge, the Spirit of Gravity, and the determination to assign guilt and responsibility for every outcome that does not live up to our prior theoretical projections lead to an intolerance never before seen. And modern intolerance has weapons at its disposal no previous time has had—from the administrative state to genetic engineering to nuclear warheads. Our intolerance is not due to an excess of difference and individuality, but to its lack.

Because we have no genuine identity, nationally or as individuals, we are mutually unsure. Had we a nonrevengeful acceptance of identity based on self-presenting difference—rather than the need to consciously construct and reconstruct ourselves—we would be far more tolerant. Assured of who we truly are, we would be far less likely to pursue that assurance by turning the Other into an enemy. To have such an identity, something that is truly one's own must be allowed to flower. The instinct of contemporary postmodernism to praise the fecundity of an-archy and fragmentation and foster it with deconstruction and ongoing critique can only exacerbate this intolerance.[15] This instinct represents a partially legitimate recoil from the fear of totalization at the hands of modern technology, markets, and the bureaucratic state. But there is a refusal to let anything congeal, a belief that ongoing critique is the only means to securing our freedom and autonomy (understood in perfectly modern terms). But something must be allowed to take root if we are ever to occupy the present in a revenge-free fashion. We live in a time when traditions have collapsed. We have no genuine *ethos*.[16] We cannot legislate and impose an *ethos*—a guided or administered mutuality, togetherness, solidarity, and patriotism, such as many communitarians advocate—what George Kateb has called an "abstract impersonation of feelings."[17] Individualism and community

15. One version of this culminates in the praise of difference in such a way that every individual must be enrolled at birth, for example, in some *old* ethnic group. This approach is atavistic and reactionary, determined to freeze in place old, conventional manifestations of difference. While it is understandable in the face of the fragmented modern world to try to hold on to something that is one's own, this approach leads only to further fragmentation; it fosters neither true difference nor openness to identity and in fact blocks the path to any *new* rootedness and solidarity actually related to "our" place and space. For example, what could be less interesting to American experience than Irishness, Germanness, Africanness, especially as manifested in customs left over from several centuries ago?

16. It is no help to be told we must *choose* among *past* theoretical traditions, as MacIntyre suggests. The postmodern task is to foster the conditions for the emergence of new traditions out of a genuine *ethos*. What is needed is a *praxis* without modern theoretical encumbrances. See MacIntyre, *Whose Justice? Which Rationality*, esp. 1–11, 124–45, 209–40, 349–403, and *After Virtue*, esp. 1–59, 222–345.

17. Kateb, *The Inner Ocean*, 226. As Kateb clearly sees, this is all connected with the Spirit of Revenge. He suggests substituting a spirit of wonder for the spirit of resentment. For Kateb wonder is occasioned by a receptivity to the mystery of "isness" or "thereness" itself. He correctly connects his understanding with Heidegger's discussion

are not opposites between which we must choose. It is precisely the play of genuine individuality conducted in a specific place that makes a distinctive community possible.[18]

Finally, everyone already lives somewhere at some time with some configuration of preexisting, shared resources. The advent of the genuinely postmodern need not imply a revolutionary break. For example, the logic of the postmodern may be antistatist without being antipolitical, pointing as it does toward smaller-scale, indigenous, face-to-face possibilities.[19] There has been, for example, in *our* American tradition, a significant debate as to the place of the central state. The Federalists argued for consolidation—and, given the circumstances at the time, they were probably correct. The Anti-Federalists argued for smaller, more face-to-face republics that would take character and virtue more seriously.[20] At the time of the founding, it was necessary to consolidate. And until slavery had been expelled and the industrial age traversed, the action of the modern state was required. But we are now beyond those points. Perhaps only now does the

---

of *Gelassenheit*. One caveat, however, is in order. Kateb opposes the secularism of liberal society to the "religious mentality" and is scornful of the latter. I would agree that when religion is used as a smokescreen to pretend to a certainty that is not available the political and moral ramifications are not attractive. This is equally true of "left" and "right" manifestations of this phenomenon, e.g., liberation theology and fundamentalism. But as I have presented the matter above, the sense of awe and wonder *is* the opening to the "religious experience," as Nietzsche used the term, or "openness to the mystery," in Heidegger's usage. Needless to say, neither should eventuate in the arrogance of certainty. But a theoretically enforced secularism coerces a society to be closed to wonder and the mysterious. This is not to say that a separation of church and state may not be perfectly prudent, only that hostility to religious experience is also a manifestation of the Spirit of Revenge.

18. This does not mean we simply step back and allow an unfettered competition of all against all in some new manifestation of social Darwinism. But the possible venue for the interaction of actual individuals is not the cosmos.

19. If I correctly understand present forces and possibilities, one can predict general parameters of the postmodern. This does not represent a wish list on my part, but is a prediction regarding a possible, sanguine deflection of present forces. The general shape of the postmodern would probably be more confederal, not simply determined by the hegemony of the modern nation-state, more participatory than bureaucratic, and more "communitarian" than cosmopolitan (albeit not on the basis of old ethnic divisions). It would preference practical reason over theoretical or instrumental reason and would retain modern egalitarian elements while integrating a respect for the aristocratic. I do not believe one can push much beyond that toward any institutional specificity.

20. I agree with Herbert Storing that the Anti-Federalists were good liberal moderns, as were the Federalists. Both agreed that the only legitimate *basis* of government was consent and the only legitimate *end* was the preservation of rights. See Storing, *What the Anti-Federalists Were For*.

Anti-Federalist possibility—which has kept resurfacing in our political debates—really present itself. Federalism, too, runs through our
collective life and its possibilities can be explored—despite having
been, especially in its states' rights permutation, frequently an excuse
for mischief. Further, there is no reason why the smaller-scale orbit
toward which the postmodern points has to focus on *old* ethnic
groups. There is no reason to remain Irish American, Chinese American, or African American when we could identify ourselves as Cali-
fornian American, Midwestern American, Dixie American, or New
England American or in terms of any number of novel, as yet unseen
bases of solidarity. We should look for the basis of commonality not
in the contingencies of distant ancestral origin, but in something indigenous to our present situation. The search for roots should be directed not merely to the past. I offer the preceding examples only to
suggest the sense in which no group of individuals is ever bereft of
shared possibilities.[21]

I am aware that what I have presented in this final section raises myriad questions both of detail and intention. Some I can anticipate; others
I am sure I cannot. I have not tried to answer every predictable question
for a variety of reasons: (1) I do not presume to be a modern author
projecting a future frame, expecting others to energetically discover
what I have buried. I aspire only to be a cointerlocutor. A multifaceted
discussion requires many other discussants; what is needed is to bring
thinking down from the clouds of the abstract universal and, to refashion a phrase from Cicero, *for a second time* force it to inquire into the

---

21. Another example emerges when we reflect on the problems of modern urban
centers. We should realize that large urban centers are altogether modern phenomena.
In an information society, centers that bring together capital, labor, raw materials, and
the rest of the infrastructure for an industrial civilization are no longer needed. One runs
against the tide of circumstance in trying to maintain urban centers as presently constituted. Decentralization and regionalism—with all they imply—no doubt have a great
deal of force behind them in the world that is coming. In fact, distinctions such as urban,
suburban, and rural will become increasingly irrelevant. I hope to return to these and
other issues in a forthcoming volume, *America after Modernity*.
   If we are ever to occupy the present in a tranquil and authentic fashion, we should
allow neither the past nor the future to take hegemony. The hegemony of the past is the
premodern alternative, that of the future the modern alternative. To find a present
within, for example, the American experience, we should look for new communities
"beyond the melting pot." The grasping for past roots, no matter how irrelevant to the
present, is a sign of anguish in the face of the loss of identity in the late-modern world.
Turning to the simple, premodern hegemony of the past will never give us a present to
occupy in the face of the anomie of a late-modern world forever "on the way" to the
future. We live in a period of transition and flux. There is no reason to glorify and magnify this into a way of life.

everyday things in the language of immediate experience. (2) In light of my argument, many questions cannot and should not be answered by us in the present. One must affirm the right of future individuals to a discussion in which they are able to do more than merely accommodate our deferred ramifications. (3) To a significant degree, I am simply unequipped to see with any clarity where the argument—assuming I have framed it well to begin with—leads in all its concrete details and must inevitably pass the baton to others. If my reflections have value, it is in starting a discussion, not in finishing it. Indeed, I am satisfied with the status of midwife. (4) Perhaps in proposing the broad outlines of a speculative alternative to late modernity, modernity might end up aiming at poles opposite its greatest vices and in Aristotelian fashion find a mean. That might open a new stage for modernity itself. That alone would be no small accomplishment. (5) Finally, there is the imperative, discussed by Heidegger, that thinking unveil itself in the appropriate way, without unveiling itself completely (*BAT* 358).

Let me finish in a fashion appropriate to my observations about the postmodern, i.e., with a thought about what is most my own. As late moderns, we stand collectively between past and future, expelled from the possibility of occupying the present with a good conscience, questioning and requestioning our past, and increasingly uncertain about the future. In those circumstances it is far easier, and more likely, that our collective gaze will be cast toward the past—either to recover it or to reject it blindly—than toward a proper integration of past, present, and future. The flight to the recovery of the past becomes all the more likely in places littered with concrete remnants of the past, whether buildings or books. Such is less the case in the United States than in most other places on our planet. Our empirical gaze does not take in nearly so many sedimented monuments to departed ages as are found elsewhere, nor does our collective national consciousness carry as many remnants of bygone eras and their various fashions and ideas. Therefore, we are probably more prone to simply dismiss the past *in toto*. We thus have a greater need than others to foster a knowledge of the past.

As the first "new nation," the first modern nation created consciously at a specific time, the United States may also plausibly be the place where modernity first reaches its concrete culmination, precisely because modernity has fewer impediments left over from the past. Americans are likely to experience the full shock of completed modernity first and most powerfully. Fortunately, we have always considered ourselves a nation on the cutting edge of history, and there is no reason why we cannot continue to do so. That is part of "our" *ethos*. If we fail to see ourselves as on the cutting edge, we, of all peoples, will drift aimlessly and frustratedly. Even the *perception* of having arrived at an end of history will not sit well with Americans. Hence we might provide the site where something genuinely postmodern first comes forth. We might have the privilege of the first glimpse of the new eternity.

Selected Bibliography

Arendt, Hannah. *Between Past and Future*. New York: Viking Press, Viking Compass, 1968.

——. *The Human Condition*. Chicago: University of Chicago Press, 1958.

Aristotle. *Nicomachean Ethics*. Translated with Introduction and Notes by Martin Oswald. Indianapolis: Bobbs-Merrill Company, Library of Liberal Arts, 1962.

Aschheim, Steven. *The Nietzsche Legacy in Germany*. Berkeley: University of California Press, 1992.

——. *The Politics*. Translated with Introduction, Notes, and Glossary by Carnes Lord. Chicago: University of Chicago Press, 1984.

Bacon, Francis. "New Atlantis." In *Francis Bacon: A Selection of His Works*, 417–57. Edited by Sidney Warhaft. New York: Odyssey Press, 1965.

Baynes, Kenneth, et al., editors. *After Philosophy: End or Transformation?* Cambridge, Mass.: MIT Press, 1987.

Beiner, Ronald. *Political Judgment*. Chicago: University of Chicago Press, 1983.

Bernstein, Richard J. *Beyond Objectivism and Relativism: Science, Hermeneutics, and Praxis*. Philadelphia: University of Pennsylvania Press, 1983.

——. *The New Constellation: The Ethical-Political Horizons of Modernity/Postmodernity*. Cambridge, Mass.: MIT Press, 1992.

——. *The Restructuring of Social and Political Theory*. Philadelphia: University of Pennsylvania Press, 1976.

Blumenberg, Hans. *The Legitimacy of the Modern Age*. Translated by Robert M. Wallace. Cambridge, Mass.: MIT Press, 1985.

Cascardi, Anthony J. *The Subject of Modernity*. New York: Cambridge University Press, 1992.

Cohler, Anne M. *Rousseau and Nationalism*. New York: Basic Books, 1970.

Connolly, William E. *Identity/Difference: Democratic Negotiations of Political Paradox*. Ithaca, N.Y.: Cornell University Press, 1991.

Connor, Steven. "Postmodernism in Architecture and the Visual Arts," in *Postmodern Culture: An Introduction to the Theories of the Contemporary*. New York: Basil Blackwell, 1989.

Cropsey, Joseph. "The United States as Regime and the Sources of the American Way of Life," in *Political Philosophy and the Issues of Politics,* 1–15. Chicago: University of Chicago Press, 1980.

Dallmayr, Fred R. "Ontology of Freedom: Heidegger and Political Philosophy." *Political Theory* 12, no. 2 (May 1984):204–34.

Deleuze, Gilles. *Nietzsche and Philosophy.* Translated by Hugh Tomlinson. New York: Columbia University Press, 1983.

Derrida, Jacques. *Of Spirit: Heidegger and the Question.* Translated by Geoffrey Bennington and Rachel Bowlby. Chicago: University of Chicago Press, 1989.

———. *Spurs: Nietzsche's Styles/Eperons: Les Styles de Nietzsche.* Introduction by Stefano Agosti. Translated by Barbara Harlow. Chicago: University of Chicago Press, 1978.

———. *Writing and Difference.* Chicago: University of Chicago Press, 1978.

Descartes, René. *Discourse on Method.* [Published with *Meditations.*] Translated with an Introduction by Laurence J. Lafleur. New York: Bobbs-Merrill Co., 1960.

Dreyfus, Hubert, and Harrison Hall, editors. *Heidegger: A Critical Reader.* Cambridge, Mass.: Blackwell Publishers, 1992.

Dunn, John. *The Political Thought of John Locke: An Historical Account of the Argument of the "Two Treatises of Government."* Cambridge: Cambridge University Press, 1969.

Farías, Victor. *Heidegger and Nazism.* Edited with a Foreword by Joseph Margolis and Tom Rockmore. Translated by Paul Burrell. Philadelphia: Temple University Press, 1989.

Ferry, Luc. *Political Philosophy: Rights—The New Quarrel between the Ancients and the Moderns.* Translated by Franklin Philip. Chicago: University of Chicago Press, 1990.

Ferry, Luc, and Alain Renaut. *Heidegger and Modernity.* Translated by Franklin Philip. Chicago: University of Chicago Press, 1990.

Foucault, Michel. *The Archaeology of Knowledge.* Translated by A. M. Sheridan Smith. New York: Parthenon, 1972.

———. *Discipline and Punish: The Birth of the Prison.* Translated by Alan Sheridan. New York: Random House, Vintage Books, 1979.

———. *The History of Sexuality.* Vol. 1, *An Introduction.* Translated by Robert Hurley. New York: Random House, Vintage, 1990.

———. *Madness and Civilization: A History of Insanity in the Age of Reason.* Translated by Richard Howard. New York: Vintage Books, 1973.

———. *The Order of Things: An Archaeology of the Human Sciences.* New York: Vintage Books, 1973.

———. *Power/Knowledge: Selected Interviews and Other Writings 1972–1977.* Edited by Colin Gordon. New York: Random House, 1977.

Fukuyama, Francis. *The End of History and the Last Man.* New York: Macmillan, Free Press, 1992.

———. "End of History?" *The National Interest,* no. 16 (Summer 1989).

Funkenstein, Amos. *Theology and the Scientific Imagination: From the Middle*

Ages to the Seventeenth Century. Princeton, N.J.: Princeton University Press, 1986.

Gadamer, Hans-Georg. *Philosophical Hermeneutics.* Translated and edited by David E. Linge. Berkeley: University of California Press, 1976.

———. *Reason in the Age of Science.* Translated by Frederick Lawrence. Cambridge, Mass.: MIT Press, 1981.

———. *Truth and Method.* Translation edited by Garrett Borden and John Cumming from 2d ed. (1965) of *Wahrheit und Methode.* New York: Seabury Press, 1975.

Galston, William A. *Liberal Purposes: Goods, Virtues, and Diversity in the Liberal State.* New York: Cambridge University Press, 1991.

Gillespie, Michael Allen, and Tracey B. Strong, editors. *Nietzsche's New Seas: Explorations in Philosophy, Aesthetics, and Politics.* Chicago: University of Chicago Press, 1988.

Gitlin, Todd. "Postmodernism: Roots and Politics." *Dissent* (Winter 1989).

Gough, J. W. *John Locke's Political Philosophy: Eight Studies.* Oxford: Oxford University Press, 1950.

Habermas, Jürgen. *Knowledge and Human Interests.* Translated by Jeremy J. Shapiro. Boston: Beacon Press, 1968.

———. *The Theory of Communicative Action: Reason and the Rationalization of Society.* Translated by Thomas McCarthy. Boston: Beacon Press, 1984.

Hartz, Louis. *The Liberal Tradition in America.* New York: Harcourt Brace, 1955.

Hassner, Pierre. "Immanuel Kant." In *History of Political Philosophy*, 3d ed., edited by Leo Strauss and Joseph Cropsey, 581–621. Chicago: University of Chicago Press, 1987.

Hegel, G. W. F. *Lectures on the Philosophy of Religion.* Translated by E. B. Speirs and J. B. Sanderson. New York: Humanities Press, 1974.

———. *Phenomenology of Spirit.* Translated by A. V. Miller. Analysis and Foreword by J. N. Findlay. New York: Oxford University Press, 1977.

———. *Philosophy of Right.* Translated with Notes by T. M. Knox. New York: Oxford University Press, 1969.

———. *The Science of Logic.* In *The Logic of Hegel*, 2d ed., revised and augmented. Translated with Notes by William Wallace. 1892; London: Oxford University Press, 1972.

Heidegger, Martin. *Being and Time.* Translated by John Macquarrie and Edward Robinson. New York: Harper & Row, 1962.

———. *Discourse on Thinking.* Translated by John M. Anderson and E. Hans Freund. Introduction by John M. Anderson. New York: Harper & Row, Harper Torchbooks, 1966.

———. *The End of Philosophy.* Translated by Joan Stambaugh. New York: Harper & Row, 1973.

———. *An Introduction to Metaphysics.* Translated by Ralph Manheim. New Haven: Yale University Press, 1959.

———. *Letter on Humanism.* Translated by Edgar Lohner. In *Philosophy in the Twentieth Century*, vol. 3, *Contemporary European Thought*, edited with Introductions by William Barrett and Henry D. Aiken, 192–224. New York: Harper & Row, 1971.

———. *Nietzsche*. 2 vols. Pfullingen: Günther Neske Verlag, 1961.

———. *Nietzsche*. 4 vols. Translated by Frank A. Capuzzi. Edited with Notes and an Analysis by David Farrell Krell. New York: Harper & Row, 1982.

———. "Nur Noch Ein Gott Kann Uns Retten." *Der Spiegel* (1974).

———. *On Time and Being*. Translated by Joan Stambaugh. New York: Harper & Row, 1972.

———. *Poetry, Language, Thought*. Translated with an Introduction by Albert Hofstadter. New York: Harper & Row, 1971.

———. *The Question concerning Technology and Other Essays*. Translated with an Introduction by William Lovitt. New York: Harper & Row, Harper Torchbooks, 1977.

———. *The Question of Being*. Translated with an Introduction by Jean T. Wilde and William Kluback. New Haven, Conn.: College and University Press, 1958.

———. "Wer ist Nietzsches Zarathustra?" *Vörtrage und Aufsatze*. Pfullingen, 1954.

———. *What Is Called Thinking*. Translated by J. Glenn Gray. New York: Harper & Row, Harper Torchbooks, 1972.

———. "What Is Metaphysics?" In *Existence and Being*, 325–61. Translated by R. F. C. Hull and Alan Crick. Introduction and analysis by Werner Brock. Chicago: Henry Regnery, Gateway Ed., 1949.

Hobbes, Thomas. *Leviathan*. Edited by Michael Oakeshott. London: Collier-Macmillan, 1962.

Kant, Immanuel. *Kant's Political Writings*. Edited with Introduction and Notes by Hans Reiss. Translated by H. B. Nisbet. Cambridge: Cambridge University Press, 1970.

Kateb, George. *The Inner Ocean: Individualism and Democratic Culture*. Ithaca, N.Y.: Cornell University Press, 1992.

Kaufmann, Walter. *Discovering the Mind*. Vol. 2. New York: McGraw-Hill, 1980.

———. *Nietzsche: Philosopher, Psychologist, Antichrist*. 4th ed. Princeton: Princeton University Press, 1974.

Kelly, George Armstrong. *Idealism, Politics and History: Sources of Hegelian Thought*. Cambridge: Cambridge University Press, 1969.

Kojève, Alexandre. *Introduction to the Reading of Hegel*. Edited by Allan Bloom. Translated by James H. Nichols, Jr. New York: Basic Books, 1969.

Kolb, David. *Postmodern Sophistications: Philosophy, Architecture, and Tradition*. Chicago: University of Chicago Press, 1990.

Lacoue-Labarthe, Philippe. *Heidegger, Art and Politics: The Fiction of the Political*. Translated by Chris Turner. Cambridge, Mass.: Basil Blackwell, 1990.

Lampert, Laurence. *Nietzsche's Teaching: An Interpretation of Thus Spoke Zarathustra*. New Haven: Yale University Press, 1986.

Lea, Frank A. *The Tragic Philosopher*. London: Methuen, 1957.

Locke, John. *Second Treatise of Government.* Edited with an Introduction by Thomas P. Peardon. Indianapolis: Bobbs-Merrill, 1952.

Löwith, Karl. *Meaning in History.* Chicago: University of Chicago Press, Phoenix Books, 1949.

Lyotard, Jean-Francois. *The Post-Modern Condition: A Report on Knowledge.* Translated by G. Bennington and B. Massumi. Minneapolis: University of Minnesota Press, 1984.

Machiavelli, Niccolò. *The Prince.* Translated with Introduction by Harvey C. Mansfield, Jr. Chicago: University of Chicago Press, 1985.

MacIntyre, Alasdair. *After Virtue.* Notre Dame, Ind.: Notre Dame University Press, 1981.

————. *Whose Justice? Which Rationality?* Notre Dame, Ind.: Notre Dame University Press, 1988.

MacPherson, C. B. *The Political Theory of Possessive Individualism: Hobbes to Locke.* New York: Oxford University Press, 1962.

Mansbridge, Jane J. *Beyond Adversary Democracy.* New York: Basic Books, 1980.

Marcuse, Herbert. *One Dimensional Man.* Boston: Beacon Press, 1964.

Marx, Karl. "Contribution to the Critique of Hegel's *Philosophy of Right:* Introduction." In *The Marx-Engels Reader,* 2d ed., edited by Robert Tucker, 16–25. New York: W. W. Norton, 1978.

————. "Theses on Feuerbach." In Karl Marx and Frederick Engels, *The German Ideology,* part 1, 121–23. Translated by Lawrence and Wishart. Edited with an Introduction by C. J. Arthur. New York: International Publishers, 1981.

Masters, Roger D. *The Nature of Politics.* New Haven, Conn.: Yale University Press, 1989.

Nehamas, Alexander. *Nietzsche: Life as Literature.* Cambridge, Mass.: Harvard University Press, 1985.

Neske, Gunther, and Emil Kettering. *Martin Heidegger and National Socialism: Questions and Answers.* New York: Paragon House, 1990.

Nietzsche, Friedrich. *Beyond Good and Evil.* Translated by Walter Kaufmann. New York: Random House, Vintage Books, 1966.

————. *The Birth of Tragedy* and *The Case of Wagner.* Translated and edited by Walter Kaufmann. New York: Random House, Vintage Books, 1967.

————. *The Dawn.* in *The Portable Nietzsche.* Translated with an Introduction by Walter Kaufmann. London: Chatto & Windus, 1971.

————. *Daybreak: Thoughts on the Prejudices of Morality.* Translated by R. J. Hollingdale. Introduction by Michael Tanner. New York: Cambridge University Press, 1982.

————. *Ecce Homo.* [Published with *On the Genealogy of Morals.*] Translated and edited with Commentary by Walter Kaufmann. New York: Random House, Vintage Books, 1967.

————. *The Gay Science.* Translated with Commentary by Walter Kaufmann. New York: Random House, Vintage Books, 1966.

———. *Human, All Too Human.* Translated by Marion Faber, with Stephen Lehmann. Introduction and Notes by Marion Faber. Lincoln: University of Nebraska Press, 1984.

———. *On the Advantage and Disadvantage of History for Life.* Translated by Peter Preuss. Indianapolis: Hackett Publishing, 1980.

———. *On the Genealogy of Morals* and *Ecce Homo.* Translated by Walter Kaufmann and R. J. Hollingdale. New York: Random House, Vintage Books, 1967.

———. *The Portable Nietzsche.* Selected and translated with an Introduction, Prefaces, and Notes by Walter Kaufmann. London: Chatto & Windus, 1971.

———. *Thus Spoke Zarathustra.* Translated with a Preface by Walter Kaufmann. New York: Penguin Books, 1978.

———. *Twilight of the Idols.* In *The Portable Nietzsche,* 463–563.

———. *Untimely Meditations.* Translated by R. J. Hollingdale. Introduction by J. P. Stern. New York: Cambridge University Press, 1983.

———. *The Use and Abuse of History.* 2d rev. ed. Translated by Adrian Collins. Introduction by Julius Kraft. New York: Bobbs-Merrill Company, Library of Liberal Arts, 1957.

———. *The Will to Power.* Translated by Walter Kaufmann and R. J. Hollingdale. Edited by Walter Kaufmann. New York: Random House, Vintage Books, 1968.

Ophuls, William. *Ecology and the Politics of Scarcity.* San Francisco: W. H. Freeman and Company, 1977.

Ott, Hugo. *Martin Heidegger: A Political Life.* New York: Basic Books, 1993.

Pangle, Thomas L. *The Ennobling of Democracy: The Challenge of the Postmodern Era.* Baltimore: Johns Hopkins University Press, 1992.

———. Introduction to *Studies in Platonic Political Philosophy,* by Leo Strauss, 1–26. Chicago: University of Chicago Press, 1983.

———. *The Spirit of Modern Republicanism: The Moral Vision of the American Founders and the Philosophy of Locke.* Chicago: University of Chicago Press, 1988.

———. "The 'Warrior Spirit' as an Inlet to the Political Thinking of Nietzsche's Zarathustra." *Nietzsche Studien.*

Pippin, Robert B. *Modernism as a Philosophical Problem: On the Dissatisfactions of European High Culture.* Cambridge, Mass.: Basil Blackwell, 1991.

Pocock, J. G. A. *The Machiavellian Moment: Florentine Political Thought and the Atlantic Republican Tradition.* Princeton, N.J.: Princeton University Press, 1975.

Pöggeler, Otto. *Martin Heidegger's Path of Thinking.* Trans. Daniel Magurshak and Sigmund Barber. 1963; Atlantic Highlands, N.J.: Humanities Press International, 1987.

Riley, Patrick. *The General Will before Rousseau: The Transformation of the Divine into the Civic.* Princeton, N.J.: Princeton University Press, 1986.

———. *Will and Political Legitimacy.* Cambridge, Mass.: Harvard University Press, 1982.

Rorty, Richard. *Contingency, Irony, and Solidarity.* New York: Cambridge University Press, 1989.

———. *Consequences of Pragmatism.* Minneapolis: University of Minnesota Press, 1982.

———. *Essays on Heidegger and Others: Philosophical Papers, Volume 2.* New York: Cambridge University Press, 1991.

———. *Philosophy and the Mirror of Nature.* Princeton, N.J.: Princeton University Press, 1979.

Rosen, Stanley. *Hermeneutics as Politics.* New York: Oxford University Press, 1987.

Rosenau, Pauline Marie. *Post-Modernism and the Social Sciences: Insights, Inroads, and Intrusions.* Princeton, N.J.: Princeton University Press, 1992.

Rosenblum, Nancy L., ed. *Liberalism and the Moral Life.* Cambridge, Mass.: Harvard University Press, 1989.

Rousseau, Jean-Jacques. *The First and Second Discourses.* Edited with Introduction and Notes by Roger D. Masters. Translated by Roger D. and Judith R. Masters. New York: St. Martin's Press, 1964.

———. *On the Social Contract.* Edited by Roger D. Masters. Translated by Judith R. Masters. New York: St. Martin's Press, 1978.

Salkever, Steven G. *Finding the Mean: Theory and Practice in Aristotelian Political Philosophy.* Princeton, N.J.: Princeton University Press, 1990.

Schacht, Richard. *Nietzsche.* Boston: Routledge & Kegan Paul, 1983.

Schmidt, Carl. *The Concept of the Political.* Translated by George Schwab. New Brunswick, N.J.: Rutgers University Press, 1976.

Schurmann, Reiner. *Heidegger on Being and Acting: From Principles to Anarchy.* Bloomington, Ind.: Indiana University Press, 1990.

Schutte, Ofelia. *Beyond Nihilism: Nietzsche without Masks.* Chicago: University of Chicago Press, 1984.

Shapiro, Ian. *Political Criticism.* Berkeley: University of California Press, 1990.

Skinner, Quentin. *The Foundations of Modern Political Thought.* 2 vols. New York: Cambridge University Press, 1978.

Smith, Gregory B. "American Postmodernism: The Case of Richard Rorty." *Political Science Reviewer,* forthcoming.

———. "Ancients, Moderns and Postmoderns." *Polity* 27, no. 4 (Summer 1995): 665–81.

———. "Cacophony or Silence: Derrida's Deconstructionism and the Possibility of Political Philosophy." *Political Science Reviewer* 18 (Fall 1988):127–62.

———. "Dialogue and Dialectic in Plato's *Phaedo:* Plato as Metaphysician, Epistemologist, Ontologist and Political Philosopher." *Polis* 10, nos. 1 and 2 (1991).

———. "The 'End of History' or a Portal to the Future: Does Anything Lie Beyond Late Modernity." In *Francis Fukuyama and His Critics,* edited by Timothy Burns. Lanham, Md.: Rowman and Littlefield, 1994.

———. "The End of History or the Beginning of a New Epoch," *The Observer* (Fall 1990).

————. "Endings, Transitions or Beginnings." *Perspectives on Political Science* (Fall 1994).

————. "Heidegger, Technology, and Post-modernity." *Social Science Journal* 28, no. 3 (Spring 1991):369–89.

————. "Heidegger's Postmodern Politics?" *Polity* 24, no. 1 (Fall 1991).

————. "Machiavelli's *The Prince* and the Abolition of the Political." *Machiavelli Studies* 2 (1988):49–72.

————. "Paths to and From Plato: A Reflection on the Origin of Political Philosophy; the Case of the *Symposium*." *Polis* (1993).

————. *Paths to and from Plato.* Forthcoming.

————. "The Post-Modern Leo Strauss?" *History of European Ideas* 19 (1994).

————. "On Leo Strauss and His Influence." *Commentary,* forthcoming.

————. Review of Richard Schacht's *Nietzsche. American Political Science Review* (Fall 1983).

————. "Who is Nietzsche's Zarathustra?: Part II." *Perspectives on Political Science* (Winter 1994).

Smith, Steven B. *Hegel's Critique of Liberalism: Rights in Context.* Chicago: University of Chicago Press, 1989.

Steiner, George. *Real Presences.* Chicago: University of Chicago Press, 1989.

Storing, Herbert J. *What the Anti-Federalists Were For.* Chicago: University of Chicago Press, 1981.

Strauss, Leo. *City and Man.* Chicago: Rand McNally, 1964.

————. Epilogue, in *Essays on the Scientific Study of Politics,* edited by Herbert Storing. New York: Holt, Rinehart and Winston, 1962.

————. *Natural Right and History.* Chicago: University of Chicago Press, 1954.

————. "Note on the Plan of Nietzsche's *Beyond Good and Evil.*" In *Studies in Platonic Political Philosophy.* Chicago: University of Chicago Press, 1983.

————. *Persecution and the Art of Writing.* Glencoe, Ill.: Free Press, 1952.

————. *Thoughts on Machiavelli.* Seattle: University of Washington Press, 1958.

————. "The Three Waves of Modernity," in *Political Philosophy: Six Essays by Leo Strauss,* edited with an Introduction by Hilail Gildin, 81–98. New York: Bobbs-Merrill, 1975.

————. *What is Political Philosophy?* Glencoe, Ill.: The Free Press, 1959; Chicago: University of Chicago Press, 1988.

Tarcov, Nathan. *Locke's Education for Liberty.* Chicago: University of Chicago Press, 1984.

Taylor, Charles. *Sources of the Self: The Making of the Modern Identity.* Cambridge, Mass.: Harvard University Press, 1989.

Tocqueville, Alexis de. *Democracy in America.* Translated by George Lawrence. Edited by J. P. Mayer. Garden City, N.Y.: Anchor/Doubleday & Company, 1969.

Vattimo, Gianni. *The End of Modernity.* Translated with an Introduction by Jon R. Snyder. Baltimore: Johns Hopkins University Press, 1988.

————. *The Transparent Society*. Translated by David Webb. Baltimore: Johns Hopkins University Press, 1992.

Voegelin, Eric. "Nietzsche, the Crisis and the War." *Journal of Politics* (May 1944).

Walzer, Michael. *Spheres of Justice*. New York: Basic Books, 1983.

Warren, Mark. *Nietzsche and Political Thought*. Cambridge, Mass.: MIT Press, 1988.

Wolin, Richard. *The Politics of Being: The Political Thought of Martin Heidegger*. New York: Columbia University Press, 1990.

Yack, Bernard. *The Longing for Total Revolution: Philosophic Sources of Social Discontent from Rousseau to Marx and Nietzsche*. Princeton, N.J.: Princeton University Press, 1986.

Zimmerman, Michael E. *Heidegger's Confrontation with Modernity: Technology, Politics, Art*. Bloomington: Indiana University Press, 1990.

Index

309–10, 316, 336–37; difference and, 338–40, 339nn. 15, 16; elitism and, 329–31, 330n.6, 332; nature and, 331–34, 332n.9; reason and, 289–91, 290n.12, 291n.13; thinking and, 324–25, 327n.4, 327–28; transition to, 276, 286–87, 286n.11, 324–28, 327n.4, 335–36, 335n.12, 340–41, 340n.19, 341n.21. *See also* Postmetaphysical age

Postmodern thinking, 170–71

Poststructuralism, 9

Practical dialectic, 45–46, 50–51

Praxis, 30n.22, 50, 53–54, 56n.2, 62–63, 89n.15, 182, 191, 199, 215–17, 216n.20, 224, 233, 235, 248, 249n.4, 309, 334, 335; in *On the Advantage and Disadvantage of History for Life,* 84–85, 86n.10, 87–88, 89n.15; as art, 180–81, 180n.12; Hegel on, 45–53, 47n.7, 48n.8, 49n.10, 51n.11, 52n.12; historicism and, 84–85, 86n.10, 87–88, 89, 89n.15; philosophy and, 134; subjectivity and, 45–53, 47n.7, 48n.8, 49n.10, 51n.11, 52n.12; theory and, 117, 131, 171, 180n.9, 226, 289–95, 290n.12, 291n.13, 292n.14, 302–3, 310, 315–16, 316n.9; thinking and, 309–10

Praxis, Spirit of Revenge and. *See* Nature, problem of

Premetaphysical thought, Being and, 232–35

Premodernity, 316

Premodern thought, 21–22, 22n.7, 331

Pretheoretical experience, dialectical thinking and, 312–16, 314nn. 3, 6, 316n.9, 322–23

Pretheoretical reality, 288–89, 316

Property: Hegel on, 58; Locke on, 28–30, 28n.19, 30n.21; Rousseau on, 35

Protomodernity, 31–32, 33

Protomodern thinkers, 18n.1, 18–20, 19n.2; Descartes, 20, 23–26, 24n.11, 25n.14, 52n.12, 228; Hobbes, 11, 18n.1, 26–29, 27nn. 15, 17, 28n.18, 47n.7; Kant, 11, 19n.2, 38–41, 38n.10, 39n.11, 40n.12, 88, 149, 225, 225n.33, 290n.12; Locke, 11, 28–31, 28n.19, 30nn. 21, 22, 47n.7; Machiavelli, 11, 15–16, 20–23, 21n.6, 23n.9, 27n.17; Rousseau, 18, 33–38, 35n.2, 36n.4, 37n.7, 47n.7, 51n.11, 180n.12. *See also* Hegel, G. W. F.

Psychologists, 138, 146

Psychology, 139

Pure resolution, 220–21, 223n.30

"Question Concerning Technology, The" (Heidegger), 244

Rational State, 58–59

Reality: as standing reserve, 239–41; theoretical relations to, 300–301

Reason, 19n.2, 27, 27n.15, 37, 41, 50–51, 82; instinct and, 76–77; postmodernity and, 289–91, 290n.12, 291n.13; in Socrates, 75–78, 77n.4; tradition and, 337–38; transformation into Will, 42, 108

Reason/Nature dichotomy, 36, 37–38; Descartes on, 24–26, 24n.11, 25n.14; in Hegel, 42–45, 43n.4; Hobbes on, 26–29, 27n.15; Locke on, 29–31, 30nn. 21, 22; Machiavelli on, 20–23, 21n.6, 23n.9; and *praxis* in Hegel, 45–53, 47n.7, 48n.8, 51n.11, 52n.12; protomodernity and, 31–32, 33. *See also* Metaphysical freedom

"Releasement to things," 260, 262–63

Religion, 101, 101n.9, 144–47, 146n.18; Heidegger and, 321–22, 339n.17; the political and, 275; postmodernism and, 294n.15

Will (*continued*)
  Nature and, 20, 21, 35; Reason
  transformed into, 42, 108; Spirit
  of Revenge and, 118–20
Will to Power, 68n.4, 93, 93n.3, 105,
  113n.23, 119, 129–30, 156, 165,
  169; in *Beyond Good and Evil*, 143–
  44, 144n.15; Heidegger on, 228,
  229, 229n.1; National Socialism
  and, 133; philosophy and, 137; in

Thus Spoke Zarathustra, 113–
  114n.24, 115nn. 25, 26
Will to Power, The (Nietzsche), 228
Women, Nietzsche on, 151–53,
  152nn. 22, 23
Work, 48, 48n.9, 52n.12
Worldviews, 237–38

Yack, Bernard, 61n.8
Yorck, Count, 225–26